From Sea to Shining Sea

THE GREAT AMERICAN
SEAFOOD COOKBOOK

From Sea to Shining Sea

THE GREAT AMERICAN

SEAFOOD COOKBOOK

BY SUSAN HERRMANN LOOMIS

Illustrations by Jamie Hogan
Preparation Illustrations by Wendy Wray

WORKMAN PUBLISHING, NEW YORK

Library of Congress Cataloging-in-Publication Data
Loomis, Susan Herrmann. The great American seafood cookbook.
Includes index. 1. Cookery (Seafood) 2. Cookery, American.
1. Title TX747.L7 1988   641.6'92   88-11400
ISBN 0-89480-585-1   ISBN 0-89480-578-9 (pbk.)

Cover and book design: Susan Aronson Stirling
Cover photographs: (left to right) Jackson Vereen, courtesy of
Chevron Chemical Company; Dennis M. Gottlieb; Susan H. Loomis.
Cover illustration by Kenneth Spengler.

Workman books are available at special discounts when purchased in bulk
for premiums and sales promotions as well as for fund-raising or educational
use. Special editions or book excerpts can also be created to specification.
For details, contact the Special Sales Director at the address below.

Workman Publishing Company, Inc.
708 Broadway
New York, NY 10003
Manufactured in the United States of America

First printing June 1988
10   9   8   7   6   5

To my loving partner and husband,
Michael T. Loomis,
who is without peer.

ACKNOWLEDGMENTS

L

ike all monumental projects, this one would never have come together without the help, expertise, and good humor of so many people.

A huge and heartfelt thank you to the fishermen and -women—many of whom you will meet in these pages—who welcomed me on their boats, into their homes, kitchens, and histories. Their characters were invariably etched with the love of their hard work, a romance of the sea, and extra doses of generosity and good humor. Special thanks to Helen and Keane Gau, Bruce Gore, Murray Bridges, Greg Cox, Chucky Clark, Allan Grow, William Grenier, Leon Fonseca, Dennis Rackliffe, Eddie Brymer, and Jim Ranson.

I had a great deal of help from people who work in state and federal offices, markets, and processing plants, particularly Kenelm M. Coons and Karla Ruzicka, New England Fisheries Development Foundation; Claude Ver Duin, Great Lakes Fisheries Development Foundation; Bob Rubin, Chicago Fish House; Larry Schweig, Five Lakes Fisheries; Donna Florio, South Carolina Wildlife and Marine Resources; Brian Paust, Alaska Seagrant; Doug Robberson, Icicle Seafoods; Jerald Horst, Louisiana Cooperative Extension Service; Alvin Folse, Big Plans Seafood; Lindsay Parker and Paul Christian, Georgia Seagrant; Larry Sims, Maryland Watermen's Association; Tommy Taylor, Humphreys County Cooperative Extension Service; John Peters, Seattle Seagrant; Jon Rowley, Fish Works!

Thanks, too, to Harry and Dick Yoshimura, and everyone else at Mutual Fish in Seattle, who have been invaluable in my enjoyment of and education about seafood; to Richard Cavanaugh, seafood buyer at the Queen Anne Thriftway in Seattle; to Stephen Cohen, seafood buyer at the Oyster Bar in Grand Central Station, New York; and to Bob Winger at Pacific Fish, for reducing the miles between East and West coasts to get me all that cod, bluefish, and sole.

Thanks to Cynthia Nims, who willingly researched, organized, and kept my office in order; to Cathy Burgett and Mary Kay Sisson for re-testing all of the recipes and giving their frank appraisals; to Marc Laderriere, who gave an enormous amount of time and tastes choosing wines for the recipes.

This book wouldn't be without the faith of Peter Workman, and the thoughtful ministrations of my friend and editor Suzanne Rafer, who is the best ever, and kept me laughing the whole time, too. Thanks to Susan Aronson Stirling for her wonderful design, and to Mardee Haidan Regan for her expert copy editing and great suggestions. I also want to thank Tina Ujlaki, Carol McKeown, and Barbara Scott-Goodman for their work on the book. Thanks to everyone at Workman for their welcome enthusiasm, and that includes Carolan Workman, Shannon Ryan, Janet Harris, Andrea Bass, Bert Snyder, and all those other great people I so enjoyed working around.

Thank you to my literary agent, Susan

Lescher, whose cheerful "I think it's a fabulous idea!" was just the response I wanted.

My profound gratitude to the experts who reviewed portions of the manuscript for accuracy, and answered endless questions—Eugene Connors, former fisherman and seafood quality expert; Richard Lord, Fulton Fish Market Information Specialist; Edith J. Langner, M.D.; Maurice Stansby, Scientific Consultant, NOAA; Marah Landolt and Fay Dong, University of Washington School of Fisheries; Brooks Takenaka, General Manager, Honolulu Fish Auction; Paul Bartram, President of Akala Products, Honolulu; Wayne Ludwigson, chef and buyer at Ray's Boathouse, Seattle; staff members of *Seafood Leader* and *Seafood Business* magazines; and Janis Harsila and Evie Hansen, National Seafood Educators.

Traveling was made easier and more comfortable in several cities with the help of Louis Richmond, Public Relations Director at the Seattle Sheraton Hotel, and Ted Durham of the Fairmont Hotel in New Orleans.

Thanks to editors at *The New York Times* who, even when they say they've had it with seafood, let me write more. And I am grateful to the late Vern Mathews, my first and most exacting editor, who encouraged me to pursue my interests and who became a cherished friend.

Special thanks to my dear friend and colleague Patricia Wells, for her constant encouragement and guidance.

For all the meals they ate, comments they made, and evenings they shared, thank you wholeheartedly to Jeff and Gayle Herrmann, Kate, Dick, Cynara, and Alexis Lilly, Mary Herrmann, John Herrmann, Karen and Chuck Malody, Randy and Chris Shuman, Jim Pridgeon and Carole Fahrenbruch, Elisabeth Hyde and Pierre Schlag, Anne Hurley, Kathy Gaspar, and our other friends.

Finally, thanks to my mother and father, Joseph and Doris Bain Herrmann, for giving me an intense interest in and appreciation of food and different cultures, and for their loving support.

CONTENTS

Part One
BEFORE YOU BEGIN

Part Two
THE RECIPES AND LEXICON

From Sea to Shining Sea

When I first began writing about seafood several years ago, I didn't expect my enthusiasm to develop into a full-blown passion. It has, though. I've become an incorrigible seafood junkie: I go to fishing ports on vacation and visit markets instead of museums. I talk with fishermen whenever I can. I attend seafood trade shows and expositions looking for characters, for what's "new" in seafood species, and for recipes. It's amazing how often I find them.

Planning the research trips for this book was a little like trying to catch eels by hand in dark water. When I was deciding which ports to visit I had to consider fishing seasons—which change by the minute—and fishermen's schedules. They are usually on the water by dawn, and if they get home by 8 P.M.—that's if they come into port at all—they're lucky.

I had to decide whether I wanted to visit ports when the fishing season was open and there was plenty of action, but few fishermen around because they were on the water, or if it would be better to go when there was no fishing, and they would be in port and able to talk. I usually opted for the busy season, for I learned that there would always be someone willing to talk, and chances of getting on a boat were much, much better.

I soon realized that making plans in advance was almost futile. When it comes to fishing, no one can plan much in advance, and I found people reluctant to commit to anything until they could sense my interest firsthand. I could see their point—what does a voice on the phone who claims to be writing a seafood cookbook have to do with getting on a wet, cold fishing boat anyway? So I made what plans I could, then took my chances for the rest.

I'll never forget my first fishing trip, braving a chilly September dawn in Maine to go lobstering with Dennis Rackliffe. I climbed on his sleek fishing boat and huddled near the exhaust pipe to try and stay warm. We sped out into the bay and I soon forgot the cold as the day turned into an exhilarating surprise. Pulling up lobster pots was like being on a treasure hunt, with the contents of each one a suspenseful mystery. Some were crowded with lively lobsters and in others the bait from the day before still remained untouched.

When we docked and returned to the Rackliffe's house, Dennis's wife, Patricia, and their three daughters, had made an apple pie, and we all enjoyed pie, conversation, and stories late into the afternoon.

From there I shivered my way through more fishing trips and fish processing plants, auctions, and markets, getting up in the middle of the night to meet eel fishermen and crabbers, oystermen and striped bass

fishermen, and to join them for a day's work.

In Maryland I saw the sun rise over the Chesapeake Bay after cold, dark hours on an oyster boat. A few days later I blistered in the sun on a Chesapeake Bay blue crab boat. In North Carolina I joined a father and his sons fishing for flounder with pound nets.

I shrimped in Georgia, catfished in Louisiana, and fished for perch on Lake Michigan, the Chicago skyline glimmering in the distance. My excitement lasted even beyond the moment I realized there was no bathroom on the boat, and we were out for a good 14 hours.

I spent four days on the open sea in Alaska, watching and helping haul in salmon, from pinks, or "humpies," to sockeyes. I gained full understanding of the southeast Alaskan saying, "humpies from hell," for it's always humpies, worth little on the market, that crowd the hooks when what fishermen hope for is a big "clatter," or group, of valuable kings.

I've seen the whole sequence in the fishing industry, from fishermen or aquafarms to market, and I am in awe of the complexity and level of cooperation necessary to get quality seafood to the consumer. Each place I visited was different, and each one had its special brand of hospitality. In some areas I couldn't get aboard a fishing vessel, no matter who or how good my contacts or efforts. Sometimes it was insurance coverage that kept me off, sometimes superstition. I never forced the issue, for spending even a day aboard someone's boat offers a very personal glimpse into his or her life.

Each fishing trip I took contributed to the respect I have for the profession, and for the people who do it because it's in their blood, and they love the independence.

FISHING FOR RECIPES

When choosing recipes for this book, I looked for ones that had a personal connection with people in or close to the fishing industry. So, I returned from each trip with as much fish and as many ways to prepare them as I could carry. I had to work fast, to make the most of the quality of fish I'd brought, and usually before I had my suitcase unpacked I was at the stove.

My husband and I had oyster nights and sole nights, Hawaiian fish nights and Creole and Cajun nights. And there were many six- and seven-recipe nights that lasted well past a decent dinner hour.

A friend gave me a 20-pound albacore tuna, and my brother—an expert fish cutter—showed me how to transform it into loins and steaks, working away with a huge filleting knife in our backyard, the picnic table being the only surface large enough to handle the fish. We had several all-tuna nights after that, which may sound like a hardship but was far from it. Tuna is one of the most versatile of fish, and baked tuna with crushed peppercorns is totally different from curried tuna, which is completely different from tuna with 40 garlic cloves.

Our friends and family had standing invitations for my recipe testing meals, which they happily accepted. Of course, the bottom line was whether or not I liked the dish, but I had to be assured that others would like it too.

I was amazed—perhaps naively so—to find such ethnic diversity in American seafood recipes. It's what makes the recipes in this book so exciting, so rich, so varied.

Now, when I bite into a piece of Alaskan salmon or halibut I think of Bruce Gore, Tom Reinholdt, and Helen and Keane Gau. I know how they catch fish and how they care for them, and I have a benchmark for perfection on my palate.

When I eat softshell crab I can follow it back to the Chesapeake Bay and all of the people at Handy Softshell Crab, Inc., in Crisfield, Maryland, who helped me get out on boats, and showed me the right way to prepare softshell crab.

When I'm offered an oyster on the half shell, I think of Randy Shuman in Willapa Bay, Washington, and remember helping him load oysters onto his barge, then shucking several dozen at home to enjoy with him and his family.

Each time I taste a crayfish (the Northwestern crawfish) I'll remember the fun of crayfishing with Guy Taylor, his zany sense of humor, and his love for the Columbia River and the work.

When I eat seafood I have a connection to it, and I hope you get the same connection in using this book, by getting to know some of the people who shared their lives and their recipes with me. I tested all of the recipes that appear here, and many more, and I chose the ones I love. No recipe was included if there were preparation problems that would be considered insurmountable in an average, well-stocked kitchen. Read these recipes and follow them to the letter if you like—I guarantee you will be pleased. But if your own tastes tell you to add a bit here, take away a bit there, do so. Recipes are guidelines, not straitjackets. Use and enjoy them, and let them lead you down your own creative paths.

Susan Herrmann Loomis

Seattle, 1988

Part One

BEFORE YOU BEGIN

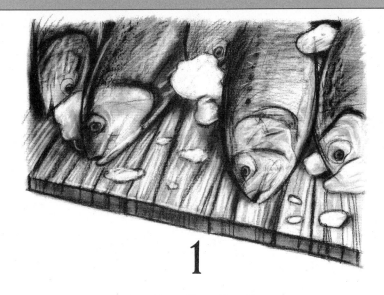

1

QUALITY SEAFOOD & HOW TO CHOOSE IT

The key to a fabulous seafood meal is quality seafood. And the key to quality seafood is confidence in knowing how to choose it.

First, get acquainted with your fish merchant. Make sure he knows when you're pleased with what you've tried, and when you're not. If he doesn't have what you want, ask for it—you'll be creating a small demand that will benefit him as well as you, because any new kind of seafood will attract other customers.

Remember, though, that seafood is seasonal, and everything is not available all the time. Be sure your demands are reasonable.

By establishing a good relationship with your fish merchant, you'll be developing trust, and creating the old-time situation of accountability. It has always worked in merchandising, and it works particularly well for seafood.

Seafood quality is notoriously inconsistent. It takes a long, long time for a fish merchant to develop good suppliers, and even when he does, there will still be inconsistencies. The only way he can protect himself is to send fish back when it doesn't meet his quality standards. He'll be eager to insist on quality if he has discerning, critical, and knowledgeable consumers. That's what this chapter on seafood quality will help you become.

Top-quality seafood, the only kind you want to eat, is bright, sparkling clean and tempting, and easy to recognize once you know how to use two simple tools.

The first is your nose. Take a sniff. Truly good-quality fish, whether it is fresh from the water or fresh-frozen, doesn't smell fishy at all. It smells fresh, like a sea breeze. When you take a deep sniff at the fish counter you should get a hint of sea brine.

If fish in a grocery store or fish market isn't fresh, you'll know it the minute you walk in the door. Any odor is an instant sign of decay, and it permeates the air. Of course, odor can be misleading—it might come from ice the fish is held in, from fishy paper wadded up in the trash, or from the unscrubbed walls of a fish case. You may find fresh fish among these conditions, but it won't stay fresh for long, and you should be extra-vigilant.

The second tool is your eyes. Take a look at the fish counter, then at the fish. The counter should be clean, the seafood cold and swaddled in ice, nicely arranged and just plain appealing.

If you see counter people handling the fish gently and picking up everything—fillets, steaks, whole fish—with both hands, you know you're in good company. Picking up fillets or steaks so one end hangs can rip them apart. Picking up a whole fish by the tail is a mistake. The weight of the fish can tear the flesh and damage the texture.

FRESHNESS CRITERIA: FISH

Whole Fish

A whole fish should look bright, firm, and glossy, as though it has just jumped from the water. If a fish is dimpled, a sign it got too warm somewhere along the line, it will be soft and lacking elasticity, and it will have an unpleasant odor.

The skin should have an even sheen with no deep net scars or holes. Except for species like salmon and herring, whose scales are very loose and fall off easily, few scales should be missing. All fish have a natural slime covering them, which should be transparent, not milky or dull.

Check the eyes. Although not a totally reliable sign of freshness, in most species the eyes should be bright and bulging naturally, and the cornea should be dark. Some species—such as salmon—have small eyes which might not conform, and an eye may be clouded from contact with ice. Also, when fish are brought up from great depths on a long line their eyes can bulge unnaturally.

Look at the gills. They should be vivid red and moist, not brown or sticky.

At this point your nose and eyes should have told you all you need to know, but if you're still in doubt, check the stomach cavity. It should be well cleaned and sweet smelling. If the rib bones are separating from the flesh, steer clear.

Touching the fish is a final freshness test. You shouldn't go around punching and poking at fish indiscriminantly, because that can damage its texture. If you've chosen a particular fish, gently press on it with your finger. It should feel firm and the flesh should spring back. If it is soft, and an indentation stays in the flesh, it isn't top-quality. Some fish, such as West Coast dover sole, hake, lingcod, and whiting do have slightly soft flesh, but they will still feel firm. If in doubt, always rely on your nose.

Fillets and Steaks

Test fillets and steaks for freshness the same way you would a whole fish. They should smell good, and look mouthwateringly bright, freshly cut and firm, their color pure and translucent so you can almost see into them.

There shouldn't be any dark red spots—an indication the fish was bruised from rough handling—or browning around the edges, which indicates blood in the flesh or dehydration and oxidation. If the flesh is separating drastically, discolored, or falling away from the bone, it was roughly handled or allowed to warm too much and is past its prime.

Fillets and steaks should never be sitting in a pool of liquid.

Not all markets have enough space to put their seafood on ice in a display case, and they sell it packaged on styrofoam plates wrapped in plastic instead. It may lack the romance of fish on ice, but it can be equally good quality and you use the same criteria to buy it. Avoid packages with liquid in them. Rub your fingers along the bottom of the package—if they come away smelling fishy, replace the package and move on.

HOW FISH IS SOLD

When purchasing fish for dinner, you can expect to find some or all of the following at the local market.

Round or Whole fish. Fish in the round are fish that are sold exactly as they come from the water—guts, gills, scales, and all.

Drawn. The name for fish that are scaled, and have the viscera and gills removed.

Dressed. These are fish that have been gutted, scaled, headed, and trimmed of their fins. Small fish in this form are called "pandressed."

Fillets. The sides of the fish that have been cut lengthwise from the backbone. They are usually ¼- to 1-inch thick. If the fillets are left connected by the back skin they are called "kited" or "butterfly" fillets. *Fletch* is the term given the 4 loins from halibut.

Chowder Pieces. Trimmings from the fillets that are economical and excellent for soups and chowders.

Portion Sizes

A little note here on how much seafood to buy. I've specified weights in all the recipes, based on the richness of the seafood—the richer the seafood, the smaller the quantity—and the preparation. If a recipe is designed to be the only course, a sort of "one dish meal," the quantity of seafood is more generous than if it is to be one course among many. As a rule of thumb, however, I think a 6- to 8-ounce portion is an ample serving. A 4-ounce serving is a bit shy, unless there is plenty to accompany it, and a 10-ounce serving is often excessive.

Tasty Neighbors

Both oysters and mussels sometimes have pea crabs—literally minuscule crabs complete with tiny legs and pincers—living in their shells. The shellfish and the crabs have a very sweet deal—the crabs never go hungry because food constantly comes their way—they intercept it on the shellfish gills, keeping the gills impeccably clean.

The pea crabs are sometimes referred to as chowder crabs, and they are completely harmless. In fact, stories are told of Maryland oystermen collecting these tiny crustaceans and selling them as chowder crabs for outrageous sums per gallon.

Pea—or chowder—crabs are easy to detect. If you bite into a mussel with one, you'll hear the soft crunch of its shell. While pea crabs are generally considered a nuisance in the shellfish industry, a clever mussel company, Blue Gold Sea Farms in Newport, Rhode Island, turned the two to five percent occurrence of pea crabs in their mussels to distinct advantage. They called their campaign the "Twin Catch," advertising their mussels as those "with the extra added bonus of the chowder crab." The strategy worked. Portraying the crab as a delicacy made their mussels more desirable in the market.

Steaks. Crosswise cuts of fish, steaks come from the larger varieties like salmon, tuna, swordfish, halibut, sturgeon, mako shark, and jumbo, whole, or large cod. The bone or piece of cartilage is usually left in and they range from about ⅝- to 1-inch thick.

Chunks. Trimmings from meaty fish such as swordfish, tuna, shark, and halibut, they are generally economical and ideal for brochettes, soups, and stews.

FRESHNESS CRITERIA: SHELLFISH

Clams and Mussels

Clams and mussels signal freshness with their shells. If they're open and don't close tight after a quick tap, then the mollusks are dead and unfit to eat. Shellfish should be kept at slightly warmer temperatures than fish, 35° to 40°F, and they should be in a moist, humid environment. If they look dry and tired, they probably are.

Oysters

Even out of the water, oysters open and close their shells naturally, and they must be placed with their cupped shell down, so their liquid, which provides the environment they need to live in, doesn't drain out. Oysters should also be kept moist and cool and their shells should be clean.

Scallops

It is natural for scallops in the shell to be open. They signal spoilage by odor, emitting an unmistakable sharp, sometimes sulfur-like smell that will cause you to make a wide berth around them.

Squid

Yes, squid are shellfish. Their shell is the clear, slim piece of cartilage inside the mantle. Look for squid that are pale colored, firm, and bright. Their thin, speckled skin shouldn't be torn or damaged, and their bright white meat should show through. The eyes should be distinct, and the tentacles firm, whole, and intact.

Geoduck

When buying live geoducks—large clams from the Northwest—look for short, fat siphons that flinch when you touch them, an indication they are still full of water, thus recently harvested and still very fresh. Though they range in color from pale beige to deep brown, this isn't any indication of quality or flavor. Within three days after they've been harvested geoducks dehydrate, their siphons elongate and start to wrinkle, and they take on a strong, fishy taste, even if they're kept alive in a tank.

Some geoducks are frozen and sold to wholesale markets, which pass them on as fillets, steaks, or chopped clams. Compared with the fresh product, the frozen product holds little interest, and if you've ever had "bad" geoduck, chances are it was frozen.

Shucked Shellfish

Your nose and eyes are critical, here, too. Both will tell you everything you need to know about the quality of shucked shellfish. An acrid, ammonia-like odor signals they aren't fit to eat.

Shucked clams should be plump and may be pinkish to yellowish, and their liquor should be clear.

Softshell clams are sold according to size:
1. Large   200 to 250 per gallon
2. Medium   350 to 400 per gallon

Hardshell clams are sold by the pound.

Seafood Contaminants

There are cases where certain seafood is contaminated with pollutants, hydrocarbons that include PCBs, DDT, and dioxin, all of which accumulate in the fatty tissue of fish. Freshwater fish and those that swim close to shore are particularly prone to contaminants. Fish from deeper ocean water are less of a problem, although predator fish such as tuna and swordfish may contain contaminants, from feeding on contaminated fish. The best advice is to be aware of the water quality in the area from which you get your seafood.

In the case of shellfish, which can fall prey to bacteria, certain pollutants or harmful algae blooms such as red tide, you can play it safe by buying shellfish only from a reliable merchant. State Health Departments are vigilant about water quality and they will inspect and publicize any problems. If water is tainted, the sale of shellfish from that water is banned for a safe period of time.

Sulfites are sometimes used in seafood processing to inhibit deterioration. A mild solution is particularly used for certain species of shrimp that develop black spots when they are exposed to air for an extended period. Ask your fish merchant about sulfites.

A phosphate dip is commonly used in the seafood industry as well, to prolong the shelf life of fish. By regulation, a solution can't be more than 10 percent phosphates, but anything more than 5 percent gives an unmistakable soapiness to fish. Thus far phosphates have not been shown to be harmful.

Oysters come naturally in a variety of shades, from celadon green to pale pink, depending on where they are from and what they've eaten. They always have a darker mantle, or edge. They should be surrounded by either clear or opalescent, not milky, liquid.

Shucked oysters are sold in plastic containers or jars, and they will keep for 4 to 5 days, refrigerated. They come in a variety of sizes.

EAST COAST OYSTERS

Name	Number per gallon
Counts or Extra Large	160
Extra Selects or Large	161 to 210
Selects or Medium	211 to 300
Standards or Small	301 to 500
Very Small	more than 500

PACIFIC OYSTERS

Name	Number per gallon
Large Pacific	less than 65
Medium Pacific	65 to 95
Small Pacific	96 to 114
Extra Small	115 to 220
Yearlings	more than 221

Mussels range in color from pale cream to vivid orange, usually edged with dark brown. They should look plump and shiny and their liquor or the water they are packed in should be clean and clear.

Scallops are most often bought shucked. They should be firm and hold their shape, slightly sticky, and free of excess liquid. Their color ranges from creamy white to light tan, sometimes with a pinkish hue, and their smell is sweet. *Sea scallops* are ivory colored. Smaller *bay scallops* are very sweet smelling and slightly brighter with a golden tone. The color of *calico scallops* ranges from pink to light brown, often with a grayish muscle attached that is somewhat less tender than the larger, lighter muscle. Unusually

Categorizing Crabmeat

A tour of a crab processing plant anywhere along the Eastern seaboard is an amazing sight. Women sit at long tables, buckets of crab on one side of them, buckets of shells on the other. Using a small knife with a sharp blade, they cut and pick the meat from the cooked crabs seemingly faster than the eye can see.

They divide the crabmeat from different parts of the crab into three separate categories of different quality.

First they extract the meat from the body, which because it comes out in large, solid lumps, is called *lump* meat. It is the best, most expensive crabmeat. It is a real luxury in salads, soups and crab cakes, or just plain, with melted butter.

Then they clean out the body shell, scraping from it the small pieces, or *flake* meat. This is also excellent quality, but it is small, and used on its own in crab cakes or salads or to extend lump meat.

The last stop is the legs, where stringy, usually darkish meat called *claw* meat, is scraped out. This is the least desirable crabmeat—it is usually somewhat tough, and is used in many dishes, from crab cakes to casseroles.

bright white scallops, those that bulge at the sides like a flabby tube and melt together, or those that have shrunk and are sitting in a pool of clear water are likely to have been soaked in phosphates to keep them fresh longer. Try to avoid these. You can recognize a spoiled scallop as soon as you get within sniffing distance, by a strong sulfur odor.

FRESHNESS CRITERIA: CRUSTACEANS

Live Crabs and Crawfish

Crabs and crawfish should be heavy for their size, spunky and full of life, ready to pinch your finger at the slightest provocation. Sometimes a crab will be watery. This is a condition that occurs just after the crab sheds its shell and sucks in water to fill its new living quarters until it grows. For Dungeness crabs, weight is a primary freshness test, but you can also test by pinching the third leg from the front of the crab. If the shell gives, it isn't full of meat.

Freshly cooked body meat from a crab is bright white and full, somewhat translucent and not dry or cottony looking. Leg and claw meat has brown and reddish coloring on it.

Soft-Shell Blue Crabs

These are the only crabs sold in their soft-shell stage. Soft-shell blue crabs should be lively, waving their tender little appendages about, though if they aren't, they can still be of good quality if they have a sheen, and are plump and fresh looking. If soft-shell crabs aren't alive, try to find out exactly when they were caught, for their shelf life out of the water is about four days, if they're carefully

Canned Fish Tip

*I*f you eat canned seafood packed in vegetable (usually soy) oil, you may want to pour off any excess and lightly rinse the seafood under water. However, the seafood absorbs some of the vegetable oil and the vegetable oil mixes with some of the oil from the seafood. The result is that the vegetable oil, which already contains some Omega-3s and has absorbed more with the natural oil from the seafood, can contribute to lowering cholesterol in the body, though it does contain a fairly substantial amount of calories.

handled and kept cool. If they look limp, flat, soggy, and dull, their taste won't be acceptable.

In the Chesapeake Bay soft-shell crab industry the crabs are graded by size, in categories with quaint names:

Name	Width
Mediums	3½ to 4 inches
Hotel Primes	4 to 4½ inches
Primes	4½ to 5 inches
Jumbos	5 to 6 inches
Whales	6 inches and over

Lobsters

A healthy lobster will be full of vigor, its tail will be tightly curled, and it will wave its claws and antennas when plucked from the water. It will also be heavy for its size.

Lobster are sold according to size, which has nothing to do with the quality of their meat. The smallest, chicken lobsters, are the most popular, though those who have eaten enormous lobsters—they can grow to weigh 45 pounds—say the meat is just as sweet, firm, and tender as that of the smaller ones. Lobsters with one claw are called culls; lobsters with no claws are called bullets.

Name	Weight
Chicken	about 1 pound
Quarters	about 1¼ pounds
Large or Selects	from 1½ to less than 2½ pounds
Jumbo	any lobster over 2½ pounds

Shrimp

Most shrimp are frozen then thawed at the retail market, except in Louisiana, Texas, and Georgia, and the Northwest, where residents have the luxury of buying them freshly caught. They should look firm and full.

Shrimp are now cultivated throughout the world, from Ecuador to Taiwan, and they come in a variety of colors, ranging from bright pink to reddish brown to shimmery gray. The color should be even, and not brownish or yellow at the edges. Shrimp rapidly develop black spots on their shells, and they are often dipped in a light phosphate solution right on board shrimp boats to retard this process.

Some black spots aren't a problem, though if the black penetrates the shell and gets on the meat they probably aren't at peak freshness. It's best to avoid shrimp with black spots, or any shrimp that are limp, or that have an ammonia odor.

"Green headless" is the market term for raw headless shrimp in the shell. Shrimp are widely sold without their heads, which are generally removed aboard ship or at aquafarms before being shipped, because the

acids in the heads cause very rapid deterioration in the meat.

Cooked shrimp should be firm, full, and pure white inside with the characteristic red coloration on the outside of the meat. They should smell sweet and somewhat briny. Crawfish, though somewhat softer, will have a pure odor too. Cooked crab, crawfish, or shrimp will smell like ammonia when they aren't fresh, so sniff carefully.

CARE AND HANDLING OF SEAFOOD AT HOME

If possible, try to make your seafood purchase right before you go home. Once you've made your choice, see that your purchase is packaged properly—don't let fillets be folded, steaks or cooked shellfish crushed, whole fish put in a bag that is too small. If you have other errands to run, ask that your seafood be packed with ice or a gel-pack, and place it out of the sun and away from heat. If you really want to protect your

What About Prawns?

There is some controversy in the industry about prawns versus shrimp. Some maintain prawns are a separate species that is similar to shrimp; others claim the terms are interchangeable. Generally, they are used interchangeably, with prawns often referring to large species of shrimp.

seafood and are traveling by car, carry a small cooler and gel packs with you so you can pop it right into a cool environment. This may sound extreme, but try it. It can simplify your life and keep your seafood in peak condition.

Once you are home, put your seafood, ice or gel pack and all in a pan on the bottom shelf of the refrigerator, where temperatures are coldest.

It's best to eat top-quality seafood the day you bring it home, but when a situation dictates that you must buy seafood ahead, or if you receive a windfall from a local fisherman that can't be eaten in a day, proper care will reduce the deterioration.

Top-quality seafood will last up to four days in your refrigerator, if properly cared for. Check the fish daily. If liquid accumulates in the bottom of the pan, drain it off and return the fish to the refrigerator. Replace the ice if necessary.

Whole fish with the skin on can be set directly on ground ice, then covered with more ice. Again, check the fish daily and pour off any liquid that collects in the bottom of the pan, and replace any melted ice.

Steaks and fillets should never be placed directly on ice, because it will leach liquid and flavor out of them. Place it, still wrapped in the paper from the fish market, in a glass or enamel pan. Either grind the ice or place the cubes in plastic bags and set them on top of the fish—if the ice isn't too heavy and the fish is firm—or around it to keep the temperature down. Then set the pan on the bottom shelf of the refrigerator.

Set shellfish still in the shell in a pan and cover them with a damp towel to keep them cool and moist. Don't put them in fresh water, or set them in ice, which will kill them. Don't pull out the byssal threads from

Edible Flowers

I frequently recommend garnishing dishes with edible flower blossoms. They are a perfect complement to seafood, and give any presentation an added spark. Flowers sold in food markets *specifically for consumption* are not treated with chemicals, and are perfectly good to eat. If you buy flowers from a flower merchant or nursery, be sure to ask if they have been treated. If you pick flowers, make sure you pick them from an area that has not been treated with any chemicals.

If you can't get fresh blossoms, use whole or finely minced flat-leaf parsley leaves or small and varied lettuce leaves such as mâche and radicchio.

mussels before you plan to use them or they will die and spoil.

Clams and mussels will last a couple of days if they are properly cared for. Oysters will last about a week. If you are in doubt, check the shells. They should be closed. If open, they should close easily when tapped (clams and mussels). If they don't, don't eat them. Give them all the sniff test.

Cooked shellfish should be handled carefully as well, and kept away from raw shellfish, for there can be a transfer of a harmful bacteria from uncooked shellfish to cooked shellfish.

Try to consume cooked shellfish the day you buy it or cook it. Otherwise, keep it on the bottom shelf of the refrigerator, surrounded by ice if possible.

Aquafarming

It's a wonderful world when all you have to do to get a fat, fresh trout or catfish, is go to the nearest supermarket and pick one up. But before putting either in your basket, there are some things you should know: There is no commercial trout fishing industry, and that trout never saw a rushing brook; and there's a good chance that catfish never snuffled along a river bottom. They were both raised on clean, controlled aquafarms.

As seafood consumption increases, farmed fish is being eaten apace with wild fish. Wild fish are increasingly hard to come by. Without exception they are capricious and don't come when baited.

On the other hand, farmed fish grow fat as commanded and come as they're bid. They're pumped out of ponds and rushed to processing plants where they're prepared for market.

Unfortunately, farm-raised fish don't tend to have good texture. Trout, for example, spend their time languidly hanging around on the equivalent of underwater street corners.

Farmed shrimp hardly fare better. At one state-of-the-art farm on Oahu, Hawaii, thousands of shrimp are crowded into raceways under big, soft, plastic bubbles. Inside, the atmosphere is totally controlled. The shrimp are constantly flicking themselves out of the water. "They don't like to touch each other and when they do it startles them, so they

jump," a scientist working there said. "But, jumping gives their meat more texture.

Farmed crawfish are generally well regarded, though they lack the depth of flavor and the pleasant texture of their wild brethren.

Shellfish farming, at least the way it's done on the West Coast, is a much happier story. Bivalves and mollusks are in their natural environment, eating the food they prefer, unencumbered. They're either sitting in large mesh, plastic bags on tables above a sandy bay bottom, in big nets hung in the water, or hanging from ropes by their byssal threads, eating food that nature sweeps up to them. They may be a little flabby from lack of exercise, but they're not controlled.

On the East Coast, farming oysters involves dredging them from their bay of origin, and transferring them to another that is considered better quality, so they can flush themselves out and develop flavor. They are generally excellent.

Aquafarming has plenty going for it. There's little fishy odor, blood, or messiness, and farmed fish are consistent. It may go a long way toward solving world hunger. But it's more complex than that. As commercial fisheries are cut back, fishermen go out of business, and less wild fish is available in the marketplace. Farmed fish steps in to fill the void. It all looks good, but it shouldn't be considered a substitute for the real thing.

FREEZING AT HOME

Without trying to sound like a broken record, the best thing to do with top-quality seafood is to eat it immediately. But if your neighbor brings over a huge salmon caught that day and you have dinner in the oven, or someone gives you a mess of wild catfish the day before you leave on vacation, it's best to freeze it.

Freezing Tips

Try not to refreeze seafood that has already been frozen and thawed. Shrimp may be frozen more than once, but it's really not a good idea to do it at home.

Try to freeze whole fish, that are cleaned with the head still on, or at least fillets with the skin still on, since the skin provides added protection. If you do freeze steaks or fillets, freeze them individually so that you can remove the amount you need.

Freeze shellfish in their shell, in ziplock bags.

Freeze crustaceans—crab, shrimp, crawfish, lobster—in their shells whenever possible, wrapped tightly in plastic wrap, then put in ziplock bags.

Frozen oily fish have about half the shelf life of frozen lean fish. Use them within two months. A good rule for other frozen seafood is to use it within a maximum of three months.

Finally, keep your freezer as cold as possible, don't crowd it, and open the door as seldom as possible.

Freezing seafood in the average home deep-freeze or refrigerator freezer won't improve its quality. Home freezers don't freeze quickly enough. Once frozen, seafood doesn't last long because its polyunsaturated fats deteriorate more quickly, say, than the saturated fats in meat and poultry. Despite all those caveats however, freezing seafood at home can be very useful and effective.

Freezing Methods

Glazing. Probably the best way to freeze any form of fish is to glaze it first.

A glaze developed by Joyce Taylor at the University of North Carolina Seagrant program works very well. It is a blend of gelatin, lemon juice, and water that protects the fish from freezer burn and oxidation. When necessary, I freeze seafood this way, and it works very well, so I have included the recipe below.

Gelatin and Lemon Juice Glaze

¼ cup bottled lemon juice
1 package unflavored gelatin

1. Combine the lemon juice and 1¾ cups water in a small saucepan. Measure out ½ cup of the mixture and reserve. Bring the remaining lemon juice mixture to a boil.

2. Meanwhile, dissolve the gelatin in the reserved liquid.

3. Whisk the gelatin mixture into the boiling lemon juice mixture. Remove from the heat and let cool to room temperature.

4. Dip whole fish, fish fillets, or steaks into the glaze. Wrap and freeze as quickly as possible.

5. To thaw, place fish on a plate or baking

sheet in the refrigerator. The glaze will melt away as the fish thaws.

Makes enough glaze for about 4 pounds of fish

Another method of glazing. For whole fish or steaks and fillets place the fish in a single layer on a baking sheet and cover them with aluminum foil or waxed paper to protect them from dehydration. Then place the fish in the freezer. As soon as the fish are very cold, remove them from the freezer and dip each piece quickly in ice cold water. A thin glaze will form. Return the fish to the freezer for about 10 minutes to allow the glaze to harden, then repeat the process about six more times, until a thick glaze has formed. Wrap the fish in aluminum foil, or place them in ziplock plastic bags and store, handling the fish carefully so the glaze doesn't chip off.

In water, in a container. One of the most common ways to freeze whole, small fish at home is in water. The easiest way to do this is to place the fish in a milk carton that has been thoroughly cleaned with soap and well rinsed. Cut the carton down, if necessary, place the fish in it, then fill it with water to within 1 inch of the top, allowing for expansion. Wrap the carton in aluminum foil, and freeze. Plastic freezer containers can also be used.

Wrapping. Whole fish, steaks, or fillets also can be wrapped in plastic wrap and frozen. Only use wrap that is made from polyvinylidene chloride or polyvinyl chloride, rather than polyethylene, which isn't an effective vapor barrier.

Note: If you buy frozen seafood, be sure to put it directly into your own freezer once you get home, unless you plan to use it that day.

Thawing Frozen Seafood

To thaw frozen seafood, place it in the refrigerator on a plate or baking sheet that will catch the liquid as the seafood thaws. Most steaks, fillets, and small whole fish will thaw in about 24 hours. Larger fish take a longer time. Don't let liquid accumulate; drain the plate frequently if possible.

If you're in a desperate hurry, place seafood in a tightly sealed plastic bag under cold running water until it is thawed. This isn't the best method, but it works in a pinch.

What About Lingering Odors?

People complain about odors that linger in the house, even though the fish they brought home was perfectly fresh.

Chances are it has nothing to do with the fish, but with the packaging it came wrapped in. Discard packaging immediately, placing it outside the house. Frying fish may leave lingering odors from the frying, but there shouldn't be any unpleasant, lingering odors from seafood.

Any bones or shells should go right into a plastic bag that gets well sealed, then put outside immediately, into a garbage can. Don't wait until the next morning, because they will begin to smell soon after they are discarded. Freeze bones, shells, and trimmings until garbage pickup day, then get rid of them.

2

PREPARING SEAFOOD

Although sparkling fresh seafood has always been available, for the longest time it was only the lucky few who could get it. Those who lived along shores and coastlines and could trap, net, or hook fish themselves, or who could pry mussels and oysters loose from their rocks, or who could plunge a "clam gun" deep into roiling sand and come forth with a slender razor clam enjoyed a bounty the rest of us hardly even knew existed.

Elsewhere, seafood for the most part, meant criminally dry fish sticks, frost-burned frozen fish, or if we were lucky, a selection of fish fillets that all looked the same, and were bought to be coated in batter and deep-fried. But that's all changed. Distribution has improved dramatically and seafood has become fashionable.

It's really no wonder. From halibut and tuna to mussels and oysters, seafood has a voluptuous array of flavors and textures. But the best part about seafood is its simple, inherent goodness, its versatility, and the ease and speed with which it can be prepared. It can be grilled, sautéed, baked, braised, poached, or fried; smoked, salted, or pickled. So it's not surprising that statistics show us to be well beyond the odd plate of fish on Friday nights.

NUTRITIONAL MERITS OF SEAFOOD

Whatever your dietary concerns, you win with seafood. Most fish, shellfish, and crustaceans are high in proteins, vitamins, and minerals, and low in total fat. Lean fish are those that have less than five percent fat. They include cod, pollock, orange roughy, and halibut, all yielding about 100 calories per four-ounce serving uncooked. Those classified as fatty species, with five to ten or more percent fat, such as salmon, mackerel, and bluefish, yield about 200 calories per serving, uncooked.

Mollusks (filter feeders that include oysters, scallops, mussels, and clams) and crustaceans generally have less than 100 calories per four-ounce serving, and contain less than two percent fat.

Triglycerides are fats carried in the blood that are stored, as body fat, for cushioning, insulation, and energy. They are made in the body from fats ingested with food.

Fats in food include those that are unsaturated and those that are saturated. Unsaturated fats, an umbrella term for fats that are liquid at room temperature and flow freely, include monounsaturated fats like those in olive oil and polyunsaturated fats like those in safflower oil. Saturated fats, like butter, are solid at room temperature and tend to clog arteries. Most seafood has about twice

as much polyunsaturated as saturated fat and the fat seafood contains is health promoting, according to Dr. Joyce Nettleton, a nutritionist, seafood expert, and author of *Seafood and Health* (Osprey Books).

Cholesterol

Cholesterol is a waxy, fat-like substance that is found in the body. It is an essential building block of all cells in the body. But there is no need for a person to ingest cholesterol, for the body produces all it needs in the liver. Cholesterol produced in the body is not a cardiac risk factor. It is an excess of cholesterol ingested with foods that poses potential cardiac risk.

Most seafood is also low in cholesterol. For example, albacore tuna, deemed a fatty fish, has 50 milligrams of cholesterol per $3\frac{1}{2}$ ounce serving and scallops have 82 milligrams of cholesterol for the same size serving. By comparison, two large eggs contain 550 milligrams of cholesterol. Squid, which appears to be relatively high in cholesterol, with about 200 milligrams (for Pacific short fin squid) per $3\frac{1}{2}$ ounce serving, is still less than those two large eggs. The current recommended cholesterol intake for healthy people is 300 milligrams a day, according to Dr. Nettleton.

The cholesterol content of foods and its affect on health may be misleading, however. There is speculation that the amount of cholesterol people eat may not raise their cholesterol levels, at least not as much as we've been led to believe, according to Dr. Edith J. Langner, a New York physician and expert on diet. What clearly raises blood cholesterol levels are saturated fats. Food high in both saturated fats and cholesterol are demons.

Those Amazing Omega-3s

Omega-3 is now the byword when speaking of seafood. Simply put, Omega-3 long-chain fatty acids, or Omega-3s, are the extra-polyunsaturated fats in fish oils. Omega-3s are essential to the body, which needs them in large concentrations. The body is thought to make very small amounts of Omega-3s, and although a certain type of Omega-3 is found in some plant oil, the most beneficial Omega-3s, and the largest amounts, come from seafood.

It is well-established that Omega-3s are beneficial to humans in a variety of ways. One of the most important appears to be that Omega-3s alter the blood to make it less likely to coagulate or clot, thereby reducing the likelihood of cardiac problems and stroke. They do this by making blood platelets less sticky, less likely to clump in the arteries.

Conclusive proof hasn't been shown for whether or not Omega-3s lower cholesterol in the blood. They don't increase it and it has been shown that the more fatty seafood consumed, the greater the possibility of a reduction in cholesterol.

The main contribution of Omega-3s is their ability to reduce triglycerides, according to Dr. Nettleton.

Very early research findings also hint that Omega-3 fatty acids may be helpful in the treatment of arthritis, migraine headaches, multiple sclerosis, diabetes, and possibly even breast cancer in women.

Fish Oil Supplements

Opinions are divided about food supplements containing fish oils, which are becoming increasingly available. Extraordinary results in lowering the fat levels in the blood with the use of fish oils have been shown. But supplements vary greatly in the amount and quality of Omega-3 fatty acids they contain.

And there are other concerns. Researchers aren't sure if isolated Omega-3s are beneficial, or if they must interact with other substances in fish to be helpful. Also, fish oil in excessive amounts can be harmful. It can interfere with blood clotting and can increase the risk of bleeding, bruising, or even stroke. No agency monitors the quality of fish oils in supplements, and they could be contaminated with harmful substances, such as pesticides and metals. Fish oils also stimulate the production of a hormone-like substance called prostoglandin E3, which increases bone loss and may raise the risk of osteoporosis.

Considering all of these issues, it is probably not a good idea to take fish oil supplements unless they are being administered under close medical supervision.

The best way to get Omega-3 fatty acids is by eating seafood. The suggested amount is about six ounces of seafood three times a week. Those who need to watch their cholesterol intake should watch their consumption of high-cholesterol seafood. Check the chart on pages 34 and 35 to get an idea of the amounts of Omega-3s and cholesterol there are in common seafood varieties.

SEAFOOD: THE INSIDE STORY

Seafood per 3½ oz (100 gm) Serving	Calories	Omega-3s gm	Cholesterol mg
Abalone	N/A	0.1	111
Channel Catfish	115	0.4	60
Clams, hardshell	54	0.24	40
Clams, softshell	62	0.24	25
Cod, Atlantic	75	0.2	45
Crab, Blue or Soft	81	0.3	80–100
Crab, Dungeness	87	0.38	60
Crab, Jonah	95	N/A	78
Crab, King	74	N/A	60
Dogfish	165	N/A	50
Eel, American	223	1.2	10
Flounder	90	0.3	50
Grouper	95	0.2	49
Haddock	83	0.2	65
Hake	87	0.4	N/A
Halibut, Atlantic	115	1.3	47
Halibut, Pacific	105	0.5	32
Herring, Atlantic	128	0.8	60
Herring, Pacific	160	1.7	75
Lobster, boiled live Maine	93	0.06	70–95
Mackerel, Atlantic	176	1.9	80
Mackerel, Pacific	129	1.1	52
Mahimahi	89	0.1	86
Monkfish	80	N/A	35
Mussels, Atlantic	80	0.43	40–65
Octopus	77	0.21	122
Orange Roughy	65	0.1	58
Oysters, Atlantic	69	0.4	55
Oysters, Pacific	79	0.7	47
Perch, Ocean	105	0.4	42

N/A: Data not available.
All values in this table are approximate.

Seafood per 3½ oz (100 gm) Serving	Calories	Omega-3s gm	Cholesterol mg
Perch, Yellow	86	0.2	90
Pike, Northern	87	0.1	40
Pollock	90	0.4	71
Pompano	165	0.6	50
Rockfish	78	0.6	35
Sablefish, Black Cod	184	1.3	49
Salmon, Atlantic	129	1.4	60
Salmon, Chinook (King)	184	1.9	66
Salmon, Chum	125	0.6	74
Salmon, Coho (Silver)	136	1.8	39
Salmon, Pink	124	2.2	52
Salmon, Sockeye	160	2.7	35
Scallops, Bay or Cape	80	0.13	N/A
Scallops, Sea	87	0.18	36

Seafood per 3½ oz (100 gm) Serving	Calories	Omega-3s gm	Cholesterol mg
Sea Trout	106	0.5	83
Shark	167	1.9	46
Shrimp, mixed species	91	0.20	150
Smelt	98	0.6	25
Snapper, Red	110	0.6	40
Snow Crab	90	0.44	N/A
Sole	88	0.1	50
Squid	95	0.8	200–300
Swordfish	122	0.2	40
Trout, Brook	108	0.3	68
Trout, Rainbow	131	0.5	56
Trout, Lake	162	1.4	50
Tuna, Albacore	172	1.3	55
Tuna, Yellowfin	124	0.6	45
Walleye Pike	93	0.2	85
Whitefish, Lake	162	0.8	60

Information in this chart was obtained from Seafood Nutrition *by Joyce A. Nettleton, D.Sc., R.D. (Osprey Books, 1985, 1987) and* Seafood: A Collection of Heart-Healthy Recipes, *by Janis Harsila, R.D. and Evie Hansen (National Seafood Educators, 1986).*

PREPARATION TOOLS

Chances are you buy or order seafood from your fishmonger cut and prepared to your specifications. This is normally the best way to buy fish, unless you have plenty of time to prepare it yourself or are lucky enough to get a whole fish directly from a fisherman. However, knowing preparation basics allows you to be versatile. Also, a whole fish keeps better than the sum of its parts, so if you steak or fillet a fish you know you're getting it fresher than if you bought it recipe-ready at the market.

You will need a few tools for preparing fish:

1. Fish scaler (optional).

2. Very sharp fish filleting knife with a flexible blade. Unless you will be working with very large fish, a 9-inch blade is sufficient.

3. Large chef's knife or medium to large cleaver, for large fish and for cutting through bones.

4. Steel to hone blades or a good knife sharpener.

5. Strawberry huller, fish tweezers, or needle-nose pliers for pulling out small bones.

6. Kitchen scissors for trimming off fins.

7. Heavy mallet.

SCALING

Scaling fish is the initial step with most species. Rub the fish with the fish scaler or the back of a chef's knife, working from tail to head (Fig. 1). Doing this under running water helps keep the scales from flying about, though the only real way to avoid the odd scale here or there is to take the fish out

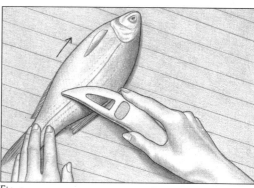
Fig. 1

in the garden where it won't matter if they scatter. Salmon have such small delicate scales that they don't need to be scaled, particularly if they are going to be grilled or baked without a sauce. Just rinse them thoroughly.

PREPARING ROUND FISH
(such as a salmon)

Dressing

1. Wash the fish, cut off the fins with scissors (Fig. 2), and trim the tail to a "V" shape. (This is for aesthetics. You may completely remove the tail if you prefer.)

Fig. 2

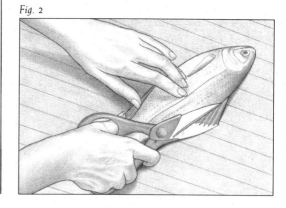

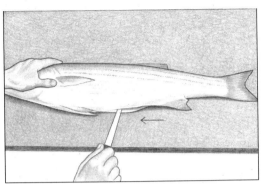

Fig. 3

2. Place the fish on a cutting board. Using the chef's knife, and resting one hand on the side of the fish, start near the tail end of the fish and make a shallow cut into and along the belly, to just below the head (Fig. 3). Be careful not to cut into the viscera (intestines), because they can release bitter acid into the flesh of the fish.

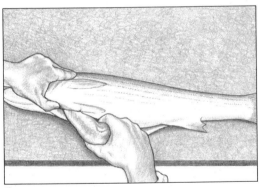

Fig. 4

3. Reach into the belly cavity with your hand and remove the viscera, which will detach easily. Just pull down, toward the tail (Fig. 4). The kidney lies along the backbone, inside a white membrane. Cut through the membrane to scrape out the kidney. Thoroughly rinse the belly cavity under very cold running water, scraping away any blood or

membrane until it is very clean.

4. If you want to leave the head on the fish, cut out the gills (the red parts behind the gill cover) by making a slit underneath the head, working the knife or the scissors in and snipping the gills where they are attached. Remove them and rinse the head very thoroughly. To remove the head, just follow the curve behind the gill cover, and

Code Words for Fish

Fresh. In seafood lingo, all fresh means is that the fish has never been frozen, regardless of its age or quality.

Flash-frozen. This is fish that is frozen on board ship or at a shore-based processing plant within hours after being caught.

Prime. This is one step below fresh-frozen fish in quality. If fish quality had a scale from 1 to 10, fresh-frozen would be a 10, prime would be a 9.

Fancy. You're planning a dinner party and want fish as elegant as your table linens, so you head for "fancy." Wait a minute. Fancy is code for previously frozen. It is between 6 and 8 on a quality scale, though it sometimes dips below that. In cases when fish has been fresh-frozen and properly thawed, it can be better than fresh. But it may have been frozen several days out of the water, or frozen, thawed and re-frozen. Chances are, if it's called fancy it is not at its best.

Bright or Silver Bright. This term technically refers to fish, particularly salmon, before they've entered freshwater to spawn, when they are still "bright" silver, and in good condition.

Fig. 5

cut right through the backbone (Fig. 5). The fish is now ready for preparing whole.

5. If you will be stuffing the fish, remove the backbone. Slip the filleting knife between the outside of the rib bones and the flesh. Start at one end and work toward the other, loosening the bones from the flesh. Repeat on the other side. Slip the knife under the backbone to loosen it and pull it out, with rib bones attached, snipping it off at each end (Fig. 6). The fish is now ready to be stuffed.

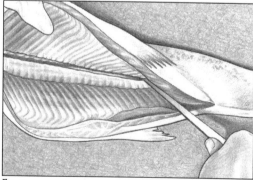

Fig. 6

Steaking

Use a very sharp chef's knife or cleaver. To cut steaks from a dressed salmon, place the

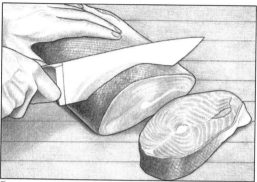

Fig. 7

fish on a board with the tail to one side. Beginning at the head end, cut slices from the fish that are about 1 inch thick (Fig. 7). Use a hard mallet, if necessary, to bang the knife through the bone, rather than sawing on it. When you get near the tail and the narrow end of the fish, cut fillets from that part of the fish.

Filleting

1. Lay the dressed fish on a cutting board with the tail toward you and the stomach to one side.

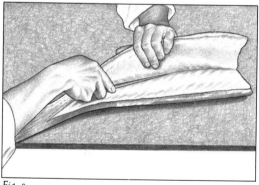

Fig. 8

2. Using a very sharp chef's knife or cleaver, cut off the head. Place one hand flat

on the fish, and cut along the backbone from the head to the tail (Fig. 8).

3. Starting at the head end, work your fingers under the flesh, gently lifting it away from the bone and cutting with the knife at the same time. Keep the knife very flat against the bone so you lose as little meat as possible, and try to make long, sweeping cuts instead of short ones. Cut until the fillet is completely separated from the backbone and the tail. Flip the fish over, and repeat the process on the other side.

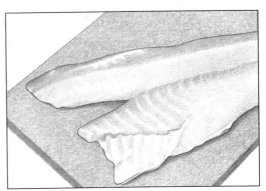

Fig. 10

remove the strip of meat which will include the bones. This is called a V-cut (Fig. 10).

You can also remove the nape and the pin bones with two cuts, which takes a large part of the meat as well. This is called a J-cut. Pull out any remaining bones with the strawberry huller, fish tweezers, or needle-nose pliers. Be careful not to grab the bones too tightly as they are soft and may break. If you still feel bones in the fillet or along the edges, just trim them out, taking as little meat with them as possible.

6. If you plan to remove the skin (which generally isn't advisable since the skin tends to hold fish together), lay the fillet flat on a board, skin side down. About ¼ inch from the tail end of the fillet, work the blade of the filleting knife between the flesh and the skin. Grab hold of the skin with your other hand and pull while you slip the knife blade between the skin and the flesh. If it is difficult, wag the skin back and forth as you push with the knife blade.

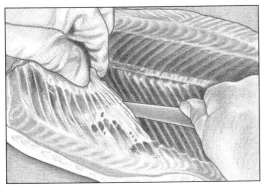

Fig. 9

4. Trim the bones from the fillet. Any remaining rib bones are very easy to see. To remove them, just cut right under them, keeping the knife blade flat against the bones, and pulling gently up on them as they detach (Fig. 9). Trim off the very fatty edge of the belly flap to clean up the fillet, and trim off any fins or pieces of skin.

5. There are bones other than the backbone and rib bones in fish, called pin bones. You can find them by rubbing your fingers along the fish, from head to tail. In many fish there is a strip of pin bones that typically runs halfway down the middle of the fillet. To remove them, make a narrow cut on either side of the bones through the fillet and

PREPARING FLAT FISH
(such as sole)

Dressing

Wash the fish and scale it. Cut off the fins with scissors and trim the tail to a "V" shape (this is for a aesthetics). You may proceed directly to "Filleting," without further dressing. If you plan to serve the fish whole, cut off the head at an angle (Fig. 11), and press

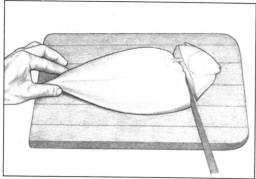

Fig. 11

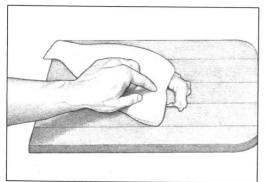

Fig. 12

on the body of the fish to force out the viscera (Fig. 12). Trim away any membranes from the body cavity, and thoroughly rinse it to remove any blood or tissue.

Filleting

1. Place your hand on the fish to hold it in place, dark side down, then make a shallow, diagonal cut with the filleting knife behind the head (Fig. 13).

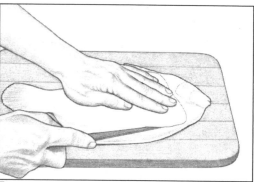

Fig. 13

2. Slip the knife blade into the cut, so that it is between the flesh and the bones of the fish. Slide the blade, keeping it flat against the bones, toward the tail, separating the fillet from the bones. Try to work in long, sweeping strokes, lifting the fillet with one hand, and cutting with the other. This is very simple—just remember to keep the knife blade flat (Fig. 14).

Fig. 14

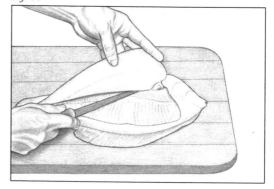

3. Hold the almost severed fillet with one hand, and with the other cut loose the fillet right down to the tail, keeping the knife blade at a slightly downward angle. Trim away the comb, or small bones, at the edge of the fillet.

4. Flip the fish over so the dark side is up. Make a shallow, diagonal cut right into the thick, fleshy part of the fish behind the head, but not through the backbone and repeat the filleting process.

5. To remove the skin from the fillet, place it on the work surface, skin side down. Holding the knife blade at a shallow angle, cut through the flesh to the skin about ¼ inch from the tail end. Keeping the blade flat and hanging on to the little flap of skin with your other hand, slide the knife blade between the meat and the skin, pulling the skin and wagging it gently back and forth if necessary, as it separates from the meat. It should detach easily (Fig. 15).

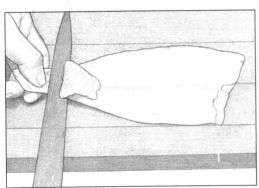

Fig. 15

6. To skin the whole fish, make a shallow cut through the dark skin at the base of the tail, but don't cut through the meat. (It is advisable to skin the dark side of the fish, leaving the light skin attached.) Using the knife blade, scrape the skin up just enough

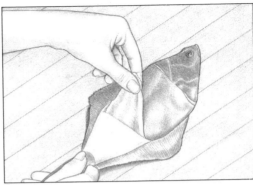

Fig. 16

so you can grasp it with your fingers. Holding the body of the fish down with one hand, pull the skin off with the other, toward and over the head (Fig. 16).

7. To stuff a flat fish, place the fish, light skin up (eyes up, if the head is still attached) on a cutting board. Use a filleting knife to cut a line down the backbone, starting from 1 inch below where the head was attached (1 inch below the mouth, if the head is left on),

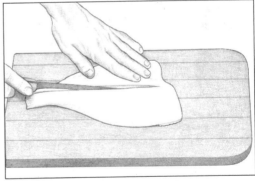

Fig. 17

Fig.17. Slide the knife between the bone and the fillet just to the upper outside edge, without cutting through at the head, tail, or sides. Repeat from the backbone to the bottom outside edge. Using scissors, snip

Fig. 18

through the backbone at either end and cut through the ribs all around. Slip the knife under the bones to detach them from the meat. Remove the bones. There is now a pocket in the fish that can be stuffed (Fig. 18).

PREPARING OYSTERS

Scrub the shells clean with a stiff vegetable brush so no debris will fall into the oyster. This is very important, as harmful bacteria can be carried on an oyster shell and can contaminate the oyster.

Shucking Oysters

There are several tricks and a measure of luck involved in shucking oysters, but anyone can learn to do it. You will need:
- Kitchen towel.
- Oyster knife, preferably with a 2½- to 4-inch blade and without a hand guard, which is awkward. Standard oyster knives are available in most cookware shops. If you have oysters with particularly delicate shells such as Olympias, you may want to use the thinner blade of a paring knife.
- Plate or tray with crushed ice on it.

1. Fold the towel so that it is several layers thick and will cover your hand. One of the shells of an oyster is more cupped than the other. Place the cupped shell down in the towel in the palm of your hand, with the hinged edge toward you (Fig. 19). Remember to keep the oyster balanced so that when it is open its liquor does not run off.

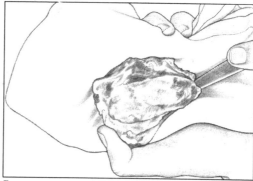

Fig. 19

2. Gently force the tip of the oyster knife into the shell at the hinged end, usually just to one side of the hinge. Work the knife in, twisting it slightly, remembering not to exert too much force, or you will find yourself with a skewered oyster, broken shells, or possibly an injury. Be patient and you will

Fig. 20

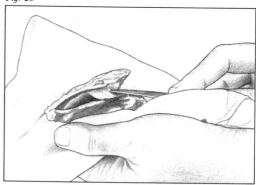

feel the shell open. Keep in mind that the oyster is nestled in the shell, rising slightly above the edge of the bottom shell, so that once the knife is in, it should be pointing up and away from the oyster (Fig. 20).

3. You need to cut the muscle that holds both the oyster to the shell and the shells together, which is toward the back of the shell. When the knife blade is inside the shell, slide it flat against the upper shell until you feel it hit, and cut through the muscle. Remove the top shell. Inspect the oyster for cuts, or for bits of shell that may have fallen in. Carefully pick out any bits of shell.

4. Finally, slip the knife blade gently under the oyster and cut the muscle that holds it in place. Detaching the oyster isn't necessary, but it is a kind concession to guests, who can then suavely slurp up the oyster without having to detach it from the shell. You may want to flip the oyster before serving, to hide any cuts.

Preparing Clams

If your clams have been cultured away from the sea or bay bottom, there is little chance they will have sand in them. But those clams that have grown in the sand do have little gritty deposits in their bellies, flotsam from their most recent meal. A mouthful of grit is extremely objectionable; it is definitely worth some effort to purge it from the shellfish.

Steam a clam open and taste it for grit. If there is some, place the remaining clams in a bucket or large bowl of salted water (⅓ cup salt mixed well with 1 gallon water). Mix in a handful of cornmeal to expedite the purging, then add the clams. Keep the clams in the salted water for about 2 hours and they will purge themselves.

Finally, scrub the shells thoroughly under cold running water with a stiff vegetable brush.

Shucking Clams

Littleneck, cherrystone, and soft-shell clams are excellent East Coast clams on the half

---

Oyster Tips

Keep them in the refrigerator covered with a damp towel, their deeper shell down, for no longer than one week before shucking.

Eat them as soon as they are shucked. If you must shuck them in advance, place ice on a plate or tray, cover it with a doubled kitchen towel, then place the oysters on it, so they are not in direct contact with the ice. Cover them with aluminum foil or plastic and don't let them sit for longer than 1 hour this way in the refrigerator.

Serve them on ice—it keeps them upright so they don't tip and lose their liquor. Place seaweed or lettuce leaves between the oysters and the ice because they should be refreshingly cold, not glacial. Kosher or coarse salt is an alternative to ice if the oysters are already cold and will be served immediately, though it will warm the oysters if they stay on it long, and it can migrate into the oyster, which isn't pleasant.

Try oysters neat, freshly shucked, without any sauce at all, just to give them a try!

shell. Butter clams, native littlenecks, Manila, and soft-shell clams are West Coast offerings to the half shell market, desirable in that order of preference. To shuck clams, you'll need an oyster knife or any sturdy, short-bladed, slim knife for the job, and a rubber glove or towel to protect your hand.

1. Place the clam in the palm of your hand, with the hinge toward the wrist.

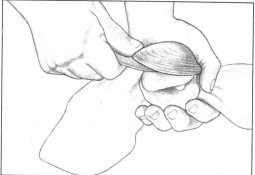

Fig. 21

2. Insert the blade between the shells to one side of the hinge, gently working it back and forth (Fig. 21). Move the knife around to sever the muscle at the hinge, then sever the adductor muscles on the top and bottom shells to free the clam. Be careful not to cut into the clam meat. Remember to keep the

Fig. 22

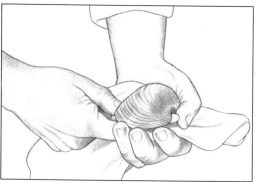

clam evenly balanced so its liquor doesn't run out (Fig. 22). Manila clams present an added challenge—they are doubled hinged across the back, so you need to be persistent when detaching the muscles there. The top shell may break—don't worry, just watch for pieces in the clam and remove them.

3. Serve the clams on ice as for oysters.

PREPARING MUSSELS

Unless they are aquacultured, and sometimes even then, mussels can arrive in your kitchen carrying whole marine environments on their shells. These are wonderful to look at—there might be tiny barnacles, little forests of seaweed, perhaps the shell of an underwater snail. The mussel shells should be scrubbed thoroughly with a vegetable brush, and the barnacles chipped off with a knife or your finger. Part of this is aesthetic, part is practical—the barnacles can chip and send shards into the mussel meats, and contamination can result from the other underwater miscellany.

Once they're scrubbed, remove the byssal threads (byssus), or beard (Fig. 23). These clumps of incredibly strong material suspend the mussels in the water as they hang from pilings and boat hulls, sometimes in the strongest currents. Try to remove the beard with your fingers by giving it a tug. If that doesn't work, use pliers, gently of course, so as not to rip the animal apart. If short of putting your foot on the mussel and yanking, you still can't get the beard all the way out, remove what you can and leave the rest. *Never remove the beard until right before you plan to cook mussels, because they will die and spoil.*

Give the mussels a good rinse and proceed.

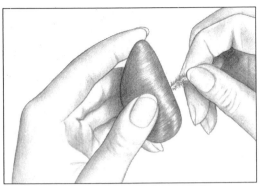

Fig. 23

Shucking Mussels

Shucking mussels is similar to shucking clams and oysters, but a trifle trickier because mussel shells—particularly from West Coast mussels—are more fragile than other shellfish. You'll need a pocket or a paring knife for this job, and a towel or glove to protect your hand.

1. Place the mussel in the towel in the palm of the hand, the hinge toward the wrist. Find the small opening on the side of the mussel shell where the byssal thread came through, and work the knife blade into that. Mussels open their shells to the side, rather than the front like clams, so work the knife

Fig. 24

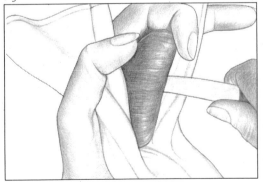

to the back and sever the muscle there, at the hinge (Fig. 24).

2. Sever the adductor muscles on the top and bottom shell to free the mussel.

3. Serve them on ice as for oysters.

PREPARING SQUID

1. To clean squid, pull the head with the tentacles from the mantle, which will also remove most of the viscera (Fig. 25). You

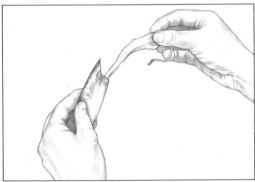

Fig. 25

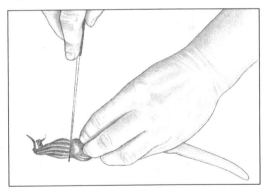

Fig. 26

may need to reach inside the mantle to remove any viscera that remains. There is a long, transparent, flexible "pen" inside the mantle, which is the bone. Pull it out and discard. Rinse the mantle under cold running water and make sure it is completely clean and empty inside.

2. If you want to remove the skin from the mantle, which is an aesthetic decision, just peel it off—it detaches easily.

3. Cut off the tentacles right in front of the eyes (Fig. 26), and using your thumb and forefinger, gently squeeze out the "beak" (a small piece of cartilage) from the center of the tentacles.

PREPARING GEODUCK

Geoducks (gooey-ducks) are not the most commonly available shellfish, but certainly one of the most talked about when they do appear, and they are delicious. To prepare them, you'll need a filleting knife.

1. Place the geoduck—both body and siphon—under hot tap water for no longer than 1 minute, to loosen the skin (Fig. 27). Plunge the geoduck into a bowl or bucket of cold water until it is cool enough to handle.

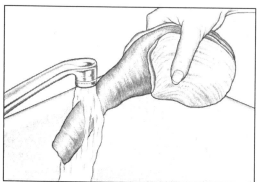

Fig. 27

2. Using a filleting knife, cut each muscle located just inside the ends of both shells to loosen the body from the shell (Fig. 28).

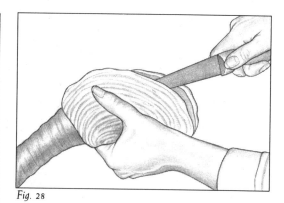

Fig. 28

When the muscles are cut, gently pull the shells away from the body meat. Cut any remaining muscle that holds the meat to the shell.

3. Peel the skin from the siphon by rubbing to loosen it, and remove any skin that is attached to the body. With a vegetable brush, vigorously brush the siphon to remove any dark coloration.

4. To remove the intestines, which are neatly encased in an orb attached to the body meat, carefully cut around them, trimming away any attaching membranes.

5. Separate the siphon from the body meat by cutting through it right at the base.

PREPARING SHRIMP

Shrimp are easy to prepare with a simple paring knife.

1. To peel raw or cooked shrimp, pull off the legs, then peel off the shell from the underside. You may want to leave just the fan of the tail shell on the shrimp, which is considered a very dressy way to serve them.

2. If you peel the shrimp, you may also want to devein them. Simply make a shallow slit right down the back with the paring knife, and remove the black vein (Figs. 29 and 30). Deveining is advisable for medium-size shrimp and larger (31 to 35 per pound; about 3½ inches long.)

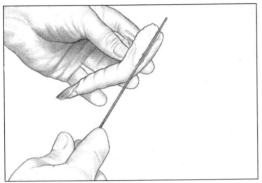

Fig. 29

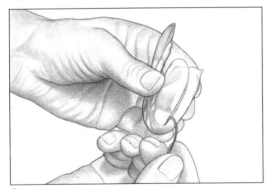

Fig. 30

Preparing Lobster

There are many ways to prepare a lobster. The American Society for the Prevention of Cruelty to Animals suggests placing the lobster on a rack in the bottom of a pan filled with cold water, and gradually bringing the water to 104°F, which feels lukewarm. This temperature lulls the lobster, and it will go limp and die. It is not cooked, and you can

proceed with any recipe calling for uncooked lobster.

Another humane treatment that isn't quite so gentle (for it you'll need a large chef's knife), is to place the lobster on a cutting board, the tail to one side, the claws to the other. Cover the tail with a towel to help you hold it still, and grasp it firmly. There is a pale cross on the back of the lobster's shell; quickly pierce the shell where the cross intersects, with the point of a large chef's knife, the sharp edge facing the tail. Push down until the blade tip hits the board. This will kill the lobster immediately.

To prepare uncooked lobster for stuffing:

1. Turn it on its back, and split it down the middle from head to tail fan, being careful not to cut through the back of the lobster shell (Fig. 31). Remove the intestines (the intestinal tract runs right down the length of the tail, Fig. 32), the sand sac from the head (Fig. 33), tomalley (greenish-gray liver) and coral (eggs), discarding the intestines and sand sac, and reserving the tomalley and coral. Quickly rinse the lobster and pat dry. Gently press the halves of the lobster apart to make room for the stuffing.

2. Crack the claws gently, so they remain intact but the meat will be easily accessible once it is baked. The lobster is now ready to stuff.

To extract uncooked or cooked lobster meat you'll need a large chef's knife, a nut pick or paring knife, and kitchen scissors (optional):

1. To remove the meat from the claws, first break them from the body by twisting. Pull off the "thumb" part of the claw, then crack the claws gently, so you don't damage the meat, by rapping them with the blunt side of a large chef's knife. The meat should

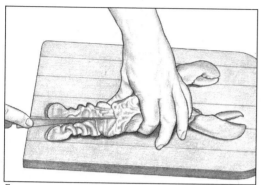

Fig. 31

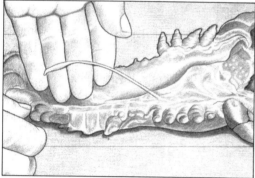

Fig. 32

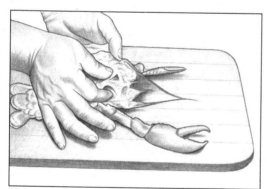

Fig. 33

come out in one piece. The legs also contain meat—just crack them gently and pry it out with a nut pick or a sharp paring knife.

2. To remove the tail meat from the shell in one piece, lay the tail on its side and press down firmly on the shell so that it cracks. (Or cut through the underside of the shell with the kitchen scissors.) Then hold the tail with two hands, under side up, and gently pull the shell away from the sides of the tail. You may need to slide your index finger between the meat and the shell to loosen the meat. Pull out the tail meat, make a shallow slit down the back, and remove the vein. The lobster tail is now ready to be cut into medallions, diced, sliced in thin strips, or cut in half.

There are several ways to prepare an uncooked lobster tail for cooking. The methods include:

1. Piggyback lobster tail: Cut through the upper part of the tail shell just to the fan, leaving the bottom of the shell intact. Extract the tail meat in one piece and clean it if necessary, by making a shallow slit down the back and removing the vein. Place the meat partially back in the shell, and it is ready for broiling.

2. Butterflied lobster tail: Cut through the upper shell from top to tail fan right through the tail meat, leaving the lower shell intact, spreading the halves apart. Remove the vein. It is now ready for broiling or baking.

3. Cutting away the undershell of the tail and removing it, leaving the meat exposed, ready for broiling.

4. Following the directions for Method 1 to remove the meat from the shell, then either dicing the tail meat, and sautéing it with other ingredients to make a light stuffing, or replacing it in the tail shell and quickly broiling it.

PREPARING CRAB

Cooked Crab

There are several varieties of edible crab, the most common of which include the Northwest's Dungeness; blue crab from Maryland, which are eaten in their soft- and hard-shell forms; the claws from stone crabs, which are marketed cooked; tanner or snow crab from the West Coast; king crab from Alaska; and jonah crab from the western Atlantic.

Crab (except for soft-shells) are most often cooked whole, then cleaned after cooking, in roughly the same manner for each species. The amount of meat they contain and its location varies depending on their habitat. Those that swim, like the blue crab, are meatiest in the body and leg joints. Dungeness crab skitter around the bottom of Northwest waters, and they have muscular legs filled with meat as well as meaty bodies. King crab are mostly legs—they look like giant, bright red and bumpy spiders on stilts, their bodies high above thin, pointy legs that are filled with meat.

The following directions are for cooked Dungeness crab, but can be applied to any crab, depending on where the meat is located. You will need a paring knife or kitchen scissors, a nutcracker, nut pick or small fork, and a large chef's knife or cleaver.

1. Grasp the top shell at the front and pull it up and away from the body (Fig. 34). Reserve the shell.

2. Turn the crab over and lift off the narrow triangular apron, removing the soft spines hidden underneath at the same time. Discard these.

3. From the top of the crab remove the white, spongy, finger-like gills that are called

Raw Fish

The sushi revolution aside, some experts counsel against eating raw fish, for it may contain parasites. Most parasites are harmless, tiny white worms. Though we recoil in horror at finding one of these in raw fish they are a perfectly natural occurrence. Only a few fish parasites are harmful to man. The best known are *anisakis*, a nematode parasite of marine fish, and *diphyllobothrium*, a tapeworm parasite of freshwater fish.

Should there be parasites in fish, they are usually removed at the processing plant in a process called "candling." Skinned fillets are put on a conveyor belt that is lit from underneath. The parasites are easy to spot because of the light shining through the fillet, and they are plucked out with tweezers. Candling largely takes care of the parasite problem.

If you do happen to find a parasite in a fillet of fish, don't throw out the fish. A parasite is more unappetizing than harmful, and you can remove it with a pair of sterilized tweezers. Rest assured too, that thorough cooking will kill any parasite. If you plan to serve raw fish, particularly salmon, first make sure it was fresh-frozen. No parasite will survive being frozen at 0°F for 72 hours. *If you can't determine from your fish merchant whether or not the fish you plan to buy for sushi or tartare was fresh-frozen, then don't buy it.*

Your best safeguard is to buy fish and shellfish from a reputable merchant. If you do encounter a problem, return the seafood. Your complaints and demand for better quality will make changes happen faster.

"dead man's fingers" and are inedible, and the firm, white intestine; discard (Fig. 35). Remove the mouth parts from the crab and discard. There will be greenish-gold viscera

Fig. 34

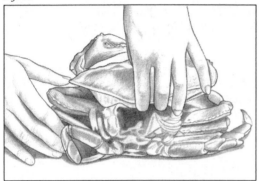

Fig. 35

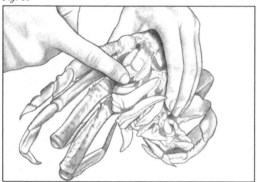

Fig. 36

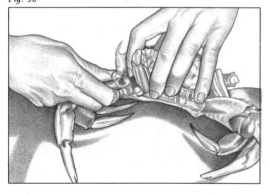

inside the body—this is the "crab butter" and it has a wonderful briny, buttery taste, prized by many. Scrape it out from the body, and also from the corners of the top shell and either save it to eat (mix it with equal parts softened unsalted butter and spread it on small toasts for a tasty appetizer) or discard it. Thoroughly rinse the crab (and the top shell if you plan to use it as a serving dish) under cold running water.

4. Holding the legs and the claws close to the body, twist them off (Fig. 36), and gently crack the shells on each with a nutcracker or the back of a sharp knife, so the meat is easily accessible. It can be picked out in large pieces with a nut pick or small fork.

5. Grasp the body and snap it in half. You may need to cut it with a heavy knife or a cleaver. The body is segmented, and the meat is separated by thin, sharp shells. Carefully pick or shake the meat out of the shell.

Live Crab

Controversy surrounds the best method for handling crab. Some say it is best to cook a crab live, others insist it is just fine to cook an already dispatched crab. There is no firm answer to the question of which is best.

Dungeness crab become very docile out of water, but to be sure, refrigerate a live crab for a couple of hours.

1. Approach the crab from the back, grab the legs on each side near the body so you are holding the crab with two hands. Crack the underside of the crab on the sharp edge of a table or a cutting board, to stun it.

2. If the top shell will be used in presentation, pull it off the crab. Clean out the viscera and trim away the gills. Cut the crab in half down the middle, removing the legs and claws and cracking them so the meat will

be accessible once it is cooked, and cutting the body into quarters, cracking it lightly as well.

3. If the shell won't be used in presentation, remove the crab from the refrigerator, lay it on its back and using a sharp knife or cleaver, cut it in half and proceed as for cleaning a cooked Dungeness crab.

Soft-shell crabs can be dressed by cutting across the crab's face at an upward angle so the eyes and scaly section of the lower mouth are removed. Then, trim away the gills on the underside and cut off the apron.

The most humane way to dispatch a crab is to anesthetize it first. Place the crab on a rack in the bottom of a pan filled with a couple of inches of cold water, and gradually bring the water to 104°F, which feels lukewarm. The crab will go limp and die. It isn't cooked and you can proceed with any recipe calling for live crab.

I Say Crayfish, You Say Crawfish.

Which is correct? That depends. If you're from the south, where the bayous and the Atchafalaya Basin team with the revered creatures, you call them crawfish. If you're currently from the Northwest—current meaning since the latter half of the twentieth century—where the lusty clawed crustaceans inhabit crystal clear, cold lakes and rivers, you call them crayfish, even though turn-of-the-century Northwesterners called them crawfish.

PREPARING CRAWFISH

The two kinds of crawfish (or crayfish) in the United States are so closely related that they are almost identical. Those from Louisiana are slimmer and smaller than those from the West Coast, and they are both prepared in the same fashion.

1. Rinse the live crawfish under cold running water.

2. The end of the tail has 5 tiny flaps on it that overlap and create a fan. Take the middle flap between your thumb and forefinger, twist it sharply clockwise, and pull. It will draw the entrails right out of the crawfish, leaving it clean and ready to cook (Fig. 37).

Fig. 37

COOKING FISH

The rule of thumb for cooking seafood is that less cooking is better. Americans have a tradition of overcooking fish, which often produces dry, tough results. Of course, undercooking it so the middle is still raw isn't the best idea either. You can rescue fish that is undercooked, but there is nothing to do about overcooked seafood but take your lumps and try to enjoy it.

Some Basic Seafood Cooking Rules

1. Keep your fish or shellfish in the refrigerator until right before you cook it to keep it as fresh as possible. Don't leave it sitting on the counter while you prepare the rest of the meal.

2. Don't work in the same area with raw seafood and cooked seafood. There is too much danger of cross contamination.

3. Cook seafood with the skin on whenever possible and appropriate. It helps fillets and steaks hold their shape and keeps moisture in whole fish. Make two or three shallow slashes across the skin of the fillet or whole fish to prevent the fish from curling while cooking.

4. If you are baking fish that is of different thicknesses, as in fillets that taper to very thin ends, fold the thin ends under so they won't overcook.

5. Try to turn fish just once, if at all, during the cooking process so there is less risk of it falling apart.

6. If cooking fish in a coating or batter, use small or thin pieces so both batter and fish cook at the same rate.

Generally, fish should be cooked until it is opaque. If you like it undercooked, cook it until the meat is opaque except for a thin translucent line running through the center of a piece of fish, or until the meat nearest the spinal column is still slightly translucent. Remember that fish will continue to cook after being removed from the heat, so allow for this by removing it just before it is done to your preference.

For shellfish, the ideal is to cook them until they open, and then about 30 seconds longer, except for pink scallops, which should be cooked 1 minute longer.

As is true in most cooking, sight and touch are more important than times. All of the recipes in this book tell you what to look for first, then give approximate times so if you are in doubt, you can fall back on timing.

Broiling and Grilling

When you are broiling or grilling fish, thoroughly oil the rack using a paper towel dipped in vegetable oil, so the fish won't stick. You don't need to use a lot of oil, just a thin layer. An oil-based marinade serves the same purpose. If you are applying a marinade, sauce, or oil to fish while it is grilling or broiling, do so with a brush so you can apply it evenly.

Broiling. When cooking fish under the broiler, put it in a shallow pan and pour about ½ cup fish stock, white wine, or marinade around it so it won't dry out.

Grilling. Fish cooked on the grill (or under the broiler) should have a soft resistance when it is done. It should be firm, but not rubbery or tough, and it should be nearly opaque through. To test for doneness, insert a metal skewer into the middle of the fish and pull it back gently so you can see into the fish. If the fish is still translucent and looks undercooked, give it more time. Remember, though, that fish will continue cooking after it is taken from the heat, so allow for that.

Test a fillet for doneness by lifting it at its thickest part, using a spatula. If it flakes, then it is done.

Certain fish benefit from cooking over

moderate heat, some adapt well to being seared. "Fish live in low gravity and they don't have a lot of tensile strength protein. They're high in albumen, like eggs, and they burn quickly. They get bitter when they're burned. You would never drop an egg in a smoking hot skillet," said Robert Del Grande, chef at Houston's popular Cafe Annie where nearly 50 percent of the menu is fish.

Some fish—swordfish and tuna specifically—may benefit from higher temperatures but generally, the fire shouldn't be so hot that the fish sizzles and gets black grill marks on it. Grill marks should be golden.

1. Preheat the grill, heating the coals until they are covered with ash. If you can hold your hand over the fire for 4 to 5 seconds without pulling it away, the heat is right.

2. Oil the grill rack.

3. Place the fish across the rungs of the rack so it has as much contact with the heat as possible.

4. If using wood briquets, try closing the lid of the barbecue, leaving the vents slightly open, for a nice, smoky flavor.

5. If you need to turn the fish, which may not be necessary if the temperature of the coals is right, turn it just once so it doesn't fall apart.

6. Grill shrimp over a slightly hotter fire than the one used for fish. They cook very quickly so watch carefully, but they should emerge with distinct, golden grill marks on them for best results.

Frying, Sautéing, Poaching, and Steaming

Frying. If you are deep-frying fish, have the oil temperature at about 375°F. This will

---

A Bone in Your Throat

*I*f you miss a bone and don't discover it until it's halfway down your throat, don't panic. Bite off a piece of bread, chew and swallow it. It will take the bone with it, out of harm's way.

---

give the fish a lovely, golden coating and allow it time to cook through. When frying fish, make sure pieces are of uniform size and thickness.

Oven-frying is a wonderful twist on pan-frying. It requires much less fat, and yet the fish gets a good, crisp coating without drying out. Heat the oven to 500°F and oven-fry the fish in enough oil to coat the bottom of the pan until it is opaque.

Sautéing. When you sauté, keep the heat to medium or medium high. If the heat is higher than that the fish will cook on the outside and get tough, while the inside remains uncooked. Cut seafood in pieces as uniform as possible, so that they cook at the same rate.

To test for doneness, insert a skewer into a piece of fish, and if it is opaque or very close to it, it's done.

Poaching. Poaching fish is a very gentle method of cooking, and one that allows you to enhance the inherent flavor of fish in subtle ways. Many different liquids can be used for poaching, and they can be flavored with herbs, spices, vegetables, and wines.

1. Put fish in a cool liquid and slowly bring it to a boil, then reduce the heat so it simmers. If you pour hot liquid over fish, it will cause the skin to wrinkle, and the fish to cook unevenly. Watch the fish carefully, and be sure not to let the poaching liquid boil vigorously, for it will break the fish apart.

2. Poaching fish with the skin on helps keep it together.

3. You will need a fish poacher if you are planning to poach a whole fish. Otherwise a deep saucepan or kettle that will hold enough liquid to cover the fish works very well.

4. If there isn't enough poaching liquid to cover the entire fish, moisten a clean cotton tea towel with poaching liquid, lay it over the fish, and keep it moist by spooning the liquid over it. This will ensure the fish cooks evenly.

Steaming. Fish that has been steamed retains its integrity better than just about any other way of preparing it. Steaming doesn't appreciably alter the shape of fish, either, so you can arrange fish on a plate, steam it, drain off any liquid that accumulates, and serve it directly from the steamer.

You can use liquids flavored with herbs, spices, and vegetables to add subtle flavors to steamed fish, or you can lay herbs and spices under and over fish, so that as it cooks, it absorbs the flavors. Whole fish to be steamed can be stuffed first, and they emerge absolutely unblemished.

1. Rub the fish all over with a light coating of oil before you steam it, so it won't stick to the plate or steamer rack.

2. Fish cooks quickly under all circumstances, but steaming seems to speed up the cooking process even more, so watch carefully. It's a great way to prepare fish quickly and with a minimum of effort.

3. Steamed or poached fish will feel firm when it is done. Insert a metal skewer at the thickest point to see if it is opaque throughout, or use the spatula test.

COOKING SHELLFISH

You've probably had clams with the texture of a rubber band, mussels like little Superballs, scallops that would have bounced if they'd hit the floor. They were all overcooked. "Less cooking is better" is a good rule for shellfish, too.

Mussels and clams lighten in color as they cook. Mussels that started out bright orange will take on a creamy orange color, and clams will lighten slightly. Mussels and clams in the shell should be cooked until they open, then for another 30 seconds.

Scallops darken slightly in color when they are cooked. For scallops in the shell (specifically pink scallops), cook them until they open, then for an additional 1 minute.

Oysters in the shell should be cooked until their shells open, then for an additional 1 to 2 minutes, depending on your preference. Oyster shells won't open completely when the oysters are cooked, so you can't judge their doneness by color unless you loosen the shell. If they aren't done, push the shell back down and cook them until they are.

Oysters lose their color definition as they cook, becoming a silver gray. A good rule for shucked oysters is to cook them just until they begin to curl around the edges.

Add pre-cooked shellfish to a warm sauce, soup, or pasta just a minute or two before serving, so it has time to warm up and cook slightly, but doesn't overcook.

Geoduck body meat is best sautéed. Cut it

Fish School

It's the first day of a three day fish school at Boston's New England Fisheries Development Foundation, down the street from the Boston Fish Pier. Students, who range from seafood importers to retail store owners and fish counter clerks, sit timidly, a baseball-style hat and fat blue folder on each desk, a slide projector at the front of the room. Maps of American and Canadian fishing grounds and posters of brightly colored fish hang on the walls, and there's a briny whiff in the air.

Before the three days are over, the students will have worn their hats to fish auctions and through major fish processors in Boston and New Bedford; they will have seen fish species from all over the world and learned to identify the most common; they will have been introduced to the baffling world of seafood nomenclature where a Boston blue is a Boston cod is an Atlantic pollock; and they will have prepared a lavish seafood meal.

Fish School provides a unique insight into the seafood industry by taking students behind the scenes, giving them gritty, wet experience not just in cooking seafood, but in judging freshness, identifying species by peering inside piscine lips to examine teeth, in watching experts cut, wash, and check fillets as the scales and water fly, and in learning how to fillet, steak and prepare whole fish, themselves. Commercial fishermen and professionals in the seafood industry teach the courses, and they tell students everything they know about seafood.

Fish school is a must for anyone in the seafood business, or anyone who wants to be. And if you're just simply mad about seafood, and want to know more about preparation and buying, with a little spice thrown in, you'll want to attend the one-day consumer program held at Boston University.

Write to the NEFDF Fish School at 280 Northern Avenue, Boston, MA 02210, or call (617) 542-7354 and ask for Karla Ruzicka.

The West Coast Fisheries Development Foundation, 812 S.W. Washington Street, Suite 900, Portland, OR 97205, (503) 222-3518 offers a similar program in Seattle, Washington, geared primarily to retailers, that gives an overview of the West Coast seafood industry. The Mid Atlantic Fisheries Development Foundation, 2200 Somerville Road, Annapolis, MD 21401-9990, (301) 266-5530 offers a comprehensive two-week session on Mid Atlantic seafoods called Fish Tech. All of the fish schools welcome the general public, whatever their background and interest.

in thin, horizontal slices which will resemble beige butterflies, and sauté it very quickly in butter, no longer than 30 seconds. Serve immediately. If you want to eat the geoduck raw, for sashimi, the siphon is best. Cut it in half lengthwise, rinse out any sand that might be inside, and pound it gently a couple of times to relax it. Then, using a sharp, thin-bladed knife, slice the siphon horizontally into paper-thin slices. If they curl, make diagonal cuts in the slices to help them lie flat. Serve with plenty of *wasabi* (green horse-radish) and eat immediately.

Squid is a unique case. What begins as a relatively tender meat can turn to firm elastic in a matter of seconds. To avoid toughness, cook it until it turns opaque. If you are sautéing squid, the right amount of time is 45 seconds to 1 minute. If you are baking squid stuffed and with a sauce, 8 to 10 minutes is right, checking to be sure it is opaque. If you don't catch it then, go ahead and let the squid cook for at least 20 minutes; this way it will pass through the tough stage and become tender again. I have found, however, that squid loses something in both flavor and texture when it is cooked longer than 20 minutes. It will still be perfectly edible cooked for a longer time, but it won't be at its prime.

COOKING CRUSTACEANS

Shrimp turn vivid pink the second they are cooked. Overcooking toughens and dries them out, so be vigilant—you want them tender and moist, so remove shrimp from the heat as soon as they change color.

Crawfish are tricky; if they are over-cooked by even a second they turn mushy. A good rule for boiling crawfish—one of the most sublime ways to eat them is boiled—is to drop them into boiling water one by one, as you clean them. After the water has returned to a boil, cook the crawfish for 8 minutes. Dropping crawfish in singly keeps the water boiling continually. The crawfish are done when they are red, and when the tail flaps have separated slightly from the tail shell.

Boiled crab and lobster signal their doneness by floating to the top of the water. When baked, lobster meat should be white through, but still very moist and not tough or dry. The same is true for crabmeat.

Part Two

THE RECIPES
AND LEXICON

3

STARTERS, SALADS, PICKLES & THINGS

irst courses are little palate teasers. Their purpose is to nudge the tastebuds awake, to get them stimulated, excited, ready for more. Starters should have fresh flavor, be attractive, colorful, and presented with panache, for the tastebuds aren't the only things that need awakening. The eyes play a large part in the success of a recipe—if it's beautiful, the palate wants it. If it isn't, the challenge is great, no matter how good the dish may taste.

Seafood is easily transformed into beautiful first courses. They can be bold like the Purslane and Smoked Trout Salad or the vivid Red and Orange Salad. Or they can be dainty still lifes like the Smoked Sturgeon with Salmon Pâté and Roe or the Oyster Salad with Artichokes.

You'll find plenty of recipes in this chapter to entice you. They are perfect starters for any meal, whether it's meat or seafood. Some will lighten a hearty meal, others anchor a light one. They all make perfect beginnings.

Smoked Sturgeon with Salmon Pâté and Roe

I love the simple elegance of this dish, which looks as lovely as it is good to eat. A hot-smoked, firm salmon, such as Northwest-style alder-smoked salmon, is best for the pâté. But you must have cold-smoked sturgeon so it will slice almost paper-thin. Try a lightly chilled Sancerre with this.

8 ounces hot-smoked salmon
1 large package (8 ounces) cream cheese, at room
    temperature
1 tablespoon fresh lemon juice
8 ounces cold-smoked sturgeon, cut into ⅛-inch slices
1 tablespoon extra-virgin olive oil
20 fresh chives
2 tablespoons salmon roe
¼ cup small flat-leaf parsley leaves, for garnish

1. Remove and discard any skin or bones from the smoked salmon. Cut the salmon into 1-inch chunks and place them in the bowl of a food processor. Pulse 2 or 3 times until the salmon is broken into small pieces. With the processor running, add the cream cheese, and then the lemon juice, and process just until well blended. Transfer the pâté to a medium-size bowl. Cover and refrigerate overnight.

2. Remove the pâté from the refrigerator 1 hour before serving.

3. To serve, arrange one-quarter of the sturgeon slices in an overlapping fan pattern on the upper two-thirds of each large dinner plate. Drizzle about ¾ teaspoon of the olive oil along the edges of the sturgeon slices.

Carefully arrange the chives on the olive oil (the oil will help keep the chives in place), so they accentuate the edges of the slices. Using 2 teaspoons, shape the pâté into small oval shapes similar to quenelles, and place 3 of them at the base of the sturgeon slices on each plate. Divide the salmon roe over each serving of sturgeon. Garnish the plates with the parsley leaves. Serve immediately.

   Makes 4 servings

Mackerel Rillettes

R illettes are typically made with pork, pork fat, a touch of goose meat, and aromatic herbs. They're a diet staple in southwest France, along with crusty sourdough bread and hearty red wine. A friend of mine, recently returned from France, was raving about the mackerel *rillettes* she'd had there. Shortly afterward I found myself with leftover mackerel and turned them into these refreshing, pâté-like *rillettes*. Though these are at their best when served with thick slices of freshly-toasted sourdough bread, they are wonderful on crackers or on warm bread fresh from the oven. Try a lightly chilled, buttery Chardonnay along with the *rillettes*.

1 cup (2 sticks) unsalted butter, softened
2 large egg yolks
1 tablespoon olive oil
¼ cup fresh lemon juice
1 medium shallot, minced
1 bunch flat leaf parsley, leaves finely minced
Salt and freshly ground black pepper
1 ½ cups cooked mackerel (see Note) or bluefish fillets
Borage blossoms and flat-leaf parsley, for garnish

1. In a large mixing bowl or the bowl of an electric mixer, cream the butter using a wooden spoon or the paddle attachment until it almost resembles whipped cream. Add the egg yolks, olive oil, lemon juice, shallots, and parsley, beating well after each addition. Season with salt and freshly ground pepper to taste.

2. Using your hands, flake the fish into the butter mixture. Fold in with a rubber spatula or flat wooden spoon. The mixture will be slightly chunky. Spoon the *rillettes* into a small bowl that holds about 2 cups, or into 8 small ramekins. Smooth the tops. Cover with aluminum foil or waxed paper and refrigerate for at least 4 hours.

3. Remove the *rillettes* from the refrigerator at least 30 minutes before serving. Garnish with the blossoms and the parsley leaves. Serve with thick slices of warm toast or crackers.

Makes 8 to 10 servings

Note: Mackerel fillets prepared in the stock used for the Mackerel and Spring Leek Broth with Coriander (see Index) are wonderful in this dish.

Gooseneck Barnacles with Aioli

*T*hese barnacles will knock your socks off. They taste like a dream—something between the most tender shrimp and the sweetest spiny lobster. Now, there are some caveats to eating them—the major one is that a tiny amount of bright orange liquid tends to spurt out of them when you begin to peel off the outer skin. It isn't harmful, it's part of the fun, but it stains clothing, so you either need to wear a napkin around your neck, or aim them out of harm's way. To eat the barnacles, which are traditionally eaten cold, but which I prefer warm, right out of the boiling water, peel off the tough outer skin that covers the neck. Dip the neck into aioli, using the shell as a handle, put it in your mouth and pull off the shell—and be prepared for a delightfully tender morsel. Try a Vinho Verde from Portugal, or a chilled rosé such as Côtes de Provence or Bandol.

1 pound gooseneck barnacles
2 bay leaves
2 tablespoons kosher (coarse) salt
1 small onion, sliced
½ lemon
6 curly green lettuce leaves
1 lemon, cut into 4 wedges
Aioli (see Index)

1. Rinse the gooseneck barnacles, rubbing gently to remove any sand or bits of shell.

2. In a large pot, combine 3 quarts of water with the bay leaves, salt, onion, and the lemon half. Bring to a boil over high heat. Add the barnacles, stir, and cook until the base of the barnacle necks turn deep pink, no longer than 4 minutes. Drain the barnacles; cover them with ice to let them cool, or serve immediately.

3. To serve the barnacles, arrange them on a platter lined with the lettuce leaves. Garnish the platter with the lemon wedges and place a dish of aioli alongside.

Makes 4 appetizer servings

The Fulton Fish Market

The Fulton Fish Market is unique in America, an eastern seaboard institution. It dates back 150 years to the days when the New York port still accommodated fishing vessels that unloaded their catch right at the market. In those days many boats docked with their holds filled with water and live, wriggling fish.

Fulton Market has had its heyday and its hard times. It still has one foot in the Dark Ages as the other runs with the technological age. Were the market to have a logo, it would have to include the omnipresent hooks in use by nearly everyone, from unloaders to buyers. The hooks come in two sizes and when they're not in use, they're slung over their owners' shoulders like a shield or a membership card.

The hooks are shocking at first, a little barbaric, like some medieval weapon. But they're incredibly useful. They help sellers and buyers keep their hands off the fish. Instead of touching and poking them, they use the smaller hooks—about 12 inches long with a short, horizontal wooden handle at one end—to hook a fish through the gills, and lift it up for examination. Or they transfer fish to different containers, or just move them aside. Larger, heavier hooks are used like handles, to move heavy boxes of fish around.

The market is one of the last vestiges of old New York, a fragrant, crumbling souvenir of an era when people on the East Coast ate fish from the Atlantic, people on the West Coast ate fish from the Pacific, and people in between ate freshwater fish.

It's a hard working place, where people curse and shout, and move thousands and thousands of pounds of seafood from all over the world, hurrying it on its way to a distant destination.

Instead of getting fish from boats, the seafood at Fulton Fish Market now comes "over the road" in refrigerated trucks that originate in ports from Florida to Maine to Chicago, Illinois. This doesn't count the trucks from Mississippi with their loads of farmed catfish.

If it doesn't come by truck it comes by plane—from the midwest, the West Coast, Africa, South America, Hawaii, Japan and Australia. Probably Fiji and Samoa too. The Fulton Fish market is an international crossroads, a melting pot of species, a virtual living, changing, thrashing museum of the world's edible seafood.

On one side of the street that splits the market in half, eighty-five separate vendors are crammed under two huge, open buildings that resemble airplane hangars and are called the "tin buildings." Others fit snugly in a warren of stalls on the other side of the street. There are no cosmetic concessions made to the consumer here. Fish of all descriptions are everywhere, in half open airline containers, boxes filled with ice where just a fin or a tail protrudes, on dollies stacked like cordwood, waiting for a delivery truck to drive up. Some are carefully placed on ice, some skid around on the floor until there's time or space to accommodate them.

Just behind the scenes—barely behind, in fact if you crane your neck you can see it all—armies of fishcutters fillet fish, knives flashing, water splashing, pack them in tidy little boxes and either shove them in cold storage or put a few out for buyers at the market.

Most of the fish and shellfish at the market are recognizable, but some are so exotic they may never have been seen before in the Northern hemisphere. In one corner rests a huge plastic sack filled with brilliantly colored reef fish from waters around the Hawaiian islands. They were probably a by-catch for a fisherman near Hawaii. He tossed them in along with a load of ta'ape or opakapaka, and they've ended up in New York City, at a stall that specializes in exotic warm water fish.

One company deals almost exclusively in tuna. Samples are taken from their tails with a narrow, hollow tube, then mashed gently between the fingers of the prospective buyer, who can determine the meat's quality by it's texture. Once the fish are graded according to quality they're butchered, and the dark red loins that still pulse with freshness are lined up on a metal table and tagged with the name of the buyers.

At another company, a bevy of large round tins filled with tiny whitebait are about to be bought by a restaurateur who will fry the tiny fish whole and serve

During the early morning hours, when the rest of New York is asleep, the Fulton Fish Market is at its busiest.

them to be eaten like peanuts.

Most remarkable at Fulton, is the range and variety of seafood to be found there. Everything from the most popular whitefish to delicate sea robins, pufferfish that blow up like balls when alarmed, to amberjacks and kingfish. And, since it's first come first serve, chefs and fishmongers are in the market at 4 A.M., when they can get their pick of the bunch.

By 8 A.M., as the rest of New York awakes, the Fulton Fish Market is gentled. Many stalls are hosed down and closed, any leftover fish tucked away in cold storage for the next day. An isolated worker cleans a batch of choice squid to take home to his family, another washes the last of the fish scales off a table. Any discarded fish doesn't hang around for long, as the street people creep in and pick it up and the Fulton Market shuts down for another day.

Crabmeat and Cheese Gratin

My mother, who is a wonderful cook, was born and raised in Oregon, and the foods of her childhood included such things as razor clams, salmon, and fresh, fresh Dungeness crab. She and my father retired in Oregon, but we spent our family life in many parts of the world and she would often mention Oregon foods and recipes, describing them as though little else could compare. Dungeness crab remains her favorite, and her cardinal rule is to do nothing that interferes with the integrity of its sweet, nutty flavor. "Somehow a touch of cheese sauce, just enough to keep the crab together, makes the flavor of crab emerge," she says, and she is right, as mothers usually are. Her crab gratin is a delightful appetizer or luncheon dish. It has a dramatic, seaside flair when served in large scallop shells, the way she likes to serve it. Try this with a clean, dry white wine or, for something special, an Oregon Gewürztraminer or Pinot Gris.

½ cup milk
1 bay leaf
1 tablespoon fresh bread crumbs
1 tablespoon freshly grated Parmesan cheese
¼ teaspoon hot paprika
1 tablespoon unsalted butter
1 tablespoon all-purpose flour
¾ cup grated white Cheddar cheese (2 ounces)
1 tablespoon heavy or whipping cream
Salt and freshly ground black pepper
6 cups loosely packed spinach (4 ounces), rinsed
10 ounces lump crabmeat, picked over
1 tablespoon minced fresh chives

1. Scald the milk and the bay leaf in a small saucepan over medium-high heat. Remove from the heat, cover, and let steep for 5 minutes.

2. Preheat the broiler.

3. Butter four 6-inch gratin dishes or scallop shells. Mix together the bread crumbs, Parmesan cheese, and paprika in a small bowl; reserve.

4. Melt the butter in a small saucepan over medium heat. Add the flour and cook, stirring constantly until golden, about 5 minutes. Reduce the heat to low. Remove the bay leaf from the milk and whisk the milk into the butter and flour mixture. Cook, whisking, until the mixture thickens. Whisk in the Cheddar and cook until it melts into the sauce. Whisk in the cream. Season with salt and pepper to taste. Remove from the heat.

5. Place the spinach in a small non-aluminum saucepan over medium-high heat. Cook, tossing in the water that clings to the leaves, just until wilted, about 5 minutes. Gently squeeze the spinach with your hands to remove most of the liquid. Finely chop the spinach. Divide among the buttered gratin dishes. Season lightly with salt and pepper.

6. Fold the crabmeat and the chives into the cheese sauce. Divide the mixture among the dishes, mounding it on top of the spinach. Sprinkle with the bread crumb and cheese mixture. Broil about 4 inches from the heat until the bread crumbs are golden and crisp, 3 to 5 minutes. Serve immediately.

Makes 4 appetizer servings

Spiced Lamb Patties and Oysters

*L*amb and oysters are an unconventional match which, if not made in heaven, was made somewhere close by. This appetizer always provokes excitement because it is unusual, and it can be a formal, or very informal, dish. The point is to eat an oyster, then take a bite of the lamb patty and a bite of buttered crusty French bread before sipping the wine. The lamb and bread soften the brininess of the oyster so just the flavor is left on the palate, which is also cleansed for the wine. Serve with a Sauvignon Blanc.

Seaweed or green leafy lettuce
1 dozen oysters, shells well scrubbed under cold
  running water, shucked
¼ cup pine nuts
8 ounces ground lamb
1 large clove garlic, minced
¼ teaspoon salt
⅛ teaspoon freshly ground black pepper
2 tablespoons fresh oregano leaves or 1 teaspoon dried
¼ teaspoon dried hot pepper flakes
1 lemon, quartered, for garnish

1. Mound a plate with crushed ice and cover it with seaweed or lettuce leaves. Arrange the oysters over the seaweed, balancing them so they don't lose any of their liquid. Cover loosely with aluminum foil and refrigerate. Remove the oysters 10 minutes before serving.

2. Preheat the oven to 300°F.

3. Toast the pine nuts in the oven just until they turn golden, about 10 minutes. Remove them from the oven and let cool. Coarsely chop the nuts.

4. In a medium-size bowl, blend the lamb with the nuts, garlic, salt, pepper, oregano, and pepper flakes, mixing well with your hands until thoroughly blended.

5. Shape the lamb mixture into 4 equal-size patties, each about ½ inch thick.

6. In a medium-size skillet over medium-high heat, cook the lamb patties until golden on the outside and cooked through, about 5 minutes on each side. Drain on paper towels.

7. To serve, place a lamb patty on each of 4 small plates. Garnish with the lemon quarters and serve the oysters, bread, and butter separately.

Makes 4 servings

Oyster Salad with Artichokes

*T*his salad combines two ingredients with surprisingly similar textures. The stark, monochromatic presentation is balanced by sprigs of chervil and finely diced shallot. This salad is best with just-shucked oysters, though jarred oysters work well as long as they are impeccably fresh, and no larger than yearlings. Serve with a lightly chilled Chablis.

4 large artichokes
½ lemon
2 tablespoons extra-virgin olive oil
1 tablespoon plus 1 teaspoon balsamic vinegar
Salt and freshly ground black pepper
4 dozen extra-small or yearling oysters, shells well
  scrubbed under cold running water
2 shallots, minced
1 small bunch chervil or flat-leaf parsley

1. Trim the stems and leaves from the artichokes, exposing the hearts. Using a small, sharp knife, remove the choke, and trim off any leaves so the heart is a neat cup shape. Squeeze the lemon half, and rub the artichoke hearts with the juice. Reserve the lemon.

2. In a small bowl, whisk together the olive oil and vinegar. Season to taste with salt and pepper. Set the vinaigrette aside.

3. Bring a medium-size pot of salted water to a boil. Add the squeezed lemon half. Add the artichoke hearts and cook until tender though still slightly crisp, about 15 minutes. Drain. Cut the artichoke hearts into ¼-inch dice. Divide the artichoke dice among 4 salad plates, placing them in a short line to one side of the plate.

4. If using oysters in the shell, shuck them, reserving their liquor. If using jarred oysters, drain them, reserving the liquor, and pick over the oysters for any bits of shell. Strain the liquor through a double thickness of dampened cheesecloth into a medium-size non-aluminum saucepan. Add the oysters and cook over medium heat until they are just warm, about 20 seconds.

5. Mince the chervil.

6. Arrange 12 oysters on each plate, next to the diced artichoke hearts. Sprinkle each portion with equal amounts of the shallots. Drizzle on the vinaigrette. Sprinkle with the chervil; serve immediately.

Makes 4 servings

Greek Oyster Puffs

*T*his recipe was submitted by Irene Mantione to the St. Mary's County National Oyster Cook-Off in Leonardtown, Maryland, and it was a winner. Easy to understand why—biting into one of these puffy little triangles is pure delight. The cheese, onions, and black pepper provide a perfect setting for moist, briny oysters, and even those who are timid about oysters eat them prepared this way. This recipe does justice to fresh oysters if you have them and don't mind shucking, but small, top-quality jarred oysters work just as well. Be sure to pick over jarred oysters and remove any bits of shell. Serve these with a chilled Puligny-Montrachet.

1 large egg, beaten
½ cup ricotta cheese
4 ounces feta cheese, crumbled (about ¾ cup)
3 scallions, trimmed, the white bulbs and light green stems finely chopped
1 small bunch flat-leaf parsley, finely chopped
Grated zest of 1 lemon
½ teaspoon freshly ground black pepper
12 sheets (about 8 ounces) phyllo dough, thawed
4 tablespoons unsalted butter, melted
24 shucked small oysters, drained and patted dry

1. In a medium-size bowl, combine the egg, ricotta, feta, scallions, parsley, lemon zest, and pepper. Set the filling aside.

2. Cut the sheets of phyllo dough in half lengthwise, to form 24 long strips. Cover the phyllo with a damp towel to keep it from drying out.

3. Working with 1 strip of dough at a time, fold the strip in half lengthwise and brush it lightly with the butter. Place 1 level teaspoon of the filling 2 inches from the end nearest you. Top the filling with an oyster. Top the oyster with a teaspoon of filling.

4. Fold the 2-inch end of phyllo over the filling. Take the lower right hand corner and

fold it over to meet the opposite edge of the dough, forming a triangle. Continue folding the triangle as though you were folding a flag, tucking the edge under at the end.

5. Preheat the oven to 400°F. Lightly oil a baking sheet.

6. Place the oyster puff on the baking sheet and brush with butter. Repeat with the remaining strips of dough and filling until you have made 24 puffs.

7. Bake the puffs until golden and crisp, 15 to 20 minutes. Serve immediately.

Makes 24 oyster puffs (4 to 6 servings)

Mussels in Balsamic Vinaigrette

Mussels are a Northwest specialty—they cling to everything from boat bottoms to pilings, and they're free for the taking in many parts of the region, as long as the water is clean. There are several mussel farms in the Northwest as well, where the mollusks hang from ropes in the water, eating the food that nature sweeps up to them. Some of the best mussel water is in Penn Cove, on Whidbey Island, about an hour from Seattle, and that's where the region's sweetest mussels come from.

This is a signature dish at Place Pigalle, a charming restaurant behind Seattle's Pike Place Market, where the expansive view of Elliott Bay seems to come right in the windows, enfolding diners as they enjoy meals made with market-fresh ingredients.

To eat the mussels, use a fork to extract the first one from its shell. Then, use the empty shell as tongs for extracting the meat from the remaining mussels. The juice at the bottom of the bowl is a reward—serve plenty of bread to sop it up. Try this with a chilled white Bordeaux.

Balsamic Vinaigrette:

¼ cup loosely-packed flat-leaf parsley leaves
2 small shallots
¼ teaspoon celery seed
2 tablespoons balsamic vinegar
1 large egg
¼ cup olive oil
¼ cup mild vegetable oil, such as safflower
Salt and freshly ground black pepper

Mussels:

⅓ cup diced bacon
⅓ cup diced celery
3 shallots, diced
2 tablespoons olive oil
3 pounds mussels, shells well-scrubbed under cold running water and bearded (see Note)
¼ cup balsamic vinegar
½ cup dry white wine, such as white Bordeaux

1. Make the Vinaigrette: Place the parsley, shallots, and celery seed in the bowl of a food processor and process until finely minced. Add the vinegar; process. Add the egg and process again. With the processor running, add the oils in a thin stream until all the ingredients are well blended. Season with salt and pepper to taste and reserve.

2. Prepare the Mussels: Cook the bacon in a small skillet over medium-high heat just until translucent, about 2 minutes. Add the celery and stir. Reduce the heat to medium, cover, and cook until the celery is crisp-tender, about 5 minutes. Add the shallots and cook, stirring constantly, until translucent, about 3 minutes. Set aside.

3. Heat the olive oil in a large non-aluminum skillet over high heat. Add the mussels and toss to coat with the oil. Add the bacon and celery mixture and toss again. Add the vinegar and wine and cook, shaking the pan. As the mussels open, transfer them to a large dish and cover to keep warm. (You may need to cook the mussels in batches—as they open remove them and add more.) Discard any mussels that do not open.

4. When all of the mussels are cooked and removed from the skillet, reduce the heat to medium. Whisk the balsamic vinaigrette into the mussel cooking liquid. Cook until heated, 2 to 3 minutes.

5. To serve, evenly divide the mussels among 6 warm, shallow soup bowls. Pour some of the liquid over each portion. Serve immediately.

Makes 6 servings

Note: Do not scrub and beard the mussels until right before you plan to use them or they will die and spoil.

Mussels and Cream

A trio of mussels on a plate with a rich spoonful of cream is a simple, elegant way to pique the appetite before a meal. Serve this with a lightly chilled Muscadet.

8 ounces mussels, shells well-scrubbed under cold
   running water and bearded (see Note)
2 tablespoons dry white wine
3 black peppercorns
1 bay leaf
½ small onion, sliced
3 tablespoons heavy or whipping cream
2 tablespoons fresh chervil leaves

1. Place the mussels, wine, peppercorns, bay leaf, and onion in a small, heavy-bottomed, non-aluminum saucepan over medium-high heat. Cover and bring to a boil. Cook until the mussels open, and then for an additional 30 seconds until slightly firm; do not overcook. Remove from the heat and remove the mussels with tongs. Discard any mussels that do not open. Reserve the cooking liquid.

2. Preheat the broiler.

3. When the mussels are cool enough to handle, remove and discard the top shell from each mussel, leaving the mussel in the bottom shell. Arrange the mussels in their shells in a flat, heat-proof serving dish, such as a small (6-inch) porcelain tart mold, propping them against each other to keep them upright. Cover the mussels with aluminum foil to keep them warm.

4. Mince the chervil.

5. Strain the cooking liquid into a clean small saucepan over high heat. Boil until the liquid is reduced to 1 tablespoon. Whisk in the cream and chervil; boil until the sauce thickens and reduces, 3 to 4 minutes.

6. Spoon equal amounts of the sauce over each mussel, filling the shell with sauce without spilling over. Lightly brown the mussels under the broiler, about 1 minute. Serve immediately.

Makes 2 appetizer servings

Note: Do not scrub and beard the mussels until right before you plan to use them or they will die and spoil.

Yakimono

*T*his traditional Japanese recipe is often served as part of *kaiseki*, a meal served before the Japanese tea ceremony. Seattle tea master Bonnie Mitchell learned to prepare this as part of her training in Japan to become a tea master. Drink sake with it or green tea, which is called *macha*, afterwards.

1 trout (12 ounces), cleaned and filleted
About 1 tablespoon salt
1 tablespoon plus 2 teaspoons sake
1 teaspoon egg white

1. Cut each fillet into 4 equal rectangular pieces. Sprinkle lightly with salt on both sides. Refrigerate for 3 hours.

2. Preheat the broiler.

3. Quickly rinse the trout under cold water to remove most of the salt; pat dry with paper towels. Thread the trout pieces onto 8 wooden skewers so they are flat. Whisk together the sake and egg white in a small bowl. Using a pastry brush, brush the mixture on one side of the trout.

4. Broil on one side, brushing frequently with the sake mixture, until the trout begins to turn opaque and slightly golden, about 2 minutes. Turn and broil, brushing with the sake mixture, until the trout is opaque but not too firm, about 2 minutes.

5. Carefully slide the trout from the skewers and serve, accompanied with small cups of sake.

Makes 8 appetizer servings

Honorine's Imperial Rolls

"These are a company dish; if they're served to you, you should know you are an honored guest."
HONORINE TEPFER

The next time you want to honor a guest, try these slender, crisp, and flavor-packed Imperial rolls. They are as impressive to look at—served on a mountain of romaine lettuce leaves with cilantro and mint alongside—as they are to eat.

Vietnamese restaurants serving top-quality food abound in Seattle, and whenever I go to one I order Imperial rolls. I've had some great ones, but this recipe, given to me by Honorine Tepfer, a Vietnamese French friend, makes the best I've had. "The filling appears homogeneous, but each ingredient maintains its own distinctive flavor so that every bite seems a little different," she said. Try these—you'll find it to be true.

There is one trick to this very simple recipe. Don't over-moisten the rice sheets. They should be pliable all the way around, but not so soft that they tear. Soak them, one at a time, for about 45 seconds. As you take one out to make an Imperial roll, slip another into the water. If you get hung up making a roll, stop and remove the soaking rice sheets from the water—you don't want them to get too soft.

The seasoning in the filling is the fish sauce—don't add salt unless you like your food quite salty.

Try a chilled Alsatian Gewürztraminer with these.

Filling:

5 dried shiitake mushrooms (about ½ ounce)

⅓ cup dried wood ear mushrooms (about ¼ ounce)

1 small package (1.7 ounces) bean threads, if possible
  Lung Kow brand

4 ounces small (36 to 40 per pound) shrimp, shelled
  and coarsely chopped

8 ounces cooked crabmeat, picked over

8 ounces boneless pork loin or beef sirloin, diced

1 medium onion, diced

2 small carrots, peeled and grated

2 large eggs

3 tablespoons fish sauce (nuoc mam)

Dipping Sauce:

1 large clove garlic, minced

¼ teaspoon sugar

6 tablespoons fish sauce (nuoc mam)

2 tablespoons fresh lemon juice

Cayenne pepper, to taste

Assembly and Cooking:

1 package (1 pound) of rice sheets (thin, crisp,
  translucent round sheets)

About 6 cups mild cooking oil, such as safflower, for
  frying

Serving:

2 large heads romaine lettuce, leaves separated,
  washed, and dried

1 cup loosely packed fresh peppermint leaves

1 bunch cilantro, stems removed

1 medium cucumber, thinly sliced

1. Prepare the Filling: Place the shiitake, wood ears, and bean threads in separate bowls and add warm water to cover each, so they are floating freely, to soften. The wood ears will soften and expand enough in about 5 minutes. The shiitake and bean threads will take up to 15 minutes. Drain all three, squeezing the shiitake and bean threads gently to remove the excess water.

2. Cut the shiitake into thin slices; coarsely chop the wood ears into good-size pieces—you want to notice their crunchy texture in the Imperial rolls. Cut the bean threads into 1-inch lengths.

3. Place the shiitake, wood ears, bean threads, shrimp, crab, pork, onion, and carrot in a large bowl; mix well. Add the eggs and mix, then add the fish sauce and mix well, until thoroughly combined.

4. Make the Dipping Sauce: Combine all of the ingredients in a small bowl; mix well. Reserve.

5. Assemble the Imperial rolls: Place the stack of rice sheets next to a large shallow baking pan or dish half-filled with water, so a rice sheet can be completely submerged.

6. Soak a rice sheet in the water for about 45 seconds. Remove and let the excess water drip off briefly. Carefully lay it flat on a work surface. Fold up the bottom edge of the rice sheet toward the center, so you now have one flat edge and a portion of the rice sheet doubled. Place 2 tablespoons of filling on the folded over portion, then roll the bottom edge up once again to enclose the filling. Fold the sides of the rice sheets toward the middle, to enclose the filling. Then continue rolling gently, but as tightly as you can from the seam side to the upper edge to make a long, slim roll. Place the roll, rolled-edge down, on a platter lined with paper towels. Repeat the process, using all of the rice sheets and filling.

7. Cook the Imperial rolls: Pour the oil into a deep-fat fryer, wok, or deep-sided skillet. You want a depth of at least 1 inch, so the Imperial rolls can float freely in the oil. Heat the oil over medium-high heat to about

375°F. When the oil is hot and lightly smoking, add several Imperial rolls to the pan. They shouldn't be crowded—I usually add 6 to a 12-inch skillet. Cook, turning frequently, until golden all over, about 15 minutes. To test for doneness, remove a roll from the oil and cut it open. If the filling holds together, it is ready. Drain the Imperial rolls on paper towels. Fry the remaining rolls.

8. To serve the Imperial rolls: Cut the stem end from the romaine lettuce leaves, leaving 6 to 8 inches of the soft, green part of the leaf. Discard the stems.

9. Pile a large platter with the nicest of the romaine lettuce leaves. Divide the mint leaves and the cilantro leaves into small bunches and place them on the platter. Pile the cucumber slices at the base of the leaves, then arrange the Imperial rolls on top of the lettuce. Serve the dipping sauce alongside, in two small bowls.

10. To eat the Imperial rolls, take a lettuce leaf and place cilantro, mint leaves, and cucumber slices on it to taste—I like a couple of cilantro leaves, 3 mint leaves, and as many cucumber slices. Place the Imperial roll on top of these, then roll it up in the lettuce leaf. Dip it in the sauce right before you eat it. Imperial rolls are delicious hot or cold—the flavors of the seafood are more pronounced when they are eaten cold, but they are more crisp when they are hot!

Makes 30 to 35 Imperial rolls (8 to 10 servings)

Abalone with Ginger Butter Sauce

The inspiration for this simple, elegant dish came from Pia Carroll, chef at the Sooke Harbour House Restaurant on Vancouver Island, British Columbia. The subtle ginger sauce and minimal cooking of the abalone accentuates its subtle, sea-breeze flavor. Contrary to popular opinion, abalone doesn't need to be pounded to tenderize it. Freezing will tenderize it very well—though if you have fresh abalone, don't freeze it for that purpose! Whether fresh or frozen, cut the abalone into medallions, and then sauté it just long enough to heat it through. If you can't get abalone try this with geoduck or lightly steamed and shelled littleneck or Manila clams. This recipe merits nothing less than an aged first-class white Bordeaux.

½ cup (8 tablespoons) plus 2 tablespoons unsalted butter, chilled
2 small shallots, minced
3 tablespoons dry white wine
3 tablespoons white wine vinegar
1 teaspoon heavy or whipping cream
2 teaspoons Pia's Ginger Purée (see Index), or to taste
2 large abalone (4½ ounces each), cut into ⅛-inch medallions
Viola flowers or small pansies (optional), for garnish

1. Melt 1 tablespoon of the butter in a small saucepan over medium heat. Add the shallots and sauté until transparent. Add the wine and the vinegar; cook until syrupy and reduced to about 1 tablespoon. Whisk in the cream. Reduce the heat to low.

2. Reserve 2 tablespoons of the chilled butter. Cut the remainder into pieces. Whisk in the butter, piece by piece, working on and off of the heat, as necessary, to keep the butter from melting before it is emulsified. Whisk in the ginger purée. Remove from the heat; keep warm in a very low oven or in the top of a double boiler over simmering water.

3. Melt the remaining 2 tablespoons butter in a medium-size skillet over medium-high heat. Add the abalone slices and cook, stirring constantly, just until heated through, about 45 seconds. Be careful not to overcook the abalone, as it will toughen.

4. Immediately transfer the abalone to a warm serving platter. Pour the ginger butter sauce over the abalone. Garnish with the flowers. Serve immediately.

Makes 4 servings

Lomi Salmon

Hawaiians are very proud of their foods, and this salmon dish is a staple of the Hawaiian diet. Nami Salz, who lives with her husband, Arthur, on the island of Oahu, was raised on the island of Hawaii and she remembers her mother making *lomi* salmon using the traditional salt salmon. "We were very poor but we always had salt salmon, and my mother used to do everything with it, from making *lomi* salmon to sprinkling it on rice," she said. (Salt salmon was, and still is, made in the Pacific Northwest and shipped almost solely to Hawaii, for use in dishes like *lomi* salmon.) *Lomi* means "to massage" in Hawaiian, and the salmon and tomatoes are "massaged" together before adding the remaining ingredients. As the ice cubes added

just before serving melt, the dish thins to become almost like a gazpacho. It is an ideal summer picnic dish. Try it with a chilled, flinty Northwest Sauvignon Blanc or a gently chilled, light French Chablis.

12 ounces kippered salmon
1 large bunch scallions, trimmed
1 teaspoon kosher (coarse) salt
3 large tomatoes, peeled, cored, and coarsely chopped
5 ice cubes

1. Remove any bones from the salmon.

2. Coarsely chop the scallions. Place in a food processor with the salt and process until very finely chopped and well mixed with the salt, about 30 seconds.

3. Place the tomatoes and the salmon in a medium-size bowl. Using your fingers, crush the salmon and the tomatoes together until well mixed. Add the scallion mixture and ¼ cup water; mix well, using your fingers or a wooden spoon. The mixture should be somewhat soupy. Refrigerate until ready to serve. (You can make this several hours before you plan to eat it.)

4. Before serving, add 5 large ice cubes, pushing them down into the *lomi* salmon. Serve immediately on small plates. The ice will keep the mixture cold and eventually melt into the dish.

Makes 6 to 8 appetizer servings

Kipper Salad with Cantaloupe and Cucumber

*T*he crisp combination of cucumber and melon, the refreshing taste of yogurt, and the smoky kippers in this salad never fail to please. It is ideal for a summer lunch or to start an elegant evening meal. You may substitute smoked trout fillets for the kippers if you like. I like to score the cucumbers with the tines of a fork before slicing them. Try this with a very lightly chilled Northwest Sauvignon Blanc.

2 medium cucumbers, washed, scored lengthwise, and
    cut into ¼-inch-thick rounds
1 cup plain yogurt
2 tablespoons Crème Fraîche (see Index) or heavy or
    whipping cream
1 tablespoon best-quality red wine vinegar
1 small bunch chives, finely chopped
1 teaspoon sugar
4 scallions, trimmed, the white bulbs and light green
    stems cut into thin rounds
Salt and freshly ground black pepper
½ large cantaloupe, peeled, seeded, and cut into thin
    crescents (you need 20)
2 cans (3½ ounces each) smoked herring fillets
    (kippers), drained

1. Blanch the cucumber slices for 1 minute in boiling salted water. Drain; run cold water over them until cool. Pat dry and reserve.

2. In a small bowl, combine the yogurt, crème fraîche, vinegar, chives, sugar, and half of the scallions. Season with salt and pepper.

3. Arrange the melon slices in a starburst pattern on 4 chilled dinner plates. Arrange the cucumber slices on and around the melon. Break the kippers into large pieces and place them on top of the cucumber. Spoon the yogurt sauce over the kipper slices, leaving some of them showing. Garnish with the remaining scallions. Serve.

Makes 4 servings

Warm Geoduck Salad

*T*his salad combines the mild, fresh, sea taste of geoduck with the nutty flavor of the oil in an intriguing warm salad. Serve as a hearty first-course or as a light lunch, with plenty of fresh, crusty bread and a refreshing Sauvignon Blanc. If you can't find geoduck, substitute Manila, butter, or littleneck clams. Steam them *just* until they open, then shuck.

1 pound geoduck siphon and breast meat, or 2 pounds
    butter, Manila, or littleneck clams, shells well
    scrubbed under cold running water
2 tablespoons red wine vinegar
1 teaspoon Dijon mustard
¼ cup plus 2 tablespoons walnut oil (see Note)
Salt and freshly ground black pepper
8 leaves curly leaf lettuce, washed and dried
1 head radicchio, separated, rinsed, and dried
3 cups dry white wine
2 shallots
1 clove garlic, crushed
6 to 8 chives
6 to 8 leaves fresh tarragon or ⅛ teaspoon dried
6 to 8 branches fresh chervil or ⅛ teaspoon dried

1. Quarter the geoduck siphon lengthwise; thinly slice. Cut the breast meat into thin slices. (If using clams, keep them whole.)

2. In a medium-size bowl, whisk together the vinegar and mustard. Slowly pour in the oil, whisking constantly. Season the vinaigrette with salt and pepper to taste.

3. Cut the lettuce leaves into fine shreds and arrange in the center of 4 plates. Garnish the plates attractively with the radicchio leaves. Set aside.

4. In a large non-aluminum saucepan over medium heat, combine the wine, 1 shallot, and the garlic. Bring to a boil. Add the geoduck and cook until it turns a pale cream color, no longer than 2 minutes. Remove from the heat; drain immediately.

5. Mince the chives, tarragon, and chervil. Add the warm geoduck and minced herbs to the vinaigrette; toss to coat.

6. Using a slotted spoon, transfer equal amounts of geoduck to each plate, placing it on lettuce. Drizzle on the remaining vinaigrette. Thinly slice the remaining shallot and sprinkle over each salad. Serve immediately.

Makes 4 servings

Note: If you can't find good-quality walnut oil, substitute extra-virgin olive oil mixed with 1 tablespoon minced walnuts.

Sillsallad - Beet and Pickled Fish Salad

*T*his vibrant salad is a traditional part of a Scandinavian smorgasbord at Christmastime. It is tart and sweet and a gorgeous pink color that manages—unlike most pink food—to look incredibly appetizing. You should probably double the recipe, because no matter how many people you serve, it will disappear almost as soon as it's put on the table. If there is any left over, it will be delicious the next day. I recommend a German wine with this, such as a chilled, estate-bottled Piesporter, from 1985.

In Scandinavia, sillsallad is usually made with home-pickled herring. Since it is difficult to find fresh small herring here, I pickle smelt for this dish. If you can't find fresh smelts, disregard the pickling instructions and substitute commercial pickled herring.

8 ounces small russet potatoes, peeled (see step 1)
8 ounces small beets (see step 1)
Salt
16 Pickled Smelts (see Index)
1 medium apple
½ cup diced dill pickle
⅓ cup diced onion
¼ cup red wine vinegar
1 tablespoon sugar
Freshly ground white pepper
½ cup heavy or whipping cream, whipped until stiff

1. Try to find potatoes and beets that are the same size. If you can't, cut the potatoes to fit the beets. Leave both whole if possible and keep a bit of the stem and root ends attached to the beets. Place the potatoes and beets in a large, non-aluminum saucepan. Add cold water to cover by about 2 inches; add 1 teaspoon of salt. Cover and bring to a boil over high heat. Reduce the heat to medium-high and cook, partially covered, until the vegetables are soft. Remove the potatoes with a slotted spoon as they are cooked, after about 20 minutes; the beets will take 25 to 30 minutes. Drain the beets.

2. When the beets are cool enough to

handle, peel them; cut into ¾-inch cubes. Cut the potatoes the same size.

3. Drain any liquid from the smelts. Cut the fish into 1-inch squares. Peel and core the apple; cut into ¾-inch cubes.

4. Place the potatoes, beets, apple, pickles, onion, and smelts in a medium-size bowl; toss together. Combine the vinegar, sugar, and white pepper to taste with 2 tablespoons water in a small bowl. Pour the sauce over the potato and smelt mixture. Toss to mix very well. Fold in the whipped cream. Transfer the mixture to a serving bowl or plate and refrigerate for 30 minutes.

Makes 4 servings

Warm Lobster Salad

This is really two salads in one—a wild green salad topped with an incredible lobster salad, separated by a piece of peppery-sweet brioche. I had it first at Arizona 206, a restaurant in Manhattan. It is the brainchild of chef Brendan Walsh, who, though he has spent little time in the Southwest, delights in incorporating Southwestern ingredients into dishes from the cuisines that inspire him—northern Italian, southwestern French, and Californian. He's very successful, as you will see from the bright colors and textures in this salad.

Use only good, heavy, live lobster for this salad—preferably those available from fall through early summer. If you can't find a good lobster, don't hesitate to use frozen Australian lobster tails, which are expensive, but not nearly as expensive as a live, late-summer lobster that gives a tablespoon of meat and a bucketful of water.

This deserves a special wine—try a very lightly chilled (not cooler than 65°F) Puligny-Montrachet or a Meursault.

2 tablespoons extra-virgin olive oil
1 tablespoon plus 2 teaspoons rice wine vinegar
Salt and freshly ground black pepper
4 cups mixed salad greens, such as mustard greens, arugula, mâche, and baby beet greens
6 ounces beef marrow bones, cut in 2-inch pieces
2 tablespoons Herb Oil (see Index)
8 to 10 ounces lobster tail and claw meat (from a 2-pound Maine lobster or a 1¼ pound Australian lobster tail), cut into ⅜-inch-thick medallions
2 roasted large red bell peppers (see Index), peeled, seeded, and diced
2 roasted, medium-size fresh Anaheim or poblano chile peppers, peeled, seeded, and diced
¼ cup Salsa (see Index)
1 avocado, peeled and cut into ¼-inch cubes
4 thick (about ⅜ inch) slices Red Pepper Brioche (see Index), toasted

1. Mix together the olive oil and the 2 teaspoons rice wine vinegar in a medium-size bowl. Season with salt and pepper to taste; reserve. Tear the salad greens into bite-size pieces; reserve.

2. Remove the marrow from the bones. Rinse and pat it dry, then cut the marrow into ⅛-inch-thick slices.

3. Heat the herb oil in a medium-size skillet over medium heat. When the oil is hot, add the lobster meat and cook, stirring constantly, until it begins to turn white, about 2 minutes. Add the bell and chile peppers and cook, stirring, until heated through, 4 minutes. Season with salt and pepper to taste.

4. Add the bone marrow, stir, and cook until it melts, 1 to 2 minutes. Fold in the salsa

and the avocado; cook the mixture for an additional 30 seconds to 1 minute, just until the avocado and salsa are warmed. Fold in the remaining 1 tablespoon rice wine vinegar; remove from the heat.

5. Quickly toss the greens in the vinaigrette and divide among 4 large dinner plates. Place a slice of the toasted brioche on top of each salad, and then top with the lobster mixture. Serve immediately.

Makes 4 large servings

Two-Cabbage Salad with Tuna

This salad is a variation on a French cabbage salad that is usually served with crisp *lardons*, or bits of bacon. The tuna here acts like *lardons*, only it is light, and adds a delicate flavor and meaty texture to the sweet cabbages. Good walnut oil is hard to find—it is often rancid, so smell it before you buy. If you cannot find it, substitute extra-virgin olive oil. Try a lightly chilled Pinot Blanc from Alsace with this dish.

7 tablespoons walnut oil
6 ounces fresh bluefin tuna, skin removed, cut into
  1 x ½ x ¼-inch pieces
2 shallots, minced
½ small green cabbage, halved, cored, and thinly
  sliced
⅓ cup best-quality red wine vinegar
Salt and freshly ground black pepper
½ small red cabbage, halved, cored, and thinly sliced
¼ cup walnuts, coarsely chopped

1. Heat 3 tablespoons of the walnut oil in a large, heavy-bottomed skillet over high heat. Add the tuna and sauté, stirring constantly, until golden, about 4 minutes. Drain the tuna on paper towels.

2. Add 2 more tablespoons of the walnut oil to the skillet. Add one-third of the shallots and cook, stirring, until just slightly translucent, about 1 minute. Add the green cabbage; toss to coat with the oil. Add half of the vinegar and cook, stirring constantly, until the cabbage is slightly wilted, 2 to 3 minutes. Season with salt and pepper to taste. Remove the green cabbage and arrange it around the outside edge of a warm serving platter.

3. Add the remaining 2 tablespoons walnut oil to the skillet. Add half the remaining shallots to the oil and cook until just translucent, about 1 minute. Add the red cabbage and toss in the oil. Add the remaining vinegar and cook, stirring constantly, until the cabbage is slightly wilted, 2 to 3 minutes. Season with salt and pepper to taste. Remove the cabbage from the skillet and mound it in the center of the serving platter. Sprinkle the remaining shallots and the walnuts over the cabbage. Scatter the tuna on top. Serve immediately.

Makes 4 large servings

Los Angeles Tuna Salad

This recipe, which always reminds me of the sun in Los Angeles, was given to me by Juan Flores, warehouse manager at Pan Pacific Fisheries on Terminal Island, California, the only tuna cannery left in the United States. He often prepares this salad for lunch for the employees, and they love it. No wonder, for it takes canned albacore tuna to new heights, with its south-of-the-border sprinkling of jalapeño chiles and tangy lime juice. Serve this atop crisp lettuce leaves with lime wedges for garnish. It's great as an appetizer or lunch dish. Don't drain the tuna unless you're really watching your weight, because the oil contains a modest amount of Omega-3 fatty acids. Try this with a white Zinfandel, for a treat.

2 cans (6½ ounces each) white albacore tuna packed in oil, undrained
¼ cup fresh lime juice
2 jalapeño chiles, stems, ribs, and seeds removed, and cut crosswise into very thin slices
1 small cucumber, peeled and cut into ¼-inch cubes
1 ripe avocado, peeled, seeded, and cut into ¼-inch cubes
1½ cups packed cilantro leaves
Salt
6 large leaves romaine lettuce, for garnish
1 lime, cut into 8 wedges, for garnish

1. Crumble the undrained tuna into a medium-size bowl, leaving it in fairly large chunks. Add the lime juice and mix well. Add the jalapeños, cucumber, and avocado; toss until well mixed.

2. Mince the cilantro leaves. Add to the salad and toss gently. Season with salt. Arrange the lettuce on a large serving platter with the stem ends toward the center. Mound the salad on the lettuce, covering the stems. Serve immediately with lime wedges for garnish.

Makes 4 servings

Wild Greens Salad with Gingered Tuna

One day when I was buying fish at Mutual Fish Company in Seattle, I saw tuna trimmings and asked what they were used for. One of the men behind the counter, accustomed to my questions about what to do with fish, winked and said, "Cook them in soy sauce, sugar, and ginger and you'll see." I did, and tossed them with mixed greens for a remarkable salad. These tiny pieces of tuna are like buried treasure as you hunt for the morsels in the deep greens. Try this with a chilled Northwest Sauvignon Blanc.

2 tablespoons light soy sauce (usukuchi)
1 teaspoon sugar
4 ounces bluefin or albacore tuna, cut into 1 x ½ x ¼-inch pieces
1 tablespoon minced fresh ginger
Green Salad with a Vinaigrette (see Index) made with greens such as arugula, purslane, escarole, and beet greens

1. Heat the soy sauce and sugar in a medium-size skillet over medium heat. Stir in the tuna and ginger, and cook, stirring often, until the pan is dry and the soy sauce has been absorbed into the tuna. Remove from the heat.

2. In a large bowl, toss the salad with the vinaigrette. Add the tuna and toss again until thoroughly mixed. Serve immediately.

Makes 4 servings

Poke Tuna

Poke (pokee) salads are common in Hawaii where they are served as snacks or appetizers. They have a base of sesame oil, and they usually include white onions and/or scallions. Some have ginger in them, others hot peppers. Tamashiro Market, one of the oldest and best in Honolulu, has an entire case of colorful poke dishes containing everything from mussels to tuna to a delicate seaweed called *ogo*. If you like your food hot, add the entire ½ teaspoon of dried hot pepper flakes. Otherwise, season the dish to your taste. Poke tuna deserves a wine with some depth, such as a chilled Pinot Noir. Give it a try!

8 ounces top-quality bluefin or yellowfin tuna, cut
    into ½-inch cubes
1 slice (2 inches thick) cucumber, peeled, seeded and
    cut into ¼ inch cubes
3 scallions, trimmed, the white bulbs and light green
    stems cut into thin rounds
2 cloves garlic, minced
¼ to ½ teaspoon dried hot pepper flakes
1 tablespoon Japanese sesame oil
1 tablespoon soy sauce
3 cups (about 1½ bunches) young spinach leaves,
    rinsed and dried
2 medium radishes, trimmed and thinly sliced
½ teaspoon toasted sesame seeds

1. Place the tuna in a medium-size bowl. Add the cucumber and scallions and mix gently. Sprinkle on the garlic and hot pepper flakes; sprinkle the sesame oil and the soy sauce over all. Mix gently but thoroughly. Cover and refrigerate for 2 hours.

2. Just before serving, cut the spinach leaves into fine shreds. Arrange on a serving plate. Mix the radishes into the poke tuna; mound the salad on top of the spinach. Sprinkle with the sesame seeds and serve at once.

Makes 4 appetizer servings

Red and Orange Salad

This is one of my favorite summer salads. I first started making it in France, where I fell in love with *carrottes rapées*, a salad of finely grated carrots in vinaigrette found in nearly every French café. I make it with leftover cooked fish or albacore tuna packed in water. Sometimes I even use a combination of cooked fish—salmon and cod or rockfish perhaps—and I always wait until I find ruby plum tomatoes bursting with juicy flavor. Serve this with a clean, crisp Sauvignon Blanc.

¼ cup plus 1 tablespoon extra-virgin olive oil
3 tablespoons fresh lemon juice
½ teaspoon Dijon mustard
Salt and freshly ground pepper
2 cloves garlic, minced
2 cups cooked coarsely flaked fish, such as salmon,
    cod, or rockfish
4 large carrots, peeled and finely grated
1 tablespoon drained capers
2 scallions, trimmed, the white bulbs and light green
    stems cut into thin rounds
½ cup fresh tarragon leaves, or 1 tablespoon dried
3 medium plum tomatoes, cut crosswise into ½-inch
    slices

1. In a small bowl, whisk together the

olive oil, lemon juice, mustard, and salt and pepper to taste. Add the garlic and mix well.

2. Place the fish in a medium-size bowl. Pour half the vinaigrette over the fish, and mix thoroughly so all of the fish is moistened with the dressing. Cover and refrigerate for 30 minutes.

3. Just before serving the salad, place the carrots in a large serving bowl. Add the capers, scallions, and tarragon and toss. Pour on the remaining vinaigrette and toss until well mixed.

4. Mound the carrots on a serving platter; arrange the fish on top. Surround the salad with the sliced tomatoes. Serve immediately.

Makes 4 generous servings

Purslane and Smoked Trout Salad

My husband worked on a farm in southern France for several months, and Dany Dubois, the lady of the farm, is a fabulous cook. One of her specialties is a purslane salad, a combination of wild purslane, warm potatoes, tomatoes, hard-cooked eggs, and a vinaigrette, alternately seasoned with smoky bacon or *confit* gizzards from the foie gras ducks she and her husband, Guy, raise. I Americanized her idea by incorporating smoked trout, and I think she would find it a worthy substitute.

Purslane grows wild in many parts of the United States, where it is sometimes called rabbit grass. Seeds for domesticated purslane are available in some specialty shops. If you can't find it, substitute an equal amount of green beans, cut into 2-inch lengths,

blanched in salted water, refreshed, and drained. Try a lightly chilled Sancerre with this salad.

1 pound russet or new potatoes, scrubbed
Salt
¼ cup olive oil
2 tablespoons best-quality red wine vinegar
3 cloves garlic, coarsely chopped
Freshly ground black pepper
1 medium smoked trout (1½ pounds), skinned, filleted, and broken into bite-size pieces
1 pound purslane, rinsed, dried, and torn into manageable pieces
1 pound ripe cherry tomatoes, stemmed and halved
2 large eggs, hard-cooked, peeled, and thinly sliced

1. Place the potatoes in a large saucepan and add enough water to cover them by 2 inches. Season liberally with salt and bring the water to a boil over high heat. Cook until the potatoes are tender when pierced with a skewer. Drain and let cool.

2. While the potatoes are cooking, make the vinaigrette by whisking together the oil, vinegar, garlic, and salt and pepper to taste in a large bowl. When the potatoes are cool enough to handle, cut into bite-size pieces. Toss in the vinaigrette until evenly coated.

3. Add the trout, purslane, and tomatoes to the bowl. Toss well, until the ingredients are thoroughly coated with the dressing. Garnish with the egg slices and serve.

Makes 6 servings

Shrimp Boats

Perhaps no one knows the glories of pink shrimp better than William Grenier. Bill has shrimped out of Petersburg, Alaska, for thirty-five years. He started with his dad in the *Charles W,* a renowned old beam trawler that was built at the turn of the century. They leased the boat from Ohmer's (now Alaska Glacier Seafood), a shrimp processor in Petersburg.

Bill Grenier hauls up a net filled with shrimp that's topped by an unexpected skate.

Now Bill runs the boat with his son, Andy, who's as hard-working a deckhand as his dad was before him.

The beam trawler is a relic in shrimping. It's inefficient, compared with the otter trawls that shrimp in other parts of the world. They have nets on either side of the boat that can pull up twice the amount of the *Charles W.* But long ago, regulations were instituted that allowed only for beam trawling out of Petersburg, in an effort to protect the shrimp stock.

At 2:30 A.M. Bill nudges the lumbering, 63-foot *Charles W* out of the dock in Petersburg and heads out in the dark through Wrangell Narrows.

Two hours later the sun is blazing on smooth blue water. Remote Kahsheets Bay, with miles of water and sky punctuated with fir-tree-covered islands, looks the closest thing to God's country I've seen. Young Andy is readying the 2½-ton net and beam to go overboard. The boat slows down to a one-knot crawl and the 50-foot-long wooden beam with the net attached swings out to the side and behind the boat.

The net is held to the beam with U-shaped irons at either end which hold it open as it drags along the bottom, sweeping up shrimp as it goes. The net, beam and all, lowers out of sight, into the water. It stays under for 45 minutes to two hours, depending on what Bill decides.

The first drag is short, about an

hour. The beam emerges dripping from the water and swings out and to the side of the boat, trailing the net. A green, meshed "trash excluder" at the top of the net holds large Dungeness crabs, seaweed, and other by-catch; they knock everything out of it back into the water, then tie the beam in place at the side of the boat. Bill attaches a huge hook to one end of the net, and a mechanical pulley hefts it up to gather the shrimp in the folds of the net. The bulging net swings over the side of the boat, above the deck, and over a sorting box. Andy releases the rope that holds the net closed and a cascade of bright pink shrimp floods the box.

The net goes back into the water, Bill goes back into the pilothouse, and Andy begins rinsing the shrimp with seawater. "They've got a brown substance in 'em," he says. "We've gotta get that out of 'em right away." Several rinsings later and Andy starts sorting the catch.

He deftly tosses out dozens of tiny flounder, tomcod, and baby crab. He also throws out a colorful assortment of shrimp with names like "Fourth of July shrimp," "Bees" (they have striped red and yellow legs), "Coon-stripes," "Side-stripes," and "Clown shrimp." They're good eating but scarce, and there is no place to sell them.

Once sorting and cleaning is finished, Andy pulls out one side of the sorting box and the shrimp drain into waiting plastic totes that hold about 165 pounds each. These are stacked and covered with wet burlap, the sorting box is cleaned, and Andy is free until the next net comes up.

Andy Grenier hoses down the shrimp with sea water to rid them of underwater flora.

Shrimping itself isn't strenuous, but finding the shrimp is, and that's Bill's department. All day he sits in the pilothouse aft, scanning the water, the radar, the sky, looking and calculating. He sees a couple of shrimp boats in the distance at his favorite shrimping grounds and mutters under his breath, "They saw me there yesterday."

It's increasingly tough to find shrimp, because they've been overharvested. The season has been cut from $10\frac{1}{2}$ to $2\frac{1}{2}$ months. "It's the shrimper's fault really," Bill says. "But we didn't have much choice if we wanted to make a living."

"See these baby shrimp?" Andy asks. "They're too small, we should be leaving them, but we don't have any choice." Andy considers his future, and that of his two children, and thinks that although he loves his work he may try to learn another trade, just in case. The thought doesn't displease him, nor his father. "So maybe we'll buy a crab boat, and start setting pots for spot shrimp," Bill says. "It won't be bad."

Squid and Wild Miner's Lettuce Salad

This recipe comes from Pia Carroll, chef at the Sooke Harbour House on Vancouver Island, B.C. Pia is a master with seafoods, and she has the freshest to work with, for much of what she cooks comes from the water right outside the door of the inn. She enhances the flavors with subtle spices, and because of the freshness of the seafood no salt is needed. You may want to use some salt, and a bit of pepper in this recipe, but taste it first to see. Try this with the driest white Zinfandel you can find.

1 pound whole small squid or ¾ pound cleaned
Salt
2 tablespoons fresh lime juice
3 tablespoons fresh lemon juice
½ cup extra-virgin olive oil
2 cloves garlic, minced
1 small carrot, cut into julienne
¼ cup diced fennel bulb
Freshly ground black pepper
4 cups miner's, Boston, or Bibb lettuce, washed
  and dried
Calendula (pot marigold) petals or borage flowers, for
  garnish (optional)

1. To clean the squid: grasp the head and tentacles in one hand and the mantle or hood in the other. Pull apart; most of the viscera will be removed from the mantle. Cut off the tentacles right in front of the eyes. Discard the viscera, eyes, and sacs. Using your thumb and forefinger, gently squeeze out and discard the beak (a small piece of cartilage) in the center of the tentacles. Slice the mantle open lengthwise. Remove the clear, cartilaginous "pen" and rinse the mantle until clean. Scrape it gently if necessary to completely clean it. Hold under running water and remove the speckled exterior membrane. Pat the mantles and the tentacles dry, and leave them whole.

2. Bring 6 cups water mixed with 2 teaspoons salt to a boil in a large saucepan over high heat. Add the mantles and the tentacles and cook until opaque, about 2 minutes. Drain, rinse with cold water, and pat dry.

3. In a medium-size bowl, combine the lime and lemon juices, olive oil, and garlic and mix well. Add the carrot, fennel, and squid; mix well. Season with salt and pepper to taste. Marinate at room temperature for 2 to 3 hours, stirring occasionally.

4. To serve, divide the lettuce among 4 salad plates. Top with the squid salad and garnish with the flower petals. You may drizzle some of the marinade over the lettuce if you desire.

Makes 4 appetizer or 2 main-course servings

Dressed Scallops

This dish is simple and delicious. There are two vital keys to its success, however. Use the freshest scallops you can get your hands on. Frozen scallops will not work! Fresh-off-the-boat scallops will, and scallops in the shell are even better. The other key—absolutely delicious olive oil. It should be light, fruity, and wonderful. Serve this with Meursault Premier Cru, a Puligny-Montrachet, or a Grand Cru Chablis—the best for the best.

8 large sea scallops (about 4 ounces), or 16 large pink
    scallops in the shell (about 12 ounces)
2 tablespoons extra-virgin olive oil
1 baguette, cut into 16 slices (each ½ inch thick)
Freshly ground black pepper
Salt
Flat-leaf parsley sprigs, borage flowers, and geranium
    petals, for garnish

1. Rinse the sea scallops and drain well. Cut into ¼-inch strips. (If you are using pink scallops, scrub the shells under cold running water, then shuck them by slipping the blade of a sharp, flexible knife between the muscle and the shell to cut the adductor muscle. Tear off the shell that is loosened; discard. Slip the knife blade between the muscle and the shell and cut it away. Trim off the mantle of the scallop, leaving just the muscle and the white or orange roe if there is any. Reserve the roe separately. Rinse well, trimming off any black parts of the mantle that remain. Cut the scallops into ¼-inch strips.)

2. Place the scallop strips in a small bowl. Cover with the olive oil and mix well. Cover and marinate in the refrigerator for 2 hours.

3. Just before serving, toast the baguette slices until golden on both sides. Generously sprinkle the scallops with fresh, finely ground black pepper, and mix well. Transfer the scallops to a serving dish, arranging any roe on top. Place the dish on a large plate, and arrange the toasts around the dish. Serve a tiny dish of fine salt alongside. (Don't be tempted to salt the scallops in advance, as the salt will "cook" the scallops where it falls, creating white marks on them.) Garnish the plate with the parsley, borage flowers, and geranium petals; serve immediately. To eat, place several scallop strips on a slice of toast, sprinkle with salt, and enjoy.

Makes 4 appetizer servings

Blini with Fish Roe and Crème Fraîche

*B*lini are wonderful any time, particularly topped with a dollop of *crème fraîche* and a spoonful of fish roe. Caviar is the obvious choice, but whitefish roe, salmon roe, even flying fish roe make a delicious, and lovely substitute.

What to drink? Champagne, of course!

1 package active dry yeast
¼ cup lukewarm water
1¼ cups milk
1 cup all-purpose flour
1 cup buckwheat flour
Salt
3 large eggs, separated
1 to 2 tablespoons unsalted butter, melted
1 to 2 cups crème fraîche or sour cream
1 container (3½ ounces) lumpfish, whitefish, or
    flying fish roe, rinsed quickly and drained

1. Five to 6 hours before you plan to serve the blini, blend the yeast with the lukewarm water. Heat the milk to lukewarm in a small, heavy-bottomed saucepan over low heat.

2. Sift the all-purpose flour, ½ cup of the buckwheat flour, and ¼ teaspoon salt into a large bowl. Make a well in the flour and add the yeast and water mixture, along with the warm milk. Gradually incorporate the flour into the yeast and milk mixture using a wooden spoon. Beat vigorously until the mixture is smooth, about 5 minutes. The batter should be the consistency of heavy cream. Cover the bowl with a cloth and let the batter rise in a warm place until doubled in bulk and half-covered with bubbles, about 2 hours.

3. Stir the batter to deflate it. Sift the remaining ½ cup buckwheat flour over the top and gradually stir it in, mixing well. Cover and let the batter rise again until doubled in bulk, about 2 hours. Add more milk if necessary—the batter should be the consistency of heavy cream.

4. One at a time, stir in the egg yolks. In a separate bowl, beat the egg whites with the pinch of salt until they hold soft peaks. Fold the egg whites into the batter; set aside for about 30 minutes.

5. Place a large skillet or griddle over medium heat and brush it lightly with the butter. When hot but not smoking, pour ⅓ cup batter onto the griddle, to make a 4-inch blini, about ¼ inch thick. Continue making blinis until the skillet is full. Cook them as you would pancakes, until they bubble on top, then flip them and brown the other side. Keep the blini warm in a low oven until all of the batter is used.

6. To serve, arrange the blini on a large, warmed serving platter. Place a large dollop of the *crème fraîche* on top of each and top that with about ½ teaspoon of the fish roe.

Makes 16 to 20 blini (4 to 6 servings)

Rockfish Ceviche

This recipe comes from Karen Malody who, as a restaurant consultant in Seattle, Washington, adds her natural flair for vividly spiced and colored foods to several of the city's major restaurants. Karen has been involved in the Seattle food scene for many years, and has long been a fan of local seafood. This is one of her favorite recipes made with one of her favorite fish, yellow eye rockfish, which is often called Alaska snapper. Any top-quality, extremely firm and fresh rockfish or snapper will do for this dish. There is no salt or pepper called for; you may want to add it, to taste. Try a lightly chilled rosé from the south of France with this, or a lightly chilled Beaujolais.

*1 pound yellow eye or other rockfish fillets or red
    snapper fillets, without skin, cut into ½-inch cubes*
½ cup fresh lemon juice
½ cup fresh lime juice
1 small white onion, diced
¼ cup diced red bell pepper
¼ cup diced green bell pepper
8 ounces ripe plum tomatoes, seeded and diced
*1 small jalapeño chile, stems, ribs, and seeds removed,
    and diced (¼ inch)*
1 cup tomato purée, preferably Progresso
1 tablespoon drained capers
1 tablespoon minced flat-leaf parsley
*¼ cup (about 12) pimiento-stuffed green olives, cut
    crosswise into thirds*
1 ½ teaspoons Worcestershire sauce
¼ teaspoon Tabasco sauce, or to taste
½ cup packed cilantro leaves, minced
2 medium-size ripe avocados
¼ cup flat-leaf parsley leaves, minced, for garnish

1. Place the cubed fish in a non-aluminum bowl and pour the lemon and lime juices over them. Mix well; the fish should be completely covered with the juices. Cover the bowl and marinate in the refrigerator for 6 to 9 hours. (At 6 hours the fish will not be completely "cooked" by the citrus juices. By 9 hours it will be "cooked," with just the tiniest bit of pink in the middle. You may leave the fish in the citrus juices up to 24 hours, if you like.)

2. Combine the remaining ingredients ex-

cept for the avocados and parsley leaves in a large, non-aluminum bowl. Mix well. Cover and refrigerate for the same amount of time you marinate the fish, at least 6 hours.

3. Drain the fish, discarding the liquid. Combine the fish with the tomato mixture, mixing well.

4. Peel and pit the avocados. Cut one into ¼-inch cubes, and add them to the ceviche, mixing gently but thoroughly. Season the ceviche to taste with salt and pepper, if desired. Cut the remaining avocado crosswise into thin slices.

5. To serve, ladle the ceviche into shallow soup bowls or onto the center of small salad plates. Garnish with the avocado slices, arranging them around the edge of the ceviche. Sprinkle with the minced parsley leaves and serve. The ceviche will hold for about 2 days, refrigerated. The ceviche should be served well-chilled.

Makes 8 servings

Coconut and Lime-Marinated Fish in Papaya

*T*his dish was inspired by a conversation with Faith Ogawa Dean, a chef in Honolulu. She suggested the combination of coconut milk and lime juice; the piles of golden papayas in markets throughout Honolulu suggested their presence here, and it is a wonderful combination. Unsweetened frozen Hawaiian coconut milk is the best, and I recommend Mendonca brand. Serve with a chilled Cabernet d'Anjou or a Côteaux d'Aix-en-Provence rosé.

8 ounces Alaska or red snapper fillet
Grated zest of 1 lime
4 tablespoons fresh lime juice
3 tablespoons unsweetened coconut milk, preferably
  Mendonca's Hawaiian-style
⅓ cup minced onion
½ small green bell pepper, diced
2 ripe papayas, at room temperature
¼ teaspoon dried hot pepper flakes
Unsweetened flaked or shredded coconut

1. Cut the fish into ½-inch squares. In a medium-size non-aluminum bowl, combine the fish, the lime zest, 3 tablespoons of the lime juice, the coconut milk, onion, and bell pepper; mix well. Be sure the fish is submerged in the liquid. Cover and refrigerate for 3 hours.

2. Just before serving, halve the papayas lengthwise and remove the seeds. Peel each half and cut a thin slice from the bottom so it will rest flat on a plate. Sprinkle the halves with the remaining 1 tablespoon lime juice.

3. Add the hot pepper flakes to the fish mixture and mix well. Evenly divide the fish mixture among the papaya halves, mounding it up over the edge. If there is extra fish mixture, place it around the base of the papaya. Serve immediately, passing the coconut alongside.

Makes 4 servings

Fresh Oyster and Salmon Tartare

The credit for this dish goes to Emile Tabourdiau, Executive Chef of the Bristol Hotel in Paris. I ate it there a couple of years ago and couldn't get it out of my mind, so I asked and he generously shared the recipe. I make this often with mildly briny Pacific oysters and flash-frozen Alaska King salmon, which is so rich and firm, and such a gorgeous color, that it adds to the brilliance of the combination. Try this with a light, delicate Blanc de Blancs champagne or a Premier Cru Chablis.

1 pound salmon fillet, coarsely chopped (see Note)
12 freshly shucked oysters, drained and coarsely
  chopped
2 large egg yolks, lightly beaten
2 tablespoons extra-virgin olive oil
Several drops of Tabasco sauce
2 tablespoons plus 1 teaspoon fresh lemon juice
1 large shallot, minced
1 bunch chives, minced
Salt and freshly ground pepper
1 ripe avocado
4 tablespoons unsalted butter, softened
3 tablespoons drained prapared horseradish
8 slices rye bread

1. Place the salmon and oysters on a chopping board, and using a chef's knife, finely chop together until combined. Place the salmon and oyster mixture in a medium-size bowl and gently mix in the egg yolks, olive oil, Tabasco, 2 tablespoons of the lemon juice, the shallot, and chives until well combined. Season with salt and pepper to taste. Cover and refrigerate for 1 hour.

2. Peel, pit, and dice the avocado. Sprinkle with the remaining 1 teaspoon lemon juice and reserve.

3. Place the butter in a small bowl and whip it with a whisk or wooden spoon until soft and light. Add the horseradish and mix well.

4. Thinly spread 4 slices of the rye bread with the horseradish butter. Top them with the remaining slices. Cut the sandwiches into 3 equal pieces.

5. To serve, mound equal amounts of the chilled tartare in the center of 6 salad plates. Drain the avocado dice, if necessary, and sprinkle around each serving of tartare. Place 2 sandwiches alongside.

Makes 6 appetizer servings

Note: In order to be sure that the salmon in this dish contains no harmful parasites (you will not be cooking it), the salmon should have been fresh-frozen. Ask your fish merchant whether the fish arrived at his market still frozen. If the answer is no or he isn't sure, don't make this recipe.

Tuna Marinated with Herbs and Lemon

What could be better than thin slices of fresh tuna slathered with olive oil, lemon juice, and fresh herbs? The lemon juice slightly "cooks" the tuna, the olive oil mellows its rich flavor, and the herbs give it a joyful little punch. I like to serve this with freshly toasted sourdough bread. Try it with a lightly chilled Pouilly Fumé.

11 ounces top-quality yellowfin tuna
⅓ cup diced onion
½ cup loosely packed fresh tarragon leaves, or 1
    tablespoon dried
2 tablespoons minced fresh dill or 1 teaspoon dried
¼ cup plus 2 tablespoons extra-virgin olive oil
3 tablespoons fresh lemon juice
Salt and freshly ground black pepper

1. Cut the skin from the tuna and discard it. Cut out the dark part of the tuna, which is the blood line—many people like it cooked, but it isn't good raw. Cut the tuna across the grain into pieces that are about ¾-inch wide, to make small "blocks" of tuna. The tuna is much easier to cut this way. Cut the blocks crosswise into very thin (1/16 inch) slices.

2. Arrange the tuna in a single layer on a serving plate. Sprinkle the onion on the tuna, covering it as evenly as possible.

3. Mince the tarragon and combine it with the dill. Sprinkle the herbs over the tuna. Drizzle the olive oil evenly over the tuna and herbs; drizzle the lemon juice over all. Refrigerate for 2 to 3 hours. Serve chilled and seasoned with salt and pepper.

Makes 4 large appetizer servings

Tuna Tartare with Red Mayonnaise

*T*his is an unusually delightful way to serve raw tuna—slathered with a spicy red mayonnaise. Make this at least 2 hours in advance, and let the tuna absorb a bit of flavor and spice from the mayonnaise.

I learned to make neat, thin cuts of tuna at Mutual Fish Company in Seattle. Follow the directions in step 1 of the recipe for Tuna Marinated with Herbs and Lemon (above). The results will be small, evenly shaped slices of tuna. Try a lightly chilled, peppery red wine with this, such as a Valpolicella, or a red wine from the Côtes du Rhône, or a Corbières.

1⅛ pounds fresh bluefin or albacore tuna, rinsed,
    patted dry, and thinly sliced
1 large raw egg yolk
1 large hard-cooked egg yolk, sieved
½ teaspoon Dijon mustard
¼ teaspoon red wine vinegar
2 cloves garlic, minced
2 tablespoons extra-virgin olive oil
5 drops Tabasco sauce
½ to 1 teaspoon Chinese chile paste, preferably
    Lan Chi brand
Salt
1 small bunch chives, minced

1. If the thin-sliced tuna isn't almost translucent, place the slices between 2 pieces of waxed or parchment paper and gently pound to thin out.

2. In a medium-size bowl, mix together the raw egg yolk, cooked egg yolk, mustard, vinegar, and garlic until quite smooth. Slowly add the oil, whisking well, to make a mayonnaise. Add the Tabasco and the chili paste to taste; season with the salt to taste.

3. Arrange the tuna slices in concentric circles on a 10-inch serving plate. Using a pastry brush, spread all of the mayonnaise over the tuna. Sprinkle with the minced chives. Cover loosely with foil, refrigerate for at least 2 hours and serve cold.

Makes 4 servings

Pink and Spiny Scallops

The Northwest's array of seafood, which already boasts astonishing variety, has been graced recently with new arrivals. They are tiny pink scallops and their almost identical cousins, spiny scallops, from Puget Sound, and they've settled in fish markets and on restaurant menus like little purple- and pink-hued butterflies, their shells dainty and perfectly formed.

They are captivating, and because the entire animal is consumed right out of the shell, scallop lovers enjoy the full, sweet richness of their meat. An added attraction is that they are served absolutely fresh, within 48 hours of being taken from the water, for there is no middle ground between the sea and spoilage. Pink and spiny scallops have a more complex flavor than the East Coast sea scallop, and are less aggressively sweet, balanced by a pleasant, oyster-like brininess and a nutty flavor usually associated with clams. At certain times during the year a small, bright orange or golden egg sac wraps around the muscle, adding a firm-textured, mildly buttery dimension to the scallop's natural sweet tenderness.

These little bivalves, whose shells seldom grow larger than three inches across, made a guest appearance at a few fish markets in Seattle several years ago. Jackie Carpenter, who then owned a Bellingham company called Westwind Seafoods, had seen them in Vancouver, British Columbia, and she introduced them to the U.S. market.

She tried to sell them as "steamer scallops," reasoning they would catch on with that name because steamer clams are so popular there. That didn't work, so she dubbed them "singing scallops," and they are still sold under that name at the Pike Place Market, downtown. "I liked the name because they puff through the wa-

Pink and spiny scallops on display at Pike Place Market in Seattle, where they are sold as "singing scallops" because they make a small popping sound in the water.

ter with their shells moving, like they're singing."

It wasn't so long ago that singing scallops began appearing regularly on restaurant menus, usually as appetizers and nearly always steamed in white wine and herbs. Some, though, are bathed in marjoram butter or cream and fennel, or spiked with garlic. What arrives at table is a bowl heaped with translucent pink shells, the plump, cream colored meat nestled inside. The shells are a bonus to take home as souvenirs.

Pink and spiny scallops occur from California to Alaska, but the only fisheries are in Washington State and British Columbia, where they have been harvested since 1985 by both divers and trawler boats. Scallops are available year-round, though there are occasional hiatuses in late summer when the occurrence of red tide, an algae bloom, prevents their being harvested. Some fans argue that pink scallops are better in spring and summer, others insist winter is the only time to eat them. It's a matter of emotion—there are no facts to back up either side.

Jim Ranson, owner of Premium Seafoods in Bellingham, Washington, is the pioneer commercial pink and spiny scallop diver in the state. He is a professional diver whose usual work involves inspecting boat hulls underwater. Diving is his passion but hulls aren't and he decided to harvest scallops about two years ago.

Ranson dives for the scallops in Puget Sound, anywhere from one to several miles from the port of Anacortes, Wash-

ington just south of Bellingham. Before stepping overboard, he looks like a tubby alien about to go on a shopping trip, suited in black diving gear, a long flashlight strapped to his head, and the scallop bag hung almost daintily over his arm.

Underwater he crawls along rocky outposts, pulling himself forward with his hands, looking for bunches of scallops whose shells are covered by a thin layer of golden sponge. Before he started using a light in the inky underwater darkness, he located scallops by putting his face right up to the rocks and feeling for the sponge.

Ranson literally picks the scallops—which detach easily—right into a seine (mesh bag) he carries on his chest. Those that escape flutter off in clouds around his head. When his time is up or his bag is full, he slowly ascends to the surface where his boat *Ogre* is waiting for him.

Once on board, the scallops are put in black plastic garbage cans pierced with holes, hefted over the stern of the boat, and sprayed with seawater from a pressurized hose, which removes the sponge, leaving the shells sparkling clean.

Aquacultured pink and spiny scallops are slowly entering the Northwest market. The growth of this industry will assure nationwide availability of these flavorful newcomers.

Clarence Barendse's Pickled Salmon

I met Clarence "Snookie" Barendse in The Logger, a bar in Knappa, Oregon, after a long, hot day on a crawfish boat. A retired salmon fisherman of Scandinavian heritage, Clarence has an abiding appetite for salmon, and he's very particular about its preparation. His recipes were as detailed and delicious as any I collected in my travels. As for salmon, he likes it any way he finds it, as long as the fish is fresh. This is his recipe, and it always gets rave reviews. It is simple to make, and I always have some on hand, to serve as a snack or an appetizer. It will keep a month in the refrigerator if you can hang on to it that long, though it's ready to eat in 24 hours. Because of the acidity in the salmon, it's best served with icy cold beer.

1 pound red king salmon fillet, skin and bones
   removed (see Note)
3½ teaspoons salt
1 cup distilled white vinegar
2 tablespoons packed dark brown sugar
1 teaspoon black mustard seed
1 teaspoon yellow mustard seed
1 tablespoon pickling spices
¼ teaspoon dried hot pepper flakes
1 medium white onion, peeled and thinly sliced

1. Rinse and pat the salmon dry. Cut crosswise in ¼-inch slices. Sprinkle 1½ teaspoons of the salt in the bottom of a shallow, non-aluminum dish that will hold all the slices in one layer. Arrange the salmon on the salt, and sprinkle on the remaining 2 teaspoons salt. Cover with foil and refrigerate overnight.

2. In a medium-size, non-aluminum saucepan, combine the vinegar, sugar, and 1 cup water. Bring to a boil. Remove from the heat; set aside to cool.

3. Rinse the salt from the salmon and pat it dry.

4. Mix the spices together in a small bowl. Alternate layers of salmon and onion in a 1-quart canning jar, sprinkling the spices on each layer so they are evenly dispersed.

5. When the vinegar and water mixture is cool, pour it over the salmon and the onions, making sure that all of the fish and onions are covered evenly with the liquid. Don't be concerned if you have some of the mixture leftover. You may want to use a chopstick to move the salmon away from the edges of the jar to let the liquid flow around the salmon.

6. Close the jar and refrigerate for at least 24 hours.

Makes 1 quart pickled salmon (10 to 12 servings)

Note: In order to be sure that the salmon in this dish contains no harmful parasites (you will not be cooking it), the salmon should have been fresh-frozen. Ask your fish merchant whether the fish arrived at his market still frozen. If the answer is no or he isn't sure, don't make this recipe.

Gravlax

*G*ravlax is the sugar-and-salt cure used in Scandinavia for salmon. The sugar and salt work together to draw the liquid from the fish and infuse it with a delicate, salty sweetness. Plenty of fresh dill adds a summery touch, and the texture of the fish, which turns almost translucent when it has fully cured, is wonderfully tender. If you are a real dill fan, don't hesitate to increase the amount used to cure the salmon. Try this with chilled vodka.

2 center-cut, flash-frozen sockeye, king, or chinook
    salmon fillets (1 pound each), scaled but with skin
    on (see Note, page 90)
3 tablespoons kosher (coarse) salt
3 tablespoons sugar
1 tablespoon white peppercorns, crushed
2 large bunches fresh dill
Mustard Sauce (see Index)

1. Rinse the salmon fillets and pat dry with paper towels. Remove any pin bones from the fillets using a sterilized strawberry huller, fish bone puller, or needle-nose pliers. Sterilize the bone remover again before putting it away.

2. Score each fillet on the skin side, making several diagonal cuts about ⅛ inch deep, so the salt and sugar will easily penetrate the meat.

3. In a bowl, combine the salt and sugar. Sprinkle 5 teaspoons of the mixture on the bottom of a 14 x 10-inch glass dish.

4. Place 1 fillet, skin side down, in the dish. Sprinkle with the crushed peppercorns and 4 teaspoons of the remaining salt and sugar mixture. Reserve 3 sprigs of dill for garnish. Lay half of the remaining dill on top of the fillet. Sprinkle 4 teaspoons of the salt and sugar mixture on the flesh side of the remaining fillet. Place it, skin side up, on the dill, as though you were reconstructing the whole piece of fish. Sprinkle the top fillet with the remaining sugar and salt mixture.

5. Cover the salmon with a sheet of waxed paper and a sheet of aluminum foil. Place a baking sheet over the top and weigh down with a 3- to 5-pound weight (canned foods

are ideal). Refrigerate for 48 hours. After about 5 hours, check the salmon: drain any liquid that has collected in the bottom of the dish. Leave the salmon in the refrigerator for at least 43 additional hours, turning it twice during that time. Once cured, the salmon will keep for about 4 days in the refrigerator.

6. To serve the gravlax, cut the skin from as much as you plan to serve, then slice the fillet into thin slices. Finely chop the remaining dill and sprinkle it over the slices. Serve with Mustard Sauce and thinly sliced pumpernickel bread.

Makes 10 to 12 appetizer servings

Mackerel Gravlax

The idea for mackerel gravlax came from Inger Johansson, a Swedish-born buyer for the Boston food distributors, Dole and Bailey, who demonstrated it at a seafood seminar a couple of years ago. Instead of using dill, the traditional gravlax herb, I use cilantro, to provide a more piquant balance to the flavor of mackerel. I serve it with a simple roast pepper purée with a hint of balsamic vinegar. It makes a wonderful first course, though we've been known to nibble on it like popcorn, sitting around watching a movie in the evening. I love this with the pepper purée as a dipping sauce, but try it too with the Mustard Sauce (see Index). Try this with a chilled, dry German Kabinett, or for a sweeter wine, a Gewürztraminer from Oregon or Alsace.

4 mackerel fillets (about 5 ounces each), skin on
2 tablespoons plus 2 teaspoons sea salt
2 tablespoons plus 2 teaspoons sugar
1 large bunch cilantro, stems removed

Bell Pepper Purée:

1 roasted green bell pepper (see Index), peeled and
  seeded
½ teaspoon balsamic vinegar
1 tablespoon cilantro leaves
Cilantro leaves, for garnish

1. Trim any pin bones from the mackerel fillets (which you can locate by running your finger along the fillet from the head end to the tail), either by pulling them from the fillet with a strawberry huller, fish bone puller, or a pair of needle-nose pliers (which should be sterilized before and after you use them), or by simply cutting them out with a very sharp knife, trying not to cut through the skin. Score each fillet on the skin side, making several diagonal cuts about ⅛-inch deep, so the salt and sugar will easily penetrate the flesh.

2. Mix together the salt and the sugar in a small bowl. Lay one-third of the cilantro leaves on the bottom of a non-aluminum baking dish, to cover an area the size of 2 mackerel fillets. Sprinkle 1 tablespoon of the salt and sugar mixture on top of the cilantro leaves. Sprinkle 1 teaspoon of the salt and sugar mixture on each of the skin sides of 2 fillets, and lay them, skin side down, on top of the cilantro.

3. Sprinkle 2 teaspoons of the salt and sugar on the flesh side of each of the 4 mackerel fillets. Cover the fillets in the baking dish with half of the remaining cilantro leaves. Place the remaining 2 fillets, skin side up, over the fillets in the baking dish. Push the top fillets gently onto the bottom fillets.

4. Cover the fillets with the remaining cilantro leaves, then sprinkle with the remaining 1 tablespoon salt and sugar mixture. Cover with waxed paper and foil and set a small plate on top. Set three 1-pound weights

on top of the plate (canned foods are ideal) and refrigerate the mackerel for 5 hours. Check the mackerel and drain off any liquid that has accumulated in the baking dish. Replace the waxed paper, foil, plate, and the weights, and refrigerate for an additional 19 hours.

5. Just before serving the mackerel, make the Bell Pepper Purée. Purée the pepper in a blender or food processor until it is smooth, then add the vinegar. Transfer the purée to a small bowl. Finely mince the cilantro and stir it into the purée. Transfer the purée to a small serving dish.

6. To serve the mackerel, remove the fillets from the baking dish; scrape off any cilantro that adheres to the fish. The flesh of the mackerel will be somewhat darkened, but don't be concerned. Using a very sharp, thin-bladed knife, slice the mackerel off the skin into the thinnest slices possible. Arrange the slices in a fan around the edge of a medium-size serving plate. Place the dish of pepper purée in the center; sprinkle the mackerel with fresh cilantro leaves. Serve with thinly sliced white or whole wheat toasts.

Makes 6 appetizer servings

Smelts in Olive Oil with Herbs and Kosher Salt

Smelts are not only gorgeous, gleaming silver with hints of olive green, but they're wonderfully tender and sweet. I like them any time, any way, though particularly like this, crisp-fried in olive oil, studded with grains of salt, and showered with herbs. Don't let the grains of salt scare you off—this is not an overly salty dish. Also, if you object to removing the smelt fillets from the bone at the table—which is very simple—buy whole, boned smelts. They won't be as flavorful, nor will they make as nice a presentation, but they will be tasty. Try this with a young, fresh Mâcon-Villages.

2 pounds smelts, cleaned, with bones in and head on

¼ cup all-purpose flour

¼ teaspoon salt

¼ teaspoon freshly ground black pepper

½ cup plus 2 tablespoons olive oil

1 teaspoon kosher (coarse) salt

2 cups loosely packed fresh tarragon, flat-leaf parsley, or basil leaves

1. Rinse the smelts and pat them dry, inside and out.

2. Place the flour on a piece of waxed paper or a plate. Season with the salt and pepper; mix well. Lightly dredge the smelts in the flour, making sure they are coated inside and out, tapping them to remove any excess.

3. Heat the olive oil in a large, heavy skillet over medium-high heat. When the oil is hot and lightly smoking, add the smelts, and cook until golden and crisp, 2 to 3 minutes on each side. Do not crowd the pan; you may want to cook the smelts in batches. Halfway through the cooking time add all of the kosher salt, so it won't dissolve in the oil, but will remain in pieces. (If you are cooking the smelts in batches, add half of the kosher salt and continue cooking.) Remove the smelts and drain on paper towels. Loosely cover with foil to keep warm. Let the oil heat again so it is very hot and lightly smoking;

add the herbs. Cook, stirring constantly, until crisp, about 2 minutes.

4. Arrange the smelts side-by-side in a row on a platter. Remove the herbs from the oil using a slotted spoon or spatula; sprinkle over the smelts. Serve immediately.

Makes 4 appetizer servings

Pickled Smelts

This is a wonderful way to prepare smelts, which are similar in flavor and texture to herring. I like to serve the small pieces of smelt with the onion slices as an appetizer, along with buttered rye bread.

Clean the fish by cutting off the head and pulling out the viscera. Cut the fish open on the belly side, from tail to head end, and lay them out flat. Work your finger under the bone at the head end and gently pull it up and out of the fish, holding the fish down with a knife blade. It should come out easily.

2 teaspoons salt

1 pound silver smelts, cleaned and boned

For the pickling liquid:

1 cup white wine vinegar

4 tablespoons water

6 tablespoons sugar

10 white peppercorns

1 teaspoon whole allspice, crushed

1 bay leaf

1 teaspoon minced fresh ginger

1 small red onion, thinly sliced

1. Sprinkle ¾ of a teaspoon of the salt on the bottom of a 12½ x 8½-inch, non-aluminum pan. Lay the smelt on the salt, and

sprinkle the remaining salt over them. Cover with aluminum foil and refrigerate for 24 hours.

2. The following day, combine the pickling mixture in a medium-size saucepan and bring to a boil over medium-high heat. Remove from the heat and let cool to room temperature.

3. Drain the smelts and pat them dry. Cut them into 1-inch-long pieces and layer the pieces, alternating with the sliced onion, in a 2-pint jar. Pour the cooled pickling liquid over all and refrigerate. They are ready to eat in 8 hours and will keep for several weeks in the refrigerator.

Makes about 2 pints pickled smelts

Octopus in Miso Paste or with Soy and Lemon

Miso paste is very common in Hawaii, and that is where the best white miso, Shiro brand, comes from. White miso paste, a mixture of rice, soy beans, salt, and vinegar, is used with seafood in a variety of ways, from a marinade to a dipping sauce. Misao Yoshimura, of Seattle's Mutual Fish Company, suggested it as a dip, with sugar and rice wine vinegar, for the cooked octopus I was buying one day. (Octopus is most often sold cleaned and cooked.) She was right, for its tart sweetness which has a flavor reminiscent of apples, is ideal with the fresh crispness of octopus.

She also suggested serving octopus with a soy and lemon sauce. I added a touch of fresh ginger and some minced chives, and it is a completely different, and equally successful, complement to the octopus. Try sake with this dish or a chilled Kirin beer.

White Miso Sauce:

3 tablespoons white miso paste, preferably Shiro brand

1 tablespoon rice wine vinegar

1 tablespoon sugar

Soy and Lemon Sauce:

9 chives

1 tablespoon light (usukuchi) soy sauce

1 tablespoon fresh lemon juice

½ teaspoon minced fresh ginger

Wasabi and Octopus:

2 teaspoons wasabi powder

¼ pound cooked octopus tentacle, cut in ⅛-inch-thick slices

1. Make the White Miso Sauce: Mix together the miso paste, rice wine vinegar, and sugar in a small bowl. Transfer to a small serving dish.

2. Make the Soy and Lemon Sauce: Mince 6 of the chives. In a small bowl, mix together the soy sauce, lemon juice, ginger, and minced chives. Transfer to a small serving dish.

3. Prepare the *Wasabi* and Octopus: Using a small spoon, mix the *wasabi* powder with 1 teaspoon water in a small dish. Shape the wasabi paste into a tiny pyramid shape.

4. Arrange the sliced octopus in fan-shaped rows on a small plate. Place the dishes of sauce at the base of the plate, and decorate the plate with the 3 remaining chives and the *wasabi* pyramid.

Makes 4 hors d'oeuvres servings

Halibut Cheeks with Pesto

*E*njoying the firm sweetness of halibut cheeks is a Pacific Northwest rite of summer. Their meat, which is strikingly similar to scallops, is a perfect foil for summery pesto. If you can't find fresh halibut cheeks use fresh-frozen, and if you don't find those, substitute either sea scallops or boned halibut steaks. Try this with a lightly chilled Meursault.

8 ounces halibut cheeks, sea scallops, or halibut steak,
  boned and cut into 4 pieces
½ teaspoon extra-virgin olive oil
Salt and freshly ground black pepper
Pesto (see Index), omitting the cheese
1 small head radicchio, separated, rinsed, and dried

   1. Rinse the halibut cheeks and pat them dry. Trim off any silvery membrane and discard it. Cut the cheeks horizontally, if necessary, to make them all the same thickness (you need not slice the scallops or halibut steaks). Rub lightly with the oil to coat all sides.
   2. Arrange the halibut cheeks in a single layer on a heatproof plate. Season lightly with salt and pepper. Top each piece with 1 teaspoon pesto. Cover and refrigerate for up to 1 hour.
   3. Bring 2 cups water to a boil in a wok fitted with a steamer rack or in the bottom of a steamer. Place the plate on the steamer rack, cover, and steam until the halibut cheeks are opaque through, about 5 minutes.
   4. To serve, arrange the radicchio on 4 warmed dinner plates, leaving a space in the center. Divide the remaining pesto among the center of the plates. Arrange the halibut cheeks on the radicchio in a flower pattern. Serve immediately.
   Makes 4 appetizer servings

Fresh Tuna-Stuffed Peppers

*T*ender, meaty albacore tuna, fresh herbs, and olive oil all set in a sweet bell pepper make this a dish everyone loves. And it's as simple to make as it is delicious. You must begin it the night before, by marinating the tuna in oil, then finish it up the next day in time for lunch or for dinner. It's ideal as a warm-weather appetizer for eight. Try this with a lightly chilled rosé of Cabernet or a chilled Cru Beaujolais.

1 pound fresh or flash-frozen loin of albacore tuna,
  skin removed, cut in 4 equal slices
1 tablespoon fresh thyme leaves, or ½ teaspoon dried
¼ cup fresh rosemary leaves, or 2 teaspoons dried
4 whole cloves
2 bay leaves
5 large cloves garlic, thinly sliced
⅔ cup plus 2 tablespoons olive oil
Salt and freshly ground black pepper
2 medium onions, thinly sliced
2 medium red bell peppers, cored, seeded, and halved
  lengthwise
2 medium green bell peppers, cored, seeded, and halved
  lengthwise
2 tablespoons drained capers
¼ cup oil-cured black olives
Sprigs of fresh rosemary, for garnish

1. Place the slices of tuna in a non-aluminum baking dish just large enough to hold them. Sprinkle on the thyme, rosemary, cloves, bay leaves, and 1 of the sliced garlic cloves; pour ⅔ cup olive oil over all. Turn the pieces of tuna a couple of times so they are coated with the oil and herbs; cover and refrigerate overnight.

2. The next morning, preheat the oven to 350°F.

3. Bake the tuna in the oil and herbs, covered, until opaque, about 15 minutes. Remove from the oven and set the dish aside until the tuna is cool enough to handle. Using your fingers, break the tuna into bite-size pieces. Mix it well with the oil in which it was baked, season with salt and pepper to taste, and refrigerate for at least 4 hours.

4. Preheat the oven to 350°.

5. Place the onions in the bottom of a 12½ x 8½-inch baking dish. Pour 1 tablespoon of the remaining olive oil over the onions and season lightly with salt and pepper. Place the pepper halves, cut sides up, on top of the onions, alternating the red and green peppers. Divide the remaining sliced garlic among the pepper halves; drizzle each one with an equal amount of the remaining 1 tablespoon olive oil. Cover the dish with foil and bake until the peppers are soft, but still keep their shape, 30 to 35 minutes. Remove from the heat and cool to room temperature.

5. To serve, add the capers to the tuna; mix well. Mound equal amounts of the tuna into the pepper halves, and garnish with the olives and sprigs of rosemary. Serve a small amount of the onions with each pepper half.

Makes 8 servings

4

CHOWDERS, SOUPS
& STEWS

When I was a child, the mention of seafood soup brought one kind to mind—creamy clam chowder, which I loved. I envisioned a wide, steaming bowl smelling sweetly of clams and thick with small chunks of potato. There was always a pat of melting butter on top and a sprinkling of red paprika.

I still cherish thoughts of clam chowder, but have since discovered and made so many different kinds of seafood soups and stews, that my definition is no longer so limited. Now my chowders are likely to be clear, bobbing with oysters and fish and spiked with lime and cilantro, or rich and studded with corn and monkfish. My soups range from a thick Chesapeake Harvest Soup that is golden with pumpkin and filled with tender crab, to a light Wanmori, with clam-shaped dumplings and delicate, clear broth. I love seafood stews, too. Simple ones made from cream poured over lobster and cooked just until the cream absorbs the flavor and delicate pink of the sweet meat, or dense ones like Bourride, a medley of white fish bathed in a garlicky sauce.

While timing in all seafood cooking is critical, cooking time for these soups and stews is minimal, so they are quick to prepare, and I often serve them to guests—even quite large groups. For although they are among the simplest seafood dishes, they have an aura of complexity and refinement that makes a meal seem special, out of the ordinary.

Monkfish and Corn Chowder

Monkfish comes into season in summer, at the same time sweet, golden ears of corn start appearing at the market. Together, they make a delightful chowder. Though the flavor the bacon adds to the chowder is essential, the bacon pieces are superfluous—they overpower the other smooth, subtle flavors. Try a chilled dry white wine, such as Vouvray, with this.

4 ounces slab bacon, rind removed, cut into ¼-inch
    dice
1 small onion, diced
1 medium russet potato, peeled and cut into ¼-inch
    dice
2 cups fresh corn kernels (about 2 ears)
12 ounces monkfish fillet, cut into ¼-inch-thick
    slices, then lengthwise in half
2½ cups milk
1 cup heavy or whipping cream
Salt and freshly ground black pepper
1 tablespoon minced red bell pepper, for garnish

1. Render the fat from the slab bacon in a medium-size saucepan over medium-high heat. When the bacon is crisp and golden, remove it from the pan. Drain on paper towels; reserve the bacon.

2. Add the onion to the bacon fat and sauté until it begins to turn translucent, about 3 minutes. Stir in the potato and reduce the heat to medium. Add enough water to just cover the potato dice. Cover the pan and cook, stirring occasionally, until the potatoes are nearly soft through, 10 to 15 minutes.

3. Add the corn and cook, stirring, until it begins to turn a brighter yellow, 2 to 3 minutes. Add the monkfish and cook until nearly opaque, about 4 minutes.

4. Add the milk and cream; cook, stirring, until very hot. Be careful not to let the soup boil. Season with salt and pepper to taste.

5. To serve the chowder, divide among 4 shallow, warm soup bowls. Garnish with the red bell pepper and serve immediately, accompanied by a crisp, green salad that has the cooked slab bacon as a garnish.

Makes 4 generous servings

Maine Fisherman's Stew

I got this hearty fisherman's dinner from Patricia Rackliffe who makes it often for her husband Dennis, a lobsterman, and their three children. It is a delectable combination reminiscent of a Portuguese salt cod dish, but with the American hallmark of egg gravy. The recipe is unusual for a stew—the ingredients are served separately—and it is very forgiving. If you cook the fish up to five minutes longer than stated in the recipe it will not be ruined. Don't let it go longer than that however, as it will become watery. If you do manage to have leftovers—which is unlikely—they make a wonderful salad the next day. Try the stew with a simple, chilled white table wine.

3 tablespoons salt
2 pounds hake or lingcod fillets
2 small onions, cut into thin rounds
1 cup white wine vinegar
4 large russet potatoes, peeled and halved
8 ounces slab bacon, rind removed
½ cup (1 stick) unsalted butter
3 tablespoons all-purpose flour
2¼ cups milk
Salt and freshly ground black pepper
4 hard-cooked large eggs, peeled and coarsely chopped
1 bunch parsley, coarsely chopped

1. Sprinkle the bottom of a large, non-metal dish with 1 tablespoon of the salt. Lay the fillets on top of the salt, cutting them if necessary to fit into the dish. Sprinkle the remaining 2 tablespoons salt on top of the fish. Cover with waxed paper and then aluminum foil. Refrigerate for 24 hours.

2. The next day, place the onion slices in a small bowl and add the vinegar. Submerge the onions in the vinegar; set aside for 1 hour.

3. Place the potatoes in a large saucepan and add salted water to cover. Cover and bring to a boil over medium-high heat. Boil until soft, about 20 minutes.

4. Cut the slab bacon into ½ x ¼ x ¼-inch pieces. Render the bacon in a medium-size skillet over medium-high heat until it is golden and crisp, about 10 minutes. Reserve the bacon and its fat in a low oven.

5. Rinse the fish twice on each side, under cold running water, to remove the salt. Place the fish in a large saucepan, and add enough cold water to cover by 2 inches. Bring the water to a boil over high heat. Remove from the heat, and drain the fish. Repeat the process. When the water comes to a boil the second time, reduce the heat to medium, and simmer the fish until translucent, 15 to 20 minutes.

6. To make the egg gravy, melt the butter in a medium-size saucepan over medium heat. Stir in the flour and cook for 5 minutes, stirring constantly. Pour in 2 cups of the milk and continue stirring until the sauce is thick. Season with salt and pepper to taste. Stir in the hard-cooked eggs. Keep warm. If the sauce thickens too much, add as much of the remaining ¼ cup milk as necessary. It should be quite thick, but pourable.

7. When the fish is cooked, drain it. Arrange the fish on a large platter and surround it with the potatoes. Sprinkle with the parsley. Serve the onions and vinegar, bacon and fat, and the egg gravy alongside. To eat this dish, mash a potato on your plate. Place the fish on top and cut it up into the potato. Top with the onions and the egg gravy, then the bacon and bacon fat.

Makes 4 servings

Southwest Chowder

This recipe comes from Stephen Pyles, owner of the Routh Street Cafe and Baby Routh in Dallas, and co-owner of Goodfellow's and Tejas in Minneapolis. Chef Pyles has a light hand with food and a knack for combining a variety of diverse ingredients to create a dish that is subtle, almost dreamy, yet startling on both the palate and the eye. Serve this with a chilled Pinot Grigio.

1 tablespoon unsalted butter
2 ounces slab bacon, rind removed and diced
1 medium red bell pepper, cored, seeded, and diced
1 medium green bell pepper, cored, seeded, and diced
⅔ cup finely chopped onion
½ cup finely chopped celery
¼ cup bourbon
1 cup dry white wine, such as Pinot Grigio
4 cups Fish Stock (see Index)
Salt
1 small sweet potato, peeled and cut into ½-inch cubes
1 snapper or grouper fillet (8 ounces), bones removed and cut into 1-inch cubes
2 medium-size ripe tomatoes, peeled, seeded, and coarsely chopped
2 dozen small oysters, shells well-scrubbed under cold running water, shucked, or petite jarred oysters
1 small handful cilantro leaves
2 teaspoons fresh lime juice
3 ounces jicama, peeled and cut into ¼-inch cubes (½ cup)
1 lime, cut into 8 slices, for garnish

1. Melt the butter in a large saucepan over medium-high heat. Add the bacon and sauté just until it starts to turn golden, about 3 minutes.

2. Add the peppers, onion, and celery. Cook, stirring constantly, until just beginning to turn soft, about 3 minutes. Add the bourbon and wine and cook until reduced by one-half.

3. Add the Fish Stock. Cover and bring to a boil. Season with salt to taste. Add the sweet potato and cook, uncovered, until

slightly softened, about 3 minutes. Add the snapper and tomatoes. Cover and cook until the grouper turns opaque on the outside, about 1½ minutes. Add the oysters and cook just until they curl around the edges, about 1 minute.

4. Just before serving, mince the cilantro and add it to the chowder with the lime juice and jicama. Season with salt to taste.

5. To serve, divide the chowder among 8 warmed soup bowls. Float a lime slice in each bowl and serve immediately.

Makes 8 servings

Bourride

The first time I had bourride, several years ago in Nîmes, France, I thought it was the best thing I had ever tasted. Silken, garlicky, studded with absolutely fresh and wonderful fish—I've never forgotten that first taste. This is an Americanized version, with an extra dose of garlic and a touch of orange. The trick to this dish is not to let the sauce boil once it is made, or it will curdle, and your efforts will have been for naught. Try a dry rosé with a spicy aroma, such as a Tavel, along with this.

Aioli:

6 large egg yolks
1 cup olive oil
10 cloves garlic, minced
½ teaspoon salt
2 tablespoons fresh lemon juice
1 teaspoon lukewarm water
Freshly ground white pepper

Toasts:

6 slices crusty white bread
2 cloves garlic

Fish:

1½ pounds white sea fish, such as Alaska or red
    snapper, John Dory, sea bream, haddock, whiting,
    or monkfish
1 medium onion, sliced
1 large sprig fresh thyme
1 bay leaf
1 stalk fennel, 6 to 8 inches long, coarsely chopped,
    or 1 teaspoon fennel seed
1 large sprig parsley
Zest of 1 orange, cut into 2¼ x ¼-inch strips
2 cloves garlic, lightly crushed
Salt and freshly ground black pepper
3 cups Fish Stock (see Index)

Garnish:

Grated zest of ½ orange
1 tablespoon minced flat-leaf parsley

1. Make the Aioli: Place 2 of the egg yolks in the bowl of a food processor and pulse to combine them. With the motor running, slowly pour in the olive oil in a very thin stream, processing until the mixture emulsifies and is very thick.

2. Pour the emulsion into a bowl and place the garlic and salt in the processor bowl. Pulse until the garlic is finely minced and combined with the salt. With the food processor running, add the emulsion, then add the lemon juice and the water. Season with white pepper to taste. Cover and refrigerate.

3. Make the Toasts: Toast the bread slices on both sides. Cut each slice into 4 small triangles. Rub the toasts on both sides with the garlic; reserve.

4. Prepare the Fish: Place the fish in a medium-size, non-aluminum skillet, saucepan, or fish poacher. Sprinkle on the onion, herbs, orange zest, garlic, and a generous sprinkling of salt and pepper. Pour in the fish stock to cover the fish (if there is not enough stock, make up the difference with water). Cover the pan and bring the liquid to a boil over medium-high heat. Reduce the heat to medium so the liquid is simmering and cook until the fish is nearly opaque, but not quite cooked through, about 10 minutes.

5. Remove the fish from the cooking liquid with tongs or a slotted spatula. Place it on a platter or in a shallow, heatproof bowl, cover loosely with foil, and place in a low oven to keep warm. Strain the cooking liquid; reserve.

6. Place half of the aioli in a medium-size bowl and whisk in the remaining 4 egg yolks. Add 1 cup of the strained cooking liquid and mix well. Pour into a medium-size, heavy-bottomed saucepan over medium heat and cook, stirring constantly, until the mixture thickens to the consistency of heavy cream. Be very careful not to let the sauce boil.

7. To serve the bourride, drain off any liquid that has come from the fish. Return the fish to the bowl, or divide it among 4 warm soup bowls. Arrange 4 of the toasts around the fish and ladle the sauce over the fish and the toasts, leaving the edges of the toasts showing. Garnish with the orange zest and parsley. Serve the remaining aioli alongside, for spreading on the remaining toasts.

Makes 4 servings

Seafood Auctions

*T*he Boston Fish Exchange, or auction as it is commonly called, is housed in a decrepit old building at the end of the Boston Fish Pier near downtown. Since 1929 fishermen have converged there to sell their catch to a crowd of buyers who arrive by 6 A.M., six days a week. Right along with the boats, however, are the semi-trucks that roll up, filled to the top with seafood from other East Coast ports.

The Boston auction is a chauvinistic place limited to selling the same 20 species it has handled for 25 years. There will be cod and cusk, hake and haddock, pollock and gray sole, dab and fluke, among others. Though monkfish, skate, and mackerel are landed, they aren't sold through the auction. Ships carrying those species go elsewhere.

At the dot of 6 A.M. the auction begins. It lasts about 15 minutes, sometimes developing into a shouting match, sometimes carried on with decorum. And, there isn't a fish to be seen; they're all still outside on the boats and semis.

Some buyers have boarded the vessels to assess the quality of fish, but most of the buying is done blind. Bidding gets tough as buyers buy only the part of the "trip," or catch, they want, with the end of the trip, or the freshest fish, going for a higher price than the beginning of the trip.

Buyers, distinguished from the handful of fishermen who attend the auction only by street clothes versus fishing clothes, cluster in the drafty old room. They run frequently to the dozen or more phones on the walls, to confer with colleagues and pass along pricing information. It's difficult for the uninitiated to understand the magnitude of what transpires at the auction. On any given day more than 50,000 pounds of fish that will soon be on its way all over the country, has changed hands.

MEANWHILE, IN NEW BEDFORD

New Bedford, Massachusetts, is the site of another historic East Coast auction.

The system is somewhat different from that in Boston. Flounder are the stars of the auction in New Bedford, and buyers here must buy an entire boat's trip, which makes bidding complicated. Before they buy they must know they can sell the fish they don't want. The phones at the New Bedford auction are in constant use and the haze of cigarette smoke is thick. Complicated or not however, the whole thing lasts just 22 minutes.

These auctions set prices up and down the coast, so what happens in New Bedford and in Boston determines the price of certain species around the country.

The Boston auction is picturesque,

and the one in New Bedford only slightly less so. They serve a purpose, but they're often regarded as unwieldy behemoths by those in the fishing industry who are interested in progress. They point to the one in Portland, Maine, as a good example of how they'd like to see auctions run.

A MODEL AUCTION

The Portland, Maine, auction is modeled after auctions in Europe, and it is conducted in a huge, controlled-atmosphere warehouse kept near 32°F. There are no species limitations and fishermen can display their entire trip, all in neat, brightly colored boxes.

Fish is unloaded at the nearby docks, repacked and iced, then brought into the auction room. One fish from each box is laid on top, to indicate the quality of the rest in the box.

It's cold inside the auction, just the way fish like it. Boxes of fish are stacked in rows, and buyers with serious expressions look them over, notebooks in hand. It's clean and tidy, and extremely civilized. "It's the only place around where you can see the fish before you buy it," Gene Connors, a former fisherman out of New Bedford said. "I've always thought it was ludicrous to buy something before you see it."

Ship captains or their representatives are present during the auction, which begins each day at 1 P.M., standing against one wall, while buyers are positioned at various points around the room. "What's your pleasure on large haddock?" asks the auctioneer, who stands on a small podium

Fish buyers assess fish before bidding at the United Fishing Agency auction in Honolulu.

as he calls and coaxes the price up. When the gavel falls captains can refuse the price if they want to, in hopes of getting more later. If the price is refused the buyer gets one chance to raise his bid.

The Portland auction is a revolutionary development in the East Coast fishing industry, which is legendary for its archaic ways and reluctance to change. It exists because almost a decade ago a group of fishermen marched up to city hall in Portland demanding improved dock space. They got it, and the most advanced auction in the country.

HILO AND HONOLULU

Hawaii hosts the other two U.S. auctions. There is a small one in Hilo, and a major auction in Honolulu. Both are display auctions that are held early each morning. The auction in Honolulu handles up to 50,000 pounds of fish a day. As Hawaiian fish becomes increasingly popular on the mainland, an increasing amount of fish goes from Hilo to Honolulu where it is put on a plane and dispersed to the four corners of the country.

Japanese Geoduck Soup

This is a simple, ethereally delicious soup that takes just minutes to prepare. The recipe calls for "kombu," which is kelp, and is readily available in most Asian groceries and many health food stores. In fact, the number of varieties of kombu is a bit overwhelming— what you want for this recipe is just plain kelp, and not one of the many seasoned varieties. This soup makes an elegant first course. Serve with a light Sauvignon Blanc.

8 ounces geoduck siphon and breast meat (½ siphon and ½ geoduck breast), littleneck, Manila, or steamer clams, shells well scrubbed under running water (see Note)
1½ pounds spinach, washed, stems removed
4 cups loosely packed watercress, washed, stems removed
1 piece kombu (kelp), 6 x 2 inches
12 small mushrooms, trimmed, washed, dried, and halved
2 tablespoons soy sauce
½ teaspoon grated fresh ginger
2 tablespoons fresh lime juice
Salt
1 scallion, the white bulb and light green stem finely chopped, for garnish (optional)

1. Cut the geoduck siphon and breast meat into thin slices.
2. Blanch the spinach and the watercress separately in boiling salted water just until they turn bright green and wilt, 30 seconds. Drain. Squeeze the greens to extract as much water as possible. Coarsely chop and divide equally among 4 soup bowls.

3. In a medium-size saucepan, bring 4 cups of water to a boil with the kombu. Add the geoduck and cook until light in color, no longer than 2 minutes. Remove the geoduck with a slotted spoon and divide equally among the soup bowls.
4. Remove the kombu from the cooking liquid; discard. Add the mushrooms and the soy sauce to the cooking liquid. Bring to a boil. Add the ginger and the lime juice; cook for 1 minute. Season with salt if necessary. Pour over the geoduck and chopped greens. Sprinkle with chopped scallions, if desired.

Makes 4 servings

Note: If you're using clams other than geoducks, steam them just until open in a medium-size saucepan, to which water ¼-inch deep has been added.

North Carolina Clam Chowder

All along the North Carolina coastline cooks and restaurants vie for the best clam chowder. Their version is water-based so there is no cream to interfere with the pure flavors of the other ingredients. I found the best at Brantley's Village Restaurant in Oriental, North Carolina, where the clams are so tender they melt in your mouth. North Carolina cooks use large chowder clams, which become tender with long, slow cooking. I prefer a lighter, quicker version of the soup, adding butter, littleneck or Manila clams at the last minute. Serve this chowder with Hush Puppies (see Index) and a crisp green salad. Try a chilled Pinot Gris, or a soft, round red table wine with this dish.

2 pounds Manila, littleneck, or butter clams, shells
   well scrubbed under cold running water
8 ounces slab bacon, rind removed, cut into
   ½ x ¼ x ¼-inch pieces
1 large onion, diced
3 medium potatoes, peeled and cut into ½-inch cubes
1 medium carrot, peeled and diced
Salt and freshly ground black pepper
½ cup loosely packed flat-leaf parsley leaves, finely
   minced

1. Combine the clams with 1 cup water in a large, heavy-bottomed saucepan. Cover and bring to a simmer over medium-high heat. Cook the clams just until they open, about 8 minutes. Remove from the heat. Drain the clams, reserving their liquor. Discard any that do not open.

2. Remove the clams from their shells and reserve them, covered, so they don't dry out. Strain the clam liquor through a double thickness of cheesecloth, and reserve.

3. Place the bacon in a large, heavy-bottomed saucepan over medium-high heat. Cook until golden. Remove the bacon; drain on paper towels. Add the onion and potatoes to the bacon fat. Cook, stirring often, until the onion is translucent, about 10 minutes. Add the carrot, the clam liquor, and 3 cups water. Bring to a boil, reduce the heat, and simmer until the potatoes are tender but still hold their shape, about 15 minutes.

4. While the soup is cooking, chop the clams into bite-size pieces. When the potatoes are tender, add the chopped clams and bacon. Continue cooking until they are heated through, about 5 minutes. Season with salt and pepper to taste.

5. To serve, divide the soup among 4 to 6 soup bowls. Sprinkle with parsley and grind plenty of pepper over all.

Makes 4 to 6 servings

Clams in Cider

*T*his is a quintessential Northwest recipe, originally prepared with Manila clams and Washington State hard apple cider. It's a terrific winter dish—hearty and delicious. Serve with chilled hard apple cider.

2 tablespoons unsalted butter
1 medium onion, thinly sliced
2 medium carrots, peeled and cut in thin rounds
Salt and freshly ground black pepper
½ cup loosely packed flat-leaf parsley leaves
1 large clove garlic, minced (do not press through a
   garlic press)
1 large head (8 cups loosely packed) curly leaf lettuce
   leaves, thinly sliced
1½ cups medium-dry hard apple cider
4 pounds Manila, butter, or littleneck clams, shells
   well scrubbed under cold running water

1. Melt the butter in a medium-size saucepan over medium-high heat. Add the onion and carrots and sauté until the onion begins to turn translucent, 3 to 5 minutes. Season lightly with salt and pepper. Stir in the parsley, garlic, and lettuce; pour in the cider. Bring the cider to a boil. Arrange the clams on top of the lettuce, and reduce the heat to medium so the cider is simmering. Cover and cook until the clams open, for 5 to 8 minutes. Discard any that do not open.

2. To serve, divide the clams, cooking liquid, and vegetables evenly among 4 soup bowls. Serve with plenty of fresh, crusty bread.

Makes 4 servings

Creamy Clam Chowder

I've eaten clam chowder from Oregon to Maryland, and I nearly always come away from a bowl disappointed. What I want is a rich, delicate, creamy soup infused with the sweet brininess of clams. This creamy clam soup is rich with diced potatoes and the smoky flavor of bacon, a touch of celery and scallions, and plenty of clams bobbing around in it. Try this with a lightly chilled Kabinett or Vouvray.

3 pounds Manila, butter, or littleneck clams, shells
  well scrubbed under cold running water
4 ounces slab bacon, rind removed, cut into
  ½ x ¼ x ¼-inch pieces
2 tender interior celery ribs, finely chopped
1 bunch (about 5) scallions, trimmed, the white bulbs
  and light green stems cut in thin rounds
2 large potatoes, peeled and cut into ½-inch cubes
1 cup milk
1 cup heavy or whipping cream
Salt and freshly ground black pepper
2 tablespoons unsalted butter, cut into 4 even pieces
¼ cup loosely packed flat-leaf parsley leaves, minced
Paprika, for garnish

1. Rinse the clams. Combine them with 1 cup of water in a medium-size saucepan. Cover and bring to a simmer over medium-high heat. Cook just until the clams open, about 8 minutes. Remove from the heat. Drain the clams, reserving the liquor; discard any that do not open.

2. Remove the clams from their shells and reserve them, covered, so they don't dry out. Strain the clam cooking liquor through a double thickness of cheesecloth; reserve.

3. Render the bacon in a heavy-bottomed saucepan over medium-high heat until crisp and golden. Remove the bacon and drain on paper towels. Add the celery, scallions, and potatoes to the bacon fat and sauté just until the scallions and celery begin to turn translucent, about 5 minutes. Add the clam liquor and 1 cup of water. Cook until the potatoes are tender but not mushy, about 15 minutes.

4. Add the milk and cream, stirring occasionally and making sure the chowder doesn't boil, until heated through, about 10 minutes. Add the clams and cook until they are heated through, 5 minutes. Season with salt and pepper to taste.

5. To serve the soup, ladle into 4 soup bowls. Top each bowl with a pat of butter, a shower of parsley, and a dusting of paprika. Pass the bacon separately. Serve immediately.

Makes 4 large servings

Oyster Stew

*T*here aren't many dishes as perfectly simple as oyster stew. Top-quality cream, whole milk, and fresh from the shell oysters and their liquor make a soup so rich, so perfect it should be eaten from a table with nothing else on it, in a plain room without furnishings. Try this with a crisp Muscadet.

2 cups heavy or whipping cream
2 cups milk
12 shucked small oysters, with their liquor
Salt and freshly ground black pepper
2 tablespoons unsalted butter, cut in 4 equal pieces
Paprika or diced red bell pepper, for garnish (optional)

1. Bring the cream and milk almost to a boil in a medium-size saucepan over medium heat. Add the oysters and their liquor, stir, and cook until the oysters are heated through, 3 to 4 minutes. Season the stew with salt and pepper to taste.

2. Ladle the stew into 4 warm soup bowls. Garnish each portion with a piece of butter and paprika or diced red pepper, if desired. Serve immediately.

Makes 4 servings

Oyster Soup with Watercress

This is a variation on a simple oyster stew. The vegetables and watercress add a refreshing lightness, and make this soup a beautiful appetizer or main course, if served with a crisp salad and fresh bread. Serve with a flinty Chablis.

12 small oysters, shells well scrubbed under cold
*   running water*
2 small leeks, cleaned, the white bulbs and light green
*   parts cuts into julienne*
2 medium carrots, peeled and cut into julienne
2 large bunches watercress, stems removed
1½ cups dry white wine
1½ cups crème fraîche (see Index) or heavy cream
Salt and freshly ground black pepper

1. Shuck the oysters, reserving the liquor. Strain the liquor through a double thickness of dampened cheesecloth; reserve.

2. Blanch the leeks and carrots separately in boiling salted water, just until tender but still crisp, about 2 minutes. Plunge directly into a bowl filled with ice water to refresh them and stop the cooking. Drain and pat dry. Using fresh water, blanch the watercress leaves in boiling salted water for 30 seconds. Remove and refresh in cold water. Drain and reserve.

3. In a medium-size, non-aluminum saucepan over high heat, bring the wine to a boil. Add the *crème fraîche* and return to a boil. Boil just until the mixture has thickened slightly, about 5 minutes. Reduce the heat to medium-low; stir in the oyster liquor. Stir in the carrots and leeks and cook until heated through, about 5 minutes. Season with salt and pepper to taste.

4. Just before serving, add the watercress to the soup. Cook just until warmed through, 3 to 5 minutes. To serve, arrange 3 oysters in the bottom of each of 4 heated soup bowls. Cover with the soup. Serve immediately.

Makes 4 servings

Robert Del Grande's Cilantro Mussel Soup

Although mussels are not indigenous to Texas, Chef Robert Del Grande, chef/owner of Cafe Annie in Houston, loves to experiment with seafood from around the country, and this soup is one of his best creations. It will make your taste buds sit up and take note. It combines very unconventional ingredients that look as beautiful together as they taste. Balancing the preserve-filled mussel shells is a delicate but worthwhile procedure. The recipe for chile preserves makes more than you may need for the soup. Save it to use in salad dressings, as a spread on crackers, or to mix with heavy cream for a vegetable dip. Serve with a lightly chilled Vouvray.

Ancho Chile Pepper Preserves:

3 dried ancho chiles
1 teaspoon red currant jelly
½ small shallot
1 small clove garlic
2 tablespoons mild honey
2 tablespoons white wine vinegar
½ teaspoon salt

Cilantro-Serrano Purée:

4 cups loosely packed cilantro leaves
1½ cups loosely packed flat-leaf parsley leaves
½ small yellow onion, halved
4 cloves garlic
2 serrano chiles, stems removed
2 tablespoons Fish Stock (see Index), or more

Mussels:

2 pounds mussels, shells well scrubbed under cold
  running water, and bearded (see Note)
1 cup dry white wine, such as a Vouvray
1 cup Fish Stock (see Index)
2 cups heavy or whipping cream
Cilantro leaves, for garnish

1. Make the Ancho Chile Pepper Preserves: In a small bowl, cover the dried ancho peppers with boiling water. Cover and set aside until very soft, about 40 minutes. Drain the peppers, squeezing out all of the water. Remove about half of their seeds. Trim off the stems. Purée with the remaining preserve ingredients in a food mill or food processor until thick and smooth. Season with salt to taste.

2. Make the Cilantro-Serrano Purée:

Place the cilantro, parsley, onion, garlic and serrano chiles in a food mill or food processor. Purée until smooth. Add 2 tablespoons of the fish stock and blend well to make a smooth, thick purée.

3. Cook the Mussels: In a large, non-aluminum saucepan, combine the mussels, wine, and fish stock over high heat. Cover and cook, shaking the pan occasionally, until the mussels open, 3 to 5 minutes. Remove from the heat. Using a slotted spoon, remove the mussels from the cooking liquid. Remove the mussel meats from their shells. Strain the mussel cooking liquid through a double thickness of dampened cheesecloth and return to the pan. Reserve 4 mussel shell halves; discard the rest.

4. Carefully fill the 4 reserved mussel shells with the Ancho Chile Preserves, mounding it well above the rim of the shell; set aside.

5. Place the pan with the mussel cooking liquid over high heat. Whisk in the cream and bring to a boil. Cook until it thickens slightly, 3 to 4 minutes. Add the cilantro-serrano purée; bring back to a boil, whisking constantly. Remove the soup from the heat. Stir in the mussels.

6. To serve the soup, use a slotted spoon to remove the hot mussels from the soup and evenly divide them among 4 soup bowls, mounding them in the middle of the bowl. Balance a mussel shell filled with ancho preserves on each mound of mussel meats. Gently ladle the soup around the mussels. Garnish with cilantro leaves. Serve immediately.

Makes 4 servings

Note: Do not beard the mussels before you plan to use them or they will die and spoil.

Chesapeake Harvest Soup

*D*riving north from Crisfield, on the southeastern shore of Maryland, in September, my husband and I came upon stand after stand of pumpkins tumbling practically onto the highway. I'd never seen so many and wanted to fill the car with them. Instead I just dreamed about ways to cook with them. We had just spent several days eating blue crab in just about every way imaginable, and I came upon this idea to combine two fall favorites—fresh, sweet pumpkin and fresh, sweet crab. Try this with a chilled Chenin Blanc, Vouvray, or Touraine.

1 live Dungeness crab (2 pounds), or 1½ cups lump crabmeat, picked over

Fish Stock:

2 pounds fish bones
2 tablespoons unsalted butter
2 medium carrots, coarsely chopped
1 large onion, coarsely chopped
2 celery ribs with leaves
1 bay leaf
1 bunch parsley stems
1 sprig fresh thyme or ¼ teaspoon dried
10 peppercorns
2 teaspoons salt

Soup:

2 pounds fresh, peeled pumpkin, cut into 2-inch pieces
3 tablespoons fresh lemon juice
Salt and cayenne pepper
3 tablespoons unsalted butter, for garnish
12 flat-leaf parsley leaves, for garnish

1. If you're using a live crab, bring a large pot of salted water to a boil over high heat. Add the crab and cook, covered, until the crab turns bright red, about 15 minutes. Drain the crab and let cool until it can be easily handled. Crack the shell, pick out the crabmeat, and refrigerate it, covered, until ready for use. Reserve the crab claw shells for the stock; discard the body shell.

2. Make the Fish Stock: Rinse the fish bones well under cold running water. In a large saucepan, melt the butter over medium heat. Stir in the carrots, onion, celery, reserved crab claw shells, and ½ cup of water. Cook, covered, until the vegetables are softened, about 10 minutes. Add the fish bones, herbs, seasonings, and 9½ cups water. Bring to a boil. Reduce the heat to low and simmer, skimming off any foam that rises to the surface, for 18 minutes. Remove from the heat. Strain and discard the solids.

3. Make the Soup: Bring a large pot of salted water to a boil over high heat. Add the pumpkin and cook until soft, about 15 minutes. Drain. Purée until smooth in a blender or food processor. You will have about 3 cups of purée.

4. Place the pumpkin purée in a medium-size saucepan over medium heat. Cook off all of the excess liquid; stir occasionally to prevent burning. Stir in 3 cups of the fish stock. Reserve any remaining stock for another use. Cook until the mixture thickens slightly, about 5 minutes. Add the lemon juice and stir; add the crabmeat. Season with salt and cayenne pepper to taste.

5. Divide among 6 soup bowls. Serve immediately, garnishing each portion with a pat of butter, a sprinkling of cayenne, and 2 parsley leaves.

Makes 6 servings

Wisconsin Fish Boil

*I*ntense orange flames shoot high into the evening sky, and the crowd stands back in awe, their stomachs rumbling. A huge pot on the fire boils over, dousing most of the flames. Then two men, their faces shiny with heat and exertion, lift baskets filled with boiled fish, potatoes, and onions from the pot and carry them inside.

The baskets are set on long tables along with plates of lemon, pumpkin, and date-nut bread, slices of dark, orange-scented rye bread, bowls of cole slaw, and a chafing dish of warm, melted butter. Diners, plates in hand, are served fish and potatoes, which must be removed gingerly from the baskets so they don't fall apart. They help themselves to the rest, and wash it down with plenty of Wisconsin beer.

This is a Door County, Wisconsin, fish boil, and a native ritual on this bucolic agricultural and fishing peninsula. It attracts people from all over—in fact, if you mention fish anywhere in Wisconsin, their first response is, "Have you had a fish boil in Door County yet?"

It's a lovely drive up Interstate 94 from Chicago to Milwaukee, then on Interstate 43 to Door County. You know you're in Door County when, on State Route 57, signs advertising "Fish Boils" appear.

Door County residents don't take their fish boils for granted, but there is a flicker of bemusement at the commotion generated by such a simple meal. "Fishermen have always done fish boils around here," said Andy Coulson, owner of the White Gull Inn in Fish Creek. According to Dan Petersen, proprietor of the Viking Restaurant in Ellison Bay, "The fishermen had pot-bellied stoves to keep them warm. They would fill a pot with lake water and stick it right down into the stove. They'd bring along potatoes and onions, throw some fish in, and boil it all up together. They ate what they wanted and threw the rest overboard."

Russell Ostrand, who has prepared fish boils at the White Gull Inn for 21 years in the evenings, after a day spent pipe fitting at the Sturgeon Bay shipyard, said fish boils were a practical way to feed a lot of people.

"We'd do them at the shipyard in the 40s and 50s," he said. "for parties. The welders and the pipe fitters—they'd come with their families—there'd be a keg of beer and lots to eat. They did 'em at the lumber camps too and for church suppers."

In the 1960s restaurants started offering them to the increasing stream of visitors. One wouldn't equate boiled fish and vegetables with gastronomic excitement, but a Door County fish boil is an uncommonly delicious presentation of unadorned local ingredients. "Some people come to the fish boil just because they're with someone who likes fish, and they say 'I'm not going to eat that junk,'" Mr. Ostrand said. "Then they taste it and love it and they keep eating. It happens all the time."

The fish used in the boil is fresh Lake Michigan whitefish, a succulent, sweet, and delicately nutty-flavored fish with white flesh. It goes so well with the small, blushing potatoes, sweet onions, and generous melted butter that it seems a natural combination. However, lake trout was used until about 10 years ago, according to Mr. Ostrand. Trout are no longer fished commercially, so whitefish has become the standard. "Trout was a lot easier to cook because it's firm, and it doesn't matter if you cook it a minute longer. Whitefish is delicate, you have to watch it so carefully," Mr. Ostrand said. "But I like 'em both!"

The fish boils are prepared outdoors in summer and winter, using standard and showy techniques. A huge, stainless-steel pot filled with water is set on a stand that sits askew over a wood fire, the pot slightly tipped to one side. Long pieces of firewood are leaned vertically around the pot, to direct the heat up and protect the fire from wind.

Large amounts of salt are added to the water for a practical reason. It makes impurities in the ingredients float to the surface—the boil never tastes salty.

Once the water boils, a stainless-steel basket that looks like a giant colander and is filled with red new potatoes and usually onions (Mr. Ostrand doesn't add onions because he thinks they mask the flavor of the fish) is set into the pot, its handles

Moments before the fish boil is ready, kerosene is poured on the fire, causing a full flame, and the impurities in the water are boiled away.

sticking well above the rim. The potatoes have a thin slice cut from each end. When asked why, Mr. Ostrand laughed: "Traditionally the ends were cut to police the work of the potato washers to make sure they didn't dump potatoes into the water without checking them."

After the potatoes and onions have boiled for 20 to 30 minutes, a smaller colander packed tight with whitefish steaks is lowered into the water. They cook for 7 to 8 minutes.

Just before the fish and vegetables are lifted from the pot, a bucket of kerosene is thrown on the fire. Flames leap and the pot boils over on its tipped side, the impurities and froth running off.

At the White Gull Inn Mr. Ostrand serenades diners, who enjoy a fish boil off china plates. At the Edgewater, where the atmosphere is more casual, waitresses rush about serving the coffee or milk which is customary in establishments that don't serve beer. It doesn't take long to eat a fish boil, and diners are welcome to go back for more, before the finale of tart and sweet Door County cherry pie.

Wanmori

This is a subtle, refined soup that, despite the lengthy recipe, is very simple to make and well worth the effort. It is often served as part of *kaiseki*, the meal served before a Japanese tea ceremony. It makes a fine, palate-cleansing, and very delicious appetizer. This serves 8 when presented in diminutive Japanese soup bowls. Otherwise it serves 4. Try this with Japanese tea or warmed sake.

10 ounces spinach

5 cups Ichiban Dashi (recipe follows)

8 medium clams (about 6 ounces total weight), shells
    well scrubbed under cold running water

6 ounces of any white-meated fish fillets, such as
    rockfish or snapper

1 large egg white

1 teaspoon fresh lemon juice

Salt

16 small oyster mushrooms

2 strips lemon zest, 2 x ½ inches, cut in julienne

1 ¼ teaspoons thin soy sauce (usukuchi), preferably
    Kikkoman brand

1. Carefully extract 16 small clusters of the innermost spinach leaves from the spinach—look for the tiniest leaves, in small bunches of three or four. Carefully wash; set aside. Reserve the remaining spinach for another use.

2. Place 2½ cups of the *ichiban dashi* in a medium-size saucepan over high heat. When it boils, add the clams and cook just until they open, 3 to 5 minutes. Remove from the heat. Remove the clams from the stock; reserve the stock.

3. Cut the fish into 2-inch pieces. Purée in a food processor. Add the egg white, lemon

juice, 2 teaspoons of the remaining *ichiban dashi* and the ¼ teaspoon salt. Purée until the mixture is elastic and holds together, about 4 minutes.

4. Remove the clams from their shells, reserving the shells. Carefully cut the adductor muscle from the shells and discard. Coarsely chop the clams. Fold into the white fish mixture.

5. Twist the halves of the clam shells apart, keeping them in pairs that will fit together. Stuff the clam shells by placing a large spoonful of the fish mixture on one half of the shell, and then covering it with the other half. Press the halves together, leaving them just slightly apart. Wipe off any excess fish mixture. Stuff all of the shells, using half of the fish mixture.

6. When all 8 clam shells are stuffed, bring the clam cooking stock to a boil in the bottom of a steamer. Place the clams on the steamer rack and steam just until the fish mixture is firm, 3 to 5 minutes. Remove the clams from the steamer. Using a sharp knife, take off one half of the clam shell. Carefully remove the cooked fish dumpling, which now resembles a closed clam shell. Keep warm in a covered container. Fill the clam shells with the remaining fish mixture and repeat the process.

7. Bring the clam cooking stock back to a boil over medium-high heat in the steamer. Add the spinach clusters and the mushrooms to the steamer. Cover and steam just until wilted, about 3 minutes. Remove the vegetables from the steamer; keep warm. Leave the steamer on the heat.

8. To serve the *Wanmori*, add the remaining *ichiban dashi* to the steamer. Bring almost to a boil over medium-high heat. Place 2 dumplings in each of 8 bowls. Top with 1 sprig of the steamed spinach leaves, 2 mushrooms,

and 2 lemon zest strips, attractively arranged. Add the soy sauce to the stock, and season with salt to taste. Divide the stock among the bowls, carefully pouring it over the other ingredients to just cover them. Serve immediately.

Makes 8 small or 4 large servings

Ichiban Dashi Basic Soup Stock

*T*his basic soup stock is a cornerstone of Japanese cuisine. Once made, it can be used in a variety of dishes. The plain *kombu* (dried kelp) and the bonito flakes are both available at Japanese groceries or specialty shops. This is a simple, but very exacting recipe. Once you've discovered how easy and flavorful this is, you'll use it often.

5 cups plus 2 tablespoons cold water
1 piece kombu (dried kelp), 2 x 2½ inches
½ cup loosely packed bonito flakes

1. Pour 5 cups of the cold water into a medium-size saucepan over medium-high heat. Add the *kombu* and bring almost to a boil. Just before the water boils, when large bubbles rise to the surface, remove the *kombu* and discard.

2. Add the 2 tablespoons cold water to the pan and immediately sprinkle on the bonito flakes. Do *not* stir the stock. Just before the mixture boils, when large bubbles rise to the surface (this will take about 5 minutes), remove the stock from the heat. Strain it through a double thickness of dampened cheesecloth. Reserve until ready to use.

Makes 5 cups

Hake Chowder

*T*his is another recipe from Patricia Rackliffe, whose husband, Dennis, is a lobster fisherman near Rockland, Maine. She has a wonderful respect for the natural, fresh flavor of seafood, and a knack for enhancing it in simple ways. This chowder is a perfect example—it is so pure and satisfying, and so simple to make, it makes you wonder why food ever need be any more complex.

Patricia suggests serving it with plenty of dill pickles and saltine crackers. Try the chowder with a chilled Entre-Deux-Mers or a Muscadet.

4 tablespoons unsalted butter
1 small onion, diced
3 medium russet potatoes, peeled and cut into ¼-inch dice
1½ pounds hake, lingcod, haddock, or any firm white fish fillets, cut into 1½-inch squares
4 cups milk
½ cup heavy or whipping cream
Salt and freshly ground black pepper
2 chive flowers, blossoms separated, or 1 tablespoon minced chives

1. Melt the butter in a large, heavy-bottomed saucepan over medium-high heat. Add the onion and sauté until it is translucent, about 4 minutes. Add the potatoes and cook, stirring frequently, until they begin to soften, about 5 minutes.

2. Stir in enough cold water just to cover the potatoes. Cover and bring the water to a boil. Cook until the potatoes are nearly soft through, about 10 minutes. Check occasionally to be sure the potatoes aren't sticking to the bottom of the pan.

3. Add the pieces of fish to the onion and

potato mixture. Cook until translucent through, about 8 minutes. Add the milk and cream; stir and heat until the soup is very hot, stirring occasionally, being careful not to let it boil. Season with salt and pepper.

4. Divide the soup among 4 warm soup bowls. Garnish with the chive blossoms.

Makes 4 servings

Mackerel and Spring Leek Broth with Coriander

*T*his broth, with its exotic perfume of coriander, distinctive flavor of mackerel, and sweetness of leeks makes a captivating first course. It is derived from a similar dish I had in France long ago. I like this broth accompanied by a bowl of steamed rice and a chilled Sauvignon Blanc.

6 small mackerel (about 3½ ounces each), filleted
1 bouquet garni (bay leaf, parsley sprigs, fresh thyme sprigs)
1 tablespoon plus 2 teaspoons coriander seed, crushed
1 cup dry white wine
1 tablespoon fresh lemon juice
1 tablespoon rice wine vinegar
½ cup olive oil
1 small onion, finely chopped
1 clove garlic, crushed
4 medium leeks, trimmed to include 2 inches of green stem, quartered lengthwise, then cut into 2-inch lengths and rinsed well
Salt and freshly ground black pepper
24 cilantro leaves, for garnish

1. Rinse the mackerel fillets and pat dry.

2. Tie the bouquet garni and the coriander seed in a square of cheesecloth. Place it, with 2 cups of water, the wine, lemon juice, vinegar, olive oil, onion, and garlic, in a large, non-aluminum saucepan over high heat. Bring to a boil, reduce the heat to low, and add the leeks. Cook until crisp-tender, about 15 minutes. Strain the broth; discard the cheesecloth bag, the onion, and the garlic. Reserve the broth and leeks separately. Keep the leeks warm, covered, in a very low oven.

3. Arrange the mackerel fillets in one layer in a large, non-aluminum skillet. Pour the broth over them and place over medium-high heat. Bring the broth to a boil; immediately reduce the heat to low. Simmer until the mackerel fillets are opaque, 2 to 3 minutes. Transfer them, as they cook, to 6 shallow, warm soup bowls, placing 2 fillets in the bottom of each bowl.

4. Divide the leeks among the bowls, arranging them on either side of the fillets. Season the broth with salt to taste. Ladle the broth over the mackerel and leeks. Garnish with a sprinkling of pepper and float 4 cilantro leaves in each bowl. Serve immediately.

Makes 6 servings

Cora Hernandez' Crab and Okra Gumbo

*C*ora Hernandez is a wonderful cook. She and her husband have lived all over the world, from Beirut to South America to the

Far East, but her culinary roots are Cajun. They now live in Kenner, Louisiana, but they spend as much time as possible at their little "camp" on the bayou, where water teeming with shrimp, crab, and the occasional sheepshead or redfish practically laps at the front door. Mrs. Hernandez often fishes from her pirogue (pronounced pee'rōg), a tiny, dug-out-like boat which she poles through the shallow bayou, a jaunty straw hat on her head. During shrimp season she and her husband resort to the motor boat and shrimp nets, bringing in enough to dry and freeze for the year.

Mrs. Hernandez makes this gumbo with crab or shrimp. If you prefer shrimp, substitute 1½ pounds for the crab, and add it about 5 minutes before you plan to serve the gumbo. Serve a lightly chilled Gigondas alongside.

½ cup mild vegetable oil, such as safflower

8 ounces okra, cut into thick rounds

¼ cup all-purpose flour

1 large onion, finely chopped

2 cloves garlic, green germ removed from the center, coarsely chopped

2½ cups Fish Stock (see Index)

1 tablespoon fresh thyme leaves or ½ teaspoon dried

¼ teaspoon cayenne pepper

¼ teaspoon freshly ground white pepper

¼ teaspoon freshly ground black pepper

2 bay leaves

8 ounces andouille or other spicy pork sausage links, cut into small rounds

1 uncooked Dungeness crab (2 pounds), or 2 pounds live blue crabs, cleaned and cut into serving-size pieces

4 cups cooked rice

1. Heat 2 tablespoons of the oil in a medium-size skillet over medium-high heat. Add the okra and cook until bright green and softened slightly, about 5 minutes. Remove from the heat and reserve.

2. Heat the remaining 6 tablespoons oil in a large, heavy skillet over medium-high heat. Whisk in the flour and cook, whisking constantly, until the *roux* is golden brown, up to 15 minutes.

3. Add the onion to the *roux*, and cook, stirring constantly, until translucent, about 5 minutes. Stir in the garlic and cook until translucent, about 3 minutes.

4. Stir in the fish stock, thyme, cayenne, white pepper, black pepper, and bay leaves. Bring to a boil. Add the okra and sausage and cook until the mixture is like a thick gravy and the okra is still bright green, about 8 minutes. Stir in the crab pieces, and cook, stirring occasionally, until they turn bright pink, about 10 minutes. Adjust the seasonings. Serve immediately, over rice.

Makes 4 servings

Silken Crab and Avocado Soup

*T*his is really a silken purée that masquerades as a soup. Served chilled, it's a refreshing blend of avocado, fish stock, tangy lemon, and big chunks of crab that beguiles with its lovely color and surprisingly light, crab-rich flavor. Its simplicity belies its elegance—don't hesitate to serve it as a first course at a formal meal. Don't overlook this soup as a simple lunch dish either. Try it with a chilled Italian Soave.

1 tablespoon unsalted butter
1 small onion, finely minced
3 ripe avocados
2 cups Fish Stock (see Index)
Grated zest of 1 lemon
3 tablespoons fresh lemon juice
½ cup heavy or whipping cream
½ cup half-and-half
10 ounces lump crabmeat, picked over
Salt and freshly ground black pepper
½ teaspoon freshly grated nutmeg

1. Melt the butter in a small skillet over medium-high heat. Add the onion and cook, stirring occasionally, until translucent but still slightly crisp, about 10 minutes. Remove from the heat; reserve.

2. Peel and pit 2 of the avocados. Purée in the bowl of a food processor or in an electric blender. Add the onions and purée. Add the fish stock, lemon zest, lemon juice, cream, and half-and-half; purée until smooth. (The onion will stay in small pieces and that is fine.) Transfer the purée to a large bowl.

3. Fold the crabmeat into the purée. Season with salt and pepper to taste. Chill for at least 2 hours before serving. (This soup is even better the day after it is made.)

4. Just before serving, peel and pit the remaining avocado. Cut it into ¼-inch dice. Taste the soup again for seasoning and adjust if necessary. Divide the soup among 6 small or 4 large soup bowls. Garnish with the avocado dice and a dash of the nutmeg. Serve immediately.

Makes 4 to 6 servings

Japanese Noodles with Salmon and Scallions

I like to think this dish was inspired by *Tampopo*, a very funny Japanese movie. My husband and I thoroughly enjoyed the film, which is about a lovely Japanese noodle-maker who wants to be the best, a handsome truck driver who helps her, and all the odd and wondrous characters and many bowls of noodles that become part of her saga to success. These noodles bear little resemblance to those in the movie—no hog's head nor whole chicken for the broth, no thrice-risen noodles—but it is lovely, hearty, and satisfying, and you can slurp if you must—as is proper with Japanese noodles. Try warmed sake with this soup.

6 cups Fish Stock (see Index)
1 package (5.6 ounces) kishimen (Japanese wheat
    flour noodles, available in Asian grocery stores)
2 cups cooked, preferably poached, salmon, flaked
    into bite-size pieces
Salt
4 large scallions, trimmed, the white bulbs and light
    green stems cut diagonally into bite-size pieces
Grated zest of 1 lemon

1. Bring the fish stock to a boil in a large saucepan over high heat. Add the noodles, partially cover the pan so some steam escapes, and cook until the noodles are softened, but still have texture, about 6 minutes. Add the salmon and cook until heated through, 1 to 2 minutes. Season with salt to taste and remove from the heat.

2. To serve the noodles, divide them among 4 shallow, warm soup bowls. Garnish with the scallions, pushing them into the soup, and sprinkle on the lemon zest. Serve immediately.

Makes 4 servings

Maine Lobster Stew

*T*his stew, really an elegant soup, is totally reliant on the best, freshest, and sweetest lobster meat possible. I suggest making this soup in late fall to early spring, when the colder water temperatures mean sweet, heavy, succulent lobster. Use only live lobster that you know hasn't been sitting in a holding tank longer than a couple of days, so its meat is still sweet. You will be delighted with the simple, delicate flavor, the lovely chunks of lobster, and the sunrise-pink color of the stew. I like to make the soup the morning of the day that I plan to serve it, so it can ripen, refrigerated, throughout the day. Serve it with a lightly chilled Vouvray.

1 ¾ to 2-pound live lobster
2 tablespoons unsalted butter
3 cups milk
1 cup heavy or whipping cream
Salt and freshly ground black pepper
2 tablespoons minced fresh chives, for garnish

1. Remove the tail and claw meat from the lobster (see Index). Cut it into ⅜-inch medallions.

2. Melt 1 tablespoon of the butter in a medium-size skillet. Sauté the lobster medallions until the skin on the outside begins to turn red, about 3 minutes.

3. Combine the milk and cream in a large saucepan over medium heat. Heat through, being careful not to let them boil.

4. When the milk and cream are hot, stir in the lobster medallions. Season with salt and pepper to taste. If you plan to serve the lobster stew immediately, continue to heat it until steaming, stirring constantly, being careful not to let it boil. Divide among 4 warm soup bowls. Garnish each bowl with a pat of the remaining butter and the chives, and serve.

5. If you plan to let the stew ripen, immediately remove it from the heat. Transfer to a bowl and let cool to room temperature. Cover and refrigerate.

6. To serve, reheat the soup slowly over medium heat, stirring occasionally, until steaming. Serve immediately, garnished with chives.

Makes 4 servings

Poseido Avgolemono

*T*his smooth, silken soup with the tang of lemon softened by whipped eggs, is a traditional Greek offering. It is usually made with chicken stock, but this version was given to me by Minas Sarris, a first-generation Greco-American fisherman, former sponge diver, and party-boat operator in Tarpon Springs, Florida. It is so light and refreshing I like to serve it between courses, as a palate cleanser, or to begin a large meal. An excellent, flavorful fish stock is a must for this dish. Orzo is rice-shaped pasta, available in most specialty-food stores. Because this dish is so light, delicate, and tangy, I don't recommend a wine with it.

4 cups *Fish Stock (see facing page), strained*
½ cup *orzo*
¼ cup *fresh lemon juice*
4 *large eggs, separated*
1 *small bunch flat-leaf parsley, minced*

1. Place the fish stock in a medium-size, heavy-bottomed saucepan over medium-high heat. Cover and bring to a boil. Add the orzo and cook until tender, about 8 minutes.

2. While the orzo is cooking, pour 2 tablespoons of the lemon juice into the egg yolks and the remaining 2 tablespoons lemon juice into the egg whites. Using a whisk, whip each mixture separately until foamy. Combine the two and whisk until pale yellow and foamy.

3. When the orzo is cooked, whisk 1 cup of the hot stock into the egg and lemon juice mixture to warm it. Pour the mixture, whisking constantly, into the stock and orzo. Remove from the heat and continue whisking until the soup is frothy and slightly thickened to the consistency of heavy cream. Ladle into 4 soup bowls. Garnish with the minced parsley. Serve immediately.

Makes 4 servings

Creamy Scallop and Garlic Soup

Don't think there's too much garlic in this soup—garlic becomes very mild and sweet when it is slow-cooked—and it is essential to the flavor. This soup is a wonderful base for chowders as well. Try adding ½ cup corn kernels freshly cut from the cob, or any leftover cooked fish, cut in bite-size pieces.

Serve with a chilled round, low acid, dry white wine such as an Alsatian Pinot Blanc.

1 *large head garlic (about 20 large cloves), separated into cloves, green germ removed from each clove*
6 cups *Fish Stock (see facing page)*
2 *medium russet potatoes, peeled and cut into ½-inch cubes*
2 cups *heavy or whipping cream*
1 *pound fresh sea or bay scallops*
Salt
3 *tablespoons unsalted butter, cut into 6 equal pieces*
Cayenne pepper
Several sprigs flat-leaf parsley, finely minced, and chive flowers, for garnish (optional)

1. Place the garlic cloves in a large, heavy-bottomed saucepan and cover with 2 cups of the fish stock. Bring the fish stock to a boil over medium-high heat. Reduce heat to low and cook the garlic, covered, until soft, about 10 minutes.

2. Add the potatoes and cook, covered, until soft, about 15 minutes.

3. Pour the mixture into a food processor or blender and purée until very smooth. Return to the saucepan. Increase the heat to medium, and add the remaining 4 cups fish stock and the cream. Cook, whisking slowly but constantly, until thickened slightly, about 10 minutes. Do not let the soup boil.

4. If you are using sea scallops, halve crosswise into 2 disks. Add the scallops to the soup and cook until translucent but still very tender, about 4 minutes. Season generously with salt.

5. To serve the soup, ladle it into 6 soup bowls. Top each bowl with a pat of butter and dust with cayenne. Garnish with the parsley and individual blossoms from chive flowers, if desired.

Makes 6 servings

Mrs. George Washington's Cream of Crab Soup

*T*his is a traditional Maryland recipe, researched and recreated by William Taylor, a Maryland caterer who calls himself the Dinner Designer. I have adapted it slightly, but it remains very true to the original. It is an almost sinfully rich soup, the kind one imagines being served at a lavish banquet in tiny white, bone china bowls with little handles on either side. Though the soup has sherry in it, I don't recommend drinking sherry along with it—try a lightly chilled German Spätlese.

2 hard-cooked large eggs
2 tablespoons unsalted butter, softened
2 tablespoons all-purpose flour
Zest of 1 lemon, minced
1½ cups half-and-half
½ cup heavy or whipping cream
2 cups milk
¼ cup medium-dry sherry
8 ounces crabmeat, picked over and flaked into
    generous bite-size pieces
Salt
Generous pinch of cayenne pepper

1. Purée the hard-cooked eggs in a food processor, or mash them until smooth with a wooden spoon. Mix in the butter, flour, and lemon zest. Scrape into a large mixing bowl.

2. Combine the half-and-half, cream, and milk in a large, heavy-bottomed saucepan over medium-high heat. Bring almost to a boil, stirring so as not to scorch them.

3. Slowly pour the cream mixture into the puréed egg mixture, whisking constantly until thoroughly incorporated. Pour it back into the saucepan and place over medium heat. Cook, stirring constantly, until the soup is very hot. Do not let it boil. Whisk in the sherry; cook for 1 minute. Remove from the heat. Stir in the crabmeat. Season with salt and cayenne pepper to taste.

4. To serve, ladle the soup into 6 warmed bowls. Dust with additional cayenne. Serve immediately.

Makes 6 servings

Fish Stock

I always have fish stock in my freezer, for making a quick soup or adding to a sauce. I freeze about 2 cups in ice cube trays, then pop the cubes out of the trays and put them in freezer bags or containers. That way I can pull out a cube or two to add to a sauce or liven up a soup. (Each cube is approximately 1½ tablespoons of stock.) I measure the remaining stock and freeze it in 1- and 2-cup lots so I always know what I have.

2 pounds bones from white fish, such as snapper, sole,
    or rockfish
2 tablespoons unsalted butter
2 medium carrots, peeled and coarsely chopped
1 large onion
Leaves of 2 celery ribs
1 bay leaf
1 bunch parsley stems
1 sprig fresh thyme
12 peppercorns
2 teaspoons salt

1. Rinse the fish bones well under cold running water until the water runs clear.

2. Melt the butter in a large, heavy-bottomed saucepan over medium heat. Add the vegetables and stir to coat with butter. Add 10 cups of water, the herbs, spices, and fish bones; bring to a boil. Reduce the heat to low. Simmer the stock for 18 minutes, skimming off any foam that rises to the surface.

3. Remove the stock from the heat. Strain, discarding the solids. When the stock is cool, either refrigerate or freeze it.

Makes 8 cups

Salmon Stock

What do you do with the bones of a whole salmon? Particularly if there is some luscious pink meat still clinging to them? Make stock to use as a base for soups or sauces . . . of course. As with any fish stock, don't let it simmer any longer than 18 minutes or it will turn bitter. And, since it has cooked for only 18 minutes, much of the flavor remains in the meat. When the stock is made, carefully remove the salmon from the bones, and use it in a salad, or soup, or in a spread for crackers.

1 ½ *pounds salmon bones and heads*
1 *tablespoon unsalted butter*
½ *medium carrot, peeled and coarsely chopped*
½ *medium onion, coarsely chopped*
½ *teaspoon salt*
1 *bay leaf*
5 *parsley stems*
5 *peppercorns*

1. Rinse the fish bones well under cold running water.

2. Melt the butter in a large saucepan over medium-high heat. Add the carrot and onion and cook, stirring, until the onion begins to turn translucent, about 5 minutes.

3. Stir in the remaining ingredients and 6 cups water. Add the fish bones. Bring to a boil, reduce the heat to medium so the water continues to boil gently, and cook for 18 minutes, skimming off any foam that rises to the surface.

4. Strain the stock. Let cool and use as a base for soups and sauces.

Makes 4 cups

5

THE SHELLFISH GANG

The first time I saw a golden Kona crab was at the Honolulu fish auction. They are gorgeous, with delicately elegant legs and swim fins, and they produce some of the sweetest, richest crabmeat I've ever tasted. One of the easiest crabs to prepare, they are very docile, and their claws are harmless.

The memory of them flashed through my mind the next time I saw Kona crabs—this time at a Seattle fish market. They're a new import, and they are going to be showing up with increasing frequency, much to my delight.

The arrival of Kona crab on the mainland is the latest proof that the bounty of shellfish and crustaceans available throughout the country is constantly increasing. There are already devotees of the Dungeness, the blue, the tanner, and the stone crab. It won't be long until we'll be making room for the Kona crab, just as we've made room for an increasing array of lobsters and oysters.

After all, it's now quite common to go into a seafood restaurant or oyster bar and be presented with a choice of more than a dozen varieties with names like Shoalwater and kumamoto, Chincoteague and Olympia. Like fine vintage wines each is unique, with its own briny flavor.

And there are plump, smoky mussels, tender clams, and beguilingly crisp, yet buttery geoduck, not to mention enough varieties of shrimp to fill the pages of an encyclopedia.

All of these shellfish and crustaceans are adaptable, versatile, and astonishingly quick to prepare. And they can't be beat for dramatic presentation. If you want to impress someone, make the Alaska Spot Prawns in Olive Oil and Garlic. It's a showstopper, and incredibly delicious. Try Alva Magwood's Shellfish Boil, too—it's a riot of color, a sumptuous combination of flavors. And no one can resist the recipes for Crawfish in Black Bean Sauce or the simple Mussel Omelette.

When you look through the recipes in this chapter, you'll find dishes that will tempt you, whether you want to plan a formal meal or a casual picnic. Try them all—you'll become a convert to the shellfish and crustacean school of simple, exquisite cooking.

Warm Scallops with Oyster Mushrooms

Scallops are so sweet, tender, and delicate that they hardly need any garnish or preparation at all. They shine in this salad, where they are simply bathed in olive oil then baked just long enough to heat them through. Serve a lightly chilled, round, low-acid white wine with this, such as an Alsatian Pinot Blanc, a slightly honeyed Orvieto, or a German Kabinett.

4 cups small spinach leaves, mâche, or small butter
    lettuce leaves
3½ ounces oyster or button mushrooms
3 tablespoons fresh lemon juice
12 large sea scallops (7 ounces), each sliced vertically
    into 4 pieces
3 tablespoons extra-virgin olive oil
Salt and freshly ground black pepper
1 small tomato, peeled, seeded, and chopped
1 small bunch chives, minced

1. Preheat the oven to 375°F.

2. Wash the spinach leaves. Drain and dry.

3. Slice the mushrooms into thin strips. Place in a small bowl and sprinkle with 4 teaspoons of the lemon juice. Mix well.

4. In a small bowl, coat the scallops with 1 tablespoon of the olive oil. Arrange the scallops in one layer on a large baking sheet.

5. In another small bowl, combine the remaining 2 tablespoons olive oil, and 1 tablespoon of the lemon juice. Season with salt and pepper to taste. Add the mushrooms and the spinach; mix well. Divide the salad among 4 dinner plates. Sprinkle the tomato over the top.

6. Bake the scallops until they are nearly opaque through, 30 to 45 seconds. The scallops cook extremely quickly so you need to watch them carefully.

7. Arrange the scallops around the spinach and mushrooms on each plate. Sprinkle the remaining 2 teaspoons lemon juice over the scallops and shower the salad with the chives. Serve immediately.

Makes 4 servings

Curried Scallops

Curry and scallops...mmm! This elegant, buttery dish is definitely the kind of thing you want to serve when the best palates you know are coming to dinner! Or for yourself when you feel like something wonderful to eat! If you're watching your butter intake, try blanching the leeks instead of sautéing them in butter. Try this with a great Chenin Blanc, such as a Côteaux du Layon, a well-chilled Clos Ste. Catherine, or a Chenin Blanc from the Loire Valley.

9 tablespoons unsalted butter
3 small leeks, trimmed, rinsed, the white parts and
    tender inner green stems cut into 3-inch lengths,
    and then cut into julienne
Salt and freshly ground black pepper
3 tablespoons Fish Stock (see Index)
1 teaspoon fresh lemon juice
1 teaspoon curry powder, preferably Sharwood's or
    Madras brand
Pinch of cayenne pepper
8 ounces large sea scallops

1. Melt 3 tablespoons of the butter in a large sauté pan over medium-high heat. Add the leeks and sauté until they are crisp-tender and the green stems still brightly colored, about 8 minutes. Remove to a plate; season with salt and pepper. Cover and keep warm in a low oven.

2. Prepare the sauce: Combine the fish stock and lemon juice in a heavy saucepan over medium-high heat. Whisk in the curry powder and the cayenne. Cut the remaining 6 tablespoons butter into small pieces. Add the butter, one piece at a time, whisking after each addition. Work on and off the heat as necessary, to keep the butter from melting before it is emulsified. Continue whisking until all the butter has been added and the sauce is creamy and smooth. Keep the sauce warm, uncovered, over gently simmering water.

3. Place a nonstick skillet over medium heat. When the pan is hot, add the scallops and cook until almost opaque all the way through, about 3 minutes per side.

4. To serve, divide the leeks among 4 small dinner plates, patting them into a small circle. Top with scallops; drizzle the curry sauce around the scallops and leeks to create a dramatic color contrast. Serve immediately.

Makes 2 main-course or 4 appetizer servings

Pink Scallops in Champagne and Sweet Cicely Sauce

This is a dish inspired by Chef Pia Carroll at the Sooke Harbour House on Vancouver Island, B.C. Pia has a wealth of fresh seafood to work with, and she always manages to use flavors that enhance its delicacy. Try mussels in this recipe if you can't find pink scallops. Sweet cicely is a feathery herb with clusters of tiny, white flowers, and a delicate anise flavor. Anise hyssop or fennel fronds may be substituted. If you don't have champagne, try a good-quality, dry white wine such as a French Sauvignon Blanc.

40 *pink scallops in the shell, or 3 pounds mussels (see Note), shells well scrubbed under cold running water*

2 *cups heavy or whipping cream*

¾ *cup champagne*

½ *cup Fish Stock (see Index)*

2 *cloves garlic, minced*

½ *cup loosely packed sweet cicely leaves or fennel fronds*

Sweet cicely flowers (optional), for garnish

1. Scrub the scallops under cold water and drain.

2. In a large, non-aluminum saucepan over medium-high heat, combine the scallops, heavy cream, half of the champagne, and the fish stock. Sprinkle on the garlic, shake the pan to mix the ingredients, and cover. Bring to a boil and cook, shaking the pan occasionally, until the scallops open, about 5 minutes.

3. Remove the scallops with tongs and transfer to a warm dish; cover and keep warm in a low oven. Add the remaining champagne to the scallop cooking liquid. Increase the heat to high and boil, stirring occasionally, until reduced by half, about 15 minutes.

4. To serve, remove the empty shell from each scallop and discard it. Arrange the scallops in their shells in a circular pattern on a serving platter or on 4 dinner plates. Mince the sweet cicely. Add to the sauce. Pour the sauce over the scallops; garnish with sweet cicely flowers, and serve immediately. If substituting mussels, serve them with both shells intact, piling them on a serving platter or plates.

Makes 4 servings

Note: Do not scrub and beard the mussels until right before you plan to use them or they will die and spoil.

Abandoned Farm Mussel Omelette

Mussel farmer Edward Myers and his wife, Julia, are true mussel fanciers, and one of their favorite ways to eat them is in this omelette, which is as heavenly as it is simple to make. Try it with a big green salad, plenty of fresh bread, and a dry, sparkling wine or a demi-sec Vouvray.

6 *large eggs*

40 *mussels, shells well scrubbed under cold running water and bearded (see Note)*

¼ *cup dry white wine*

5 *black peppercorns*

1 *bay leaf*

1 *small onion, sliced*

Freshly ground black pepper

2 *tablespoons unsalted butter*

2 *tablespoons minced fresh chives*

1. Break the eggs into a large bowl and whisk well.

2. Combine the mussels, wine, peppercorns, bay leaf, and onion in a medium-size, non-aluminum saucepan over medium-high heat. Cover and cook until the mussels open, 3 to 5 minutes. Cook for an additional 30 seconds, so they firm up without overcooking. Remove the mussels from the heat; discard any that do not open. When they are cool enough to handle, remove the mussels from their shells; discard the shells.

3. Strain the mussel cooking liquid through a double thickness of dampened cheesecloth; return to the pan. Reduce to ¼ cup over medium-high heat. Remove from the heat.

4. When the mussel cooking liquid has

cooled slightly, whisk it into the eggs. Season with pepper (the mussel cooking liquid provides the salt).

5. Melt the butter in an omelette pan or small skillet over medium-high heat. When the foam subsides and the butter is just beginning to turn golden, reduce the heat to medium. Pour the eggs into the pan. Stir constantly with a fork, keeping the fork flat, and pulling the uncooked eggs from the sides of the pan into the middle, and tipping the pan at the same time so the uncooked eggs run to the edges.

6. When the edges are set, cook for about 15 seconds to brown the bottom slightly; the middle should still be soft. Add the mussels, distributing them evenly over half of the top of the omelette. Sprinkle on the chives. Slide the omelette onto a warm serving platter, folding one side over the mussels as it slides out of the pan. Serve immediately.

Makes 4 first-course or 2 generous main-course servings

Note: Do not scrub and beard the mussels until right before you plan to use them or they will die and spoil.

Poached Eggs with Mussels and Cream

There are times when poached eggs can be the most wonderful food on earth. They become very elegant here with mussels and a cream sauce, but they retain a comforting, homey appeal. These make a lovely brunch dish, with a light champagne, or a fine evening meal with a lightly chilled Alsatian Riesling.

Abandoned Farm Mussels

Edward Myers is a mussel pioneer—he sold wild mussels way back in the fifties, when few Americans knew how delectable they were. In 1971 he started the first mussel farm in the United States—Abandoned Farm, in Damariscotta, Maine, where he produces first-class mussels—they come without crunchy pearls ("the only smart thing a mussel does is avoid eating the worm that eventually becomes the pearl," he said) or pea crabs, and their meat is plump, sweet, and firm.

Mr. Myers journeyed to Spain to learn about mussel farming, and there he saw suspended raft culture, rafts floating on the water, with lines hanging below them thick with blue mussels. He returned home and adapted the Spanish idea to a system of connected tires that float on the water.

When Mr. Myers has a mussel order, he takes a small barge rigged with a hoist out to the tires, hefts one up to see if it has what he wants, then drags the tire behind him on his way back to the dock, so the mussels are clean when he arrives.

Erudite, hysterically funny in a dry, philosophical manner (he has a degree in philosophy from Princeton), Mr. Myers is committed to making mussel culture work, against all odds. And the odds have certainly come and gone at Abandoned Farm. He lost almost all of his mussels to a freak storm in 1978. But he's bounced back. "You ask me why I'm staying small?" he said. "Because I'm looking at 70, and this is as big as I want to get."

1 cup white wine, such as Johannisberg Riesling

3 shallots, minced

1 bouquet garni (bay leaf, parsley sprigs, fresh thyme sprigs)

1 clove garlic, chopped

Freshly ground black pepper

2 pounds mussels, shells well scrubbed under cold running water and bearded (see Note)

2 tablespoons distilled white vinegar

8 whole large eggs

⅔ cup heavy or whipping cream

2 large egg yolks

Salt

8 slices white bread, each slice trimmed into a 4-inch round and toasted

2 tablespoons minced fresh flat-leaf parsley

1 tablespoon diced red bell pepper

1. Combine the wine, shallots, bouquet garni, garlic, and a generous amount of pepper in a large, non-aluminum saucepan over high heat. Bring to a boil. Add the mussels, cover, and cook, shaking the pan occasionally, for about 5 minutes. Remove the mussels as they open to avoid overcooking them; discard any that do not open. Strain the cooking liquid through a sieve lined with a double thickness of dampened cheesecloth, reserving the bouquet garni. Transfer both to a medium-size, heavy-bottomed, non-aluminum saucepan.

2. Remove the mussels from their shells. Discard the shells and reserve the mussels, covered, so they stay warm.

3. To poach the eggs, fill a large, non-aluminum skillet about two-thirds full of water. Add the vinegar. Bring to a boil over high heat. Reduce the heat to medium-high, so the water is boiling gently. One at a time, break the whole eggs into a small bowl and slide them into the water. You can poach up to 4 eggs at a time, if the skillet is large enough to keep them from touching. Spoon water over the eggs to cook them evenly. When the whites have solidified and the yolks have lightened on top, gently remove the eggs with a slotted spoon and transfer them to a bowl filled with lukewarm water. Finish the mussel preparation immediately.

4. Bring the mussel cooking liquid to a boil with ⅓ cup of the heavy cream over medium-high heat. Cook until the mixture is reduced by half, about 5 minutes. Reduce the heat to low. Whisk together the egg yolks and the remaining ⅓ cup cream. Whisk into the reduced mixture, and cook, whisking constantly, until the sauce thickens enough to coat the back of a spoon. Season the sauce with salt and pepper to taste.

5. To serve, place 2 toast rounds in the center of each of 4 warmed dinner plates. Top each round of toast with 1 drained poached egg. Divide the mussels among the plates, placing them on top of the eggs and toast. Coat each portion with one-fourth of the sauce. Sprinkle on the parsley and bell pepper; serve immediately.

Makes 4 servings

Note: Do not scrub and beard the mussels until right before you plan to use them or they will die and spoil.

Doug's Deep-Fried Clams

Doug's Seafood, a fish market and cafe, on Park Street in Rockland, Maine, may not seem a promising place to stop, but those who live anywhere near Rockland know better. Doug's happens to be the best place around for everything from fresh haddock to lobster rolls and fried clams.

I can take or leave lobster rolls—lobster meat and mayonnaise in an oval bun—but I could become addicted to his fried clams. They're shucked fresh then fried, and they emerge sweet, tender, and crisp, the way only fresh clams can be. Try a good pale ale to quench your thirst.

2 pounds Manila, butter, or littleneck clams, shells well scrubbed under cold running water, then shucked and drained
2 large eggs
1 cup finely ground saltine crackers
¼ teaspoon cayenne pepper
2 cups mild vegetable oil, such as safflower, for frying
Tartar Sauce (see Index)

1. Line a baking sheet or platter with a double thickness of paper towels. Arrange the shucked clams in a single layer on the towels. Cover with another double thickness of paper towels. Refrigerate for at least 1 hour to give the clams a chance to dry.

2. Whisk together the eggs in a medium-size bowl. Whisk in 1 teaspoon water and continue to whisk until somewhat frothy.

3. Place the cracker crumbs in a shallow dish or bowl. Add the cayenne pepper.

4. Set a wire rack on a baking sheet. One at a time, dredge the clams in the egg wash, then in the cracker crumbs, shaking off any excess. Place the clams on the rack and set aside to dry in the coolest spot of the kitchen for 30 minutes. (Be forewarned that if you omit this step the clams will still be excellent, but you and your kitchen will be covered in fat from the minor explosions the wet clams make when they hit the oil.)

5. Heat the oil until hot but not smoking (about 375°F) in a wok or a deep-fat fryer. Working in batches, fry the clams, without crowding, until golden, 2 to 3 minutes. Turn them so they brown evenly. Remove with a slotted spoon or spatula and drain on a double thickness of paper towels.

6. If you want to serve the clams all at once, keep warm in a low oven. Otherwise, serve in batches, which won't take long since they cook very quickly. Serve immediately, with the tartar sauce alongside.

Makes 4 small servings

Oven-Roasted Clams Vinaigrette

This recipe is great as an appetizer for four, or as a main course for two hungry clam fans. It is also wonderful for a crowd. Just increase the amounts to feed the number of guests you plan to serve. Roasting clams just until they open allows them to retain their fresh-from-the-sea sweetness. To eat, just dip them into the flavorful sauce and pop them in your mouth. Serve these with plenty of crusty bread for sopping up the sauce and the clam nectar that collects in the baking dish. Serve this with an Aligoté or Muscadet.

2 pounds Manila, butter, or littleneck clams, shells well scrubbed under cold running water
¼ cup extra-virgin olive oil
1 small bunch chives, minced
1 small clove garlic, minced
1 teaspoon white wine vinegar
Salt and freshly ground black pepper to taste

1. Preheat the oven to 450°F.

2. Place the clams in a large, ovenproof baking dish. Bake until they open, 8 to 10 minutes.

3. While the clams are baking, whisk together all of the remaining ingredients in a small bowl. Divide the sauce between 2 small dishes or ramekins. To eat the clams, use a small fork or your fingers to remove the clams from their shells; dip them into the sauce.

Makes 4 servings

Broiled Clams in Pepper Butter

This recipe makes a generous amount of the pepper butter. You may want to adjust the amount you use on the clams. The arugula is for garnish, but don't leave it on the platter! The leaves wilt slightly with the heat of the clams and the melted pepper butter, and they are delicious. Try this with a chilled Entre Deux Mers or an Aligoté.

3 pounds littleneck, butter, or Manila clams, shells
    well scrubbed under cold running water
1 clove garlic
2 tablespoons fresh oregano leaves or 1 teaspoon dried
1 cup (2 sticks) unsalted butter, at room temperature
3 tablespoons fresh lemon juice
Salt and freshly ground black pepper
2 roasted red bell peppers (see Index), peeled and
    seeded
4 cups arugula leaves, rinsed well and dried

1. Shuck the raw clams, discarding the top half of the shell. Loosen the clams from the bottom shell by sliding the blade of a sharp knife under the meat and cutting the muscle. Leave the clam in the shell. (This can be done up to 2 hours in advance.) Refrigerate shucked clams, covered with aluminum foil so they don't dry out.

2. Preheat the oven to 500°.

3. Place the garlic and oregano in a food processor and process until finely chopped. Add the butter, lemon juice, salt and pepper and process until the mixture is well blended and light and fluffy. Add the roasted peppers and process quickly with a few short pulses. The mixture should be thoroughly combined but the peppers should be in small pieces, not puréed.

4. Place the clams in an ovenproof baking dish, and top each with 1 to 1½ tablespoons of the butter mixture. Bake until the clams are opaque and cooked through and the butter is melted, about 5 minutes.

5. While the clams are baking, arrange the arugula leaves on an oval serving dish. Remove the clams from the oven and arrange them on the arugula leaves. Pour any melted butter in the baking dish over the top and serve immediately.

Makes 4 servings

Razor Clams in Lime-Butter Sauce

Razor clam season generates front-page news excitement in the Northwest. Daily newspapers in Seattle never fail to have a picture of hearty souls on the beach, pant legs rolled up and shovels (or "clam guns") in hand, as they bend to search for the clams in the sand. Within 24 hours of the opening of the season, razor clam signs fly at fish markets. It's a short season—lately lengthened by fresh Alaskan razor clams that equal those from Oregon and Washington in sweetness and flavor. In this recipe the razor clams are barely cooked, then served with citrus lime-butter sauce. The sauce is a little unconventional—the first time I made it I began with a traditional butter sauce, but when I cooked the razor clams they yielded a delicious juice, which I couldn't bear to waste. So I added it to the sauce and it was a winner. If you can't find razor clams, go ahead and use littlenecks, butter, or Manila clams and add half their juices to the sauce. Try a lightly chilled Sylvaner or a Muscadet with this.

8 tablespoons (1 stick) unsalted butter

1 shallot, finely chopped

2 tablespoons fresh lime juice

1 tablespoon heavy or whipping cream

8 ounces shelled razor clams, cleaned and halved
   lengthwise, or 1 pound littleneck, butter, or
   Manila clams, shells well scrubbed under cold
   running water

Grated zest of 1 lime

Salt and freshly ground pepper

Fennel fronds, for garnish (optional)

1. Melt 1 tablespoon of the butter in a small, heavy-bottomed skillet or saucepan over medium heat. Add the shallot and cook, stirring constantly, until translucent, about 5 minutes.

2. Add the lime juice and cook until the mixture is reduced to 1 tablespoon, about 5 minutes. Add the cream and reduce the mixture by half, an additional 2 to 3 minutes. Reduce the heat to low and keep warm.

3. Melt 1 tablespoon butter in a medium-size skillet over medium-high heat. Add the razor clams and cook just until they turn opaque and give up their juice, about 4 minutes. Remove from the heat, cover, and keep warm. (If using regular clams, add them to the melted butter, cover and cook, shaking, until they open. Discard any that do not open.)

4. Cut the remaining 6 tablespoons butter into small pieces. Raise the heat under the lime and cream mixture to medium and whisk in the butter, one piece at a time. Do not add a second piece until the first is incorporated. Work on and off the heat as necessary to keep the butter from melting before it is emulsified. Continue whisking until all of the butter is added and the sauce is thick and creamy. Whisk in the lime zest. Whisk in the liquid from the razor clams (or half the liquid from the hard-shell clams). Season the sauce with salt and pepper to taste.

5. To serve, transfer the razor clams (or the hardshell clams in the shell) to a warmed serving platter. Pour the sauce over the clams; garnish with fennel fronds. Serve immediately.

Makes 2 servings

Mark Miller's Clams with Red Chile Pesto Sauce

Mark Miller is the chef/owner of the Coyote Cafe, a serendipitous restaurant in Santa Fe, New Mexico. He has traveled widely in Latin America, and his inspirations come from many different areas and cultures. In this recipe, which includes no salt, you may use 12 dried ancho chiles if you cannot find dried New Mexican chiles (both are relatively mild, flavorful chiles). This can be served as a thick soup or as a sauce over pasta. Try this with a chilled dry Gewürztraminer from Oregon or the Napa Valley, or a white Zinfandel.

6 dried ancho chiles
6 dried New Mexican (anaheim) chiles
Boiling water
¼ cup pine nuts
5 large cloves garlic, unpeeled
¼ cup plus 2 tablespoons extra-virgin olive oil
1 tablespoon fresh oregano or 1 teaspoon dried
Grated zest of 1 lemon
¼ cup fresh lime juice
30 littleneck, butter, or Manila clams, shells well
    scrubbed under cold running water
2½ cups Fish Stock (see Index)
Cilantro leaves, for garnish

1. Place the dried chiles in a large skillet over medium-high heat. Roast, turning frequently and being very careful not to burn them, until they are hot through and begin to smell toasted, 4 to 5 minutes.

2. When the chiles are cool enough to handle, remove the stems and the seeds and place the chiles in a large bowl. Pour enough boiling water over to cover. Cover the bowl and let soak until very soft, about 40 minutes. Drain the chiles.

3. Preheat the oven to 350°.

4. Scatter the pine nuts on a baking sheet. Toast in the oven, stirring occasionally, until golden, about 8 minutes.

5. Simultaneously, place the garlic cloves with the 2 tablespoons olive oil in a small, ovenproof pan; stir to coat the garlic cloves with oil. Cover and roast in the oven until very soft and golden, but not overcooked and dry, about 20 minutes. Remove from the oven to cool. Peel the garlic and reserve the soft pulp.

6. If using dried oregano, place it in a small skillet over medium heat. Toast until it begins to smell pungent, about 3 minutes.

7. Combine the chiles, garlic pulp, lemon zest, and oregano in a food processor or blender. Purée until smooth. With the machine running, add the remaining ¼ cup olive oil and process until thoroughly blended. Add the pine nuts and process until they are coarsely chopped. Season the pesto with lime juice to taste.

8. Combine the clams and fish stock in a large non-aluminum saucepan over medium-high heat. Cover and cook, shaking the pan occasionally, until the clams open, about 5 minutes. Remove the clams with tongs as they open. Discard any that do not open. Increase the heat to high and reduce the cooking liquid by half, 8 to 10 minutes. Whisk in the chile pesto.

9. To serve, divide the clams among 4 soup bowls. Ladle the pesto mixture over them. Garnish each bowl with several cilantro leaves. Serve immediately.

Makes 4 servings

Shellfish and Wild Rice with Saffron and Lemon

The idea for this dish came from Mary Pelham, in Darien, Georgia. She uses the fresh and abundant Georgia seafood in a variety of ways. In a region where most of the fish is rolled in cornmeal and fried, Mrs. Pelham's recipes are a breath of fresh air.

Wild rice and shellfish is one of Mary's favorite combinations, and I find it as delicious as it is unconventional. Try a chilled Verdicchio, Muscadet, or dry Vouvray along with this.

1 cup uncooked wild rice

3 cups Fish Stock (see Index) or water

Grated zest of 1 lemon

1 tablespoon fresh lemon juice

1 ½ teaspoons loosely packed saffron threads

Salt and freshly ground black pepper

1 ½ pounds mussels, shells well scrubbed under cold running water, and bearded (see Note)

1 ½ pounds small clams, shells well scrubbed under cold running water

1 cup heavy or whipping cream

12 ounces bay scallops

1 lemon, peel and pith removed, sectioned

1 tablespoon finely chopped fresh chives

1. Combine the wild rice and fish stock in a medium-size, heavy-bottomed, non-aluminum saucepan over medium-high heat. Cover and bring to a boil. Add the lemon zest, lemon juice, and 1 teaspoon of the saffron threads. Reduce the heat to medium, cover, and cook until two-thirds of the kernels have split, 45 to 50 minutes. Remove from the heat and reserve. Season with salt and pepper to taste, if desired.

2. While the rice is cooking, pre-cook the shellfish. Combine the mussels with ¼ cup water in a large, heavy-bottomed saucepan over high heat. Cover and cook, shaking occasionally, just until the shells open, about 3 minutes. (Some of the mussels may open sooner than 3 minutes. If so, remove them to a bowl as they open, so they don't overcook.) When all of the mussels are cooked, remove them from the pan; discard any that do not open. Add the clams to the pan, cover, and cook over high heat just until they've opened, about 2 minutes. (Some of the clams may open sooner than 2 minutes. If so, remove them as they open so they don't overcook.) Discard any that do not open. Drain the shellfish, reserving them and their cooking liquid separately.

3. When the clams and mussels are cool enough to handle, remove the meats from the shells, discarding the shells. Cover the shellfish meats so they don't dry out.

4. In a medium-size, heavy-bottomed saucepan, bring the cream and half the reserved shellfish cooking liquid to a boil over medium-high heat. Cook until reduced by half, or until the consistency of heavy cream is reached. Lightly crush the remaining ½ teaspoon saffron with your fingers or in a mortar and pestle. Stir into the hot cream.

5. Add the scallops to the saffron cream. Cook until they begin to turn opaque, about 4 minutes. Add the clams and mussels and cook until heated through, about 2 minutes. Cut the lemon sections into small pieces. Stir the lemon and chives into the saffron cream. Season with salt and pepper to taste.

6. Arrange the wild rice on a warm serving platter. Using a slotted spoon, place the shellfish and lemon pieces on top of the rice. Pour the sauce over the shellfish, letting it seep out from under the rice for a very attractive presentation. Serve immediately.

Makes 4 generous servings

Note: Do not scrub and beard the mussels until right before you plan to use them or they will die and spoil.

A Little Story About Lobster

Unlike the stereotypical grumpy, taciturn lobsterman, Dennis Rackliffe has a teasing laugh in his eyes. He's been a Maine lobsterman all his life and he loves the work.

Bundled in warm clothes and orange rubber overalls, Dennis walks a hundred yards from his Sprucehead, Maine, home, to his sleek, slim, and elegant 38-foot lobster boat. His nephew and deckhand Daren, whose nickname is "Bubba," comes along, bringing a couple of lobster pots and a big thermos of coffee.

The boat has an open cabin at the stern that barely protects from licks of frigid wind. The only warmth comes from an exhaust pipe that runs up through the cabin roof. Dennis and Bubba complain of the cold as the purring engine drives the boat out into Wheeler's Bay. They forget the temperature soon enough as they check the loran, fathometers, and radar, equipment that makes the job of hunting lobsters a little easier. "These things just show me where I am and what's out there with me," says Dennis.

Dennis grew up in Sprucehead and most of his family still lives there, within shouting distance, on a small, bucolic point they all call the "neighborhood." His father and grandfather were lobstermen before him. "Twenty years ago there were just 12 lobstermen in Wheeler's Bay. Now there are 21," Dennis says. There are just as many lobster, but they're smaller and fewer per boat. And Maine lobstermen feel the pinch from imported Canadian lobster, which constitute nearly 25 percent of all lobster consumed in the United States.

Dennis would like to see limits put on the number of lobster fishermen. "Lobster licenses should cost $10,000 a year," he said. "That way only serious fishermen would do it."

Bubba, who at 18 already has the blood of a fisherman, doesn't hear any of what Dennis says. He scans the choppy water for buoys, rubs his gloved hands together to keep warm, and claims he'll fish all his life, seduced by the craggy beauty of Maine and the silence. He gives a wild shout as he spots the first buoy that signals a lobster pot. Daylight flickers on the horizon as Dennis hauls up the pot with a hydraulic hook and line. A huge wire pot comes lumbering out of the water, and they balance it on the edge of the boat.

Dennis sizes up the catch, which includes a sculpin, several crab, and one "keeper," as he calls a legal-size lobster. As he unhooks the latch that keeps the trap's door shut, Bubba says, "We've got a secret way to keep out 'pickers,'" referring to poachers who empty pots at night. "Nobody gets into these traps but us."

September is usually a slack month for lobster, perhaps because they feel the water cooling, which causes them to be-

Dennis Rackliffe's state-of-the-art lobster boat during a quiet moment in Wheeler's Bay, Maine.

come dormant. Though it's slow, a few lobsters come up in each pot. They can't keep females, so Bubba notches their tails with a paperpunch-like tool as a signal to the next lobsterman, and tosses them overboard. Sometimes females come up laden with eggs—called "berries"—inside their cupped tails. These too go overboard. They measure others, from right behind the eye to the end of the body—keeping only those who fall between the limits of $3^3/_{16}$ and 5 inches.

Bubba slips thick bright yellow rubber bands over their claws, so they don't start gnawing on each other. Lobster's favorite food is other lobster, though they also eat shellfish, worms, and the herring and alewives used as bait. The rubber bands are modern replacements for the wooden pegs that old-timers stuck in the hinge of one claw. Sometimes a big, thorny old lobster comes up with the remains of a peg in its claw. "My grandfather used 'em," Dennis says. "He spent all winter whittling wooden pegs." Some lobstermen still use plastic pegs, though they pose a risk of infection to the lobster.

Once bound, the lobsters are tossed into a sectioned wooden box, to size them and keep them separated. When fish come up in the pots, Dennis stuns them and tosses them in the bait sack—traditionally knit by girlfriends, wives, and mothers—closes the latch and heaves the trap back overboard.

This goes on all day, one trap after the other, until it is nearly dark again and 400 pots have been checked. It's been a typical work day, with one surprise: a pot that is completely filled with one huge lobster. Dennis extricates him and his claws extend nearly three feet. "This guy's an old friend. See he's got a peg in him. We pull him up now and then," Dennis says. He strokes his tail affectionately, then drops him overboard with a smile. "He weighs more than 15 pounds. At $2.40 a pound to the fisherman, he would have been a nice catch. They could keep him in Massachusetts. We can't here—the laws are stricter here than anywhere."

Dennis heads the boat to a nearby dock. He sells his catch for a premium price to a man who will sell them along the roadside. Dennis turns 12 percent of the day's take over to Bubba and heads the boat home.

With the workday done, Dennis searches the sky for eagles, then points out a stark, bright house and its lighthouse on a point. "That's Andy's house," he says, referring to the painter Andrew Wyeth, and settles into the romance of a day on the water. "It's sure beautiful out here," he says.

Oyster Roast for a Crowd

William Taylor, a caterer who hails from southern Maryland, suggested this recipe for roasting oysters. I follow it religiously, usually in early spring, when the bivalves are still firm and plump and a spate of warm days calls for barbecues and outside dining. You don't need fine weather, however—I know a couple who celebrate New Year's Eve with an oyster roast.

I prefer roasted oysters dipped in lemon butter, but be sure to have Old Bay Seasoning and Tabasco sauce on hand for those who like theirs with a spicy kick. An oyster roast for many will move more smoothly if you have two barbecues going and if someone is willing to shuck for guests. Cover a large table with newspaper, and be sure to have plenty of paper napkins or rolls of paper towels about and small forks for eating the oysters. Serve a flinty Chablis.

1 cup (2 sticks) lightly salted butter
Juice of 1 lemon
10 dozen oysters, shells well scrubbed under cold
  running water
1 small can (6 ounces) Old Bay Seasoning or 1 small
  bottle (2 ounces) Tabasco sauce (optional)

1. Prepare a grill with charcoals. Ignite and let it burn until the coals glow red and are covered with ash. Set the grilling rack over the fire.

2. Melt the butter in a small, heavy-bottomed saucepan over low heat. Spoon off as much foam as possible, add the lemon juice and stir. While you prepare the oysters, keep the lemon butter warm on top of the grill cover if possible. If not, keep warm in a low oven.

3. When the charcoal is ready, arrange enough unopened oysters on the grill, cupped shell down, to cover it. Cover the grill and roast until the shells open slightly, 10 to 15 minutes.

4. To shuck the oysters, pry open the shells and slip a knife blade under and over the oysters, cutting loose the muscle.

5. Dip the oysters in the lemon butter. Sprinkle with Old Bay Seasoning or Tabasco, if desired.

Makes 10 to 20 servings

East Coast Crab Cakes

Crab cakes are to Maryland what bubbles are to soda. Everywhere you go in Maryland, from restaurants to roadside stands you'll find crab cakes, and they range from sublime to awful. Everyone in Maryland, it seems, has an opinion about crab cakes. Some like them round and light like balls, others insist they should be flat and dense. I prefer crab cakes that are mostly crab, with just a few other ingredients to enhance their flavor and keep them from falling apart. I searched all over Maryland for the perfect crab cake to no avail. Not until I reached South Carolina and the home of friends Ruth Ann and Frank Shuman did I find perfection. Ruth Ann has made crab cakes for years and she uses a traditional Maryland recipe "with a little extra crab." Serve these with coleslaw and a light Chardonnay.

½ cup soft fresh bread crumbs

1 large egg

About 5 tablespoons mayonnaise

2 scallions, trimmed, the white bulbs and light green
   stems minced

1 tablespoon chopped fresh parsley

1 teaspoon dry mustard

½ teaspoon salt

¼ teaspoon freshly ground black pepper

1 pound lump crabmeat, picked over

1 tablespoon unsalted butter plus 1 tablespoon bland
   vegetable oil, such as safflower, for frying

1. In a medium-size bowl, mix together the bread crumbs, egg, 4 tablespoons of the mayonnaise, the scallions, parsley, and the seasonings. Add the crabmeat and mix gently. If the mixture is too dry, add the remaining 1 tablespoon mayonnaise. (Add additional mayonnaise if the mixture will not hold together and is still dry.)

2. Shape the mixture into 6 patties.

3. Heat the butter and oil in a large skillet over medium-high heat. When the oil is hot and lightly smoking, add the crab cakes and cook until golden, about 5 minutes on each side. Serve immediately with coleslaw.

Makes 4 to 6 servings

Diana Fonseca's Fried Soft-Shell Crabs

Soft-shell crabs are a time-honored delicacy from the Chesapeake Bay to Grand Isle, Louisiana. Diana Fonseca of Des Allemands, Louisiana, frequently prepares them for her fisherman husband, Leon, and the crew of his fish processing plant, and she marinates them in a milk, egg, and cayenne mixture that imparts a gentle heat. Nutritional controversy surrounds deep-fat fried foods, with good reason. But somehow, soft-shell crabs just aren't right if they aren't embraced in a crisp coating, and a dozen crabs fried in 2 cups of oil actually absorb a scant ½ cup of the oil. Accompany these with a lightly chilled American Sauvignon Blanc.

2 cups milk

2 large eggs

2 teaspoons cayenne pepper

1 dozen soft-shell crabs, trimmed

2 cups mild vegetable oil, for frying

1 cup all-purpose flour

¾ teaspoon salt

1. The night before you plan to cook the crabs, whisk together the milk, eggs, and cayenne pepper in a medium-size bowl. Cover and refrigerate.

2. The next day, place the crabs in a single layer in a flat glass or enameled dish. Pour the milk mixture over them, and refrigerate them, turning once, for 2 to 4 hours. (The longer you marinate them the more they will absorb the pepperiness of the marinade.)

3. Heat the oil in a wok or large saucepan, to 350°F. While the oil is heating, combine the flour and salt in a shallow dish. Remove the crabs from the marinade. One at a time, dredge them in the flour mixture, coating well on all sides.

4. Fry the crabs in the hot oil until golden, about 3 minutes on each side. To serve, place the crab atop a green salad.

Makes 4 to 6 servings

What Is Surimi, Anyway?

I t is those candy-cane looking sticks of imitation crab meat; curled, stubby, and orange-colored imitation shrimp or lobster tails; and whitish disks called imitation scallops that are showing up in restaurant and salad bar seafood salads, and at fish counters across the country.

What is it made of?

It's minced whitefish, usually Alaska pollock, but sometimes New Zealand hoki, and perhaps soon East Coast menhaden, with the bones, the skin, and most of the fat and flavor removed. This processing is done on the fishing grounds, and the resulting white, rubbery paste is frozen in 22-pound blocks and then sent to surimi plants for further processing.

When it arrives at one surimi plant in the Pacific Northwest, it is thawed and thrown into a giant blender. Other ingredients are added according to a customer's request. Additions are usually sugar, salt, crab or shrimp meat, and juice (crab juice is a by-product of the Alaska crab industry, where most Dungeness crab are cooked in water before being shipped out of state), egg whites, starch, and polyphosphates for preservatives. But that's not all. Additives might also include monosodium glutamate, vegetable oils, and seasonings for texture and bulk.

The mixture, which is now called *kamoboko*, has a firm, gelatinous texture. It is extruded onto a belt in wide, thin sheets or "ribbons," which are cooked and

cooled, then run through a machine called a "slitter," which cuts it into thin strands. The strands are rolled into ropes, washed in blood red dye, cut into lengths and wrapped in clear plastic, or chopped for salad chunks. It is usually labeled "imitation crab."

Other surimi plants may use a different system, but they are all producing the same, basic product. Everyone is divided as to what to call it—imitation shellfish, fake crab and shrimp, crab- or shrimp-meat, surimi, or *kamoboko*. One industry magazine, intent on fairness and without regard for product appeal, has decided to call it what it is—surimi-based shellfish analogue.

The technique for making this analogue was borrowed some 10 years ago from Japan, where *kamoboko* has long been popular. If you've ever had a piece of brightly colored fish cake floating in soup or perched on salad in a Japanese restaurant, that's *kamoboko*. If you've ever tasted it, you know how bland and rubbery it is.

The Food and Drug Administration governs surimi-based analogue labeling. So far, it has required that analogues be labeled "imitation" when they're sold in supermarkets. However, little legislation governs restaurants or delicatessens. When customers order a seafood salad at a fast-food restaurant, they are likely to be getting a hefty amount of surimi-based shellfish analogue as part of the package.

Crab and Cucumber Salad

Petersburg, Alaska, a charming town of mostly gravel streets and gorgeous, steel gray water vistas, has a legendary affinity with Norway. The phone book reads like a listing of classic Norwegian names, and the regional dishes include smoked black cod and boiled potatoes, *lutefisk*, fish pudding, and wonderful, hearty pastries. I spent three lovely days there and saw a brown bear just outside of town, bald eagles hunkering on the docks, and more salmon, crab, and pink shrimp than I could count. As I searched for recipes, every road led to the Sons of Norway Fedrelandet Lodge, and every cook said, "I put my best recipe in the Sons of Norway Cookbook—please take it from there."

So I have. I adapted this recipe, which was contributed by Karen Bennett, a resident of Petersburg. It is wonderfully refreshing, and the cucumber highlights the nutty sweetness of Dungeness crab. You may substitute lump blue crab meat in this recipe. Serve a clean, "appley" Chardonnay.

2 medium cucumbers, washed and scored lengthwise
with the tines of a fork
¾ teaspoon salt
1 tablespoon white sesame seeds
2 tablespoons rice wine vinegar
1 teaspoon sugar
1 teaspoon peanut oil
½ teaspoon Japanese sesame oil
8 ounces Dungeness or lump blue crabmeat, picked
over
Freshly ground white pepper

1. Cut the cucumbers into very thin slices. Place in a bowl and sprinkle with the salt. Toss and refrigerate for 30 minutes.

2. Toast the sesame seeds in a small skillet over medium-high heat, stirring constantly, until they are golden brown. Set aside. the heat and reserve.

3. In a medium-size bowl, combine the vinegar, sugar, and oils. Rinse the cucumber slices to remove most of the salt; pat them dry. Add to the sauce and toss to coat thoroughly. Add the crabmeat and toss gently to mix well. Season with white pepper to taste.

4. Divide the salad among 4 chilled plates.
Makes 4 main-course servings

Alvin Folse's Crawfish Boil

This is a crawfish boil I enjoyed with Alvin Folse and his family (see box, following page). Everything, from the crawfish to the potatoes and celery, bursts with subtle and not-so-subtle spices and wonderful flavor. I treasure the memory of that meal, and I recreate it at home whenever I can get good, fresh crawfish. Serve plenty of ice-cold beer along with this—you'll be glad you did.

7 pounds fresh crawfish
¼ cup plus 1 tablespoon kosher (coarse) salt
2 tablespoons cayenne pepper
¼ cup Chackabay Crab and Shrimp Boil (see Note)
4 large onions, peeled
4 smoked sausages (about 4 ounces each), cut into 2-
inch lengths
2 pounds new potatoes, washed
1 bunch celery, ribs separated and cut into 4-inch
lengths

1. Rinse the crawfish well in several changes of water.

2. In a very large pot, bring 3½ gallons of water to a boil over high heat. Add the salt. Add the cayenne pepper and the Chackabay seasoning and stir. Cut the onions halfway through, horizontally. Add to the water. Boil for 15 minutes.

3. Add the sausages, potatoes, and celery. Cook until the potatoes are crisp-tender, 10 to 15 minutes. Add the crawfish, deveining them just before you drop them in; let the water return to a boil. Cook until the crawfish are red, about 8 minutes. Remove from the heat. You can serve the crawfish immediately. Just drain them, discarding the liquid, and pile on a serving platter or in the center of a newspaper-covered table with the potatoes and sausages. Be sure to have plenty of paper towels on hand.

4. Though the crawfish, vegetables, and sausages will be quite spicy, if you want to let them absorb more spice without overcooking, place the pot in a sink half-filled with cold water for 10 to 15 minutes. Serve.

Makes 7 to 10 servings

Note: Chackabay Crab and Shrimp Boil is available in specialty stores in Louisiana, or you can write to Chackabay Crab and Shrimp Boil, 102 Landry Lane, Thibodaux, Louisiana 70301. It costs between $1.30 and $1.60 a package.

If you can't find Chackabay brand crab or shrimp boil, use any other good-quality brand, such as Zatarain's, which is readily available at most supermarkets and fish markets, or use pickling spices.

A Louisiana Crawfish Boil

I was melting from the heat in downtown New Orleans one spring day, when Alvin Folse, the owner of Big Plans Seafood, a processing plant in Des Allemands called. "We're havin' a crawfish boil out at my cousin's, and we'd like you to come," he said. I needed no further encouragement. When I arrived, Alvin and his cousin, O.J. Blouin, had an aluminum beer keg with one end cut off standing on a short tripod over a propane flame. The keg was two-thirds full of bubbling salted water and Alvin went to work. He took the top off the biggest jar of cayenne pepper I've ever seen and poured half of it in the water, along with a batch of other seasonings, which turned the water brilliant red.

He added two sacks of potatoes, a sack of onions, and a couple bunches of celery. Before adding the onions he cut halfway through them, so they would cook evenly. Lengths of spicy smoked *andouille* sausage went in too, and finally, when the water boiled, so did 40 pounds of prime Belle River crawfish.

He cranked up the propane, and the water returned to a boil almost instantly. After exactly 10 minutes, Alvin turned off the heat, gave the crawfish another stir, and let them sit for about 8 minutes. "You can let 'em sit as long as you want—the longer they sit the hotter they get!" he said. He scooped out crawfish, potatoes, onions, and sausages and piled it all on the newspaper-covered picnic table, and we sat down to a feast.

Crawfish in Black Bean Sauce

This dish is as wonderful as it is fun and messy to eat. Serve it with plenty of paper napkins and be prepared to regale yourself in the earthy flavor of black beans and the sweet succulence of crawfish. Also, serve a big bowl of cooked white rice alongside, and spoon the sauce over it. Try a simple red table wine alongside.

2½ pounds large fresh crawfish
2 tablespoons Chinese fermented black beans
2 large cloves garlic, coarsely chopped
2 tablespoons minced fresh ginger
½ cup Fish Stock (see Index)
2 teaspoons soy sauce
2 tablespoons mirin (Japanese sweet cooking wine)
1 teaspoon chili paste with soy bean, preferably Lan Chi brand
2 tablespoons safflower or peanut oil
2 scallions, trimmed, the white bulbs and light green stems coarsely chopped

1. Rinse the crawfish well in several changes of water.

2. In a small bowl, use a wooden spoon to mash the black beans, garlic, and ginger into a paste. In another bowl, stir together the fish stock, soy sauce, mirin, and chili paste. Reserve.

3. Heat the oil in a wok or large skillet over medium-high heat. While the oil is heating, clean the crawfish by twisting the middle plate of the tail fin and pulling on it, so the viscera are removed with it. When the oil is hot, add the crawfish and stir to coat with oil. Add the fish stock mixture and the black bean paste; stir well and bring to

> ## "Forty pounds of crawfish will feed 16 normal people, or 6 Cajuns."
>
> ALVIN FOLSE, DES ALLEMANDS, LOUISIANA

a boil. Cover and cook, stirring occasionally, until the crawfish shells turn red, 5 to 8 minutes. Stir in the scallions; serve immediately.

Makes 4 servings

Oregon Crawfish Boil

This Oregon recipe is from Ida Olsen, who used to cook crawfish for the whole town of Knappa, Oregon, in the 1930s and 1940s when her husband, John, fished for them. John was a commercial salmon fisherman—he fished crawfish from the Columbia River for fun and sold most of them to Jake's Famous Crawfish restaurant in Portland. He'd put big boxes on the night train in Knappa, and they'd travel the 70-odd miles to Portland, where Jake's would pick them up in the morning. "They can live as long as two months out of the water," Richard Olsen, John and Ida's son, told me. He's the one who prepares crawfish now, following his mother's recipe, which has been carefully written in a family cookbook. "This is a sorta kinda' recipe," he said. "It's a matter of salt." Once the water comes to a boil, devein a crawfish by twisting the middle flap of the tail fin and pulling on it—the intestines come right out; add the crawfish to the boiling water. "The water stays boiling or near it, and they all cook at roughly the same time, because the deveining goes fast," Richard said. Hot or cold, serve these spiced crawfish Oregon-style, on a newspaper-covered table with a big bowl of potato salad on the side and plenty of cold beer. This recipe can be increased forever—just increase everything in proportion. Try a beer from a small American brewery, such as Red Hook or Anchor Steam.

½ cup salt

4 to 5 cloves garlic

1 large carrot, cut into 1-inch-long pieces

4 sprigs fresh dill

1 cup dry white wine

½ teaspoon each ground cloves, freshly grated nutmeg, ground allspice, curry powder, and cayenne pepper

2 tablespoons pickling spice

2 dozen large fresh crawfish (about 1½ pounds), rinsed

In a large pot, combine the salt, garlic, carrot, dill, wine, and spices with 3 quarts water. Bring to a boil over high heat. Devein the crawfish and add them to the boiling water one at a time. When the water returns to a boil, cook until the crawfish are bright red, 5 to 10 minutes. Set the pan with all the crawfish in it into a sink filled with cold water to stop the cooking. Drain the crawfish. Serve hot or cold.

Makes 4 servings

Alaska Spot Prawns with Lime Juice and Ginger

The idea for this recipe comes from Mary Pelham, renowned in the Darien, Georgia, region for her culinary prowess. She uses rock shrimp, which are very similar to spot prawns in their lobster-like flavor and texture. Rock shrimp are hard to come by outside of Georgia, and any good-quality shrimp will be delicious prepared this way. Be sure to serve this dish with plenty of fresh, crusty bread for sopping up the cooking juices, and a chilled American Sauvignon Blanc. If you do find rock shrimp, remove the hard shell by placing the shrimp on a work surface, swim fins down. Hold it by the tail and, using a soupspoon, rap the shell. It will crack so you can peel it off.

1 pound medium (31 to 35 per pound) Alaska spot prawns, rock shrimp, or shrimp, peeled and deveined

1 tablespoon minced fresh ginger

Juice of 1 medium lime

¼ teaspoon dried hot pepper flakes

Salt

1. Preheat the oven to 450°F.

2. Rinse the prawns and pat them dry. Arrange them in one layer in an ovenproof glass, enameled, or porcelain baking dish. Evenly sprinkle on the ginger, lime juice, and pepper flakes. Lightly salt them.

3. Bake until the prawns are opaque but still tender, not overly tough, about 8 minutes. Transfer the prawns and their cooking juices to a warmed serving platter and serve.

Makes 4 servings

Prawns Braised in Olive Oil and Garlic

This recipe comes from Thor Plancich, a Seattle-based fisherman who seems always to have a ready supply of spot shrimp, also known as Alaska spot prawns, gifts from his shrimping friends. Thor claims this is the best way to prepare any kind of shrimp or prawn. It is certainly one of the most dramatic, for it ends up a pile of bright pink prawns glistening with olive oil and pungent with garlic. Serve with a chilled Pinot Grigio or Aligoté, and plenty of freshly made, crusty bread to sop up the garlicky olive oil.

½ cup olive oil
10 cloves garlic, coarsely chopped
1 tablespoon kosher (coarse) salt
2½ pounds large (26 to 30 per pound) spot shrimp, in their shells
1 lemon, cut into 6 wedges, for garnish

1. Heat the olive oil in a large skillet over medium-high heat.

2. When the oil is hot but not smoking, add the garlic and sauté until it begins to turn translucent, 2 to 3 minutes. Add the salt and the prawns and toss to coat with oil. Cook, stirring occasionally, just until the prawns are pink, about 5 minutes.

3. Remove from the heat; transfer the prawns to a large serving platter, mounding them in the center. Pour the cooking juices over the prawns. Garnish with the lemon wedges. Serve immediately.

Makes 4 generous servings

Salonika Shrimp

The first time I had this dish, at Sofi's restaurant in Los Angeles, I was astounded by the herbiness of the feta cheese, the slightly firm but tender sweetness of the shrimp, and the appealing size and texture of the orzo. It is a fabulously simple, flavorful, and elegant dish. Chef and owner Sofi Konstantimidis insists on using 100 percent sheep's milk feta, preferably Bulgarian or French, which are generally milder and fresher than Greek or Israeli fetas. Try this with a fruity red Greek wine such as Cava Boutari or a good Beaujolais.

2 cups orzo (rice-shaped pasta)
Salt
1½ tablespoons unsalted butter
1 large bunch fresh dill, the leaves snipped off the stems
½ bunch fresh basil, stemmed
2 tablespoons virgin olive oil
3 cloves garlic, minced
1 pound ripe plum tomatoes, peeled, cored, and coarsely chopped
1 pound medium (31 to 35 per pound) shrimp, peeled and deveined
Freshly ground black pepper
2 tablespoons fresh oregano or 2 teaspoons dried
9 ounces feta cheese

1. To cook the orzo, bring 6 cups of water to a boil in a large saucepan. Add 2 teaspoons salt. Stir in the orzo. Cook until the orzo is *al dente* (tender but still firm to the bite) and has doubled in size, about 7 minutes. Drain well. Return to the pot and add the butter; mix well to coat all of the orzo. Set aside.

2. Butter four 6-inch porcelain baking dishes. Mince the dill and basil.

3. Heat the olive oil in a large skillet over medium-high heat. Add the garlic and sauté just until it begins to turn translucent, 3 to 5 minutes. Add the tomatoes, dill, and basil; cook until the tomatoes are slightly soft, but still hold their shape, about 10 minutes. Add the shrimp and cook, stirring occasionally, just until they turn pink but are still somewhat limp, 3 to 4 minutes. Season lightly with salt (the feta cheese is quite salty, so don't overdo it) and pepper to taste. Remove from the heat and reserve.

4. Preheat the oven to 500°F.

5. While the tomato mixture is cooking, mince the fresh oregano, or crush the dried oregano with your fingers, just enough to release the perfume. Crumble the feta into a small bowl. Add the oregano and toss until the oregano and cheese are blended.

6. To assemble, divide the orzo among the baking dishes, spreading it out in an even layer. Top with the shrimp and tomato mixture. Crumble the herbed feta over the top. Bake just until the feta begins to melt, about 5 minutes. Serve immediately.

Makes 4 servings

Seared Shrimp with Spinach and Pickled Garlic

A friend calls this "Christmas shrimp" because of the color scheme. This dish evolved over time, as I experimented with shrimp, searching for fresh, simple accompaniments. The spiced shrimp highlight the smooth, fresh green flavor of the spinach, and the tomatoes wrap it all in a tart-sweet sauce. Be sure to prepare the Pickled Garlic at least a week before you plan on serving this dish. Accompany this with a chilled American Sauvignon Blanc.

4 bunches spinach, washed and stemmed
3 tablespoons extra-virgin olive oil
Grated zest of 1 lemon
5 cloves garlic, minced
Salt and freshly ground black pepper
2 pounds medium (31 to 35 per pound) shrimp, peeled and deveined, shells reserved
2 small carrots, peeled and sliced in rounds
½ medium onion, coarsely chopped
1 small celery rib, coarsely chopped
¼ cup coarsely chopped fresh chives
1 small handful fresh tarragon leaves or 2 teaspoons dried
1 large sprig flat-leaf parsley
5 cups Fish Stock (see Index)
1 cup dry white wine, such as Sauvignon Blanc
4 large tomatoes, peeled, cored, and coarsely chopped
2 tablespoons unsalted butter
1 tablespoon fresh lemon juice
Pickled Garlic (recipe follows)

1. In a large, non-aluminum pot, cook the spinach in the water that clings to the leaves over medium-high heat until wilted but still bright green, about 5 minutes. Drain and gently press out the excess liquid. Reserve.

2. In a large bowl, whisk together 2 tablespoons of the olive oil, the lemon zest, a little less than half of the garlic, and a pinch of salt and pepper. Add the shrimp, toss, and refrigerate.

3. Combine the shrimp shells, carrots, onion, celery, chives, tarragon, and parsley in a large non-aluminum sauté pan. Add the fish stock and wine; bring to a boil over high

heat. Reduce the heat to medium-low and simmer for 20 minutes.

4. Strain the shrimp stock and discard the solids. Return the stock to the pan and boil over medium-high heat until reduced by half, to about 2½ cups. Add the tomatoes, and cook until the sauce is slightly thickened and reduced to about 1½ cups, about 20 minutes.

5. Place the remaining 1 tablespoon olive oil in a large skillet over medium-high heat and heat until the oil is hot and a wisp of smoke dances off the surface. Add the shrimp, its marinade, and the remaining garlic, and cook, stirring occasionally, just until the shrimp have curled, are bright pink, and firm though not tough or rubbery, 5 to 6 minutes. Remove from the heat and reserve.

6. While the shrimp are cooking, melt the butter in a medium-size skillet or frying pan. Add the spinach and cook, stirring constantly, just until the spinach is heated through and coated with the butter. Season with salt and pepper to taste.

7. Just before serving, add the lemon juice to the tomato sauce. To serve, divide the spinach among 4 dinner plates, pressing it out slightly to make a thick circle on the plate. Top with the shrimp; spoon the tomato sauce over all. Sprinkle each serving with 1 tablespoon of pickled garlic. Serve the remaining pickled garlic alongside.

Makes 4 servings

Pickled Garlic

Although this pickled garlic goes specifically with the Seared Shrimp with Spinach, it is wonderful to have on hand to add to everything from a summer seafood salad, to succulent grilled or steamed fish. It is simple to make and it will keep for about 1 month.

1 cup garlic cloves

1½ cups white vinegar

¾ teaspoon salt

2 bay leaves

20 peppercorns

10 coriander seeds

1 large branch fresh thyme or ½ teaspoon dried

5 juniper berries

1. Slice each garlic clove in half lengthwise, and remove the green sprout inside. Thinly slice each garlic half crosswise.

2. Bring the vinegar and 1½ cups water to a boil in a medium-size non-aluminum saucepan over high heat.

3. Place the spices, herbs, and garlic in a clean, heatproof glass jar. Pour in the vinegar mixture and screw the lid on tight. Let sit for 1 week before using.

Makes about 1 cup

Alva Magwood's Shrimp, Oyster, and Clam Boil

"You don't want to be pinchy with your seafood—it's the flavor of the seafood that you want."

Words to live by, from Alva Magwood, who lives just outside Charleston, South Carolina, in Mount Pleasant. She's been involved in the seafood business for more than 40 years, helping her husband, "Junior." Junior is a shrimper, and they have a dock where they buy shrimp from others. One of the benefits of living in Mount Pleasant and shrimping is abundant seafood, which Alva turns into sumptuous meals at least twice a day for the "crew," her husband, three sons, and daughter. This recipe is one of her favorites, and it's an easy one for a group of people. It's beautiful, too, for it looks like a fall harvest when it's served up. If you make this at the end of summer, oysters will just be returning to their firm, sweet condition—try to get those from the coldest waters possible. With this serve a dry white wine such as Pinot Gris, Aligoté, Rully, or a dry Sauternes such as Château "R" or "G."

1 pound yams or sweet potatoes, peeled, halved lengthwise, and cut into 1½-inch pieces
2 medium russet potatoes, peeled, halved lengthwise, and cut into 2-inch-long pieces
2 tablespoons crab or shrimp boil seasoning, preferably Zatarain's brand, or pickling spice
¼ teaspoon salt
1 pound clams, shells well scrubbed under cold running water
6 oysters, shells well scrubbed under cold running water
8 ounces hot Italian sausage, cut into 2-inch lengths
2 large ears fresh sweet corn, husked and halved crosswise
2 tablespoons unsalted butter, cut in 4 equal pieces
4 ounces small (36 to 42 per pound) shrimp in their shells

1. Place the yams and potatoes in a large, heavy-bottomed saucepan, over medium-high heat. Add ¾ cup water, 1 tablespoon of the crab boil, and the salt. Cover and bring to a boil. Reduce the heat to medium and cook until the potatoes are nearly soft through, about 10 minutes.

2. Add the clams, oysters, Italian sausage, and corn in that order, so the corn is on top. Sprinkle the remaining 1 tablespoon crab boil over the corn; dot the butter on top.

Cover and bring the water to a boil. Cook until the corn is bright yellow, the clams open, and the oysters are either open or very close to it, about 7 minutes. Discard any clams or oysters that do not open.

3. Add the shrimp, placing them over and around the corn. Cook until they turn pink, 4 to 5 minutes.

4. Remove from the heat and serve right from the pot, into shallow soup bowls or large rimmed plates, or divide the mixture among the bowls or plates and serve.

Makes 4 servings

Shrimp and Garlic with Artichokes and Bell Peppers

Sweet, lovely pink shrimp, dusky red and green peppers, nutty artichokes—they blend here to make a wonderful first course or elegant luncheon dish. Serve with a clean, American Sauvignon Blanc or a Sancerre with some age.

1 roasted red bell pepper (see Index)
1 roasted green bell pepper (see Index)
½ cup extra-virgin olive oil
1 teaspoon balsamic vinegar
¼ teaspoon coarsely ground black pepper
6 cloves garlic, coarsely chopped
1½ pounds medium (31 to 35 per pound) shrimp, peeled and deveined
½ teaspoon dried hot pepper flakes
4 large artichokes
1 tablespoon salt
1 lemon, halved

1. Slice the peppers into very thin strips.

2. Place the pepper strips in a large bowl, add 5 tablespoons of the olive oil, the balsamic vinegar, and the black pepper; mix well. Set aside at room temperature.

3. Heat the remaining 3 tablespoons olive oil in a large skillet over medium heat. Add the garlic and sauté until translucent, about 5 minutes. Add the shrimp and hot pepper flakes and sauté just until the shrimp turn pink, about 5 minutes. Scrape the shrimp, garlic, and any remaining oil into the bowl of pepper strips. Mix well. Set aside to marinate at room temperature for 1 hour.

4. Trim off all of the artichoke leaves and the stems, leaving just the heart and the choke.

5. Fill a large, heavy-bottomed saucepan with 1 gallon of water. Add the salt and the lemon halves; bring to a boil over high heat. Boil the artichoke bottoms until tender but still somewhat firm, about 15 minutes. Drain and let cool. When the artichoke bottoms are cool enough to handle, scrape out the choke using a stainless-steel teaspoon.

6. Thinly slice the warm artichoke bottoms and arrange them in a sunburst pattern on each of 4 warm dinner plates. Remove the shrimp and pepper strips from the marinade with a slotted spoon. Mound them in the center, so some of the artichoke bottoms show. Pour the remaining olive oil and vinegar marinade over the shrimp and the artichoke slices. Serve immediately.

Makes 4 servings

Shrimp and Sausage Purloo

Once you hit South Carolina, purloo becomes an institution. "Purloo" is the word for pilau, or pilaf, in the Gullah dialect—a country dialect that is still used in some parts of South Carolina. I first tasted purloo at Robertson's Cafeteria, a relic from the 1950s just outside Charleston that serves down-home, regional foods. I loved its soft, comforting texture and the pure flavors that come from the vegetables and shrimp. A touch of Worcestershire sauce, which I have decided is the most common seafood seasoning in America, provides the only seasoning, aside from salt and pepper. For something a little different, try a light red wine with this, such as an Italian Dolcetto or just about any Pinot Noir. Otherwise, a Vouvray or German Kabinett goes well here too.

1½ pounds small (36 to 42 per pound) shrimp, peeled and deveined
3 tablespoons Worcestershire sauce
4 ounces slab bacon, rind removed, cut into ¼-inch dice
1 large onion, diced
1 large green bell pepper, cored, seeded, and diced
8 ounces okra, cut into ⅜-inch rounds
8 ounces smoked sausage (kielbasa), cut into ¾-inch rounds
1 cup long-grain white rice
Salt and freshly ground black pepper

1. Place the shrimp in a medium-size bowl with the Worcestershire sauce. Stir well. Marinate, covered, in the refrigerator for 30 minutes.

2. Meanwhile, cook the bacon in a saucepan or a deep skillet over medium heat until it is golden and has rendered most of its fat, about 7 minutes. Transfer the bacon to paper towels to drain.

3. Add the onion and the bell pepper to the bacon fat and cook, stirring frequently, until the onion is translucent, about 3 minutes. Add the okra and sausage and stir to coat with the bacon fat. Add the rice, and cook, stirring, until it begins to turn translucent, about 2 minutes. Add 2 cups water, ½ teaspoon salt, and the cooked bacon. Cover and cook until the rice is just cooked through and has absorbed the water, 20 to 25 minutes. Check the rice occasionally while it is cooking, to see if it needs additional water. If it does, add it 1 tablespoon at a time. Season with salt and pepper to taste.

4. Stir the shrimp and Worcestershire sauce into the rice mixture, pushing the shrimp into the rice. Cover and cook just until the shrimp are pink, 3 to 5 minutes. Serve immediately.

Makes 4 servings

Squid with Chanterelles, Cream, and Prosciutto

*T*his dish is as pretty to look at as it is delicious to eat. The play of textures and flavors makes it a conversation stopper, every time. It was inspired by a visit to Seattle's Pike Place Market, where chanterelle mushrooms, the duff of a Douglas fir forest still clinging to them, demanded to be purchased, and hunks of prosciutto at De-Laurenti Specialty Foods nearly jumped out of the cooler into my shopping bag. The desire for a hearty meal, a shopping bag full of wonderful ingredients, and the serendipity of a gorgeous summer day resulted in this. Try it with a dry Sauternes such as Château "R," or a lightly chilled Chianti, and invite your family and friends to share.

1 pound squid, cleaned
2 tablespoons unsalted butter
1 large shallot, finely chopped
8 ounces small chanterelles, brushed clean
1 tablespoon olive oil
4 ounces dried rotini pasta
4 ounces dried spaghetti
¾ cup Crème Fraîche (see Index) or heavy or whipping cream
3 ounces prosciutto, cut into thin strips
2 tablespoons fresh tarragon leaves or ½ teaspoon dried
Salt and freshly ground black pepper

1. Cut the squid mantles into ¼-inch-thick rounds. Leave the tentacles whole. Rinse well, pat dry, and refrigerate until ready to use.

2. Bring a large pot of salted water to a boil over high heat.

3. Meanwhile, melt the butter in a heavy-bottomed saucepan over medium-high heat. Add the shallot and cook until translucent, about 3 minutes. Add the chanterelles and cook, stirring, until softened, 8 minutes.

4. When the pot of water is boiling, stir in the olive oil. Add both kinds of pasta and cook until *al dente* (tender but still firm to the bite), 8 to 10 minutes.

5. While the pasta cooks, finish the sauce. Drain any liquid from the squid. Add the squid to the chanterelles and cook, stirring,

until white at the edges, about 30 seconds. Stir in the *crème fraîche* and prosciutto and cook until the squid is completely white, about 5 minutes. Finely chop the tarragon leaves; add to the sauce. Season with salt and pepper to taste.

6. Drain the pasta. Return it to the cooking pot and add the squid and chanterelle sauce. Toss well to thoroughly coat the pasta. Transfer to a warm serving platter. Sprinkle with coarsely ground black pepper; serve immediately.

Makes 4 servings

Squid Salad with Honey Citrus Dressing

*T*his is a delicately flavored salad that will cause your tastebuds to snap to attention. The tender squid marinates in citrus juice and honey to emerge succulent and gently sweet and sour. The squid are cooked whole because they tend to retain more flavor that way. Try this with a chilled American Chenin Blanc.

3 tablespoons salt
1 pound whole squid
Grated zest and juice of 1 lime
3 tablespoons fresh lemon juice
⅓ cup extra-virgin olive oil
2 teaspoons mild honey
2 shallots, diced
2 cloves garlic, diced
1 head of escarole, separated, washed, and torn into bite-size pieces

1. In a large saucepan, bring 3 quarts of water and the salt to a boil. Add the squid and cook for 4 minutes. Drain and rinse under cold running water until cooled.

2. To clean the squid, pull the head with tentacles from the mantle, which will also remove most of the viscera from the mantle. Slice the mantle open lengthwise, remove the clear, cartilaginous "pen," and rinse the mantle until it is clean. Scrape gently, if necessary, to completely clean it. Cut off the tentacles right in front of the eyes and, using your thumb and forefinger, gently squeeze out the "beak" (a small piece of cartilage). Pat the mantles and the tentacles dry. Leave the tentacles whole; cut the mantle lengthwise into 1-inch strips. Reserve.

3. In a medium-size bowl, combine the lime zest, lime juice, lemon juice, oil, honey, shallots, and garlic; mix well. Add the squid, stir, and marinate, stirring occasionally, at room temperature for at least 2 hours.

4. Just before serving, drain the squid, reserving the marinade. Place the escarole in a large bowl and pour the marinade over it. Toss and divide the escarole among 4 plates. Top each salad with squid and serve immediately.

Makes 4 first-course or 2 main-course servings

Calamari Stuffed with Mozzarella

*P*at Devito, a seller at Caleb Haley's fish stall in New York's Fulton Fish Market, told me about this recipe while he was cleaning squid one early morning after the rush of the market. It is a homey dish replete with spicy flavors and textures that range from the tenderness of mozzarella-stuffed squid to the crispness of peppery friselli, an Italian pepper-studded biscuit. Try to find the plumpest, ripest tomatoes you can, and be generous with the amount of basil, for along with the final drizzle of olive oil, it gives this dish the shine of summer.

Pat buys the friselli at his local Italian bakery in Brooklyn. For those who can't buy them, they are easy to make (see Index), and essential to this spicy dish. Serve with Chianti.

4 tablespoons olive oil

1 medium onion, minced

4 cloves garlic, minced

4 pounds tomatoes, peeled, seeded, and coarsely chopped

2 bay leaves

2 small hot chiles, such as jalapeño or serrano, stemmed, seeded, and minced, or 1 teaspoon dried hot pepper flakes

8 large (about 8 inches long) squid, cleaned, with tentacles and mantles separated

Salt and freshly ground black pepper

12 ounces fresh mozzarella cheese, thinly sliced

2 bunches fresh basil, stems removed

16 Friselli (see Index)

1/4 cup freshly grated Parmesan cheese (optional)

1. Heat 2 tablespoons of the olive oil in a large skillet over medium heat. Stir in the onion and cook, covered, until translucent, about 10 minutes.

2. Add two-thirds of the garlic; stir and cook until softened, 1 to 2 minutes. Add the tomatoes, bay leaves, and chiles; stir and reduce the heat to low. Cover and cook, stirring occasionally, until the tomatoes are soft but not mushy and the sauce is somewhat rough and chunky, about 1 hour.

3. Preheat the oven to 375°F.

4. Wash the squid in cold running water; pat dry. Season the inside of the mantles with salt and pepper.

5. Cut each slice of mozzarella into 4 strips. Stuff equal amounts of the cheese into each mantle, arranging the strips in a layer along one side. Using three-fourths of the basil leaves, divide them among the mantles, stuffing the leaves on top of the mozzarella and gently pushing them in. Close the edges of the mantles with flat toothpicks.

6. Arrange the squid side-by-side in a 12½ x 8½-inch ovenproof dish. Stir the remaining garlic and the squid tentacles into the tomato sauce. Season with salt to taste; remove and discard the bay leaves. Pour the warm sauce over the squid. Bake until the squid are opaque but not tough, 12 to 15 minutes.

7. Place 4 friselli in the center of each of 4 dinner plates. Remove the squid from the oven and place two squid on top of the friselli on each plate. Cover the squid and friselli with tomato sauce; set aside for 2 to 3 minutes to allow the sauce to soak into the friselli.

8. Meanwhile, mince the remaining basil leaves. Drizzle the remaining 2 tablespoons olive oil over the squid, sprinkle with the basil, and dust with Parmesan cheese, if desired.

Makes 4 servings

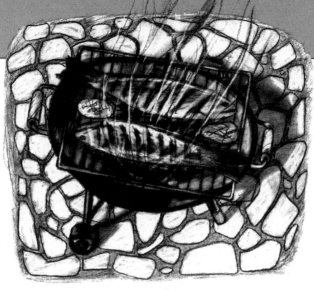

6

SEAFOOD ON THE GRILL

Grilling and smoking give a feeling of serendipity to foods. A backyard isn't necessary; neither is warm weather. You can set up a small grill on a terrace in Manhattan and create the illusion of the great outdoors, or get a smoker going in midwinter and bring a succulent piece of salmon indoors, the aroma of summer clinging to it.

Not only do grilling and smoking add a whole new dimension to seafoods, giving new meaning to the words moist and succulent, but they create a festive ambience.

All you need for successful grilling are a sturdy barbecue, good briquets—those made from wood are best—and a small space for cooking out of doors. For smoking you need either a smoker such as Little Chief brand, for long-smoked seafoods, or a simple, covered barbecue for quick-smoked foods.

When you want to evoke the outdoors and the relaxation of summer's warmth, you'll find what you're looking for in this chapter.

Greek-Style Grilled Grouper

*T*his recipe comes from Minas Sarris, a party-boat operator and former fisherman in Tarpon Springs, Florida. Minas is a first-generation American, born of Greek parents, and he loves to cook. His recipes are all geared to the Florida climate, with big, hearty flavors spiked with lemon juice and lots of olive oil. I love grouper—which has large, white flakes, a faint sweetness, and a round "nutty" flavor that comes on slowly— and I serve it with garlic-fried potatoes, Tzaziki (see Index), and a chilled Northwest Chardonnay or Sauvignon Blanc.

1½ pounds grouper fillet
¼ cup virgin olive oil
3 to 4 tablespoons fresh lemon juice
2 tablespoons fresh oregano leaves, coarsely chopped,
*   or ½ teaspoon dried*
Salt and freshly ground black pepper

1. Rinse the grouper and pat dry. Cut it into 4 equal pieces.

2. In a small bowl, whisk together the olive oil, 1 teaspoon of the lemon juice, the oregano, ¼ teaspoon salt, and a generous amount of pepper. Place the grouper in a shallow, non-aluminum dish, and pour the mixture over it. Turn to completely cover with the marinade. Refrigerate for 1 hour, turning it at least once.

3. Prepare charcoal for a medium-size fire in a barbecue. Let it burn until the coals glow red and are covered with ash. Thoroughly oil the grill, using a paper towel dipped in vegetable oil. Set the grill in place. Remove the grouper from the marinade, shaking off as much excess as possible, and place it on the grill. Cook, without turning, until the grouper is just opaque through, about 6 minutes, testing it often by piercing it with a skewer or knife and pulling it back slightly to see into the meat.

4. Add the remaining lemon juice to the marinade. When the grouper is cooked, transfer it to a warm serving platter; pour the marinade over it. The heat of the fish will sufficiently heat up the marinade. Serve immediately.

Makes 4 servings

Russ Wohlers' Hot Alder-Smoked Salmon

*R*uss Wohlers is part-owner of Ray's Boathouse and Ray's Downtown, two of Seattle's signature seafood restaurants. He, along with Wayne Ludvigsen, head chef at Ray's, have been key players in the quality improvement in Seattle's seafood over the past seven years. They both work tirelessly, searching for the best seafood available, often buying it directly from the fishermen.

When Russ wants smoked salmon he smokes his own, using the following recipe. It produces slightly sweet, slightly salty salmon that is mouth-wateringly rich and tender.

I use a Little Chief brand electric smoker, which is very efficient and takes up very little room. You can easily adjust the smokiness of the fish. If you prefer very smoky fish, moisten the chips before adding them to the smoker, and add more every hour. For a less smoky fish just add dry chips.

I like to serve the salmon fresh from the smoker, with vegetables and a crisp green salad. Try it with a luscious, rich Sauvignon Blanc or a rich Puligny-Montrachet.

2 pounds silver or king salmon fillets

Brine (enough for up to 4 pounds of salmon):

⅔ cup granulated sugar
⅔ cup packed brown sugar
⅔ cup salt

3 cups alder, fruit, or hickory chips, soaked in water
to cover for at least 20 minutes

1. Rinse the salmon and pat dry. Remove as many bones as possible using a strawberry huller, fish bone puller, or needle-nose pliers. Cut the salmon crosswise into serving pieces. Arrange the salmon in a single layer in a large, shallow, non-aluminum dish.

2. In a large bowl, combine the brine ingredients with 2 quarts water. Mix well. Pour the brine over the salmon. Cover and refrigerate for 24 hours.

3. Plug in the smoker and let it heat to about 300°F.

4. Remove the salmon from the brine. Rinse well and pat dry.

5. Place the salmon on a plate or a wire rack and let it sit, uncovered, at room temperature long enough to form a pellicle (slight skin) on the surface, about 30 minutes. The surface of the salmon will look shiny and will feel dry and somewhat sticky. (If you want to speed up this process, place a fan near the salmon and let it blow directly on it for about 10 minutes.)

6. Remove a handful of wood chips from the water and squeeze the excess water from them. They should still be quite damp. Place

Traditional Northwest Salmon

The Indians of the Northwest revered salmon. After they had ceremoniously barbecued the first spring-run salmon, allowing its spirit to rise with the smoke from the fire and to observe the thankfulness of the people, they carefully took the still-intact bones and set them back in the river pointing upstream, to ensure the salmon's return the following year.

Salmon was traditionally baked over alder wood coals by Northwest Indians. The head was cut from the fish (to be boiled in a stew for another meal), the fish was split, and the backbone was removed, leaving the meat intact. It was gently laid out flat, then slid between the split halves of a stake made from old-growth western red cedar. The stake was secured closed, and thin cedar sticks were wedged between the salmon and the stake, to hold the fish out like a sail on a mast. The stake was pounded into the ground near the coals, leaning slightly over the smoke. The salmon was baked until cooked through but still moist, and sometimes brushed with seal oil to enhance its succulence.

If you've got a backyard, you probably won't want to tear it up to recreate a Northwest Indian salmon barbecue, and the good news is that you don't have to. You can get the same mouthwatering succulence and subtle smoky flavor using a small, electric smoker and the recipe for Russ Wohlers' Hot Alder-Smoked Salmon (see facing page).

them in the smoker pan and place the pan in the bottom of the smoker. Wait for about 5 minutes to give them a chance to start smoking.

7. Place the salmon, skin side down, on a rack in the smoker, and smoke until it has achieved the consistency you desire. If the salmon is to be a main course, let it smoke for about 2 hours. For a firmer, rich salmon suitable as an appetizer, let it smoke for about 2 hours and 40 minutes. For a very firm salmon, let it smoke for 4 to 6 hours, checking occasionally. You will need to add a handful of wood chips every 1 to 1½ hours.

8. To serve as a main course, transfer the salmon from the smoker to a warmed dinner platter. Serve with boiled new potatoes and lightly dressed green salad.

Makes 4 servings

Barbecuing Tips

Mike Okoniewski has a couple of tips on how best to cook salmon. He says the fire should have burned relatively low—start it about 40 minutes ahead of time. Once the salmon is on the grill and has been cooking for about 3 minutes, check it. If the juices from the salmon and the marinade are bubbling merrily, the fire is perfect. If they are sizzling furiously, the fire is too hot, and you should carefully spray some water on the coals (making sure you don't cause ashes to fly onto the salmon—use a spray bottle with a very fine mist) or open the cover of the barbecue to cool the fire down. "It doesn't hurt the fish to cook it slowly, but you can ruin it if you cook it too fast," Mike says.

Barbecued Alaska Salmon

This recipe comes from Michael Okoniewski, processing supervisor at the Seafood Producer's Co-op in Sitka, Alaska. He started preparing salmon this way years ago when he lived in Chignik, a tiny town on the Alaska Peninsula, and, since he moved to Sitka four years ago, he's been the official chef at barbecues the co-op holds several times a year for fishermen and staff.

Mike prefers to use red king salmon that weigh more than 30 pounds, have been frozen at sea, or are less than four days old, reasonable preferences for someone in the Alaska seafood business. For those of us who rarely see salmon that large, a top-quality king salmon fillet works beautifully, and gives the best, moistest result, because of its high fat content. Try silver (coho) salmon if you can't find king, and adjust the cooking time accordingly.

The salmon cooks more evenly if you cut the fillet(s) crosswise in half. You can remove the thin end of the fillet after about 12 minutes, when it will be cooked, and leave the thicker part of the fillet on the fire to continue cooking.

Try a lightly chilled American Gewürztraminer or a light, red Graves from Bordeaux with this dish.

Fish:

1 fillet (2 to 3 pounds) king, silver, or sockeye salmon
¼ teaspoon salt
1 clove garlic, minced
⅓ cup minced onion

Marinade:

⅛ teaspoon cayenne pepper

1 teaspoon Tabasco sauce

1 teaspoon Worcestershire sauce

1 tablespoon dry white wine

1 teaspoon fresh lemon juice

2 tablespoons soy sauce

½ teaspoon sugar

1 teaspoon sake

1 teaspoon minced fresh ginger

2 cloves garlic, minced

Sauce:

4 tablespoons unsalted butter

⅓ cup packed brown sugar

2 teaspoons fresh lemon juice

2 teaspoons dry white wine

1 large clove garlic, minced

¼ teaspoon Tabasco sauce

Pinch of cayenne pepper

⅓ cup minced onion

Salt

Garnishes:

2 lemons, very thinly sliced

1 large white onion, very thinly sliced

1. Rinse the salmon fillet and pat dry. Remove as many bones as possible using a strawberry huller, fish bone puller, or needle-nose pliers.

2. Sprinkle the salmon very lightly with the salt. Rub the garlic into the salmon; sprinkle on the minced onion, pressing it gently into the fish. Place the salmon on a large, non-aluminum dish or platter that can go into the refrigerator. (If you don't have a dish or platter large enough to hold the whole fillet, cut the fillet crosswise in half and place it on 2 dishes or platters.)

3. Mix together the marinade ingredients in a small bowl. Pour over the salmon. Cover with aluminum foil and refrigerate for 3 hours.

4. Make the sauce: Melt the butter in a small skillet or saucepan over medium heat. Stir in the brown sugar. Add all of the remaining sauce ingredients and cook until well mixed. Season with salt and set aside in a warm place, so the sauce will stay liquid and the butter in the sauce won't harden.

5. Prepare a good-size fire in a barbecue using mesquite charcoal, or use regular charcoal and soak 1 cup of mesquite or fruit wood chips in water to cover for at least 20 minutes.

6. The fire is ready when the coals glow red and are covered with ash. (If you have not used mesquite charcoal, squeeze the water from the wood chips, and place the chips around the edge of the fire, so they smoke lightly.) Thoroughly oil the grill using a paper towel dipped in vegetable oil. Set the grill in place. Place a piece of aluminum foil on the grill that is about 2 inches larger on all sides than the salmon. (The aluminum foil should not cover the entire grill. The smoke should be able to come up and around it.) Lay the salmon on the aluminum foil; pour any marinade left in the dish or platter over the salmon. Cover the grill, making sure the vents on the top and bottom of the barbecue are open. Cook for 5 minutes.

7. Uncover the barbecue and pour ¼ cup of the sauce over the salmon. Cover and cook for 5 minutes. Repeat the process, using the remaining sauce. Cook for 2 minutes.

8. Check the salmon. If the thinner end of the fillet is opaque through, or nearly so, remove from the fire. The thicker part of the fillet will still be uncooked in the middle.

Cover and cook for 3 minutes or until the salmon is opaque through.

9. Pick up the edges of the aluminum foil to remove the salmon from the grill. Transfer to a work surface. To serve the salmon, either cut individual pieces, removing the fish from the skin with a metal spatula or a knife blade, and place them on the center of warm plates, or transfer the entire fillet to a warm serving platter. Garnish the plates or the platter with the lemon and onion; serve immediately.

Makes about 6 servings

Lime- and Ginger-Grilled Salmon

*T*his is a wonderful way to prepare salmon for a crowd. The lime and ginger are perfect complements to the fish. The butter adds a touch of moisture and protects the salmon from the smoke. You must either use mesquite charcoal to build the fire, or place 1 cup of moistened, drained wood chips around the fire, so it smokes lightly just before you place the salmon on the grill. You don't want an overpowering flavor of smoke on the fish, just a hint.

Try this with a lightly chilled Pouilly Fumé, or a clean American Sauvignon Blanc. To prepare this salmon for two people, cut the ingredients by half.

1 salmon fillet (2 pounds)
½ teaspoon salt
¼ teaspoon freshly ground white pepper
¼ teaspoon freshly ground black pepper
2 tablespoons minced lime zest
2 tablespoons minced fresh ginger
1 teaspoon fresh lime juice
4 tablespoons unsalted butter, melted

1. Rinse the salmon fillet and dry. Cut crosswise into 4 equal pieces. Remove as many bones as possible using a strawberry huller, bone puller or needle-nosed pliers.

2. Prepare a good-size fire in a barbecue. Let it burn until the coals glow red and are slightly covered with ash.

3. Season the salmon with the salt and pepper. Sprinkle on the lime zest and the ginger and press them gently into the salmon. Thoroughly oil the grill using a paper towel dipped in vegetable oil. Set the grill about 3 inches above the coals.

4. Place the pieces of salmon on a sheet of aluminum foil that is about 2 inches larger than the salmon. The foil shouldn't cover the grill; you want the smoke to flow up and around it. Place on the grill. Stir the lime juice into the melted butter; pour half of it over the salmon, moistening the pieces all over. Cover the barbecue, making sure the vents in the top and bottom are open. Cook for 8 minutes. Pour the remaining lime butter over the salmon. Cover and cook until the salmon is just opaque through, about 7 minutes. Check for doneness by making a cut in the thickest part of the salmon and pulling back the meat.

5. Transfer the salmon on the aluminum foil to a work surface. To serve, remove from the skin by sliding a sharp knife or a spatula between the fish and the skin.

Makes 4 servings

Robert Del Grande's Broiled Salmon

I love the flavors of this dish, and Chef Del Grande of Cafe Annie in Houston is a master at combining the sun-splashed ingredients of Texas with seafood. He jumps regional boundaries here by using rich salmon, playing it with smoky tomatoes and garlic. This dish recreates the flavors of outdoor grilling for those who don't have access to a barbecue. Try a lightly chilled red such as Côtes du Rhône Villages, a light Zinfandel, a Bouzy Rouge, Chinon, or Bourgeuil.

Roasted Tomato Sauce:

8 ripe plum tomatoes (about 2 pounds), stem ends
  removed
1 shallot, peeled
2 cloves garlic
1 jalapeño chile, stemmed
¼ cup chicken stock
1 cup loosely packed cilantro leaves
2 tablespoons unsalted butter
Salt

Garlic Cream:

8 large cloves garlic, unpeeled
2 tablespoons extra-virgin olive oil
⅓ cup sour cream
½ cup heavy or whipping cream
½ teaspoon fresh lime juice
Salt and freshly ground black pepper

Fish:

4 salmon fillets (about 7 ounces each)
Juice of 1 lime
Cilantro leaves, for garnish

1. Preheat the oven to 350°F.

2. Make the Roasted Tomato Sauce: Place the tomatoes, shallot, garlic cloves, and jalapeño in a small roasting pan. Roast them until the tomatoes are blistered and the shallot is soft, about 40 minutes.

3. Transfer the vegetables to the bowl of a food processor; purée. Scrape the purée into a medium-size, non-aluminum saucepan. Whisk in the chicken stock. Bring the mixture to a boil over medium-high heat. Reduce the heat to low. Finely chop the cilantro. Add it to the sauce with the butter. Season with salt to taste. Keep warm over very low heat.

4. Make the Garlic Cream: Place the garlic cloves and olive oil in a small roasting pan. Cover with foil and roast until the garlic is very soft, 15 to 20 minutes. Check occasionally; do not let the garlic brown.

5. Remove the garlic cloves from the oven; preheat the broiler.

6. Peel the garlic. Crush the cloves in a mortar or in a small bowl using the back of a spoon. In a medium-size bowl, combine the crushed garlic, the olive oil in which it cooked, sour cream, heavy cream, and lime juice; mix well until smooth and thin enough to pour. Thin with 1 to 2 tablespoons of water if necessary. Season with salt and pepper to taste.

7. Place the salmon on a broiling pan. Drizzle with the lime juice. Broil until the fillets are opaque in the center and slightly firm, 3 to 4 minutes on each side.

8. To serve, divide the roast tomato sauce among 4 warm dinner plates. Top each portion with a salmon fillet; drizzle the garlic cream over the salmon. Garnish with cilantro leaves. Serve immediately.

Makes 4 servings

Chicago Wholesale Fish Markets

The offices of the Chicago Fish House look as if they belong to a posh interior designer more than to a purveyor of seafood. Decorated in cool blues and greens, there's a quiet reception area, a luxurious conference room, and a series of neat, efficient offices each with it's own computer terminal, where hushed business is transacted.

Just a few steps down the hallway is another world, what looks like a city newsroom. At least 20 salespeople are either on the phone, dashing through double doors with slips of paper in their hands, or yelling to each other over the short dividing walls that form separate cubicles. This is the nerve center of the Fish House, where hundreds of species of seafood from all over the world are bought and sold.

"Nobody here just sits in their office," said Bob Rubin, Director of Research and Development. "We're all in and out of the cooler eight to ten times a day, keeping up on what's fresh."

The Chicago Fish House is something of a phenomenon in the seafood industry. Started in 1930 by three brothers, Theodor, Carl, and Harry Mitsakopoulos, it has grown to be the largest wholesale purveyor of fish in the Midwest, and one of the three largest in the country.

Still owned and operated by the Mit-sakopoulos family, it has succeeded where other fish wholesalers have failed. "We're here 18 hours a day," Jack Mitsakopoulos said as he passed hurriedly by the conference room. "You succeed in this business by having someone to open the door at midnight, when the fish truck arrives. And by not eating lunch for 40 years." The real key, he claims, is making sure fish is delivered on time, in top-quality condition. This is done in the company's 20 trucks, which are in constant contact with the main office by radio phone.

Just behind the sales office is a cold room where at least a dozen men work in plastic aprons and rubber boots filleting, steaking, and skinning tuna, catfish, whitefish, and red snapper among other fish. They service hundreds of accounts throughout the country, processing fish to order down to plucking bones from whitefish fillets.

The company handles about 150 tons of fresh fish per week, from all over the world. They have a rotating stock of five million pounds of frozen fish, all neatly stacked in icy warehouses. Some of the seafood goes right into the Chicago Fish House retail store next door. "It's our only retail store, and it's really there so we can bring our clients in and train them to handle fish," Bob Rubin said.

The success of the Chicago Fish

House is due to the quality of their sea-food and service, and also to a progressive attitude that had them hire Bob, who has worked in the seafood industry since 1957 and who knows it inside and out, and Nancy Abrams, a consultant who works with Chicago Fish House accounts on everything from menu planning and nutrition to seafood handling and staff training.

PICK FISHERIES

Not far from the Chicago Fish House is another quality wholesale fish purveyor who is as different from them as night is from day. At Pick Fisheries, established more than 65 years ago in the old Fulton Street fish market area of Chicago, tables filled with boxes of iced fish sit on a loading dock. Retail customers slither around on the wet dock, poking at fish, lifting conch to test how meaty they are, sniffing to make sure everything is up to their standards. It's like an old-time fish market and conditions are far from elegant, but they, and the seafood, obviously have appeal.

One morning an international clientele was doing a brisk business, communicating in a variety of languages with the staff. Meanwhile, an aproned crew rushed around filling orders and hefting boxes into a fleet of refrigerated trucks that would soon be released into Chicago traffic. Owner Robert Kornblatt surveyed the business from a central office on the loading dock. It was 8:30 A.M. and he'd been there since long before dawn.

PENTECOST FISH

Pentecost Fish is another midwest original. It was established in 1862, and owner Robert Santoro claims it is the oldest full-line fish house in Chicago, and one of the first seafood distributors in the Midwest.

It has been in the Santoro family since the early fifties, and Mr. Santoro has watched it grow from an antiquated city loft building where they loaded trucks at the curb and did the bookkeeping by hand, to its current, fully computerized, 11,000 square foot facility that sells more than 35,000 pounds of fresh and frozen seafood daily, primarily to Midwest retail chains and restaurants.

Pentecost Fish built their new facility in 1983. "We ran a relatively small business for a long time," Mr. Santoro said. "But the future of this business is so good that if you remain status quo people will pass you by. We decided to expand in 1980 and we've continued expanding ever since."

Twenty-five employees do everything at Pentecost from operating computers, to cutting fish into portions, to holding seminars for dieticians about proper use and handling of seafood. They handle about six hundred different items, from local Great Lakes whitefish to Australian lobster tails. The key to their success? "We have good competition, which is the best thing that ever happened to the fish business."

Sandy Shea's Stuffed Salmon

Sandy Shea owns Chez Shea, an elegant, restaurant upstairs from Seattle's Pike Place Market, with an astounding view of Elliott Bay and the San Juan Islands beyond. Sandy has impeccable taste and style, and she offers a menu replete with fresh, inspired ideas.

Sandy prepares this recipe in summer, for parties on the deck of her house. The cooking time and amount of liquid the wild rice absorbs will depend on its quality—choose the finest, longest grain wild rice you can, preferably that from St. Maries, Idaho. Also, the cooking time for the salmon will vary depending on what species you have. Sockeye generally cooks more quickly than silver salmon. This is a truly great dish—try a great white wine along with it, such as a chilled Puligny-Montrachet or another great white Burgundy.

1 cup wild rice

3 cups Fish Stock (see Index)

*1 fresh or fresh-frozen sockeye or silver (coho) salmon
    (5 pounds), cleaned, with head removed*

1 teaspoon mild vegetable oil, such as safflower

Salt and freshly ground black pepper

3 tablespoons unsalted butter

2 shallots, diced

2 cloves garlic, diced

¼ cup hazelnuts, coarsely chopped

*8 ounces chanterelle mushrooms, brushed clean and
    very coarsely chopped*

1 tablespoon minced fresh ginger

2 cups fresh or frozen blackberries

1 large bunch fresh tarragon or flat-leaf parsley

1. Bring the wild rice and fish stock to a boil in a medium saucepan over medium-high heat. Reduce the heat to medium, cover, and cook until softened and about two-thirds of the kernels split, about 45 minutes. Some unabsorbed fish stock may remain. Remove from the heat.

2. Rinse the salmon and pat dry. Lightly rub the oil all over the salmon. Sprinkle the cavity generously with salt and pepper.

3. Prepare a large fire in a barbecue.

4. Melt the butter in a large skillet over medium-high heat. Add the shallots and the garlic and sauté just until they begin to turn translucent, 2 to 3 minutes. Add the hazelnuts; sauté for 1 minute. Add the chanterelles and stir to thoroughly coat with butter. Cook, stirring constantly, until they begin to soften, 4 to 5 minutes. Stir in the wild rice and any fish stock that wasn't absorbed. Add the ginger, mix well, and remove from the heat. Gently fold in the blackberries. Season the stuffing with salt and pepper to taste.

5. Place the tarragon sprigs on a piece of heavy-duty aluminum foil large enough to hold and fold up around the salmon. Lay the salmon on the sprigs, then spoon as much stuffing as you can into the belly cavity of the salmon. Let some of the stuffing spill out onto the aluminum foil. (There may be leftover stuffing, which is fine. Place in an ovenproof serving dish and keep warm in a very low oven.) Bring the foil up and fold loosely around the salmon, pinching it together at the ends so it encloses the tail and the collar of the fish, but leaving it open at the top over the body of the fish.

6. Thoroughly oil the grill using a paper towel dipped in vegetable oil. When the coals are still fiery red with some flames licking at them, spread them out in a single layer and place the grill about 3 inches above them. Place the salmon in the aluminum foil on the grill, making sure the foil is open wide to expose the fish to the smoke. Close the barbecue, leaving the top and bottom vents open. Cook the salmon until opaque through, 30 to 35 minutes.

7. Remove the salmon in the foil from the barbecue. Using 2 long, metal spatulas to support the weight of the fish, remove the fish from the foil and transfer to a long serving platter. Spoon any stuffing on the platter as well. Serve the remaining stuffing on the side. Serve immediately.

Makes 8 to 10 servings

Grilled Marinated Tuna on a Bed of Kale

Kale and tuna have similar personalities— they're both assertive yet subtle, and they go extremely well together. This is a great early fall dish—serve it after the first frost, when the sugar in kale is again coursing through its veins. If it's too cold for the barbecue, it is easy to prepare the tuna in the broiler. Try a chilled herbal, clean and crisp Oregon or Washington Sauvignon Blanc, such as an Arbor Crest or a Shafer 1986.

Marinade and Fish:

5 tablespoons extra-virgin olive oil
2 tablespoons white wine vinegar
¼ teaspoon dried hot pepper flakes
¼ teaspoon salt
¼ cup fresh oregano leaves, or 2 teaspoons dried
4 cloves garlic, germ removed, finely minced
4 tuna steaks (6 ounces each)

Kale:

2 pounds kale, ribs and stems removed
2 tablespoons extra-virgin olive oil
1 medium-size red onion, coarsely chopped
½ teaspoon sugar
¼ teaspoon freshly ground black pepper
Salt
6 chive flowers, for garnish

1. In a small bowl combine all of the marinade ingredients; mix well. Place the tuna steaks in a single layer in a porcelain, enameled, or glass dish. Pour the marinade over the tuna, turn the steaks to coat well, and refrigerate for 1 hour.

2. Prepare charcoal for a medium fire in a barbecue, or preheat the broiler.

3. Blanch the kale leaves in a large pot filled with boiling, salted water, until they turn a brighter green and have softened slightly, about 3 minutes. Drain well. Gently squeeze out the excess liquid with your hands; pat dry. Cut the kale into very narrow, even strips; reserve.

4. Heat the oil in a large non-aluminum skillet over medium heat. Add the onion and sauté just until it begins to turn translucent, about 5 minutes. Add the kale, sugar, pepper, and ¼ cup water. Cook, stirring, until the kale has softened, about 8 minutes.

5. Drain the tuna steaks and pour the marinade into the kale. Cook over low heat, stirring occasionally, until the kale is quite limp. Season with salt to taste. Keep warm.

6. Thoroughly oil the grill using a paper towel dipped in vegetable oil. When the coals glow red and are covered with ash, place the tuna steaks on the grill (or under the broiler). Cook until they begin to turn opaque, but have a very thin, pinkish line in the very center, no longer than 3 minutes per side if the steaks are ½ inch thick,

slightly longer if they are thicker.

7. To serve, divide the kale among 4 warm dinner plates, flattening it out a bit. Place a tuna steak on top of each portion. Separate the petals of the chive flowers and sprinkle them over the tuna. Serve immediately.

Makes 4 servings

Greek-Style Rosemary-Grilled Swordfish Kebabs

This recipe was inspired by a visit to Tarpon Springs, Florida, a small Greek community that used to be famous for its natural sponge industry. Innovative sponge gathering techniques were introduced to Tarpon Springs at the turn of the century by an immigrant from Greece, where sponge gathering is traditional. His success attracted others from Greece, and they created a Greek community at Tarpon Springs.

The sponge industry has declined, and Tarpon Springs has become a tourist attraction and a fishing port. The Greek atmosphere is strong, and the people I talked with there were full of Greek recipes, similar to this one. It reminds me of the clear, blue water off Tarpon Springs, the lush greenery that borders the shore, and all the Greek restaurants and pastry shops that send wonderful aromas into the air.

If you can't find yellow zucchini, go ahead and use only green. Serve this with Garlic Fried Potatoes (see Index) and a rich, full-flavored Cabernet Sauvignon.

1¼ pounds swordfish steak, cut about 1 inch thick
½ cup olive oil
1 cup loosely packed, coarsely chopped oregano leaves, or 3 tablespoons dried
3 tablespoons rosemary leaves, crushed, or 1 teaspoon dried
Grated zest of 1 orange
Coarsely ground black pepper
3 small green zucchini, trimmed and cut into 1-inch rounds
2 small yellow zucchini, trimmed and cut into 1-inch rounds
Salt

1. Rinse the swordfish steak and pat dry. Cut into 1-inch cubes.

2. Place the cubes in a medium-size bowl and pour the olive oil over them. Add the oregano, rosemary, orange zest, and black pepper; toss to mix well. Cover and refrigerate for 24 hours, tossing occasionally.

3. Prepare a good-size charcoal fire in a barbecue. Thoroughly oil the grill using a paper towel dipped in vegetable oil. Set the grill in place.

4. Thread the swordfish cubes on skewers, interspersing them with alternating pieces of green and yellow zucchini. Pour any remaining marinade over the kebabs; sprinkle all over with salt. Drain any excess marinade off the kebabs right before you put them on the grill, so the oil doesn't drip on the coals and cause them to flame up. (This will happen a bit anyway, which is fine, but you don't want to incinerate the kebabs.) When the flames are still licking at the coals, place the kebabs on the grill. Grill, turning every 2 minutes, until the fish is opaque through and the zucchini are dark golden and crisp, 8 minutes. Serve immediately.

Makes 4 servings

Grilled Smoky Trout

*T*his is a wonderful, flavorful way to grill trout so they emerge crisp and golden. The aromatic scallion and thyme lend a subtle, alluring flavor to the trout from the inside, the sweet fruit wood bathes the trout from the outside. Try this with a chilled dry white wine such as Pinot Grigio.

1 cup fruit wood chips, for grilling
4 rainbow trout (about 1 pound each), cleaned with
  heads on
Salt and freshly ground black pepper
8 small sprigs fresh thyme or ½ teaspoon dried
4 scallions, trimmed
6 tablespoons extra-virgin olive oil
½ cup loosely packed flat-leaf parsley leaves, finely
  minced

1. Prepare a fire in a barbecue and let it burn until the coals glow red and are covered with ash, about 20 minutes. Soak the wood chips in water to cover for at least 20 minutes.

2. Rinse the trout and pat dry. Generously season the cavity of each trout with salt and pepper. Place 2 thyme sprigs inside each trout (or sprinkle the cavities with the dried thyme).

3. Cut the scallions lengthwise in quarters; trim to the exact length of each trout's cavity. Place on top of the thyme sprigs. Close the cavities, securing each with a small metal skewer.

4. Drain the wood chips; sprinkle evenly over the coals. Thoroughly oil the grill using a paper towel dipped in vegetable oil. Set the grill in place. Cover the barbecue for 2 to 3 minutes to let the smoke build up inside, making sure to leave the vents on the bottom and top open.

5. Rub the trout on each side with half of the olive oil. Place on the grill, and cook until opaque through but not firm or dry, 4 to 5 minutes per side. Drizzle the trout with the remaining 3 tablespoons olive oil. Sprinkle with parsley; serve immediately.

Makes 4 servings

King Mackerel with Skorthalia and Tzaziki

*I*f you need a hit of summer, whatever the season, try on this recipe for size. With the flavor of Greek oregano, a touch of hearty skorthalia (potato and garlic purée), and cool, yogurt and cucumber tzaziki—you can't go wrong. If you can't get king mackerel, try Hawaiian *ono* (or wahoo). Swordfish or blacktip shark would also work well here. Try this with a Cava Boutari.

4 pieces king mackerel or ono fillets (4 to 6 ounces
  each), about 1 inch thick
4 teaspoons extra-virgin olive oil
Salt and coarsely ground black pepper
16 short tender sprigs fresh oregano, rinsed and patted
  dry, or 1 teaspoon dried oregano
Skorthalia (see Index)
Tzaziki (see Index)
Additional fresh oregano, for garnish

1. Rinse the fish and pat dry.

2. Prepare a medium-size charcoal fire in a barbecue.

3. Place each piece of fish on a 12-inch

square piece of aluminum foil. Drizzle each piece with 1 teaspoon of the oil; season generously with salt and pepper. Place 4 sprigs of oregano across each piece. Bring the aluminum foil up and fold loosely around each piece of fish, leaving the foil open at the top. (This will allow the fish to bake and grill at the same time, keeping it very moist, but allowing a hint of wood smoke flavor.)

4. When the coals glow red and are covered with ash, thoroughly oil the grill using a paper towel dipped in vegetable oil. Set the grill in place and put the fish on it. Cover and cook until the fish is just opaque through, about 13 minutes.

5. Slip a sharp knife or a metal spatula between the meat and the skin of the fish and transfer each piece of fish to the center of a warmed dinner plate.

6. Place about ¼ cup of skorthalia on and to the side of each piece of fish, over the sprigs of oregano, so it drapes over one side of the fish. Garnish with the additional oregano. Serve immediately accompanied by a bowl of tzaziki.

Makes 4 servings

Sturgeon Grilled in Corn Husks

Some time ago as Karen Malody, a friend, restaurant consultant, and wonderful cook, was leaving our home after dinner, she rolled down the window of the car and said, "Have you ever cooked any fish in corn-husks?" then sped off into the night. I hadn't, and it intrigued me. The following day I saw some Columbia River sturgeon at the mar-

ket, its meat a gorgeous translucent pink, and I couldn't resist. I picked up some packaged corn husks—they're much easier to use than fresh ones—several ears of fresh Yakima Valley corn (possibly the best in creation!), and peppers from the Pike Place Market, and had a go. This is the dish I came up with, and it's wonderfully good and surprisingly quick and easy to prepare. Each packet has fresh corn kernels inside, and I like to serve corn on the cob alongside, since it seems no one—including myself—can ever get enough during the season. Try this with a clean, appley Northwest Chardonnay.

4 sturgeon steaks (8 ounces each), skin removed
Salt and freshly ground pepper
½ package (4 ounces) dried corn husks
1 large jalapeño chile
1 large green bell pepper, cored, seeded, and diced the size of corn kernels
1 large red bell pepper, cored, seeded, and diced the size of corn kernels
2 cups fresh corn kernels
1 large yellow or green pattypan squash or zucchini, trimmed and cut into 8 slices
4 medium cloves garlic, finely minced
¼ cup loosely packed fresh tarragon leaves, coarsely chopped, or 2 teaspoons dried
8 teaspoons crème fraiche (see Index) or sour cream
8 lengths (each 18 inches) of household string, soaked in water
16 lengths (each 16 inches) of household string, soaked in water

1. Preheat the broiler. Prepare a large charcoal fire in a barbecue.

2. Rinse the sturgeon steaks and pat dry. Cut in half, crosswise, to make 8 small sturgeon steaks. Season on both sides with salt and pepper.

3. Run water over the corn husks just until softened slightly and pliable, about 30 seconds.

4. Broil the jalapeño until blackened on all sides. Remove from the heat, cover with a towel or foil. When cool enough to handle, remove skin, stem, and seeds. (You may want to wear rubber gloves to protect your hands from the chile's oil which can burn eye and mouth tissue if you rub your hands there by mistake.) Finely mince the chile; reserve.

5. Combine the bell peppers and corn kernels in a medium-size bowl; mix to distribute.

6. To assemble the sturgeon in corn husks: Smooth out 2 of the largest corn husks, about 6 inches wide at the wide end. Place one husk flat on a work surface; place the other over it, placing the narrow end of the top husk about 2 inches from the edge of the wide end on the lower husk, to make a "square" of cornhusk.

7. Have all of the ingredients close at hand, in the order they will be used. First, arrange one-eighth of the squash slices in the center of the cornhusk "square." Sprinkle with salt and pepper. Top with one-eighth of the garlic and one-eighth of the tarragon. Place 1 piece of sturgeon on top. Sprinkle one-eighth of the jalapeño over the fish. Top with ½ cup of the pepper-corn mixture and 1 teaspoon *crème fraîche*.

8. Lay a 3- to 4-inch piece of cornhusk over the mixture. Slip 2 of the 16-inch pieces of string under the corn husks, each about 2 inches from an end. Slip an 18-inch piece of string under the length of the corn husks. Bring the 2 shorter pieces of string around the sides of the corn husks, overlapping the edges of the top cornhusks. Securely tie the strings. Fold the top and bottom ends of the cornhusks together as though you were wrapping a package, bringing the ends up and over the packet. Tie with the longer piece of string. You will have a tidy packet, with none of the fish or vegetable mixture showing.

9. Repeat with the remaining ingredients to make 8 packets.

10. When the coals glow red and are dusted with ash, thoroughly oil the grill using a paper towel dipped in vegetable oil. Set the grill in place about 3 inches above the coals.

11. Place the packets on the grill, close, leaving the vents open, and cook for 18 minutes.

12. To serve, either place a packet on each of 8 warm dinner plates and cut the strings before serving, or stack the packets on a serving platter, make sure each guest has a sharp knife, and let them open the packets themselves. Serve with corn on the cob.

Makes 8 servings

Grilled Barracuda with Red Pepper and Sesame Sauce

The Red Pepper and Toasted Sesame Sauce on this barracuda is a specialty from Hawaii. The sauce is gutsy and slightly smoky from the pulverized sesame seeds, the barracuda is white, moist, and meaty—some think its delicate flavor resembles salmon. Try this with a French Chablis or a substantial California Chardonnay with some age.

1 piece (2 pounds) barracuda, bone-in, or 1 salmon
    fillet (2 pounds)
2 teaspoons mild vegetable oil
Salt and freshly ground black pepper
Hawaiian Red Pepper and Toasted Sesame Sauce (see
    Index)

1. Prepare charcoal for a fire in a barbe-cue. Thoroughly oil the grill using a paper towel and vegetable oil. When the flames subside, place the grill about 3 inches above the coals.

2. Rub the barracuda all over with the oil. Season inside and out with salt and pepper.

3. When the coals glow red and are lightly covered with ash, place the barracuda on the grill. Cover, leaving the top and bottom vents open; cook until the barracuda is nearly opaque on the underside, about 8 minutes. Carefully turn the barracuda, cover, and continue cooking until opaque through, about 8 minutes. (If you are using salmon, grill it skin side down only, 10 to 12 minutes.) Look at the fish occasionally to check its progress; remove from the grill sooner, if necessary.

4. While the barracuda is cooking, heat the Hawaiian Red Pepper and Toasted Sesame Sauce over low heat; keep warm.

5. To serve, fillet the barracuda, placing 1 piece on each of 4 warm dinner plates. Spoon equal amounts of sauce over each serving. Garnish with the sesame seeds and the scallions (from the sauce recipe). Serve immediately.

Makes 4 generous servings

Grilled Marlin Brochettes with Marinated Eggplant

When I saw striped marlin in the market I knew immediately I wanted to pre-pare it, skewered with vegetables, on the grill, along with luscious Japanese eggplants. Marlin is very firm and usually quite lean, so marinating is essential. Also, cooking the brochettes at the edge of the fire assures that the marlin will stay tender and won't dry out, as does brushing the brochettes frequently with the marinade. Try this with a rousing Côtes du Ventoux, a Côtes du Rhône, or a light Zinfandel. If you can't find marlin, use swordfish or shark.

¾ cup olive oil
1 jalapeño chile, trimmed, with seeds, and minced
¾ cup loosely packed cilantro leaves, coarsely
    chopped
1 teaspoon coriander seed, crushed
12 ounces striped marlin, swordfish, or shark steaks,
    rinsed, patted dry, and cut into 1-inch cubes
8 small Japanese eggplants
4 small onions, peeled
2 red bell peppers, cored, seeded, and cut into 1-inch
    squares
2 green bell peppers, cored, seeded, and cut into 1-inch
    squares
12 small cherry tomatoes, stemmed

1. Combine ½ cup of the olive oil, the jalapeño, cilantro, and coriander seed in a medium-size bowl. Add the cubed fish and toss. Marinate in the refrigerator for 2 hours.

2. Place the eggplants in a baking dish;

pour the remaining ¼ cup olive oil over. Marinate at room temperature for at least 1 hour.

3. About 25 minutes before you plan to serve, prepare charcoal for a good-size fire in a barbecue. Thoroughly oil the grill with a paper towel dipped in vegetable oil. When the coals glow red and are lightly covered with ash, set the grill in place.

4. Precook the onions in salted boiling water until crisp-tender, about 5 minutes. Drain well, and halve vertically.

5. Using 4 long metal skewers, thread bell peppers, onions, cherry tomatoes, and marlin, beginning and ending with squares of bell pepper. Make sure to skewer the onions horizontally so the layers don't fall off.

6. Arrange the eggplants in the center of the grill, and cook, turning, until completely softened, about 10 minutes. Brush the brochettes liberally with the remaining marinade. Arrange the skewers toward the outside of the grill; cook, turning frequently and brushing them lightly with oil, just until the marlin is opaque through and the vegetables are cooked, about 8 minutes.

7. Serve the brochettes with the eggplants arranged alongside.

Makes 4 servings

Blue Marlin with Mango Salad

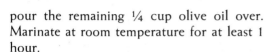

*T*his dish is inspired by a combination of cultures found on the Hawaiian Islands. The Koreans make a fruit and vegetable salad called *Namul*, which is seasoned with sesame oil, garlic, and vinegar. A typical Hawaiian condiment is mango chutney, which tastes like a sweet and sour jam. The sauce here is a combination of the two, and it is a perfect complement to the lean, meaty texture of grilled blue marlin. If you can't find marlin, substitute swordfish. Try this with a dry White Zinfandel.

3 tablespoons extra-virgin olive oil
4 marlin or swordfish steaks (5 to 6 ounces each)
2 large ripe mangos, peeled and pitted
2 scallions, trimmed, the white bulbs and light green stems cut into thin rounds
Grated zest of 1 lime
2 tablespoons fresh lime juice
1 teaspoon minced fresh ginger
1 jalapeño chile, seeded and minced
2 cloves garlic, minced
Salt to taste

1. Place the olive oil in a flat dish. Add the fish steaks and turn to coat with the oil. Refrigerate for 1 hour, turning once.

2. Cut the mangos into ¼-inch dice and place them in a medium-size bowl. Add all of the remaining ingredients and stir. Refrigerate for 1 hour.

3. Prepare charcoal for a medium-size fire in a barbecue.

4. When the coals glow red and are covered with ash, thoroughly oil the grill using a paper towel dipped in vegetable oil. Set the grill in place. Place the marlin steaks on the grill. (If the fire is very hot, place the marlin steaks at the edge of the grill.) Cook, brushing lightly with any remaining olive oil, until the marlin is opaque throughout, about 5 minutes.

5. To serve, place the marlin steaks on 4 warm dinner plates; spoon the mango salad on top and alongside. Serve immediately.

Makes 4 servings

Sapelo Island Mullet

My husband Michael and I went to Sapelo Island, Georgia, to find what we'd heard described as the best smoked mullet in the world. We found that a boat ferried tourists across to the island several times a week, so we hopped on at the appointed time. We fell into conversation with Cornelia Bailey, who turned out to be tour director, and who said that, since we'd bought tickets, we were obliged to go on her guided tour with the rest of the tourists. Unfortunately smoked mullet and mullet smokers were not included in Cornelia's tour. It is, apparently, a local delicacy prepared by people at their homes, with very little available for sale.

I suppose it was the expression on my face and her natural friendliness that made her say, as we docked on Sapelo, "We'll work something out—just follow me."

Once on land she led us to a white station wagon where her husband, Julius (whom everyone calls Frank, but who seems to prefer Julius), awaited. She gave him orders: "Take these folks around the island. Tell 'em all there is, and find 'em someone smokin' mullet." We were set for the time of our lives. Julius took us on a grand tour, driving through the woods on this tiny island that is half bird sanctuary, half "community" to a population of 80 people who've lived there for generations. We drove around every house in the community, looking for the telltale wisp of smoke that would signal mullet on the fire. We found none. Julius was angry with himself, for he'd already smoked last night's catch and given most of it away. By that time we didn't care. He and Sapelo had us under their spell.

People on the island raise a few cows, catch and smoke a lot of mullet, work by day over on the mainland, and return to the paradise of Sapelo each night. Those who don't work on the mainland make their way weaving gorgeous broom grass baskets, grape vine wreaths, and lovely, grape vine baskets. Cornelia has many jobs in addition to that of being the island's official tour director. Among them is making folk dolls, an art she learned from her grandmother. Julius works for the University of Georgia, which has a research station on the sanctuary half of the island, housed in a wonderful old mansion originally built by J.P. Reynolds.

Our tour of the island was over, and Julius took us home and presented us with a foil-wrapped package as we left the house to catch the boat back to the mainland. Inside were two fat, smoked mullet that he'd saved for the family. "Don't y'all worry—I'll be catching some more tonight," he said, brushing off our refusal of his gift, and we left with light hearts, and some incredibly delicious smoked mullet.

Grilled Aweo-Weo with Garlic

I couldn't resist buying an aweo-weo the first time I saw one. It's a friendly looking little fish with round, limpid eyes that tastes like a cross between bluefin tuna and mackerel—in other words, fabulous. Aweo-weo are reef fish from Hawaiian waters, and they won't show up at fish markets frequently, because their numbers are relatively few. Brooks Takenaka, general manager of the United Fishing Agency Ltd. fish auction in Honolulu, says that when he was a student at the University of Hawaii, he used to fish for them and they weighed at least 2 or more pounds. "We'd put a line over the rocks with many hooks, all baited. We'd pull it up a few minutes later and there'd be an aweo-weo on each hook." Now they're smaller, but they're no less delicious.

Mackerel work well in this recipe. In fact, this recipe should really have been written for mackerel, which are much more common. But with the choice of naming a recipe after mackerel or aweo-weo, what would you do? Serve this simple dish with a full-bodied red wine, such as a Valpolicella.

4 aweo-weo or mackerel (about 1 pound each), cleaned
  with heads on
¼ cup plus 1 teaspoon virgin olive oil
Salt and freshly ground black pepper
12 cloves garlic, thinly sliced crosswise
1 large bunch flat-leaf parsley

1. Prepare charcoal for a good-size fire in a barbecue. Let it burn until the coals glow red and are covered with ash. Thoroughly oil the grill using a paper towel dipped in vegetable oil. Set the grill in place.

2. Lightly rub the aweo-weo all over with the 1 teaspoon oil. Sprinkle generously with salt and pepper inside and out. Place on the grill and cook until opaque through, 5 to 8 minutes per side.

3. While the aweo-weo are cooking, combine the remaining ¼ cup olive oil with the garlic in a small saucepan over medium heat. Cover and cook until the garlic is translucent and soft, about 15 minutes.

4. To serve, arrange the parsley on a large serving platter. Place the aweo-weo on the parsley. Pour the olive oil and garlic over the fish. Serve immediately.

Makes 4 servings

Georgia Hickory- or Apple-Smoked Mullet

T his recipe is based on the technique used by Julius Bailey of Sapelo Island, Georgia, who makes some of the finest smoked mullet found anywhere. We like a nice dry Spanish red wine with this.

(Sapelo Island is worth a detour, if you're in the area. Stop by the tourist office in Darien, Georgia, for information.)

4 mullet (9 ounces each), cleaned with head removed
⅔ cup kosher (coarse) salt
1 cup apple wood chips, for the fire
About 1 teaspoon mild vegetable oil

1. Rinse the mullet well inside and out. Trim off all of the black membrane from the stomach cavity.

2. Cut a mullet open down its full length, working toward the tail from the belly cut made to clean it. Gently press the mullet open. To remove the backbone and rib bones, use a very sharp knife (flexible if possible), and cut between the rib bones and the fish. You will be working toward the backbone. Cut right down to the backbone, keeping the knife close to the rib bones and being careful not to cut through the skin at the back. Repeat on the other side. Using a pair of kitchen shears, snip right along the backbone to remove it from the fish. This may leave a rough part of the backbone in the fish, but don't worry as you will be removing the fish from the skin and serving it in small pieces once it is cooked. Remove any pin bones with a strawberry huller, fish bone puller or needle-nose pliers. Trim any belly flaps without meat from the mullet, and trim the collar, so you have nice, butter-flied fillets. Butterfly the remaining fish.

3. Place the fillets in a non-aluminum baking dish and sprinkle with the salt, covering them in an even layer. Refrigerate for 30 minutes.

4. Prepare charcoal for a medium-size fire in a barbecue. Place the apple wood chips in a small bowl and add warm water to cover. Soak for at least 20 minutes. When the coals glow red and are half-covered with ash, squeeze most of the water from the wood chips and sprinkle them on the coals. Thoroughly oil the grill using a paper towel dipped in vegetable oil. Set the grill in place. Close the barbecue, leaving top and bottom vents open, for about 5 minutes, to allow the smoke to build up.

5. Remove the mullet from the refrigerator and rinse off all of the salt. Pat dry with paper towels. Rub with the oil, particularly on the skin side.

6. Place the mullet, skin side down, on the grill. Cover and cook until the fish is firm, 40 to 45 minutes. (You may leave it longer if you like rather dry smoked fish, or remove it sooner if you prefer fish with just a touch of smoke.)

7. When the mullet is cool enough to handle, remove the meat from the skin, keeping it in somewhat larger than bite-size pieces. Serve atop a green salad (see Index) or tossed into buttered fettuccine.

Makes 4 servings

Smoked Creole-Marinated Mullet

Mary Pelham, a Darien, Georgia, cook who spends her days nourishing students at Darien's Todd Grant Elementary School and her evenings and weekends working in the garden and cooking for her husband and family, says this recipe for mullet is one of their favorites. The gently spiced creole sauce is made in advance so the fish can marinate in it overnight. The sauce plays off the distinctive flavor of the mullet to make a soul satisfying dish. It can be served hot or cold, accompanied with a big green salad and a cool glass of beer. If you can't find mullet, try this dish with bluefish or mackerel. Reserve any leftover marinade for another use, for instance to spread on freshly made pizza dough. It freezes well and is nice to have on hand.

Serve the mullet with a Corbières or an Oregon blended Pinot Noir.

4 mullet fillets (4 ounces each)

4 ounces slab bacon, rind removed, cut into 1 x ½ x
   ¼ inch pieces

1 medium onion, finely chopped

1 large green bell pepper, cored, seeded, and finely
   chopped

3 celery ribs, finely chopped

2 pounds ripe tomatoes, cored and coarsely chopped,
   or 1 can (28 ounces) whole tomatoes

1 tablespoon Worcestershire sauce

¼ teaspoon hot paprika

1 cup hickory or fruit wood chips, for the fire

1. Remove any bones from the mullet fillets. Rinse the fish and pat dry. Refrigerate until ready to use.

2. Fry the bacon in a large saucepan over medium-high heat until golden and most of its fat is rendered. Remove the bacon and drain on paper towels.

3. Add the onion, bell pepper, and celery to the bacon fat; sauté until the onion is translucent, about 10 minutes. Stir in the tomatoes, Worcestershire sauce, and paprika. Reduce the heat to low. Cook until the sauce is a thick and chunky purée, about 1½ hours. Remove from the heat; set the creole sauce aside to cool.

4. The night before you plan to serve the mullet, rub the fillets all over with the creole sauce. Cover and refrigerate.

5. Prepare charcoal for a small fire in a barbecue. Place the wood chips in a bowl and add water to cover. Soak for at least 20 minutes.

6. When the coals have burned down, glow red and are covered with ash, squeeze the water from the wood chips and add to the fire. Thoroughly oil the grill using a paper towel dipped in vegetable oil. Set the grill in place. Close the barbecue for 3 to 4 minutes, to allow smoke to build up inside. Place the mullet fillets with the sauce covering them on the grill. Cover and cook until the mullet is opaque and somewhat firm, 8 to 10 minutes.

7. Transfer the mullet to a serving platter. Garnish with the reserved bacon. Serve either hot or at room temperature.

Makes 4 servings

The Petersburg Black Cod Special

Petersburg, Alaska, seems to be the home of black cod or sablefish. A great deal is caught there, and it usually goes right in the smoker to get a light sheath of alder smoke flavor. Then it is steamed and served with creamed peas and small, boiled potatoes.

I prefer black cod grilled. Grilling brings out the moistness, and the fish browns so beautifully that no one can resist it. Black cod is very forgiving—if you leave it on the grill a bit too long it doesn't matter—its high oil content keeps it moist and succulent. Try a nice, simple white wine alongside.

2 black cod steaks (12 ounces each), cut 1 inch thick
Salt

1 cup milk

1 bay leaf

1 pound small new potatoes, washed, with a strip of
   peel removed around the center of each potato

4½ tablespoons unsalted butter

Freshly ground black pepper

1 cup wood chips, preferably alder

1½ tablespoons all-purpose flour

2 cups small fresh or frozen peas

1. Rinse the cod steaks and pat dry. Sprinkle the steaks on one side with 1 tablespoon of salt. Place in a non-aluminum baking dish, and sprinkle them on the other side with another 1 tablespoon salt. Refrigerate for 30 minutes.

2. Meanwhile, scald the milk with the bay leaf in a small, heavy-bottomed saucepan over medium-high heat. Remove from the heat, cover, and let steep for 10 minutes. Discard the bay leaf.

3. Place the potatoes in a large, heavy-bottomed saucepan and add water to cover by 2 inches. Add 1 tablespoon salt, cover, and bring to a boil over high heat. Boil until the potatoes are soft through, but not mushy, 15 to 20 minutes. Drain and return to the pan. Add 2 tablespoons of the butter; swirl to coat the potatoes with butter. Season with salt and plenty of coarsely ground black pepper. Keep warm over very low heat or in a low oven.

4. Prepare charcoal for a small fire in a barbecue. Place the wood chips in a bowl and add water to cover. Soak for at least 20 minutes.

5. Remove the black cod steaks, rinse off the salt, and pat dry. Place the steaks on a wire rack or plate and let air-dry for about 15 minutes, to form a slight pellicle or skin on them.

6. Season the black cod steaks generously with pepper. When the coals glow red and are covered with ash, squeeze the water from the wood chips and add the chips to the fire. Set the grill about 3 inches above the coals. Place the fish on the grill. Cook, without turning, until opaque through, and the flakes have just begun to separate, 15 to 18 minutes. (The steaks are delicate and may break apart if turned.)

7. Meanwhile, to prepare the cream sauce, melt 1½ tablespoons of the butter in a small, heavy-bottomed saucepan over medium-high heat. Add the flour and cook, whisking constantly, until the mixture froths light yellow, about 4 minutes. Reduce the heat to medium, and slowly whisk in the milk. Whisk and cook the sauce until slightly thicker than heavy cream, about 4 minutes.

8. Melt the remaining 1 tablespoon butter in a small saucepan over medium heat. Stir in the fresh peas, and cook until they turn bright green, 1 to 2 minutes. Season lightly with salt and pepper. (If you are using frozen peas, thaw quickly in a medium-size saucepan over low heat, swirling the pan until they are bright green, about 1 minute. Drain the peas.) Stir the peas into the cream sauce; keep warm over very low heat.

9. To serve, cut the black cod steaks lengthwise in half. Place each half steak on one side of a warm dinner plate. Divide the creamed peas among the plates, placing them to the side of the black cod; do the same with the potatoes. Serve immediately.

Makes 4 servings

Grilled Bluefish

This simple preparation was suggested to me by caterer William Taylor, in Great Mills, Maryland. He says it's one of the best ways to prepare succulent bluefish, and I have to agree. Serve the bluefish with a small arugula salad (see Index)—the smoky flavor of the arugula is a wonderful complement to the smoky succulence of the bluefish. Try this with a lightly chilled, nice white Burgundy from 1979, 1981, or 1982, such as a Meursault or a Puligny-Montrachet.

1 cup mesquite, cherry, or hickory chips (optional; see
    step 1)
3 tablespoons unsalted butter
1 tablespoon fresh lemon juice
2 small scallions, trimmed, the white bulb and light
    green stems cut into thin rounds
1 pound thick bluefish fillet, cut into 4 equal pieces
1 teaspoon mild vegetable oil, such as safflower
Salt and freshly ground black pepper

1. Prepare charcoal for a medium-size fire in a barbecue, using mesquite charcoal if possible. If you don't have mesquite charcoal, use regular charcoal and soak 1 cup of mesquite, cherry, or hickory chips in water to cover for at least 20 minutes.

2. Melt the butter in a small saucepan over low heat. Add the lemon juice and scallions and keep warm over very low heat or on the barbecue grill cover while the fish is cooking.

3. Rub the bluefish all over with the oil. Season lightly with salt and pepper.

4. When the coals are glowing red and covered in ash, thoroughly oil the grill using a paper towel dipped in vegetable oil. (Wring out the wood chips, if you are using them, and scatter them over the coals.) Set the grill in place and let heat for 1 to 2 minutes. Place the bluefish, skin-side down, on the grill. Cover the barbecue, leaving top and bottom vents open. Cook until the bluefish is opaque through, about 8 minutes.

5. Transfer the fish to the center of 4 warm dinner plates. Spoon the lemon butter over the bluefish. Serve immediately, with an arugula salad on the side.

Makes 4 servings

Grilled Shrimp and Wild Green Salad

The dog days of summer always push us outdoors, where we set up the barbecue for seafood, meats, and vegetables, and base most of our meals around greens from the garden. A fisherman friend presented us with some fresh-frozen spot prawns, and they evolved into this boisterous salad, which calls for good friends and plenty of German Kabinett or an off-dry Alsatian Gewürztraminer.

Fire:

1 cup hickory, alder, or fruit wood chips

Marinade and Shrimp:

½ cup peanut oil
Juice of 1 lime
Grated zest of 2 limes
Grated zest of 1 orange
4 cloves garlic, coarsely chopped
1 teaspoon Sambal Odelek (Indonesian chili paste—
    available in most specialty shops)
Salt
1 pound medium (31 to 35 per pound) shrimp in their
    shells

Salad:

8 cups mixed salad greens such as red chicory, butter
    lettuce, escarole, red oakleaf lettuce, mâche,
    purslane, or arugula
Nasturtium flowers, for garnish
1 orange, peel and pith removed and sectioned, for
    garnish

1. Prepare the fire: Place the wood chips in a small bowl and add water to cover. Let the chips soak for at least 20 minutes. Prepare a medium-size fire in a barbecue.

2. Whisk together all of the marinade ingredients in a medium-size bowl.

3. Skewer the shrimp on 4 long, metal skewers. Baste them with some of the marinade.

4. When the coals glow red and are covered with ash, drain the wood chips and put them on the fire. Thoroughly oil the grill using a paper towel dipped in vegetable oil. Set the grill in place. Place the skewers on the grill. Grill the shrimp, turning frequently, until opaque through and curled into a loose curve, 5 to 8 minutes. The shrimp should be elastic, not firm or dry.

5. When the shrimp are cool enough to handle (almost immediately), remove shells. Place the shrimp in the marinade and toss to coat. Set aside to marinate for 45 to 60 minutes.

6. To serve, drain the shrimp, reserving the marinade. Toss the salad greens with the remaining marinade; arrange on a large platter. Top with the shrimp. Garnish the salad and platter with the flower blossoms and orange sections. Serve immediately.

Makes 4 large or 6 average servings

Sage-Grilled Marinated Sardines

*T*his classic Mediterranean combination speaks of summer evenings on a terrace, a cool glass of Sauvignon Blanc, and sage leaves fresh from the garden. If you can't find sardines, try this with mackerel.

1 pound sardines, cleaned
Salt and freshly ground black pepper
2 red bell peppers, cored, seeded, and cut into 2-inch-wide strips
2 large onions, cut into ½-inch slices
1½ cups loosely packed fresh sage leaves, ½ cup dried sage
½ cup olive oil

1. Rinse the sardines and pat dry. Season the stomach cavities with salt and pepper. Place the fish in a large, non-aluminum dish or pan. Arrange the peppers and onions alongside in a single layer.

2. Gently crush 1 cup of the sage leaves (¼ cup dried) and place them in a small bowl. Pour the olive oil over the leaves, mix, and pour over the sardines and vegetables. Cover and refrigerate for 1 hour.

3. Soak the remaining ½ cup sage leaves (¼ cup dried) in water to cover. Prepare charcoal for medium-size fire in a barbecue. Thoroughly oil the grill using a paper towel dipped in vegetable oil.

4. When the coals glow red and are covered with ash, set the grill in place. Place the strips of red pepper and onions on the grill. Cook until browned and softened, but not quite cooked through, 6 to 8 minutes. Push them to the outside edge of the grill to keep warm.

5. Squeeze the water from the sage leaves and sprinkle the leaves on the coals. Shake the oil from the sardines and place them on the grill. Cook until opaque through and crisp on the outside, about 3 minutes per side. Reserve the marinade.

6. Transfer the sardines to a large serving platter. Pour the reserved marinade over them. Arrange the vegetables alongside the sardines; serve immediately.

Makes 4 servings

7

IN THE OVEN

Just thinking about the Tuna with Peppercorns or the Sotterley Oyster Pye in this chapter gets my mouth watering. My thoughts turn to sharing a meal with friends and family, for the dishes in this chapter lend themselves to entertaining.

Many of the recipes can be assembled in advance, then the dish can be popped in the oven as guests arrive, or at the appropriate moment during the meal. You can keep your eye on it without being glued to the oven—check it once or twice, then pull it out just when it's cooked to perfection.

Some of the dishes can be prepared and cooked in advance as well, like the Salmon Piroghi Alaska, which is fabulous and created to be eaten at room temperature.

But don't just save these recipes for when guests come to dinner. They will delight you with their bright, delicious flavors anytime.

Wild Louisiana Catfish

*I*t was sultry and inky black at 5 A.M. when I pulled up to Big Plans Seafood, a processing plant in Des Allemands, Louisiana. I had a rendezvous to go catfishing with one of the best catfish fishermen in the area, a Cajun named Leon Fonseca.

I followed Leon, part-owner of Big Plans, to nearby Bayou Des Allemands, where we left our cars and clambered onto his 24-foot, aluminum-hulled boat. We meandered down the bayou in the dark, following Reno Fonseca, Leon's nephew, also a catfish fisherman.

Leon pointed out duck blinds and alligator traps as we traveled. The bayou took a turn, Leon opened the throttle, and we were suddenly flying along the bayou and out onto Lake Salvador, which teems with catfish in summer.

Leon knows the lake better than most of us know our neighborhoods. He whipped the boat right and left, seeing landmarks when all I saw was water, and he knew which among a small forest of spindly poles sticking out of the water were holding his nets poised just off the bottom of the lake.

It was barely dawn when we pulled up next to Reno. New Orleans, 25 miles distant, shimmered in the background. Reno was already hauling in a net full of small catfish. "Leon, he always know where to get the catfish," Reno said, as Leon ignored him. We watched Reno and his partner pile fish into the center of the boat, rinse them off, and cover them with burlap before we zoomed off.

On our way back to Big Plans we sidled up alongside Leon's sons' boat, out in the middle of the lake. They were pulling big black drums from gillnets, and we collected a boatful to deliver, then meandered back down Bayou Des Allemands. As we went, Leon pointed out small wax myrtle bushes that were stuck in the bayou bottom to act as traps for softshell crab, and a small alligator floating on the water's surface.

Back at Big Plans Seafood, the crew was processing catfish from the day before. They're washed, cleaned, and their tough skin is removed by machine. It's tricky working with the fish, most of which are prime and less than 11 inches long. "I had to learn how to do it," Bobbye Murry said as she ran the slithery fish against the machine's razor-sharp blade. It is so well regulated it actually cuts the close-fitting skin from the fish without taking the membrane that's just under the skin.

Most of the catfish are delivered to New Orleans, where they're considered a delicacy. The crew at Big Plans enjoys them too, and both Diana Fonseca, Leon's wife, who admits to learning the secrets of Cajun cooking from her husband, and Polly Folse whose husband, Alvin, is a partner in Big Plans with Leon, love to cook the catfish and bring delicacies into the processing plant often, for the crew to enjoy.

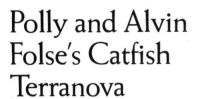

Polly and Alvin Folse's Catfish Terranova

*P*olly and Alvin Folse are owners with Leon and Diana Fonseca of Big Plans Seafood, in Des Allemands (pronounced 'daze allmen'), Louisiana. They showed me through their processing plant, introduced me to many of the people in Des Allemands who deal in seafood, and shared many a dish, and recipe, with me. This is one of their favorites, made with the incomparable catfish that are caught in nearby Lake Salvador (see Wild Louisiana Catfish in box). If you can't find wild catfish, try rainbow trout. This dish merits your favorite crisp, young, dry white wine, such as an Orvieto.

4 small catfish (about 6 ounces each), cleaned, with
*   heads on*
½ teaspoon cayenne pepper
½ teaspoon salt
8 tablespoons extra-virgin olive oil
1 small onion, finely chopped
6 cloves garlic, minced
¼ cup loosely packed fresh thyme leaves or
*   2 teaspoons dried*
½ cup loosely packed fresh oregano leaves or
*   1 tablespoon dried*
½ cup loosely packed flat-leaf parsley
2 tablespoons fresh bread crumbs
2 tablespoons freshly grated Parmesan cheese

1. Preheat the oven to 400°F.

2. Rinse the catfish and pat dry. Mix together the cayenne and salt in a small dish; season the catfish inside and out.

3. Oil a 12½ x 8½-inch glass or porcelain baking dish, using 1 tablespoon of the oil. Place the fish in the dish, leaving some room between them. Refrigerate them until the sauce is nearly ready.

4. Heat the remaining 7 tablespoons oil in a medium-size skillet over medium heat. Add the onion and sauté until it begins to turn translucent, about 3 minutes. Add the garlic and sauté until the onions are completely translucent, about 10 minutes. Finely mince the herbs. Add the herbs to the onion and garlic. Remove from the heat.

5. Pour the onion, garlic, and herb mixture evenly over the fish, scraping all of the oil over them. Bake in the oven for 8 minutes. Combine the bread crumbs and Parmesan. Sprinkle the fish with the mixture. Continue baking until the fish are opaque—check this by making a tiny slit right behind the head—no longer than an additional 15 minutes. Serve immediately.

Makes 4 servings

Crisp Parmesan Catfish

*T*he idea for this recipe comes from the Catfish Farmers of America, in Humphreys County, Mississippi. It is a wonderful way to cook just about any small fish, wild or farmed. The cheese is a nice contrast to the tender, mild meat. Oven frying is one of the simplest ways to prepare fish. Pop them in the oven, check once to see if they are done, and before you know it, the fish are crisp-crusted outside, succulent inside. If you are using catfish, they will be skinned when you buy them. If you are using trout, go ahead and follow the recipe—the skin is very edible, and very tasty. Try this with a crisp, young, American Chardonnay or a Mâcon-Villages.

1 tablespoon mild cooking oil, such as safflower
8 catfish or rainbow trout (about 8 ounces each), cleaned, with heads on
6 tablespoons freshly grated Parmesan cheese
2 tablespoons all-purpose flour
¼ teaspoon salt
¼ teaspoon freshly ground black pepper
½ teaspoon hot paprika
1 egg, beaten
2 tablespoons milk

1. Preheat the oven to 500°F. Coat the bottom of a 12½ x 8½-inch baking dish with the oil.

2. Rinse the fish and pat them dry.

3. Combine the cheese, flour, salt, pepper, and paprika in a shallow dish. In another shallow dish, beat the egg with the milk and mix well.

4. Using one hand, dip the fish in the egg and milk mixture, coating well. Transfer the fish to the cheese and flour mixture, picking the fish up with the other hand to dredge until well coated. The process is much easier and tidier if you use one hand to dip the fish in egg and the other to dip them in the dry ingredients.

5. Place the catfish, leaving space between them, in the prepared baking dish. Bake until opaque through, neither too soft nor overly tough, about 15 minutes. Check for doneness by making a tiny slit right behind the head of one of the fish. The meat should be opaque through. Serve immediately.

Makes 4 servings

Sole Paupiettes with Zucchini and Tomato Cream

This recipe is based on one from Chef Henry Barbour, a professor in the Boston University Hotel Administration Program, who teaches cooking to participants of the New England Fisheries Development Foundation's Fish School. Chef Barbour's class is definitely the most entertaining segment of a very entertaining three-day course, set up for retailers in the seafood trade.

When I attended the class he planned six dishes for about 20 students to prepare. We began cooking at about 5 P.M., and it was well after 10 P.M. when we sat down to taste our creations. Chef Barbour selected about 10 wines for us to blind taste with the meal and gave each of us a carefully thought out score sheet. Not only did we learn the basics of seafood preparation, but we learned a bit about wine pairings too. Needless to say, it was well after midnight before any of us were on our way home. Try this with a light, delicate, dry white wine such as a Sauvignon Blanc or a French Chardonnay, a Sancerre, or a Touraine.

2 sole fillets (8 ounces each)
1 large shallot, minced
1 medium-large zucchini, trimmed
½ cup loosely packed fresh basil leaves
Salt and freshly ground black pepper
2 tablespoons dry white wine
¾ cup Fish Stock (see Index)
¾ cup heavy or whipping cream
4 ounces plum tomatoes, peeled, seeded, and diced

1. Rinse the sole fillets and pat dry. Halve the fillets lengthwise, to make 4 thin strips.

2. Preheat the oven to 350°F.

3. Generously butter an 8½-inch square ovenproof baking dish. Sprinkle with the shallot.

4. Cut the zucchini lengthwise into paper-thin slices, so thin you can almost see through them. Finely mince the basil leaves.

5. Lay the strips of sole flat on a work surface. Lightly season with salt and pepper. Place as many slices of zucchini as needed to cover over each fillet, leaving about ½ inch at either end. (If you need to, piece together slices of zucchini to fit.) Lightly season the zucchini with salt and pepper. Reserving 1 tablespoon of basil, sprinkle with the remaining minced basil.

6. Carefully roll up the sole fillets, jelly roll fashion, to contain the zucchini and basil. Attach the ends with toothpicks.

7. Stack any remaining strips of zucchini on top of one another; cut crosswise into very thin slices. Sprinkle them over the shallot in the baking pan; lightly season with salt and pepper. Stand the sole paupiettes on top of the zucchini, with the spiral ends showing. Pour the wine around the sole. Cover the dish with aluminum foil. Bake until the sole is opaque through, 10 to 15 minutes.

8. While the sole is cooking, place the fish stock in a small, heavy-bottomed, non-aluminum saucepan. Reduce to ¼ cup over high heat. Add the cream and bring to a boil. Reduce the heat to medium-high and cook until the sauce reduces to about ½ cup, about 10 minutes. Add the reserved 1 tablespoon basil and the diced tomatoes. Season to taste. Cook until the tomatoes are heated through, 1 to 2 minutes.

9. To serve, remove the toothpick from each paupiette. Scoop it from the baking dish, taking one-fourth of the zucchini and the shallot with it; place in the center of a warm dinner plate. Spoon equal amounts of the tomato cream sauce over the paupiettes. Serve immediately.

Makes 4 servings

Jahnssen's Temptation

We had Swedish visitors in Seattle one summer, and they were amazed at the Scandinavian neighborhoods of the city and especially of the community of Poulsbo, which is just a couple of hours outside Seattle. "It looks just like my village at home," Hans Kremb said. One evening while they were with us, they prepared this dish, which they said is a Scandinavian classic, designed with the climate of the Netherlands in mind. Once you've tasted it you'll understand the name—it's so tempting you may want to finish the whole thing at one sitting. While I wouldn't advise it—it is extremely rich and filling—the combination of flavors is delectable. It is also indestructible—make it the night before, bake it for just 1½ hours, let it cool, and freeze it. To finish cooking, just pop it in the oven for 30 to 45 minutes at 350°F. It makes a hearty main course, with a crisp salad and cool Aligoté or Pinot Grigio.

2 tins (3½ ounces each) flat anchovy fillets packed in oil

4 medium-size russet potatoes, peeled and thinly sliced

Freshly ground black pepper

2 medium onions, thinly sliced

1½ cups heavy or whipping cream

¾ cup loosely packed flat-leaf parsley, minced

1. Preheat the oven to 400°F.

2. Drain the anchovy fillets, reserving the anchovies and the oil separately.

3. Generously butter a 1½-quart baking dish. Cover the bottom with half the potato slices. Sprinkle with pepper. Add a layer of half the onions; top with the anchovies, laying them side-by-side. Top with the remaining onions; season with pepper. Make a top layer with the remaining potatoes. Drizzle the oil from the anchovies over all. Pour in the cream. Bake for 20 minutes.

4. Reduce the oven temperature to 300°F. Continue baking until the potatoes are cooked through and golden on top, about 1 hour and 10 to 20 minutes. Garnish with the parsley. Serve immediately.

Makes 4 to 6 servings

Sotterley Oyster Pye

This is a traditional Maryland recipe, researched and recreated by William Taylor, a Maryland caterer and historian. Mr. Taylor relives the history of Maryland through its cuisine, catering lavish banquets using traditional recipes, often in historic homes such as Sotterley Mansion, for which this pie is named. Oyster pie is wonderful—it sounds unusual and it is. Every time I serve it, people literally clamor for more. I like to use golden hominy, for a touch of color, but white is fine. Also, cut a fanciful design in the top crust before you bake it. Serve this with a fruity white wine such as a Piesporter Riesling.

Pie Pastry:

2 cups all-purpose flour

¼ teaspoon salt

⅔ cup chilled unsalted butter

½ to ¾ cup ice water

Béchamel Sauce:

2 to 2¼ cups milk

1 bay leaf

4 tablespoons (½ stick) unsalted butter

¼ cup all-purpose flour

Liquor reserved from oysters (see Filling)

Salt and freshly ground white pepper

Pinch of cayenne pepper

Generous pinch of ground mace

Filling:

2 dozen small (yearling) oysters, drained

3 hard-cooked large eggs, peeled and thinly sliced

1 can (14½ ounces) white or golden hominy, drained and rinsed

Salt and freshly ground white pepper

Mace

1. Make the Pastry: Combine the flour and salt in a large bowl. Using a sharp knife, finely shave the butter onto the flour. Toss with a fork to mix the butter with the flour. Sprinkle in ½ cup of the ice water, while tossing the flour mixture with a fork until the pastry is moist enough to form into a ball, but not too wet. Add more water if the pastry is dry. Wrap the pastry in waxed paper. Chill for at least 1 hour or overnight.

2. Roll out two-thirds of the pastry into a 12-inch circle. Line the bottom and sides of a 10½-inch removable bottom tart pan with the dough; crimp the edges. Roll the remaining pastry into an 11-inch circle for the top of the pie. Trim into a neat round. Place on a baking sheet. Chill crusts for 30 minutes.

3. Preheat the oven to 400°F.

4. Line the bottom crust with a sheet of aluminum foil; place another sheet of foil over the top crust. Weigh down both crusts with baking weights or dried beans. Bake both crusts at the same time. After 8 minutes remove the foil and weights from the top crust. Continue baking until golden, 7 to 12 minutes more. Remove the foil and weights from the bottom crust after 10 minutes of baking. Continue baking until golden, 10 to 15 minutes more. (You can make the pastry the night before, but don't bake it until the day you plan to use it.) Cool the crusts on a rack. Leave the oven on.

5. Make the Béchamel Sauce: In a small saucepan, scald 2 cups of the milk with the bay leaf over medium heat. Remove from the heat, cover, and set aside to steep for 5 minutes. Discard the bay leaf.

6. Melt the butter in a heavy-bottomed saucepan over medium heat, being careful not to brown it. Whisk in the flour and cook, whisking constantly, for 3 minutes. Pour in the warm milk, and cook, whisking constantly, until thickened. Whisk in the oyster liquor and additional milk, if necessary, to make a thick, but pourable sauce—like pudding. Season generously with salt, white pepper, cayenne, and mace to taste. The sauce should be well seasoned.

7. Remove the sauce from the heat. Add the oysters and stir gently until mixed in.

8. Cover the bottom crust with the egg slices. Sprinkle the hominy over the eggs; season with salt and pepper. Pour in the hot oyster sauce, spreading evenly to the edge of the pastry. Dust with additional mace.

9. Gently set the top crust in place. Set the pie on a baking sheet. Bake until the pie is hot through, 12 to 15 minutes. Be careful not to brown the pastry or overcook the oysters. If the pastry begins to brown, cover loosely with aluminum foil.

10. Remove from the oven. Remove the sides of the pie pan. Serve immediately.

Makes 10 first-course or 6 main-course servings

Salmon Piroghi from Alaska

Alaska has a large Russian population which has influenced that state's culture, art, language, and food. Piroghi—or peroche or pirok—is a Russian dish I first encountered in Sitka at a wonderful native Alaskan dinner. I loved the salmon and the rice in pastry, and my neighbor there, an elderly Tlingit Indian lady, said she often adds cabbage to hers. This dish is rich and elegant, and it deserves a similar wine—try a chilled Rully or Muscadet.

Pastry for a Two-Crust Pie (see Index), chilled
6 tablespoons unsalted butter
1 small green cabbage, cored and thinly sliced
Salt and freshly ground black pepper
1 tablespoon fresh lemon juice
½ teaspoon freshly grated nutmeg
1½ cups cooked white rice
1 tablespoon Fish Stock (see Index), chicken stock, or dry white wine
2 cups cooked salmon, preferably poached, crumbled into fairly large pieces
4 hard-cooked large eggs, peeled and thinly sliced
2 tablespoons minced fresh chives
1 large raw egg
1 teaspoon cold water

1. Roll out half the pastry dough into a 12-inch circle. (Keep the remaining dough in the refrigerator.) Line the bottom and sides of a 10½-inch, removable bottom tart tin with the pastry dough and crimp the edges. Chill for 30 minutes.

2. Preheat the oven to 425°F.

3. Melt 2 tablespoons of the butter in a large skillet over medium-high heat. Add the cabbage and stir to coat with butter. Cook, stirring frequently, until pale green and limp, about 7 minutes. Remove from the heat; season lightly with salt and pepper. Reserve.

4. Melt the remaining 4 tablespoons butter in a small saucepan over medium heat. Add the lemon juice; set aside in a warm place.

5. Pierce the bottom pastry all over with the tines of a fork. Line the crust with a sheet of aluminum foil and weigh it down with baking weights or dried beans. Bake until pale golden, about 10 minutes. Remove from the oven; cool slightly on a wire rack. Reduce the oven to 400°F.

6. To assemble the piroghi, spread half of the cabbage on the baked crust, pressing it into an even layer. Season lightly with salt, pepper, and nutmeg. Top with an even layer of rice; season more generously with salt, pepper, and nutmeg. Pour the fish stock evenly over the rice. Top with the salmon; season lightly. Place the hard-cooked eggs over the salmon in an even layer; season. Top with the remaining cabbage; season lightly with salt, pepper, and the remaining nutmeg. Press down on the mixture gently. It will still be mounded above the edges of the tart tin, but don't be concerned.

7. Stir the chives into the melted lemon butter; pour evenly over the top of the cabbage.

8. Whisk together the egg and the water in a small bowl, to make an egg wash. Paint the wash on the cooked edges of the bottom crust with a pastry brush. Roll out the remaining pastry dough and fit it over the filling, pressing it onto the egg-washed edges of the bottom crust to seal. It doesn't matter if you need to patch the top pastry to make it fit, for it will all bake together and look beautiful when you remove it from the oven. Paint the top crust generously with the egg wash (don't try to use all of the egg wash—it would make the top crust soggy). Pierce steam vents in the top crust in several places with the tip of a sharp knife.

9. Bake the piroghi until deep golden brown, about 25 to 30 minutes. If the top browns too quickly, cover it loosely with aluminum foil. Remove from the oven, and let it cool for 10 to 15 minutes before serving. To serve, cut into 6 or 8 wedges. This is also delicious cold.

Makes 6 to 8 servings

Wayne Ludvigsen's Pan-Fried White Sturgeon

This recipe is from Wayne Ludvigsen, the Executive Chef at Ray's Boathouse and Ray's Downtown, in Seattle, Washington. Wayne has been with the Ray's restaurants for more than a decade, and during that time he's directed his considerable energy toward developing a network of seafood suppliers who sell top-quality fish to him direct. Some fishermen even bring their boats right up to the dock at Ray's Boathouse to unload.

When he isn't searching for seafood sources, Wayne is supervising a kitchen, making dishes that are simple, fresh, and clean, and that don't mask the seafood itself. This is one of Wayne's favorites, and when sturgeon is in season, it is on the menu at Ray's. If sturgeon isn't available, try swordfish or tuna steaks, both of which will cook more quickly than the sturgeon because they are leaner. Brown them for 2 minutes per side, but reduce the cooking time by half. To check for doneness, make a tiny slit in the center of a steak with a very sharp knife, or insert a metal skewer and pull back gently on the meat so you can see the interior.

Try this dish with a chilled Chardonnay from California's Napa Valley or a Meursault.

6 sturgeon, swordfish, or tuna steaks, cut 1 inch thick (about 7 ounces each)

4 tablespoons clarified unsalted butter (see Note)

2 large mushrooms, thinly sliced

¼ teaspoon salt

¼ teaspoon freshly ground black pepper

¼ cup all-purpose flour

⅔ cup dry white wine

3 large shallots, finely chopped

2 cups Fish Stock (see Index)

1 cup heavy or whipping cream

¼ cup Pernod (anise-flavored liqueur)

2 tablespoons unsalted butter, chilled, cut into pieces

Grated zest of ½ lemon, for garnish

1. Rinse and pat the sturgeon dry and refrigerate until just before use.

2. Preheat the oven to 350°F.

3. In a small skillet, heat 1 tablespoon of the clarified butter over medium-high heat. Add the mushrooms and sauté just until limp, 2 to 3 minutes. Remove from the heat and reserve.

4. On a shallow plate, mix the salt, pepper, and flour. Lightly dredge the sturgeon steaks, shaking off the excess. In a large skillet over high heat, heat the remaining 3 tablespoons clarified butter until it begins to brown. Add the sturgeon and cook until golden, about 2 minutes per side. Place the sturgeon in an ovenproof dish; cover with foil. Bake until the fish is opaque through, about 10 minutes (about 5 minutes for swordfish or tuna).

5. Meanwhile, drain and discard any butter that remains in the skillet used to brown the sturgeon. Over high heat, deglaze the pan with the white wine and stir, scraping up any browned bits. Add the shallots and fish stock; cook until the sauce reduces to about one-quarter of its original volume and you can draw a streak across the bottom of the pan with a wooden spoon, 15 to 30 minutes.

6. Add the cream and the Pernod, and reduce until the sauce is thick enough to coat the back of a wooden spoon, about 5 minutes. Whisk in the butter one piece at a time and continue stirring until completely emulsified. Add the mushrooms.

7. To serve, spoon the sauce evenly in the center of 6 dinner plates. Place the sturgeon on the sauce but slightly to one side of the plate. Garnish with the zest; serve immediately.

Makes 6 servings

Note: To make clarified butter: In a heavy-bottomed saucepan, melt 10 tablespoons unsalted butter over medium-high heat. Skim any foam from the surface of the butter. Remove from the heat and let cool. Drain off the clear butter on the top; discard the milk solids at the bottom of the pan. Clarified butter can be made several weeks in advance. Keep covered and refrigerated.

Baked Snapper with Peppers and Artichokes

This dish from Seattle gourmet Willie Fisch is a cinch to prepare, pure poetry to eat. He created it one night as I stood in his kitchen watching in fascination. I make it often, because I love the jaunty fish sitting upright on its belly, surrounded by fresh and vividly colored vegetables. It's a pleasure to look at and a bigger pleasure to eat. Try a chilled Vouvray with this.

⅓ cup plus 1 tablespoon Greek or other strong
   flavored olive oil
1 pound small new potatoes, scrubbed
Salt
1 snapper (4 to 6 pounds), cleaned, with head on
3 cloves garlic, green germ removed, cut into thin
   strips (about 1 tablespoon)
1 piece ginger (1½ x 1 inch), peeled and cut into thin
   strips (about 1 tablespoon)
Freshly ground black pepper
1 medium onion, peeled and cut into ⅛-inch slices
1 medium yellow bell pepper, cored, seeded, and cut
   into ⅛-inch rings
1 medium red bell pepper, cored, seeded, and cut into
   ⅛-inch rings
1 pound baby artichokes, stemmed and peeled down to
   the light, tender leaves, or 1 can (8 ounces)
   artichoke hearts in brine, rinsed and drained
8 scallions, trimmed
⅓ cup dry white wine such as Vouvray
¼ cup fresh sage leaves, coarsely chopped, or 1
   tablespoon dried
2 bay leaves

1. Preheat the oven to 375°F. Oil, with the 1 tablespoon of olive oil, an enamel or porcelain baking dish large enough to hold the fish.

2. Place the potatoes in a large saucepan and add enough water to cover them by 2 inches. Season liberally with salt and bring the water to a boil over high heat. Cook until the potatoes are nearly done, but still somewhat crisp in the middle. Drain, cool, and cut the potatoes into quarters.

3. Rinse the snapper and pat dry. Cut 4 slits 2 inches long and ½ inch deep in each side of the fish. Stuff equal amounts of the garlic in each slit. Divide ½ tablespoon of the ginger equally among the slits in the fish, pressing it in firmly. Season the cavity with salt and pepper.

4. Separate the onion into rings and spread them over the bottom of the baking dish. Place the fish on its belly atop the onions, so it is sitting upright. You may need to curl it slightly to fit into the pan. Lean the pepper rings upright against the fish from head to tail, alternating colors and overlapping the rings slightly.

5. Cut the fresh artichokes in half (canned artichoke hearts should stay whole) and place them and the potatoes on top of the onions. Sprinkle the remaining ginger over the vegetables. Lay half the scallions on each side of the fish.

6. Drizzle the remaining olive oil over the fish and the vegetables, then drizzle the white wine over all. Sprinkle generously with salt, pepper and sage, nestle the bay leaves in the vegetables, and cover the dish tightly with aluminum foil.

7. Bake until the fish is opaque through, about 1 hour, checking it periodically. The cooking time will vary depending on the size of the fish. When the fish is cooked, remove

it from the oven and let it sit for about 10 minutes before serving.

Makes 6 servings

Redfish Sauce Piquant

*T*he redfish gained national recognition when Cajun Chef Paul Prudhomme introduced his now-famous blackened version. So much redfish was taken from the Gulf of Mexico, that authorities became concerned about the population, and they slapped a ban on the amount of bull, or large redfish, that can be landed. The ban doesn't concern most Cajuns I talked with, for it's the smaller "puppy" drum they covet, and there is no ban on taking those.

Sauce piquant is a staple in the Acadian region of Louisiana—it bathes everything from baby catfish to dried reconstituted shrimp. You might consider making a double batch of sauce piquant and freezing what you have leftover, for it is a wonderful sauce to have around. I slather it on dough for pizzas, use it cold as a dip—the possibilities are endless.

Try to get a whole fish for this recipe, for it makes a dramatic presentation. But if you can't, go ahead and smother fillets in the sauce and reduce the cooking time accordingly. And leftovers, if you happen to have them, are delicious warm or cold. Though redfish is delectable, several other fish are equally good, and will work very well in this recipe. Try substituting any kind of snapper.

Try a fruity red wine, such as Côtes du Rhône, with this dish.

1 redfish (2 pounds), scaled and cleaned, with head on
½ cup mild cooking oil, such as safflower
½ cup all-purpose flour
2 pounds fresh tomatoes, peeled and coarsely chopped
2 medium onions, diced
1 large bell pepper, cored, seeded, and diced
2 bunches scallions, trimmed, the white bulbs and light green stems finely chopped
1 long celery rib, finely chopped
4 cloves garlic, minced
¼ cup Louisiana brand hot sauce
6 drops Tabasco sauce, or more to taste
2 tablespoons Worcestershire sauce
1 tablespoon fresh oregano leaves, minced, or ¼ teaspoon dried
5 bay leaves
½ lemon, peel and pith removed, and sectioned
Salt and freshly ground black pepper, to taste

1. Rinse the redfish inside and out. Trim off any dark membranes from the cavity, and scrape the backbone clean, using a sharp knife. Refrigerate until ready to use.

2. Make the roux: Heat the oil in a large skillet over medium heat. Add the flour and cook, stirring constantly, until dark brown, about 10 minutes. Add all of the remaining ingredients except for the black pepper. Mix well and bring to a boil, stirring frequently so it doesn't stick. Reduce the heat to medium-low; cook, stirring occasionally, until the sauce becomes quite thick, about 1½ hours.

3. Preheat the oven to 400°F.

4. Oil a 14 x 10-inch glass or enamel baking dish.

5. Season the redfish inside and out with salt and pepper. Cut shallow, ⅛-inch-deep diagonal cuts in the redfish on both sides. Remove and discard the bay leaves from the

sauce piquant; pour a thin layer of sauce in the bottom of the baking dish. Lay the redfish on top and cover with the remaining sauce. Bake until the redfish is opaque through but not dry, about 30 minutes. Check for doneness by making a small slit near the backbone.

6. To serve, either present the whole fish at the table, right from the oven, or fillet it in the kitchen, placing half a fillet, skin-side up, in the center of each of 4 warm dinner plates. There is a generous amount of sauce, but it will all be eaten—you'll see. Spoon the sauce over the fish and serve immediately, with a crisp green salad.

Makes 4 servings

Bruce Naftaly's Broiled Sturgeon with Lemon Thyme

Bruce Naftaly is one of Seattle's best chefs. He was a pioneer in searching out individual farmers who would supply him with fresh, untreated produce, meat, and seafood. He has a huge network of suppliers now, who furnish him with everything from fresh cheeses aged in straw to the best, freshest fish, because they know he won't take anything else. Thanks to Bruce, and to his partner Robin Sanders, other chefs in Seattle have followed suit, creating an increasing network of farmers to supply them.

Bruce serves this sturgeon dish at his small restaurant, Le Gourmand, near Seattle's Ballard district. Try it with a chilled white Burgundy, such as Saint-Veran or Montagny.

4 sturgeon steaks cut 1 inch thick (about 7 ounces each)
Salt
¾ cup dry white wine
¼ cup sherry vinegar
1 large shallot, minced
1 teaspoon fresh lemon or common thyme leaves, or ¼ teaspoon dried
8 tablespoons (1 stick) unsalted butter, cut into cubes
Freshly ground black pepper
8 sprigs fresh thyme or flat-leaf parsley, for garnish

1. Preheat the broiler.

2. Rinse the sturgeon steaks and pat dry. Season lightly with salt. Place on a broiler pan. Broil 4 inches from the heat for 10 minutes, turning frequently, until golden and just opaque through. Transfer to a heatproof dish, cover, and keep warm in a low oven.

3. Make the sauce: In a medium-size non-aluminum saucepan over medium-high heat, combine the wine, vinegar, and shallot. Bring to a boil and reduce to 1 tablespoon, about 10 minutes. Stir in the thyme. Slowly add the butter, a cube at a time, whisking after each addition. Work on and off the heat as necessary, to keep the butter from melting before it is emulsified. Season with salt to taste.

4. To serve, place the sturgeon on warm dinner plates; lightly season with pepper. Divide the sauce among the plates, pouring it to one side of the sturgeon. Garnish with the sprigs of thyme or parsley. Serve immediately.

Makes 4 servings

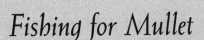

Fishing for Mullet

My husband and I were driving from St. Petersburg across Tampa Bay, and we saw fishermen casting huge nets and bringing in loads of flopping, jumping fish onto the man-made beach alongside the turnpike. We stopped to take in the scene and talked with fisherman Michael Rabada. He's fished for mullet most of his life, and mostly right from that spot.

Mike and his father, John, stood on the beach and gazed out at the water, while traffic whizzed by just feet away. They were looking for a black mass in the water—the color of hundreds, sometimes thousands, of the black-backed fish. Suddenly Mike jumped into his 21-foot skiff and streamed out into the water to surround the fish with his net. "Mullet move two to three miles in eight minutes when they're running," Mike said. "You have to move fast."

Once thrown, he dragged the net toward shore, bringing the teeming, jumping fish along with it. The water was shallow, and Mike cut the engine many feet offshore, jumped in the water, and with help from his crew, brought the net ashore. The impressive mass of fish were summarily loaded into the back of a waiting truck, which, when full, took them to the roe processor.

Mike and his dad usually save a half dozen prime mullet for themselves. They set up a camping stove and fry up some roe, some milt, and a good batch of fillets for lunch. Watching their pure enjoyment in eating the fish, whose meat is sweet and tender, you'd think it was a rare treat. Not so. They have it nearly every day!

Rosemary-Baked Mullet with Peppers

Mullet are common in the backwaters and bayous of Florida and the Gulf of Mexico, where they're caught primarily for their big, golden roe. It is cut from the fish, cleaned, packaged in small plastic bags, frozen, and most of it sold directly to Taiwan, where it is an expensive delicacy. The sweet, tender meat of the fish is usually sold for bait, turned into soap, or worst of all, discarded.

I like the roe, but the milt, which resembles veal sweetbreads, is my favorite—second to the sweet fillets, of course. The following recipe is what I do with mullet in my kitchen, and it speaks to me of sandy beaches and summertime. If you can't find mullet, try this recipe with mackerel. Serve it with a light, American Merlot.

2 mullet (12 ounces each), cleaned, with head on
Salt and freshly ground black pepper
2 large sprigs fresh rosemary, or 1 teaspoon dried
5 tablespoons olive oil
2 tablespoons fresh rosemary leaves, or 2 teaspoons dried
¼ cup plus 2 teaspoons fresh lemon juice
2 medium green bell peppers, cored, seeded, and cut into ¼-inch-thick strips
2 medium onions, cut into ¼-inch-thick slices
4 cloves garlic, slivered crosswise
½ cup loosely packed fresh basil leaves, or ¼ teaspoon dried
Rosemary sprigs, for garnish

1. Rinse the mullet. Scrape off any black membrane from the stomach cavity; pat dry. Refrigerate until ready to cook.

2. Preheat the oven to 500°F.

3. Season the cavity of the mullet with salt and pepper. Place 1 rosemary sprig inside each fish. Pour 3 tablespoons of the oil in a large baking dish with deep sides. Add the fish, leaving some room between them. (If you don't have a dish large enough, use 2 baking dishes.) Season the fish generously with salt and pepper. Turn and season on the other side. Sprinkle the rosemary leaves over the mullet. Bake for 5 minutes. Pour the ¼ cup lemon juice over the mullet. Continue baking until they are opaque through, an additional 5 minutes.

4. Five minutes before the mullet are cooked, heat the remaining 2 tablespoons oil in a large skillet over medium-high heat. Add the bell peppers, onions, and garlic, and sauté until the peppers turn a brighter shade of green, 3 to 4 minutes. Coarsely chop the basil. Stir in the basil. Stir in the remaining 2 teaspoons lemon juice. Season with salt and pepper to taste. Cook for 1 minute, and remove from the heat. The vegetables should be crisp-tender and sprightly.

5. Place the fish on a large, warm serving platter, leaving space between them. Spoon the pepper and onion mixture between the fish. Garnish with rosemary sprigs. Remove the fillets at the table, giving each person one fillet. Alternatively, fillet the fish and place each fillet on a warm dinner plate. Spoon the vegetables alongside and garnish each plate with a rosemary sprig. Serve immediately.

Makes 4 servings

Greek-Marinated Bluefish with Potato Salad

Bluefish has deep-colored, almost blue meat that lightens to a soft ivory when it is cooked. It is incomparably tender, rich, and delicious, and it dresses up any meal, any preparation. I love it marinated in olive oil and lemon juice just long enough to give it a fresh tang, then quickly broiled and served with Rosemary Potato Salad (see Index). Try this with a chilled, dry rosé champagne, for a little difference.

2½ pounds thick bluefish fillets, bones removed
Salt and freshly ground black pepper
¼ cup olive oil
2 tablespoons fresh lemon juice
¼ cup loosely packed fresh rosemary leaves or 1
   tablespoon dried, lightly crushed
Rosemary sprigs, for garnish
Lemon wedges, for garnish

1. Rinse the bluefish fillets and pat dry. Lightly season with salt and pepper. Place the fillets in a shallow, non-aluminum dish.

2. Combine the olive oil, lemon juice, and rosemary in a small bowl; pour over the fillets. Turn the fillets once to coat with the marinade. Refrigerate for 2 hours.

3. Preheat the broiler.

4. Cover a broiler pan with aluminum foil. Set the pan 2 to 3 inches below the heat source to preheat. Remove the bluefish fillets from the marinade, reserving the marinade for basting. Place the fillets in the pan. Broil, basting at least twice, until just opaque through, 8 to 10 minutes. (The time will vary

depending on the thickness of the fillets.)

5. To serve, arrange the fillets on a serving platter, garnish with the rosemary sprigs and lemon wedges and serve immediately.

Makes 4 to 6 servings

Macadamia Mahimahi in Coconut Milk

Mahimahi is ubiquitous in Hawaii, and a visit to the islands really isn't complete without at least one mahimahi meal. Despite its popularity, however, many Hawaii residents aren't nearly as fond of it as are visitors, though it appears on nearly every restaurant menu.

I was delighted when, on my first visit to Hawaii, I found myself surrounded by the sight and scent of coconuts and macadamia nuts, and I tasted truly fresh, wonderful mahimahi. When I returned, I couldn't wait to combine them all in one dish, and it works beautifully. The succulent, firm meat of the mahimahi is perfectly balanced by the exotic flavors of the nuts and the coconut.

Mahimahi is a member of the dolphin family, though no relation to Flipper, who is (was) a porpoise, or to any of those smiling creatures we see at Sea World. They are large and long, their skin tinged with gorgeous bright blue and yellow. They are among the last fish brought into the Honolulu fish auction each day, because they don't hold up well outside of refrigeration. As one buyer put it, "When you see the mahimahi, it's the light at the end of the tunnel—the auction is nearly over." Buyers circulate among rows of mahimahi in search of females, who, with their streamlined heads, give more meat per pound than males, much of whose body weight is in their high, bony foreheads and large, blunt heads.

If you want to go all out with this dish, serve a lightly chilled Meursault. Otherwise, try a Chardonnay.

1 ½ pounds mahimahi fillet
Salt and freshly ground black pepper
1 cup whole salted macadamia nuts
1 cup unsweetened coconut milk, preferably
   Mendonca's Hawaiian-style brand

1. Preheat the oven to 350°F.
2. Rinse the mahimahi fillet and pat dry. Cut the fillet diagonally into four 1-inch-wide pieces. Place them in a 12½ x 8½-inch baking dish in a single layer. Season with salt and pepper on the top side.
3. Sprinkle half the macadamia nuts over the fish, then pour the coconut milk all around the fish. Bake until the mahimahi is opaque through, about 18 minutes.
4. Coarsely chop the remaining ½ cup macadamia nuts. Sprinkle over the mahimahi. Serve immediately with the coconut milk as sauce.

Makes 4 servings

Haddock with Mustard Cream

Haddock is a delicious, big-flaked white fish with a subtle sweetness akin to scallops. The sweet cream and mustard and the sweetness of the onions bring out the flavor of the haddock and make this a hearty, yet sophisticated dish. Serve it with a large green salad, plenty of fresh, crusty bread for sopping up the sauce, and a chilled white Burgundy or Chardonnay. If you can't get haddock, lingcod makes a good substitute.

1½ pounds haddock fillet, cut into 4 serving pieces
2 cups heavy or whipping cream
3 tablespoons whole-grain mustard
Salt and freshly ground black pepper
2 large onions, thinly sliced

1. Rinse the haddock and pat dry. Refrigerate until ready to use.

2. Preheat the oven to 350°F.

3. Mix together 1½ cups of the cream and the mustard in a medium-size bowl. Season with salt and pepper to taste. Add the onions and toss until coated. Pour the onions and cream into a 12½ x 8½-inch baking dish; cover with aluminum foil. Bake until the cream is bubbling and the onions are crisp-tender, about 25 minutes.

4. Season the haddock with salt and pepper. Submerge in the onion mixture, turning once to coat with a thin layer of cream. Pour the remaining ½ cup cream over the fish; cover with aluminum foil. Bake until the haddock is opaque through, about 10 minutes. Serve immediately.

Makes 4 servings

Teriyaki Mackerel

*F*irm, flavorful mackerel lends itself to the intriguing salty-sweetness of teriyaki. While the recipe calls for the fish to be left in the marinade for 2 hours, which gives it a lovely flavor, an additional hour won't hurt the fish and it will enhance the teriyaki flavor. Mackerel cooks very quickly—watch it carefully under the broiler so it doesn't overcook. Be sure to leave the skin on the fillets to hold them together while they marinate and cook. It peels off very easily once cooked. Try this with white rice, a crisp Cucumber Salad (see Index), and a chilled Northwest Chenin Blanc.

4 mackerel fillets (6 to 8 ounces each), boned, with skin on
Teriyaki Marinade (see Index)

1. Rinse the mackerel fillets and pat dry. Check them for bones and remove as many as you can.

2. Place the fillets in a shallow porcelain or glass dish. Pour the marinade over the fillets. Refrigerate the fillets for 2 hours, turning once.

3. Preheat the broiler.

4. Place the fillets, skin side down, in a shallow baking dish or on a piece of aluminum foil. Spoon several tablespoons of the marinade over the fillets. Broil 4 inches from the heat until opaque, 4 to 5 minutes. Remove from the heat. Serve immediately.

Makes 4 servings

Black Cod Misoyaki in Ti Leaves

*I*n Hawaii, black cod misoyaki is ubiquitous, and it is often served wrapped in large, shiny green ti leaves. The already unctuous black cod (or sablefish) is made even more so with the sweet, appley miso mixture. The carrot and scallions add a flash of color, and the ti leaves gives a hint of earthiness, though their major contribution is exotic appeal. Don't worry if you can't find ti leaves; go ahead and use aluminum foil.

Try this with a clean, young Chardonnay, such as Rully or Montagny, from the Côtes Challonais in Burgundy.

2 black cod steaks (about 8 ounces each) cut ¾ to 1
*   inch thick*
Misoyaki (see Index)
8 ti leaves
1 small carrot, peeled and cut into julienne
2 scallions, trimmed and cut into julienne

1. Rinse the black cod steaks and pat dry. Halve lengthwise, removing the bone. Place half of the *misoyaki* in a small, non-aluminum shallow dish or baking pan. Lay the black cod on top, pushing the steaks into the miso mixture. Spread the remaining miso mixture on top, and on the sides, to coat thoroughly. Use all of the miso mixture to give the requisite flavor. Cover and refrigerate for 24 hours.

2. Preheat the oven to 350°F. (You can't test this dish for doneness, so be sure you bake it for the correct amount of time, and that your oven is correctly calibrated.)

3. Lay a ti leaf flat on a work surface. Place a piece of black cod steak in the center of the leaf; trim the leaf so the ends will wrap up and over the piece of cod, overlapping by at least 2 inches. Place one-fourth of the carrot and scallion julienne on top of the black cod. Wrap the ti leaf up and around it. Slip another ti leaf under the black cod, trim, and wrap up and over the length of the fish to cover any exposed sides, making a completely enclosed packet. Secure the packet with kitchen string, tying it as you would a package. (If you are using foil, tear pieces 10 to 12 inches long. Fold over the top and side edges and press closed to seal the packet.) Repeat with the remaining pieces of black cod and ti leaves.

4. Place the packets in a non-aluminum, 12 x 8½-inch baking pan. Bake for 20 minutes for fish that is opaque through.

5. To serve, place a packet in the center of each plate. Remove the strings at the table, and let each guest open his own packet.

Makes 4 servings

Jack Crevalle Baked in Salt with Herb Oil and Pickled Garlic

Jack crevalle is like several fish in one—it is a relative of pompano, which it resembles; its meat, which turns a dark ivory when cooked, is similar in texture to mackerel, but its flavor is more like albacore tuna. I love it baked in salt. It stays moist, and its flavor takes on a surprising complexity—almost as though you taste the clean, clear sea it swims in. In order for the fish to be cooked through in the time stated in the recipe, they must weigh exactly 1 pound—a couple ounces under is better than over. The salt forms an uneven crust around the fish as it bakes, so when you get ready to remove it, sweep away as much salt as you can, then tap at the parts that have crusted over, to break them.

If you don't have the Pickled Garlic on hand, and don't want to make it, thinly slice 4 cloves garlic and poach the slices in the Herb Oil over low heat for 15 minutes.

Try a chilled Pouilly Fumé with this dish.

2 jack crevalle or mackerel (1 pound or less each),
   cleaned, with head on

7 cups kosher (coarse) salt

8 teaspoons Herb Oil (see Index)

¼ cup Pickled Garlic (see Index), drained and diced

1. Preheat the oven to 350°F.

2. Rinse the jack crevalle thoroughly inside and out. Pat dry.

3. Pour 1 cup of the kosher salt on the bottom of a non-aluminum 12½ x 8½-inch baking dish. Lay the fish in the pan, and pour the remaining 6 cups salt over them to completely cover from head to tail. It should look like you have a baking dish mounded with nothing but salt.

4. Bake the fish for 25 minutes.

5. Remove from the oven. Brush away as much salt as you can from the top of the fish, then gently but firmly tap at the salt crust that will have formed over them. You want to remove as much salt as possible in the pan so that it doesn't get onto the fish when you remove the skin. Using a long spatula, remove the fish from the pan and transfer them to a work surface. Using the blade of a sharp knife, gently scrape the skin from the top fillet of the fish. Remove the top fillet from a fish, and transfer it to the center of a warm dinner plate. (You may cut out the dark strip of meat from the fillets if you like. It is more strongly flavored than the rest of the meat.) You may also need to trim bones from the edge of the fillet.

5. Pull the tail of the fish up and away from the bottom fillet—it should come right out. Trim any bones from the fillet, then flip it over and scrape the skin off. Transfer to the center of a warm dinner plate. Repeat with the second fish.

6. Drizzle 2 teaspoons of herb oil over each fillet. Sprinkle with equal amounts of the diced pickled garlic. Serve immediately.
Makes 4 servings

Seabass Fillet in Parchment

Seabass is incomparably tender and moist. It is considered of such high quality that it is often sold for sashimi. I love it cooked, like this, in a parchment envelope so it steams and bakes at the same time, the gentle aromas of the fish, herbs, and spices puffing out as guests open them at the dinner table. This recipe is as easy to make for one as it is for a crowd. Try this with a Cru Beaujolais for a very elegant meal.

4 seabass fillets (6 to 8 ounces each)

2 teaspoons chili paste with soy bean, preferably Lan
   Chi brand

4 teaspoons Japanese sesame oil

1 large white onion, thinly sliced

2 teaspoons finely minced fresh ginger

2 teaspoons mild (low sodium) soy sauce, such as
   Kikkoman

1. Preheat the oven to 450°F. (You can't test this dish for doneness, so be sure you bake it for the correct amount of time, and that your oven is correctly calibrated.)

2. Rinse the seabass fillets and pat dry. Cut four 12-inch squares of parchment. Place a seabass fillet at the end of each piece of paper. Rub ½ teaspoon of the chili paste into each fillet. Pour 1 teaspoon of sesame oil over it. Divide the onions among the fillets. Sprinkle each with ½ teaspoon ginger and

½ teaspoon soy sauce.

3. To close the parchment paper, brush the edges lightly with water. Fold the free half over the fish, closing it like a book. Fold the edges of the parchment paper over, making a very narrow fold. Make another fold, this time crimping the edges as you go to fold the paper around the fish and vegetables.

4. Place the packets on a baking sheet. Bake until the paper is golden brown, 5 minutes. Remove from the oven; let sit for 2 minutes. Serve, explaining to the guests that they should slit the paper open with their knives and lift out the fish. Remove the empty packets.

Makes 4 servings

Turkish Fish in Parchment

Dick Lilly is a Seattle newspaper reporter and native Seattleite with an abiding love for things Northwestern—sailing, seafood, and Northwest beaches. He prepares several seafood specialties, always to rave reviews. He brought this recipe back from a several-year stint in Turkey as a member of the Peace Corps, and it evokes the hot sun and clear waters of the Mediterranean. Though it originally called for swordfish, he uses a variety of firm-fleshed, white fish such as lingcod or haddock.

It's a delight to open the crisp parchment packets at the table, and reveal the colors and wonderful aromas within. I like to use red onions and yellow or green bell peppers,

depending on what is available. Try with a chilled white Burgundy or a dry Riesling from Alsace.

1 lingcod fillet (1 pound)
Salt
2 small russet potatoes, peeled and cut into ¼-inch dice
Coarsely ground black pepper
8 ounces tomatoes, cut into large (1 x ½ x ½-inch) pieces
1 large red onion, diced
1 medium green bell pepper, cored, seeded, and cut into ¼-inch dice
¼ cup loosely packed fresh oregano leaves, or 1 teaspoon dried
4 teaspoons olive oil
4 ounces French or Bulgarian feta cheese, at room temperature, crumbled into pea-size pieces

1. Rinse the lingcod and pat dry. Remove any bones with a strawberry huller, fish bone puller, or needlenose pliers. Cut crosswise into 4 equal serving pieces.

2. Preheat the oven to 450°F. (You can't test this dish for doneness, so be sure you bake it for the correct amount of time, and that your oven is correctly calibrated.)

3. Cut four 12 x 15-inch sheets of parchment paper.

4. Bring 2 quarts of water to a boil with 2 teaspoons salt in a large saucepan over high heat. Add the potatoes, return to a boil, and cook until slightly tender, but still crisp, about 1 minute. Drain; set aside to cool to just warmer than room temperature.

5. Generously season the fish on all sides with salt and pepper.

6. Place 1 piece of fish on the bottom third of a sheet of parchment paper. Top with one-fourth of the tomatoes, onion, bell pepper, and potatoes. Coarsely chop the

fresh oregano (slightly crumble the dried oregano between your fingers or using a mortar and pestle). Sprinkle one-fourth of the oregano over all; season with salt and a generous amount of pepper, and drizzle with 1 teaspoon olive oil. Brush the edges of the parchment paper with water, fold the top half of the paper over to meet the bottom half, as though you are closing a book. Make a very narrow fold all the way around the edges of the paper, then make another fold around the edges, crimping as you go, to close the paper around the fish and vegetables. Place the packet on a baking sheet, and repeat with the remaining ingredients. You will need 2 baking sheets to hold the 4 packets.

7. Bake until the parchment is puffed and golden brown all over, about 13 minutes.

8. Place a packet on each dinner plate. Give each guest a sharp knife to cut open the parchment envelope, or have them unfold it. (Since the parchment paper can become soggy by the time you finish eating the fish, you may suggest that people lift the fish and vegetables off the paper onto the plate.) Serve the feta cheese alongside, for sprinkling over the fish and vegetables.

Makes 4 servings

Halibut in Parchment Paper with Spring Vegetables

The advent of spring halibut from Alaska is a joyous occasion in the Northwest. The sun finally comes through bright and clear, gardens produce tender spring vegetables, and tons of fresh halibut are flown down from Alaska, its translucent, pale, pale green meat begging to be poached, steamed, or grilled.

Cooking halibut in parchment assures that its essence, flavor, and texture remain intact. Open the packets at the table, so diners can appreciate the bouquet of aromas that emerge. Try it with a clean Chardonnay that isn't over-oaked.

1 medium cucumber, peeled, halved lengthwise, seeds removed
8 baby carrots, peeled
8 small radishes, quartered lengthwise
1 pound slim asparagus stalks, tips only
4 halibut steaks (6 to 8 ounces each)
Salt and freshly ground black pepper
2 shallots, finely minced
3/4 cup loosely packed fresh tarragon leaves
4 tablespoons extra-virgin olive oil

1. Preheat the oven to 450°F. (You can't test this dish for doneness, so be sure you bake it for the correct amount of time, and that your oven is correctly calibrated.)

2. Bring a large pot of salted water to a boil over high heat. Have a large bowl of ice water ready.

3. Cut the cucumber into 2-inch lengths, then into very thin strips, 1/8 x 1/8 inch.

4. Blanch the carrots until crisp-tender, about 4 minutes. Using a slotted spoon or strainer, remove the carrots and plunge them into the ice water. When cooled, pat dry and reserve. When the water returns to a boil, blanch the radishes, leaving them there just until the water returns to a boil. Transfer to the ice water. Repeat with the asparagus tips.

5. Cut four 24 x 12-inch sheets of parchment paper. Place 1 halibut steak at one end

of the parchment, leaving about 2 inches of paper at the bottom. Season the fish generously with salt and pepper. Top the steak with one fourth of the vegetables, shallots, and tarragon. Season again with salt and pepper. Drizzle on 1 tablespoon of the olive oil.

6. To close the parchment paper, moisten the edges of the paper with water. Fold the free half of the parchment paper over the fish, closing it like a book. Fold the edges of the parchment paper over, making a very narrow fold. Make another fold, this time crimping the edge as you go to fold the paper around the fish and vegetables. Assemble 3 more packets using the remaining ingredients.

7. Place the packets on a baking sheet. Bake until the parchment paper is puffed and brown, 10 minutes.

8. Place a packet on each of 4 warm dinner plates. Serve immediately, explaining to the guests that they should slit the paper open with their knives and lift out the fish and vegetables from the paper. Remove the empty packets before digging in.

Makes 4 servings

Spotted Seatrout with Bacon and Tomato Sauce

*T*his is a variation on a traditional Louisiana dish, with bacon laid under and on top of the trout as it cooks, instead of incorporated into the soft tomato sauce. It keeps the trout moist while oven-frying and imparts a gentle smokiness to the trout's nutty meat. If you can't find seatrout, substitute catfish or brook trout. Try a Pouilly Fuissé with this dish.

2 seatrout, brook trout, or catfish (1 pound each), cleaned, with heads on and fins trimmed
Salt and freshly ground black pepper
Scant 8 ounces good-quality slab bacon, sliced into ⅛-inch-thick strips
1 medium onion, coarsely chopped
2 pounds plum tomatoes, stem ends removed, or 1 can (28 ounces) whole tomatoes, quartered
1 tablespoon fresh lemon juice
1 teaspoon sugar
1 tablespoon fresh oregano leaves or ½ teaspoon dried
1 teaspoon Louisiana brand hot sauce or Tabasco sauce

1. Preheat the oven to 400°F.

2. Rinse the seatrout and pat dry. Season with salt and pepper inside and out.

3. In a medium-size skillet over medium-high heat, partially cook the bacon until soft and the fat is translucent, about 5 minutes. Remove from the heat. Reserve the bacon strips and the skillet of bacon fat separately.

4. When the bacon strips are cool, arrange half of them in a 12½ x 8½-inch ovenproof baking dish that can come to the table. Place the seatrout on top; cover with the remaining bacon.

5. Place the onion in the skillet of reserved bacon fat. Cook over medium-high heat until the onion begins to turn translucent, about 5 minutes. Place the trout in the oven. Bake until opaque through, 20 to 25 minutes.

6. While the trout are baking, add all of the remaining ingredients to the onion and bacon fat. Cook over medium heat until the sauce has thickened, but is still pourable, about 25 minutes. Season to taste. Keep warm over low heat.

7. Remove the trout from the oven. Pour the tomato sauce over and around them, and serve immediately, presenting the dish at the table before filleting.

Makes 4 servings

Kay and Kyle Vanderpool's Tuna with Peppercorns

I spent an evening with the Vanderpools aboard their boat, The Pursuit, at the boat dock in Honolulu. They were waiting to unload a recent catch of bottom fish for the Honolulu auction. The Vanderpool's real fishing speciality is tuna, which they catch on hook and line and land individually on the carpeted deck of their boat. Both of the Vanderpools like to cook, as does their daughter and chief deckhand, Sonja, and this remarkable tuna with peppercorns is an easy Vanderpool specialty. Try this with a Côtes du Rhône.

1 pound tuna
Salt
1 tablespoon black peppercorns, coarsely ground
1 tablespoon unsalted butter
2 large onions, thinly sliced
¼ cup dry white wine, such as a French Riesling
2 tablespoons minced fresh chives

1. Preheat the oven to 300°F.
2. Rinse the tuna and pat dry. Season lightly with salt all over; press the pepper

into it, covering all surfaces.

3. Melt the butter in a medium-size cast-iron or enameled roasting pan over medium-high heat. Add the onions; toss to coat with butter. Season with salt and pepper. Cook until softened very slightly, about 5 minutes. Remove from the heat. Add the wine.

4. Place the tuna on top of the onions. Bake for 20 minutes. Turn the tuna over and continue baking until almost opaque through, an additional 25 minutes. Remove from the oven.

5. Garnish with the chives. Serve immediately if you like the tuna pale pink in the center. Let sit for about 10 minutes if you like the tuna cooked through.

Makes 4 servings

Salt Cod, Potato, and Onion Gratin

T his is a soul-satisfying dish, with its American roots in the cobbled streets of Boston, where cod, onions, potatoes, and cream are like national treasures. Soaking the cod removes the salt, so it isn't unusual to add some for seasoning. Try it with a crisp green salad and a bottle of Aligoté, for a simple, hearty meal with a touch of elegance.

1 pound skinless and boneless salt cod
1 pound russet potatoes, peeled and thinly sliced
Salt and freshly ground black pepper
1 tablespoon unsalted butter
3 small red onions, thinly sliced
1¼ cups heavy or whipping cream
1 small bunch parsley, finely minced

1. Soak the salt cod in plenty of cold water (about 3 gallons) at room temperature for 24 hours, changing the water at least three times.

2. Generously butter a 12½ x 8½-inch baking dish.

3. Place the potatoes in a large saucepan and cover with cold, salted water (1 teaspoon per 2 quarts of water is a good proportion). Bring to a boil over high heat. Reduce the heat to medium-high; boil gently until the potatoes are tender, but not mushy. Drain the potato slices very well. Layer in the bottom of the buttered baking dish. Season lightly with salt and pepper.

4. Melt the butter in a large skillet over medium heat. Add the onions, cover, and cook, stirring frequently, until soft and beginning to turn pale golden, about 20 minutes. Layer on top of the potatoes. Season lightly with salt and pepper.

5. Preheat the oven to 400°F.

6. Drain the cod. Place in a large saucepan and add cold water to cover by 2 inches. Slowly bring to a boil over medium-high heat. Reduce the heat to medium-low and poach the cod until it begins to flake and come apart, about 15 minutes.

7. Drain the cod very well. Using your fingers, flake the fish on top of the onions, discarding any bones and spreading it out evenly over the surface of the dish. Pour the cream over all; season lightly with salt and pepper. Cover with aluminum foil. Bake until heated through and bubbling, 20 minutes.

8. To serve, remove the aluminum foil. Grind pepper over the top of the gratin. Sprinkle with the parsley and serve.

Makes 4 to 6 servings

Monkfish Gratin

Monkfish, or goosefish, anglerfish, or devilfish as it's alternately called because of its unattractive mien, isn't referred to as "poor man's lobster" for nothing. Its sweet, crustacean-like texture and flavor are illustrated perfectly here. If you can't find monkfish, substitute large sea scallops and reduce the cooking time by about 2 minutes. Flying fish roe, which are tiny, almost translucent fuschia-colored granules, give a spark of color to this golden dish, as do salmon eggs. Try this with a top-quality, balanced California Chardonnay, or a Pouilly Fumé.

½ cup (1 stick) unsalted butter, melted
¾ cup fresh bread crumbs
3 cloves garlic, finely chopped
⅓ cup minced fresh parsley
3 tablespoons fresh lemon juice
Salt and freshly ground black pepper
1½ pounds monkfish, cut at an angle into bite-size medallions
Salmon eggs or flying fish roe, for garnish

1. Preheat the oven to 400°F.

2. Brush 4 to 6 oval gratin dishes or scallop shells generously with some of the melted butter. Sprinkle with half of the bread crumbs.

3. In a small bowl, combine the remaining butter with the garlic, parsley, 2 tablespoons of the lemon juice, and salt and pepper to taste. Add the monkfish and mix thoroughly. Divide the mixture among the gratin dishes. Sprinkle with the remaining bread crumbs.

4. Bake until the monkfish is opaque through, 8 to 10 minutes. Drizzle with the remaining lemon juice. Serve immediately.

Makes 4 servings

Rosemary Gaspergoo

When I first spotted the name gaspergoo I fell in love with the fish, even before tasting it. Once I had, I found its bright white, tender meat of an almost incomparable sweetness. Gaspergoo is very common in the bayous of Louisiana, and in late spring—gaspergoo season—signs for the fish are all along the road. Having a translator along helps, of course, for as I drove down to Grand Isle, in south Louisiana, and saw signs for "goo" all along the way, I wasn't quite sure what was being offered! This is a very unconventional preparation for gaspergoo—normally it is rolled in cornmeal or flour and deep-fried. Try a Côtes du Rhône with this, for a real treat.

2 small gaspergoo, rock cod, or snapper (1 to 1½
*   pounds each), cleaned, with heads on*
1 teaspoon mild vegetable oil, such as safflower
Salt and freshly ground black pepper
1 piece ginger (2 x 2 inches), peeled and cut in thin
*   strips*
4 large branches fresh thyme or ¼ teaspoon dried
12 sprigs fresh rosemary or ¼ cup dried
½ cup dry white wine
4 sprigs fresh rosemary for garnish

1. Preheat the broiler.
2. Rinse the fish and pat dry. Rub them all over with the oil. Season with salt and pepper inside and out. Divide the ginger and thyme between the stomach cavities.
3. Place the rosemary in a shallow, non-aluminum 12½ x 8½-inch ovenproof baking dish. Lay the fish on top. Pour the wine all around.
4. Broil until the gaspergoo are golden and opaque on top, about 5 minutes. Turn and broil until opaque through, an additional 5 minutes.
5. Fillet the gaspergoo. Garnish with a sprig of the rosemary or several rosemary leaves and serve.

Makes 4 servings

8

ON THE STOVE OR THEREABOUTS

If anyone had told me four years ago that I'd be singing the praises of deep-fried yellow perch, or a big pot of poached fish, I would have looked at them cross-eyed. Everyone knows, I might have said, that fried foods are bad for you, and really, what could possibly be appealing about poached *anything*, especially fish?

Well, have I learned a thing or two! Now one of my favorite dishes is the Poached Halibut with Tuberous Begonia Petals—it is stunningly simple, pure, and delicious. And deep-fried yellow perch vies with crispy nuggets of deep-fried tilapia accompanied by lychees as a favorite meal to serve when friends come to visit. I've measured the amount of oil that properly fried foods absorb—it's negligible, truly.

Many of the dishes in this chapter have distinct ethnic origins, making them particularly exciting, unusual, and impressive to serve. And they taste simply wonderful.

There's mahimahi with salted

turnip, a Chinese influenced dish from a Hawaiian native who insisted it was one of the simplest and best things in the world to eat (I agree), and cinnamon-spiced Portuguese hake, from Cape Cod. There are Cuban dishes, Japanese dishes and Scandinavian dishes, and they all reflect our heritage. More important, at least for me, is that they make me want to rush to the fish market and then to the stove, so I can create their heady aromas, and sit down to a stop on a culinary seafood voyage.

Wisconsin Fish Fry

Come Friday night in Wisconsin, everyone's out for a fish fry. It's an all-you-can-eat meal that used to center around sweet yellow perch from the Great Lakes, when there was plenty of it. Now, as often as not, the fish in the fry is pollock from Alaska. It may not be as delicate, but it's firm and tasty.

A good beer batter is the secret to a fish fry. It should be light and crisp, and keep the fish moist without obscuring its flavor. The traditional accompaniments to a fish fry are golden crisp Potato Pancakes, Coleslaw, and Applesauce (see Index for all three recipes), and, as you will see, it makes a fine meal.

You may use just about any white fish fillet—judge the cooking time by the texture of the flesh. For example, lingcod will take longer to cook than yellow perch. But none of it takes much longer than 4 minutes per piece of fish. Try a chilled, appley Chardonnay, lightly chilled Eau Claire beer from Wisconsin, or Chimay beer from Belgium.

1½ pounds white fish fillets, such as yellow perch,
    lingcod, or rockfish
1⅓ cups all-purpose flour
Salt
Large pinch of cayenne pepper
2 large egg yolks, beaten
1 tablespoon unsalted butter, melted
¾ cup regular beer
6 cups mild vegetable oil, such as safflower
Freshly ground black pepper
2 large egg whites

1. Rinse the fillets and pat dry. Cut them into 4 x 2½-inch pieces. Refrigerate until ready to use.

2. Whisk together the flour, 1 teaspoon salt, and the cayenne in a large bowl. Make a well in the center, and add the egg yolks and butter. Add the beer to the ingredients in the well and stir, then quickly whisk the flour into the liquids. Set aside for 1 hour.

3. Heat the oil in a deep-fat fryer or a heavy-bottomed large saucepan to 375°F.

4. Season the fish with salt and pepper.

5. Beat the egg whites with a pinch of salt until they form stiff peaks. Fold into the beer batter. Dip as many pieces of fish as you will fry in each batch into the batter, shaking off any excess. (You do not want too thick a coating of batter, and do not be alarmed if the batter doesn't evenly cover the fish. It will expand immediately when it hits the hot fat, so the fish will be completely encased.)

6. Working in batches, fry the fish in the hot oil until golden, about 4 minutes. Drain on paper towels. Let the oil heat up between batches.

7. Either serve the fish as it is cooked or keep warm in a single layer on a baking sheet in a low oven. (Don't keep it too long in the oven, or the batter will become soggy.)

Makes 4 servings

Mathilde's Fish Cakes with Fried Onions

*I*n the Scandinavian community of Petersburg, Alaska, fish cakes are as common as raindrops. You won't find them in restaurants—they're the culinary jewels of the home, and everyone's recipe is a shade different. Feelings about fish cakes run high in any Scandinavian community: In Seattle not long ago, a local newspaper ran a story about fish cakes, with recipes, and the hullabaloo that followed lasted for weeks—letters agreeing and disagreeing, pointers for where the best fish cakes in town could *really* be found, what was in them or should be.

This recipe for fish cakes is one of the best. I claim no credit for it, for it was given to me by Anne Thompson, a matriarch of Petersburg. Her husband was a fish buyer in the town, which meant she always had plenty of fish for experimentation. Mrs. Thompson has a wonderful collection of recipes that she let me peruse one day, and when I came across these—likely the hundredth fish cake recipe I'd seen in my three-day stay in Petersburg—they sounded a cut above. "I got those from an old friend years ago, they are real good," Mrs. Thompson said. I trusted her judgment, for my path to find her had been strewn with praise for her cooking abilities and natural good taste. Here, then, are Mathilde's fish cakes—as homey and simple, yet elegant and wonderful as can be. They are traditionally served with slow-cooked, buttery onions. I love them with *crème fraîche* or sour cream too. Try these with a lightly chilled white Graves or an Orvieto.

Onions:

3 tablespoons unsalted butter
2 large onions, thinly sliced
Salt and freshly ground black pepper

Fish Cakes:

1 pound lingcod, boned
1 large egg
1 small onion, minced
1 tablespoon potato flour (potato starch)
½ teaspoon finely ground black pepper
1 teaspoon freshly grated nutmeg
½ teaspoon ground ginger
1½ teaspoons salt
1¼ cups milk
½ cup (1 stick) unsalted butter, melted
1 tablespoon unsalted butter
1 tablespoon mild vegetable oil, such as safflower
¼ cup loosely packed flat-leaf parsley leaves, minced
1 cup crème fraîche or sour cream, for garnish

1. Prepare the Onions: Melt the butter in a large skillet over medium heat. Add the onions and stir to coat. Cover and cook, stirring occasionally, until softened and beginning to turn golden, 10 to 15 minutes. Season with salt and pepper to taste. Remove from the heat; reserve.

2. Make the Fish Cakes: Cut the lingcod into 1-inch squares. Place in the bowl of a food processor and process until the cod is completely ground and is almost fluffy looking. Add the egg and onion; process until thoroughly combined. Add the potato flour and seasonings; blend again. With the processor running, slowly pour in the milk. When thoroughly incorporated, add the melted butter and process until well combined.

3. Heat the 1 tablespoon butter with the oil in a large skillet over medium heat. When

hot but not smoking, add the fish cake mixture in heaping tablespoonfuls, pressing down on each one to make it about 1½ x 2 inches, and more oblong than round. Cook until the cakes are golden and puff slightly, about 4 minutes; flip and cook until golden on the other side, about 4 minutes. Place the fish cakes on a paper towel-covered baking sheet and keep warm in a low oven until the remaining fish cakes are cooked.

4. Reheat the onions and butter, stirring occasionally, over medium heat. Arrange the fish cakes on a large, warm serving platter; surround with the onions. Sprinkle the onions with the parsley; serve the *crème fraîche* on the side. Serve immediately.

Makes 4 to 6 servings

Chinese-Style Buffalo Fish

*T*his recipe, which is adapted from one in *Chinese Cooking on Next to Nothing*, by Kenneth H. Lo, grew out of my curiosity about buffalo fish. Whenever I go to the fish market, I see people buying buffalo fish. I must stare, for, without fail, they tell me how delicious it is and how I should take one home, dredge it in cornmeal, and fry it. That has never appealed to me, so I decided to try and prepare it in a stew of some kind. When I saw this recipe, I knew it was the right one. And it is. The sauce is rich and somewhat earthy, and it complements the earthy flavor and slightly soft texture of the buffalo fish, yet mellows it as well. Buffalo fish is a very sweet fish with a fair amount of bones, particularly near the head end, so be aware

of them as you eat. Try it with a chilled, light white wine, such as a Pinot Grigio.

1 buffalo fish or carp (3½ to 4½ pounds) cleaned, with head off
Salt and freshly ground black pepper
2 tablespoons all-purpose flour
¼ cup soy sauce
¼ cup sweet sherry
3 tablespoons mild vegetable oil
1 tablespoon very fine fresh ginger julienne
2 medium onions, thinly sliced
1 medium green bell pepper, cored, seeded, and thinly sliced
2 tablespoons lard
3 scallions, trimmed, the white bulb and light green stems cut diagonally into thin slices

1. Rinse the buffalo fish inside and out. Trim off any membrane from the cavity, if necessary; rinse again and pat dry. Generously season the stomach cavity with salt and pepper.

2. Cut the fish into 6 steaks, each 2 inches thick.

3. In a shallow dish, combine the flour with 2 teaspoons of salt.

4. Dredge the fish steaks in the salt and flour, making sure they are well-covered. Shake off any excess.

5. Combine the soy sauce and sherry with ¼ cup water in a small bowl; reserve.

6. Heat the oil in a large skillet over medium-high heat. When the oil is hot, add the ginger, onions, and bell pepper; cook, stirring constantly, just until the onion is limp, about 4 minutes.

7. Transfer the onions, green pepper, and ginger to a bowl or plate. Add the lard to the pan. When hot, reduce the heat to medium. Add the fish steaks and lightly brown on both sides, 2 to 3 minutes per side. Return

the onions, bell pepper, and ginger to the pan. Add the soy and sherry mixture; mix gently to coat the fish and vegetables with the sauce. Cover and cook until the fish is opaque through, 7 to 8 minutes.

8. To serve, sprinkle with the scallions and serve it from the skillet for an attractive, informal presentation. Alternately, transfer the pieces of fish to a shallow serving bowl or platter. Arrange the onions, bell pepper, and ginger on and around the fish. Pour the sauce over all and sprinkle with the scallions. Serve immediately.

Makes 4 to 6 servings

Salmon and Peas in Ginger Butter

*T*his dish embodies spring in the Northwest, when the first, brilliant red sockeye start to show, peas come fresh and crisp from the garden, and thoughts turn to light, elegant, fine-weather meals. Try this with a lightly chilled, young white Graves from Bordeaux, or a Sancerre.

1 salmon fillet (1 pound), sockeye if possible

Scant ½ teaspoon mild vegetable oil, such as safflower

¼ cup Fish Stock (see Index)

2 tablespoons dry white wine

1 cup (2 sticks) unsalted butter, chilled

Salt and freshly ground black pepper

2 teaspoons Pia's Ginger Purée (see Index), or to taste

12 ounces sugar snap or snow peas, trimmed

½ cup shelled fresh peas

½ teaspoon minced fresh ginger

1. Rinse the salmon fillet and pat dry. Cut the fillet crosswise, holding the knife blade at a 45 degree angle, into 8 slices. Rub the slices lightly all over with the oil. Place on the rack of a fish poacher or steamer. Refrigerate until ready to use.

2. Bring the stock and wine to a boil in a small, heavy-bottomed non-aluminum saucepan over medium-high heat. Boil until reduced to about 1 tablespoon. Reserving 1 tablespoon butter, begin adding the remaining butter, one piece at a time, whisking well after each addition. Work on and off the heat, as necessary, to keep the butter from melting before it is emulsified. Season with salt and pepper to taste. Add the ginger purée, to taste. Keep the pan of sauce warm in a bowl or pan filled with hot water.

3. Melt the remaining 1 tablespoon butter in a large skillet over medium-high heat. Add the pea pods and cook, stirring, until they begin to turn bright green, about 4 minutes. Add the shelled peas and cook until bright green, 3 to 4 minutes. Remove from the heat; reserve.

4. While the peas are cooking, bring water in the bottom of a fish poacher or steamer to a boil over high heat. Place the salmon on a rack in the poacher, cover, and steam until opaque throughout, 4 to 5 minutes. Remove from the heat.

5. To serve, arrange the pea pods and all but 1 tablespoon of the peas on the bottom of a large warm platter. Arrange the salmon slices on top; coat with the ginger sauce. Sprinkle the minced ginger and the reserved peas over all. Serve immediately.

Makes 4 servings

Fishing in Alaska

They're called "swivelnecks" in southeast Alaska, because they're constantly turning their heads from side to side, to check the lines on either side of the boat for fish. The rest of the world calls them troll fishermen, and they catch some of the best quality wild fish available.

Helen and Keane Gau have been troll fishermen in southeast Alaska for 25 years, and their story is unique. Keane owned a bar in Spokane and had never been on a boat, but he always dreamed of being a fisherman. When he and Helen got together they moved to the Washington coast and bought a sailboat. "We didn't know you couldn't fish from a sailboat," Helen said. "So we did, for nearly 25 years."

Now, the Gau's fish outside of Sitka, from a small power boat that skips across the water like a piece of styrofoam. It's called the Adagio, which translates as "music played slowly, with feeling" and that's how they see the present.

Keane and Helen were among the first fishermen to clean and bleed their fish at sea. They still do, then put the fish in slush ice to keep them fresh between visits to port every couple days.

Tasks are clearly delineated aboard the Adagio. "There's a lot of macho in fishing," Helen said, as Keane left the cabin to go check the lines. "The stern is his 'office,' and I don't go back there until it's time to clean the fish."

Suddenly, at the sound of a bell tinkling, Helen shouts "King salmon knockin' heavy on the line!" The bell is called a "gerlie" and it sits at the top of the trolling pole, to signal a fish on the line. Helen can tell by the sound of it, and by the way the spring at the end of the line, called a "tattletale," vibrates, what kind of fish they've hooked.

Keane activates a hydraulic pulley that brings the line slowly out of the water. He unsnaps the individual lines attached to it, and transfers them to a line

A view of the village of Sitka from Bruce Gore's boat, the Triad.

strung across the stern of the boat. When he sees a king salmon on the hook end, he attaches a length of rubber hose called a "rubber snubber" to his end of the line, so the fish can play out a bit more, and use up some of its energy before being pulled in and stunned.

Keane gently pulls fish right up to the boat, reaches over and knocks them on the head with a stick that looks like a baseball bat with a nail sticking out of one side. He hooks the fish through the gills with the nail and hauls it on deck. He cuts out the gills which severs an artery, and the still-beating heart pumps out most of the blood. He covers the fish with wet burlap, and once it's had a chance to cool down it becomes Helen's territory.

A small wooden trough on the starboard stern holds the fish steady, belly up, while Helen spreads the belly flaps and scrapes the blood from the backbone using a knife with a spoon lashed to the handle end, so she can cut with one end, and scrape with the other. She scrapes down the belly walls with the spoon, pushing out any remaining blood until the water she rinses them with comes clean. When she's finished, the fish goes back on deck to cool for another hour or so before it's put in the tank of slush ice.

Later in the day there's a lull in the action, and we're all sitting in the cabin. Keane and Helen reminisce about their lives as Alaska fishermen. "It's changed. Big boats back when we started are little boats now," Helen said. "But fishermen are the same. They're the greatest bunch in the world. They'll do anything for each

Helen Gau removes a bonus of fat, firm roe from a just-caught salmon.

other," she says. "Except tell you where the fish are," adds Keane.

Bruce Gore fishes from Sitka too. Like Keane, Bruce is considered a top-notch fisherman.

Bruce grew up around the fishing business in Longview, Washington. When he caught and sold his first fish at age 5 he was hooked on the business. He crewed on seine boats in Alaska during college, then bought his own boat. "We used to pack the fish around unrefrigerated and uncleaned, looking for a buyer," he said. That was common practice then, though a few, like the Gaus, had different ideas. In the 1970s Bruce realized some-

(continued on next page)

(continued from previous page)

thing was wrong. "The domestic market was a dumping ground and all the good fish went for export," he said. "When the dollar got strong I said to heck with imports, sold my old boat and designed and built the Triad."

The classy, 44-foot boat is like an ocean liner in miniature, at least compared with most fishing boats. The cabin was hand-crafted by a carpenter, and finished by Kathy, Bruce's wife, and it's as comfortable as a suburban living room. The deck is all organization and efficiency, and the engine room, whose rumbling growl is effectively muffled, is so clean you could eat off the floor, if there was room in the maze of wires and pumping, humming parts that make the Triad go. In the freezer hold, apparent magic takes place.

It isn't really magic, it's all carefully designed by Bruce, who doesn't leave much to chance. His equipment is state-of-the-art, so fish can be flash-frozen and glazed at sea, then delivered in peak condition. When they thaw, they glisten, every scale is in place, and they look as beautiful as when they first came out of the water.

Bruce has a "deckhand, puller, crewman, I don't know what I'm called," said Tom Reinholdt, and together they get the job done. After a day in Sitka, Bruce heads the Triad out on a late summer afternoon. The salmon hunt is on.

He stops the boat in Sam Sing Cove at about 10 P.M. It's still light outside, as it will be all night, except for a quick hour when darkness flits across the sky.

I'm up by 5 the next morning, a slug-a-bed compared with Bruce and Tom, who've been up since 3:30 A.M. It's a slow morning. Tom is outside checking the lines. He's pulled in a couple silver salmon and is hosing them down. Bruce's eyes are riveted on the surrounding water. There isn't much else to see, except a cluster of boats on the horizon where, apparently, there's action.

He decides it isn't worth it to pick up the gear and head over there. "I follow my hunches to find fish," Bruce says. "You can't follow other boats—you're just following someone else's fish.

Bruce has four radios on simultaneously, and their snowy crackle creates constant background noise. Like all fishermen, Bruce belongs to a "code-group," of four or five other fishermen who tell each other over the radio when they've found fish, in code, and that's what he listens for. It also provides diversion in twenty-hour long days, when the fish are only biting casually, and there's time to sit.

"What kills you is getting a fish here and there," Bruce said. "What's good is if you get a couple, then you get a clatter, then you get some more, all day long." A 'clatter' is a group of fish on the lines all at once.

When that happens, both men jump to work, hauling in fish as fast as they can. After a clatter, the deck is crowded with fish. There are a dozen or more huge, sweet-smelling king salmon. Then there's an assortment of sleek silvers, a slim sockeye, and many pink salmon, all flopping around on deck with a rhythm you could dance to even though they've

Bruce Gore displays a king salmon at the end of a gaff hook.

been stunned, and are emitting a strong, unpleasant odor. Pink salmon, or 'humpies' as they're called, are the bane of an Alaska trollfisherman's life. They take up room on the lines, they're difficult to work with, and they sell for practically nothing. In southeast Alaska they've been christened "humpies from hell."

Bruce catches most of the fish when it's busy, hefting them on deck with a grace and rhythm born of years of practice. When there's no more room on deck, Tom starts to clean them.

He sets each fish in a Plexiglas cleaning trough, and cleans them much the same way Helen Gau does. He goes a few steps further, however, flushing each fish with saltwater, literally massaging the blood out, and grooming it with tweezers and a toothbrush, so the fish fairly sparkle. The cleaned fish are covered with wet burlap and left on the deck to cool and drain, then cleaned again.

Tom inserts a plastic tag into the collar of each fish that reads 'Bruce Gore—Triad Fisheries, Inc.,' "There's never been this kind of accountability in the industry," he said. Following Bruce's lead, fishermen in other places are now doing similar things. Bruce descends into the hold, that's kept at about 27 below zero, to take the fish Tom hands down. When they're frozen to the core, usually within three days, Bruce will dip them in a sugar-and-water glaze as protection against dehydration.

When Bruce began freezing fish at sea he realized quickly that producing good fish wasn't enough. He's had to be zealous about getting his fish to market, and overcoming the stigma attached to "frozen" fish. When he first started, he hand-carried his fish to restaurants and supermarkets, to explain his processing methods, and why his fish costs more per pound.

It's paid off, at least in the Seattle-area, where most of his fish is sold. Everyone who knows even a little bit about fish knows a Bruce Gore fish means the highest quality.

Panaché of Steamed Seafood with Basil Butter Sauce

This dish is elegant, simple, and pristine. The play of textures and colors in the tiny brochettes is wonderful, and you may mix and match—substitute just about any firm, white meat fish for the shark and the monkfish. You must have salmon, though, for it adds flair as well as flavor. The fish for this dish is cut into very small pieces, which makes for somewhat dainty, elegant skewers. Try a chilled dry Loire white wine with this, such as a Vouvray, a Touraine, or a Saumur.

6 ounces mako shark steak, cut in small cubes,
   slightly less than ½ inch
5 ounces skinless salmon fillet, preferably sockeye, cut
   in small cubes, slightly less than ½ inch
4 ounces monkfish, cut in small cubes, slightly less
   than ½ inch
4 tablespoons extra-virgin olive oil
1 tablespoon fresh lemon juice
Salt and freshly ground black pepper
8 ounces squid-ink or spinach spaghetti or fettuccine
4 crawfish, rinsed
8 clams, rinsed

Sauce:

1 tablespoon balsamic vinegar
1 teaspoon fresh lemon juice
1 tablespoon extra-virgin olive oil
1 teaspoon minced orange zest
4 tablespoons (½ stick) unsalted butter, chilled and
   cut into small pieces
Salt and freshly ground black pepper
½ cup loosely packed fresh basil leaves

1. Place the cubes of fish in a small bowl. Add 3 tablespoons of the olive oil, the lemon juice, and a pinch of salt and pepper; toss to coat thoroughly. Marinate in the refrigerator for 30 minutes.

2. Remove the fish cubes from the marinade, reserving the marinade. Thread the cubes on 8 short, wood or metal skewers, alternating the fish so the colors are distributed. Refrigerate until right before you put them in the steamer. (The fish skewers should not be assembled more than 15 minutes in advance.)

3. Bring a large saucepan of salted water to a boil over high heat. Stir in the remaining 1 tablespoon olive oil; add the pasta and stir to separate the strands. Cook until al dente, tender but still firm to the bite, 8 to 10 minutes. Drain the pasta well. Return it to the pan and add the reserved marinade. Toss to coat; keep warm in a low oven.

4. While the pasta is cooking, bring 2 cups of water to a boil in the bottom of a steamer. Devein the crawfish. Place the crawfish and clams in the steamer. Cover and steam for 2 minutes. Either shift the clams and the crawfish in the steamer to make room for an even layer of skewers, or remove them from the steamer just long enough to add the skewers, and replace them, on top of the skewers if necessary. Cover and steam until the pieces of fish are nearly opaque through, the clams are open, and the crawfish are bright red, 4 to 5 minutes.

5. While the fish is cooking, prepare the sauce: Combine the vinegar, lemon juice, and oil in a small non-aluminum saucepan over medium-high heat. Bring to a boil. Stir in the orange zest. Add the butter, a few pieces at a time, whisking constantly after each addition and working on and off the heat, as necessary, until all the butter is

added and the sauce is smooth and creamy. Season with salt and pepper to taste. Mince the basil and whisk into the sauce.

6. To serve, evenly divide the pasta among 4 warm dinner plates. Place 2 skewers of fish on top of the pasta, and evenly divide the clams and the crawfish among the plates. Serve the sauce alongside.

Makes 4 servings

The Moors Restaurant's Peixe Com Molho Tomate

This Portuguese recipe comes from My-lan Costa, owner of the Moors Restaurant in Provincetown, Massachusetts. Each year Provincetown is the site of the "Trash Fish Banquet," a huge meal sponsored by the Center for Coastal Studies in Provincetown and local restaurants, to promote underutilized species of fish and shellfish—mussels, monkfish, hake, ocean pout, mackerel, and squid. With a line-up like that, Trash Fish start to sound pretty tasty. The array of creations at the Trash Fish banquet are enough to convince anyone that there is more in the sea than cod and orange roughy.

There are wonderful surprises in every bite of this dish. One of the biggest is that the flavor and texture of the fish come through the robust flavors of the sauce. At the Moors this dish usually features hake, though just about any firm, white fish will do. Try this with a light, dry, firm and elegant red wine, such as a red Graves from Bordeaux.

3 tablespoons plus 1½ teaspoons mild vegetable oil, such as safflower
1 small white onion, thinly sliced
1 large green bell pepper, cored, seeded, and thinly sliced
8 ounces mushrooms, brushed clean and thinly sliced
1 pound ripe plum tomatoes, peeled and quartered
3 cloves garlic, coarsely chopped
½ cup full-bodied red wine
2 teaspoons sugar
¾ teaspoon ground cumin
¾ cup loosely packed fresh basil leaves, or ½ teaspoon dried
1 tablespoon fresh thyme leaves, or ½ teaspoon dried
¼ teaspoon dried hot pepper flakes
¾ teaspoon Tabasco sauce, or to taste
4 ounces linguiça or chorizo (spicy sausage available from Italian or specialty delicatessens), cut into thin rounds
4 ounces coppacolla (available from Italian or specialty delicatessens) or smoked ham, diced
2 pounds hake, lingcod, haddock, or snapper fillets cut into 6 equal pieces
Salt and freshly ground black pepper
1 cup loosely packed flat-leaf parsley leaves, minced

1. Heat 3 tablespoons of the oil in a large non-aluminum saucepan over medium-high heat. When the oil is hot, add the onion, bell pepper, and mushrooms; sauté until the onions are translucent, about 5 minutes. Stir in the tomatoes and garlic. Cover, bring to a boil, and cook, stirring occasionally, until thickened somewhat, about 5 minutes.

2. Stir in the wine, sugar, cumin, basil, thyme, pepper flakes, Tabasco, *chorizo, coppacolla,* and ½ cup water. Cover and bring to a boil, stirring occasionally. Reduce the heat to medium and cook, uncovered, stirring occasionally, until the sauce is thick but

some liquid remains, about 45 minutes.

3. About 10 minutes before the sauce is finished, bring 2 cups of water to a boil in the bottom of a wok, steamer, or fish poacher. Lightly rub the pieces of fish all over with the remaining 1½ teaspoons oil. Season lightly on both sides with salt and pepper. Place the fish on a plate or steaming rack, cover, and steam until opaque through, about 8 minutes. Transfer the fish to a warm serving platter or 16 warm dinner plates.

4. Stir the parsley into the sauce. Spoon the sauce over and alongside the fish. Serve immediately.

Makes 6 servings

Stephen Pyles' Blue Cornmeal Catfish with Pecans

This recipe is like a treatise on southwest ingredients—pecans, blue cornmeal, catfish. Stephen Pyles, chef and owner of the Routh Street Cafe in Dallas, Texas, grew up around catfish—his family served it fried at their truck stop restaurant, with tartar sauce and hush puppies. This recipe is a lighter, contemporary twist on that. Try a lightly chilled, toasty American Chardonnay.

Pecan Butter:

⅓ cup pecan halves
2 tablespoons unsalted butter
1 tablespoon minced fresh chives
1 jalapeño chile, stemmed, seeded, and minced

Butter Sauce:

⅓ cup Fish Stock (see Index) or chicken stock
⅓ cup dry white wine, such as Vouvray
⅓ cup white wine vinegar
1 tablespoon minced shallot
2 tablespoons minced fresh mint marigold leaves or 2 teaspoons dried mint marigold or tarragon
1 cup (2 sticks) chilled unsalted butter, cut into tablespoon-size pieces
1 tablespoon fresh lime juice
Salt and freshly ground black pepper

Catfish Fillets:

¾ cup mild vegetable oil, such as safflower, for frying
2 large eggs, beaten
½ cup buttermilk
1 cup cornmeal, preferably blue
¼ teaspoon salt
¼ teaspoon freshly ground black pepper
4 catfish fillets (4 to 6 ounces each), rinsed and patted dry
1 tablespoon minced fresh chives, for garnish

1. Preheat the oven to 300°F.

2. Make the Pecan Butter: Place the pecans in a cake pan. Toast in the oven, stirring occasionally, until golden, about 15 minutes. Set aside to cool.

3. Finely chop the pecans in a food processor, pulsing on and off. Add the butter, chives, and jalapeño; process until puréed, about 2 minutes. Scrape into a small bowl; chill until ready to use, but at least 1 hour.

4. Make the Butter Sauce: Bring the fish stock, wine, vinegar, shallot, and 1 tablespoon of the mint marigold to a boil in the top of a medium-size non-aluminum double boiler over medium-high heat. Boil until reduced to 2 tablespoons. Reduce the heat to medium. Whisk in the butter, one piece at a

time, working on and off the heat, as necessary, to keep the butter from melting before it is emulsified. Whisk in the remaining 1 tablespoon mint marigold and the lime juice. Cut the chilled pecan butter into bits. Whisk in the pecan butter as you did the unsalted butter, until thoroughly incorporated into the sauce. Season with salt and pepper to taste. Keep the sauce warm over a bowl or pan of hot water.

5. Prepare the catfish: Heat the oil in a large skillet over medium-high heat.

6. In a medium-size bowl, whisk together the eggs and buttermilk. Pour the mixture into a shallow dish. In a shallow plate, mix the blue cornmeal with the salt and pepper. Dip the fish fillets in the egg and buttermilk mixture; dredge in the blue cornmeal to coat completely. Shake off any excess.

7. When the oil is hot and a wisp of smoke dances off the surface, fry the fillets until golden on both sides and opaque through, about 4 minutes per side. Drain on paper towels.

8. To serve, pour the sauce in the middle of 4 warm dinner plates. Place a catfish fillet on top of the sauce. Garnish with the chives. Serve immediately.

Makes 4 servings

Aromatic Portuguese Hake

*T*his delectable recipe has a distinct Portuguese flavor. It comes from Cape Cod, where many Portuguese people, originally from the Azores, immigrated for the fishing. They brought a rich culinary legacy in sim-

ple, aromatic, and hearty food. This recipe was inspired by one in *Peter Hunt's Cape Cod Cookbook*, published in 1954. It works well with cusk, haddock, or hake. Why not match the roots of the dish with chilled dry, white Vinho Verde from Portugal? Or try any dry white wine with this dish.

1½ pounds hake fillet, cut into 4 equal pieces
3 tablespoons unsalted butter
1 pound onions, sliced (4 cups)
2 tablespoons all-purpose flour
1 tablespoon white wine vinegar
¼ teaspoon each ground cloves, allspice, and cinnamon
¼ teaspoon saffron threads, gently crushed with a mortar and pestle
½ teaspoon ground cumin
Salt and freshly ground black pepper
2 tablespoons finely minced flat-leaf parsley

1. Rinse the hake and pat dry. Refrigerate until ready to use.

2. Melt the butter in a large skillet over medium-high heat. Add the onions, and sauté until nearly translucent and beginning to turn gold, about 10 minutes. Stir in the flour and cook, stirring, until it turns dark gold, about 5 minutes. It will stick to the bottom of the pan a bit, but don't worry, just keep stirring the onions and don't let the flour burn.

3. Add 2 cups water, the vinegar and all of the spices; mix well, scraping up any browned bits on the bottom of the pan. Cook, stirring constantly, until the sauce has thickened slightly, about 5 minutes. Season generously with salt and pepper.

4. Season the pieces of hake on each side with salt and a generous amount of pepper. Place the fish in the sauce, turning once to coat the pieces with it, and making sure they

are nestled well in the onions. Cover and cook until the hake is opaque through, about 10 minutes. (The sauce, which will be quite thick, will bubble and boil merrily—scrape the bottom of the pan occasionally, moving the fish around gently to get at it.)

5. Remove from the heat. Transfer the fish and sauce to a warm serving platter and garnish with the parsley, or garnish with the parsley and serve as is, from the pan.

Makes 4 servings

Trout with Hazelnuts and Butter

There is something magical about trout with hazelnuts. The crunch of the nuts adds interest and wonderful, rich flavor, and lemon makes it all stand up and shout. The skin of the trout peels off easily, for those who don't care to eat it, though in my mind if you remove the skin, you remove a great deal of the flavor. Farm-raised trout are raised in such pristine conditions that the skin is very edible; wild trout generally come from wonderful, clean rushing water, and they are recommended here. You may want to try this same preparation with petrale or lemon sole. Try this with a very lightly chilled white Burgundy.

4 rainbow trout (6 ounces each), cleaned with head on
Salt and freshly ground black pepper
¾ cup whole hazelnuts
½ cup (1 stick) unsalted butter, clarified (see Index)
¼ cup all-purpose flour
2 tablespoons fresh lemon juice
2 tablespoons minced fresh chives

1. Rinse the trout and pat dry. Season the stomach cavities with salt and pepper.

2. Preheat the oven to 350°F.

3. Place the hazelnuts in an ovenproof pan and toast in the oven until golden and the skins split, 12 to 15 minutes. Remove and wrap them in a tea towel; set aside for 5 minutes, until cooled somewhat. Rub in the towel to remove as much of the skin as possible. Discard the skins; coarsely chop the hazelnuts.

4. Heat 3 tablespoons of the clarified butter in a large skillet over medium-high heat.

5. While the butter is heating, combine the flour with ¼ teaspoon salt and a generous grinding of pepper in a shallow dish. Dredge the trout in the flour, coating thoroughly.

6. When the butter is hot, gently slide the trout into the pan. Fry until light golden on each side and just opaque through, 3 to 4 minutes per side.

7. While the trout are frying, heat the remaining clarified butter in a small saucepan over medium heat. Stir in the lemon juice and hazelnuts; add the chives.

8. Remove the trout from the pan; pour the butter and hazelnut sauce over them. Alternatively, fillet the trout and serve the fillets individually, with the butter and hazelnut sauce poured over all.

Makes 4 servings

Honorine's Salty Fish

Honorine Tepfer is a Vietnamese-French artist and a fabulous Vietnamese cook. She lived in Seattle for a long time and, while there, she had so many friends and relatives clamoring for her recipes that she wrote a lovely cookbook, *Honorine's Vietnamese Cookbook,* in 1976. Honorine visits Seattle often, from her home in Paris, France, and once when she was here she gave me her book, which includes this incredible recipe. It exalts Honorine's devotion to *nuoc mam,* or fish sauce, a staple seasoning in Vietnamese food. She even composed an ode to it, which is printed in the introduction to her book:

> *If I were granted just one wish*
> *I'd pick a sea of fermented fish*
> *When I run out of that dear Nuoc Mam*
> *Just lay me down and sing a psalm.*

Honorine recommends *nuoc mam* from Hong Kong, though Thailand also produces a good quality sauce. This dish demands good white rice and a Spinach Salad (see Index) alongside. As Honorine explained, "You take a bite of fish, a bite of rice, then a bite of salad, in traditional Vietnamese fashion." Try this with a chilled, very toasty Chardonnay or white Burgundy.

1 swordfish or tuna steak (1 pound)
1 tablespoon peanut oil
½ cup fish sauce (nuoc mam)
1 large jalapeño chile, seeded and cut into medium
    julienne, or ¼ teaspoon dried hot pepper flakes
2 tablespoons sugar

1. Rinse the fish and pat dry.
2. Heat the oil in a medium-size skillet (that is just larger than the piece of fish) over medium-high heat. Add the fish and brown lightly on each side, about 1 minute per side.
3. Combine the fish sauce and ¾ cup water in a small bowl. Pour over the fish. Add the jalapeño; bring the liquid to a boil. Reduce the heat to medium-low, cover, and cook for 25 minutes. Carefully turn the fish,

cover, and continue cooking for 20 minutes more. Do not think this is too long—the fish will be moist and succulent.
4. About 5 minutes before the fish is to be removed from the heat, combine the sugar and 1 tablespoon water in a small saucepan over medium-high heat. Cook until the mixture caramelizes and is deep gold. Remove from the heat. Add 2 tablespoons of the fish cooking liquid to the caramel, stirring to combine.
5. Transfer the fish to a warm serving platter. Stir the caramel into the fish cooking liquid. Pour the cooking liquid over the fish. Serve immediately.

Makes 4 servings

Skate Sauce Gribiche

Skate is a much-ignored treasure of the sea, though it shouldn't be for its meat is white and tender, and its taste is sweet. Once prepared, it looks gorgeous on a plate, the deeply ribbed, fan-like shape of its meat a delight to the eyes.

One of my favorite ways to serve skate is with a sauce *gribiche,* a common preparation in France, where skate is very highly regarded. I got the idea from a restaurant in Paris, La Cagouille, and I make it often at home. Sauce *gribiche* goes well with many kinds of seafood because it heightens flavors and makes for a zesty, colorful preparation.

If I get skate with the skin on, I prefer to pre-cook it in a court bouillon to loosen the skin from the meat and remove any whiff of ammonia. Even very fresh skate has a tiny hint of ammonia, which increases with age. As long as skate is fresh, however, and it will last up to a week if it is carefully handled and kept cold, the ammonia isn't troublesome and will be removed by cooking in court bouillon.

If I get skate with the skin off, I still cook it for just a few minutes in court bouillon. I always prefer to finish cooking skate in a steamer, for it is gentler on the meat.

Serve this with a chilled, white Chenin Blanc or a buttery Chardonnay.

1 tablespoon plus 1 teaspoon red wine vinegar
1 tablespoon plus 1 teaspoon sherry vinegar
2 tablespoons plus 2 teaspoons extra-virgin olive oil
1 tablespoon plus 1 teaspoon mild vegetable oil, such as safflower
¼ cup diced red onion
2 tablespoons diced cornichons (small French pickles)
1½ teaspoons drained small capers
½ teaspoon Dijon mustard, or to taste
Salt and freshly ground black pepper
Court Bouillon (see below)
2 pounds skate wing
2 large hard-cooked eggs, yolks and whites minced separately
¼ cup flat-leaf parsley leaves

1. Place the vinegars in a small bowl. Using a wire whisk, add the oils in a thin stream, whisking constantly until emulsified. Add the onion, cornichons, capers, and mustard; mix well. Season generously with salt and pepper; reserve. (The sauce gribiche can be prepared several hours in advance.)

2. Bring the court bouillon to a boil over medium high heat. Slide the skate wing into the court bouillon. Reduce the heat to medium, and simmer the skate until it begins to turn white at the edges and the skin begins to wrinkle, about 5 minutes. (If the skate wing is already skinned, cook it just until it begins to turn white at the edges, 2 to 3 minutes. Add additional boiling water if the court bouillon doesn't completely cover the skate wing.) Transfer the skate to a work surface and let cool.

3. To skin the skate, using a sharp-bladed knife, gently scrape off all of the skin and any gristle underneath it (easily identified—it is a clear, jelly-like substance), being careful not to disturb the pattern of the skate wing. There is a thin layer of brown meat on the skate wing as well, which you may cut away if you like, though it isn't necessary.

4. Bring 2 cups of water to a boil in a saucepan or a wok fitted with a steaming rack. When the water boils, add the skate wing. Cover and steam until the skate is opaque through, about 8 minutes if the wing is thin, or for about 10 minutes if the wing is about 2 inches thick.

5. While the skate is steaming, mince the parsley leaves.

6. To serve, cut the skate wing vertically into 4 pieces. Carefully arrange on 4 warmed dinner plates. Pour equal amounts of the sauce gribiche over the skate wing. Garnish with equal amounts of the egg yolk, egg white, and parsley. Serve immediately.

Makes 4 servings

Court Bouillon

3 cups dry white wine, such as Vouvray
2 tablespoons white wine vinegar
2 medium onions, cut into thick slices
Several sprigs of flat-leaf parsley
4 whole peppercorns
2 bay leaves
1 whole clove

1. Combine all of the ingredients in a large non-aluminum saucepan along with 4 cups cold water. Bring to a boil over high heat. Reduce the heat to medium, and simmer for 30 minutes.

2. Strain the court bouillon, discarding the solids, before using as a cooking liquid.

Makes about 2 quarts

Flounder à la North Carolina

Murray Bridges, a flounder fisherman in Kitty Hawk, North Carolina, likes flounder best when it is smothered in what he calls "steak gravy," a water-base sauce chock full of sweet onions. This version of Murray's recipe calls for the flounder to be slowly cooked on top of the stove, set on a bed of lemon-tinged spinach, and smothered with the requisite onions. I don't know if it would be called a steak gravy, but it sure makes the flounder taste great. You may substitute petrale sole for the flounder, if you like. Try this with a lightly chilled, clean white wine such as an Alsatian Sylvaner.

4 tablespoons unsalted butter
4 medium onions, finely chopped
Salt and freshly ground black pepper
2 pounds fresh spinach, stemmed and washed
2 tablespoons fresh lemon juice
4 flounder fillets (6 to 7 ounces each)
¼ cup dry white wine
¼ cup Fish Stock (see Index)
2 tablespoons chopped fresh mixed herbs or parsley

1. Melt 2 tablespoons of the butter in a medium-size skillet over medium-high heat. Add the onions and stir. Reduce the heat to medium, cover, and cook, stirring occasionally, until translucent but not coloring, about 25 minutes. Season with salt and pepper to taste. Keep warm over low heat.

2. While the onions are cooking, place the spinach in a large non-aluminum saucepan over medium-high heat. Cover and cook in the water that clings to its leaves just until the spinach has reduced in volume and the leaves are soft but still bright green, 5 to 7 minutes.

3. Drain the spinach; gently squeeze out some but not all of the liquid. Coarsely chop. Place the spinach in a small bowl and add the lemon juice. Toss until well mixed. Cover and keep warm in a low oven.

4. Melt the remaining 2 tablespoons butter in a large skillet over medium heat. Add the flounder fillets, season with salt and pepper, and pour the wine and stock around the fillets. Cook until opaque on one side, about 6 minutes. Gently turn, season with salt and pepper, and cook until opaque through, 4 to 5 minutes.

5. Evenly divide the spinach among 4 warm dinner plates, spreading it out in the center of the plate. Top with a flounder fillet; spoon the onions over the top. Dust with pepper; sprinkle with the herbs. Serve immediately.

Makes 4 servings

Alligator Creole

This recipe comes from Bob Sturgeon, a native Floridian transplanted to Seattle, who imports fresh-frozen, farm-raised Florida alligator meat into Seattle, where 'gator fans snap it up as fast as it arrives. No wonder—farm-raised alligator meat is mild and tasty, with a texture similar to pork but with a much more delicate flavor. Though alligator isn't exactly seafood, it lives in water and it's always spoken of in a seafood context, which is why this recipe is here. I serve this over white rice seasoned with 4 whole cloves, a small onion cut in thin rings, and a bay leaf. Try this with a slightly chilled Beaujolais.

2 tablespoons unsalted butter
1 large green bell pepper, cored, seeded, and diced
1 large onion, coarsely chopped
1½ cups diced celery
1 pound ripe plum tomatoes, cored and coarsely chopped
⅓ cup dry white wine, such as Vouvray
1 tablespoon fresh lemon juice
1 teaspoon Worcestershire sauce
2 bay leaves
4 whole cloves
¼ teaspoon hot red pepper flakes
Salt and freshly ground black pepper
1½ pounds alligator meat, cut into bite-size pieces

1. Melt the butter in a large non-aluminum skillet over medium high heat. Add the bell pepper, onion, and celery. Sauté, stirring frequently, until the vegetables are translucent, about 10 minutes.

2. Stir in the tomatoes. Add the wine, lemon juice, and Worcestershire sauce. Stir in the bay leaves, cloves, and hot pepper flakes. Season with salt and pepper to taste.

3. Bring the mixture to a boil over high heat. Add the alligator, stir, and return to a boil. Reduce the heat to medium low, cover, and cook, stirring occasionally, until the alligator is cooked and tender, about 40 minutes.

4. Remove the bay leaves and the cloves if you can locate them; correct the seasoning, if necessary. Serve immediately.
Makes 4 servings

Karl Beckley's Sturgeon with Anchovy Butter

Sturgeon from the Columbia River, which courses through Idaho, Washington, and Oregon, is one of the finest fish in the world. Sturgeon aficionados consider it the sweetest there is. Karl Beckley of Seattle's Green Lake Grill, serves sturgeon often, in season, which is generally three times a year—in the spring, fall, and winter—and this is one of his favorite recipes. Try this with a balanced American Chardonnay—not too oaky or over-rich.

4 sturgeon steaks (about 7 ounces each), cut 1 inch thick
1 anchovy fillet packed in olive oil, drained
¼ cup milk
½ cup (1 stick) plus 2 tablespoons unsalted butter, at room temperature
3 sprigs parsley, leaves coarsely chopped
2 teaspoons drained capers
1 small clove garlic, finely minced
1 teaspoon fresh lemon juice
Pinch of freshly ground white pepper
4 sprigs parsley, for garnish

1. Rinse the sturgeon steaks and pat dry. Refrigerate until just before cooking.

2. Soak the anchovies in the milk for 15

minutes. Drain, and discard the milk. Coarsely chop the anchovies.

3. In a medium-size bowl, work ½ cup of the butter until soft and creamy. Add the chopped parsley, anchovy, capers, garlic, lemon juice, and white pepper; mix until well blended. Shape the mixture into a long roll; wrap in parchment or waxed paper; refrigerate until needed, but at least 2 hours. (The butter can be prepared up to a week in advance if it is carefully wrapped and refrigerated.)

4. Just before cooking the sturgeon, cut the anchovy and caper butter into 12 equal slices.

5. Melt the remaining 2 tablespoons butter in a large skillet over medium-high heat. When the butter begins to brown, add the sturgeon steaks and cook until browned and firm, and not quite opaque through, about 6 minutes on each side. Do not overcook.

6. To serve, place a sturgeon steak in the center of each dinner plate. Arrange 2 slices of the anchovy and caper butter on top of each steak. Garnish with the parsley sprigs. Serve immediately.

Makes 4 servings

Ken Koval's Stuffed Eggplant Croustades

Cajuns always know what they are about with food. Stuffed eggplant is a regional treasure in southern Louisiana, and it is a dish made in heaven. The eggplant is either steamed, blanched, or deep-fried, and it is always stuffed with seafood, whether it be shrimp, crab, or white chunks of grouper. I got the idea for this recipe from Ken Koval, at Vive la Difference just outside Lafayette, Louisiana. He serves a dish very similar to this, and I absolutely loved it when I had it there. I like a vigorous dry red wine with this, one that isn't at all woody and has plenty of bright fruit, like a young Chianti or a Côtes du Rhône.

4 tablespoons extra-virgin olive oil
3 cloves garlic, minced separately
1 large bunch flat-leaf parsley, stemmed and finely minced
Freshly ground black pepper
1 pound medium (31 to 35 per pound) shrimp, shelled and deveined
4 same-size eggplants (about 8 ounces each) or 2 eggplants (about 1 pound each), peeled
Salt
2 shallots, finely minced
Cayenne pepper
4 ounces slab bacon, rind removed, cut in ½ x ¼ x ¼-inch pieces
1 medium-size white onion, diced
2 tablespoons fresh lemon juice
1 medium-size ripe tomato, peeled, seeded, and diced
1½ quarts mild vegetable oil, such as safflower, for frying
1 large egg
½ cup all-purpose flour

1. In a medium-size bowl, combine 2 tablespoons of the olive oil, 1 clove garlic, half of the parsley, and ½ teaspoon black pepper. Stir in the shrimp and coat with the mixture. Cover and refrigerate. (This can be done in the morning for preparation of the dish in the evening or simply a couple of hours before preparation.)

2. Cut the ends off of the eggplants to give them a uniform shape. Cut the eggplants

crosswise in half. Scoop out the eggplant, leaving a ¾-inch shell all around. Sprinkle the inside of each eggplant "cup" with salt (you will have 4 or 8 cups, depending on the size of eggplant you use) using a total of 2 teaspoons of salt. Invert on a wire rack or 2 layers of paper towels. Drain for 20 minutes. Pat dry.

3. Bring a large saucepan of salted water to a boil over high heat. Add the eggplant pulp and cook until soft, 15 to 20 minutes. Drain the eggplant pulp. Transfer to a medium-size bowl; mash with a fork until smooth but still somewhat chunky.

4. Heat 1 tablespoon of the olive oil in a medium-size saucepan over medium-high heat. Add the shallots and cook, stirring constantly, until soft, about 8 minutes. Reduce the heat to medium. Stir in the eggplant pulp and cook, stirring occasionally, until thick enough to mound on a spoon. Season with cayenne pepper—the purée should be quite spicy. Remove from the heat; cover and keep warm.

5. Fry the bacon in a medium skillet over medium-high heat until golden. Remove the bacon with a slotted spoon; drain on paper towels. Add the remaining 1 tablespoon olive oil to the bacon fat and place over medium-high heat. When hot, add the onion. Reduce the heat to medium and cook until the onion begins to turn translucent, about 3 minutes. Add the remaining 2 cloves minced garlic and cook, stirring frequently, until almost translucent, about 2 minutes. Stir in the lemon juice and tomato. Cook, stirring, until the tomato softens somewhat but still keeps its shape, about 5 minutes. Reduce the heat to low; keep warm.

6. Heat the mild oil to 350°F in a large, heavy-bottomed saucepan or deep-fat fryer.

7. Whisk the egg with 1 teaspoon water in

a small bowl. On a sheet of waxed paper, combine the flour, ½ teaspoon salt, and ¼ teaspoon cayenne.

8. One at a time, roll the eggplant shells in the flour, coating evenly. Roll in the egg mixture. Dredge again in flour, working quickly and making sure they are evenly covered. Tap off any excess flour. (This is somewhat messy. Just work quickly, touching the eggplants as little as possible.)

9. Working in batches if necessary, add the eggplant halves to the fat. Fry, turning, until deep golden brown on all sides, about 8 minutes. (The cooking time is the same for the small and the large eggplants.) Drain on paper towels; keep warm in a low oven.

10. While the eggplant shells are frying, reheat the tomato mixture over medium heat. Stir in the shrimp and marinade. Cook just until the shrimp are pink, about 5 minutes. Add the remaining parsley and the bacon; stir. Season with salt and pepper to taste.

11. To assemble the dish, place the eggplant *croustades* in the center of 4 warm dinner plates. Place ¼ cup of the eggplant purée (2 tablespoons if you are using small eggplants) in the bottom of each *croustade*. Top with equal amounts of the shrimp mixture, mounding it slightly over the top of the eggplants. Evenly divide the remaining shrimp mixture among the plates, arranging it so it wraps around one side of the *croustades*. Wrap the remaining eggplant purée around the other side of the *croustades*. Garnish with additional minced parsley, if desired, and serve.

Makes 4 servings

Steamed Salmon with Corn, Bacon, and Cream

This dish was "created" aboard the fishing vessel, *Triad*, in the waters off Sitka, Alaska. Because skipper Bruce Gore and deckhand, Tom Reinholdt, freeze their catch at sea in a freezer hold that stays somewhere around –30°F, carrying food isn't a problem. Tucked away in the hold was everything from vanilla ice cream to hand-cut pork chops to frozen vegetables. I chose corn, and teamed it with sweet boiling onions, cream, and bacon, which we enjoyed with silver salmon. Try this with either a clean or a slightly more rich, chilled American Chardonnay.

4 salmon steaks (5 ounces each), boned
½ teaspoon mild vegetable oil, such as safflower
4 ounces slab bacon, rind removed, cut into ½ x ¼
   x ¼-inch pieces
1 small onion, finely chopped
2 cups fresh or frozen corn kernels
1 cup heavy or whipping cream or crème fraîche
Salt and freshly ground black pepper

1. Rinse the salmon and pat dry. Rub all over with the oil. Refrigerate until ready to use.

2. Cook the bacon in a large skillet over medium-high heat until it is crisp and golden, about 8 minutes. Drain on paper towels; reserve.

3. Add the onion to the bacon fat and sauté until translucent but still somewhat crisp, about 5 minutes. Add the corn and cook until it begins to turn a brighter yellow,

3 to 5 minutes. Stir in the heavy cream and bacon. Bring the mixture to a boil. Cook until the cream is thick enough to coat the back of a spoon, about 5 minutes. Season with salt and pepper to taste. Keep warm over low heat.

4. Meanwhile, in the bottom of a steamer, bring 2 cups water to a boil over high heat. Season the salmon with salt and pepper. Place on the steamer rack. Cover and steam until opaque through, about 5 minutes.

5. To serve, divide the corn mixture among 4 warm dinner plates; place the salmon on top. Grind black pepper over all. Serve immediately.

Makes 4 servings

Salmon with Salal Berry Sauce

The two major ingredients in this recipe, salmon and salal berries, characterize the Northwest more than just about any other foods. Salmon have swum in Northwest waters for centuries—at one time so thick the waters gleamed with their silvery sides. Shiny, thick-leaved salal bushes grow beneath Douglas fir forests, along highways, and on almost any patch of ground that's free. In midsummer, when the salmon run thick, salal bushes are heavy with berries that hang from stalks like little bells in a row. Their dusky flavor is a wonderful complement, particularly to rich king salmon. Blueberries are an admirable substitute for salal berries. Whichever berry you choose, use a few from the sauce to garnish the salmon steaks—the pale pink and deep purple make a stunning combination. To make this even more special, try a brut rosé champagne. A white Burgundy would be excellent as well.

1 salmon fillet (1½ pounds)
1½ quarts Fish Stock (see Index)
1½ cups fresh or frozen salal berries or blueberries
1 tablespoon fresh lemon juice
1 tablespoon unsalted butter
Salt and freshly ground black pepper
Flat-leaf parsley sprigs, for garnish

1. Rinse the salmon and pat dry. Use a strawberry huller, fish bone puller, or needle-nose pliers to remove any remaining bones. Cut into 4 serving pieces.

2. In a large, non-aluminum skillet, bring the fish stock to a boil over medium-high heat. Add the salmon fillets, reduce the heat so the stock is simmering, and cook, basting the salmon with the stock until it is opaque but still resilient, 5 to 8 minutes.

3. Using a slotted spatula, remove the salmon to an ovenproof plate. Cover and keep warm in a low oven.

4. Strain the fish stock, returning it to the skillet. Boil the stock over medium-high heat until reduced to about 1 cup.

5. Meanwhile, combine ½ cup of the salal berries with the lemon juice in a food processor and purée. The purée will be somewhat coarse. Add the berry mixture to the reduced fish stock; cook until the sauce has thickened slightly, 2 to 3 minutes. Add the butter to the sauce and whisk until completely emulsified. Season with salt and pepper to taste and keep warm over very low heat.

6. Just before serving, add the remaining 1 cup berries to the sauce and cook until heated through, about 2 minutes.

7. To serve, divide the sauce among 4 warm dinner plates, spooning it into a circle in the center of the plate. Reserve about 2 tablespoons of the berries in the sauce, for garnish. Carefully place each piece of salmon fillet on top of the sauce. Garnish with some of the reserved berries and a sprig of parsley. Serve immediately.
Makes 4 servings

Poached Halibut with Tuberous Begonia Petals

I went out to the Herbfarm in Fall City, just outside of Seattle, to teach a cooking class one summer day, and found managers Carrie Van Dyck and Ron Zimmerman excited by the news they had just learned from an associate gardener and cook that tuberous begonia blossoms are edible. Ron handed me a blushing pink petal and I took a tiny bite. My taste buds were immediately won by a beguiling kaleidoscope of tart and tender flavors. I couldn't wait to team the petals with the halibut steaks I'd brought. I guarantee this dish will startle you with its beauty and capture your taste buds for good. This dish deserves an equally lovely wine—try a lightly chilled, clean and flowery Condrieu.

4 halibut steaks (6 ounces each)
4 tablespoons unsalted butter
1 tablespoon fresh lemon juice
1 clove garlic, finely minced
2 cups well-seasoned Fish Stock (see Index)
Salt and freshly ground black pepper
About 20 tuberous begonia petals

1. Rinse the halibut steaks and pat dry.

2. Melt the butter in a small saucepan over medium heat. Stir in the lemon juice and garlic; keep warm over very low heat.

3. Bring the fish stock to a boil in a large, non-aluminum skillet over medium-high heat. Reduce the heat to medium so the stock just simmers. Add the halibut steaks, and season with salt and pepper to taste. Cover and cook until the halibut steaks are opaque through, about 5 minutes.

4. Transfer the halibut steaks to the center of 4 warm dinner plates. Tuck 4 or 5 of the begonia petals underneath the halibut steaks on one side, overlapping them slightly and working as quickly as you can. Drizzle the garlic and lemon butter over the steaks and onto the plate, on the side of the halibut opposite the petals. Serve immediately.

Makes 4 servings

Malia Crump's Tilapia with Ginger

Malia Crump, who raises frogs on the northern shore of Oahu, gave me this recipe, which is based on the African fish, tilapia. There are several tilapia farms not far from Malia and tilapia are becoming increasingly available on the mainland as well.

The meat from farm-raised tilapia is pristine, white, and slightly sweet. Though it can be a tad soft, I find it the most interesting of the fish currently being farmed, for it has good flavor and texture.

Once tilapia are scaled, their skin is quite edible, and serving them whole, on a platter, with sauce poured over them and scallions sprinkled on top, makes for a very exotic presentation. Try this with a chilled Sauvignon Blanc.

2 tilapia, ocean perch, or rock cod (1 pound each), cleaned, with heads on
Salt and freshly ground black pepper
¼ cup plus 2 tablespoons soy sauce
2 tablespoons sugar
2 large cloves garlic, minced
2 tablespoons minced fresh ginger
¼ cup fine cornmeal
3 tablespoons mild vegetable oil, such as safflower
2 large scallions, trimmed, the white bulbs and light green stems cut in thin diagonal slices

1. Rinse the tilapia inside and out and pat dry. Generously season the stomach cavities with salt and pepper.

2. Mix together the soy sauce, sugar, garlic, ginger, and ½ cup plus 1 tablespoon water in a small bowl. Stir well.

3. In a shallow plate, mix the cornmeal with ¼ teaspoon each of salt and pepper. Dredge the tilapia in the cornmeal, using your hands to press it onto the fish to coat thoroughly from head to tail.

4. Heat the oil in a large skillet over medium-high heat. When the oil is hot but not smoking, add the tilapia and fry until brown on one side, about 3 minutes. Turn and brown the other side. Reduce the heat to medium, and stir in the soy sauce mixture. Turn the fish again, cover, and simmer until opaque through, 4 to 5 minutes.

5. Transfer the tilapia to a warm serving platter. Pour the sauce over them and sprinkle the scallions on top. Alternately, fillet the tilapia and place a fillet in the center of each of 4 warm plates. Divide the sauce over the fillets. Garnish with the scallions and serve.

Makes 4 servings

Fishing in Chicago

A small but vital commercial fishing industry on the Great Lakes may be one of the country's best-kept secrets. In an area whose culinary and economic reputation rests on aged beef, deep-dish pizza, and amber waves of grain, fish seems out of place. But in fact, the Great Lakes' supply of fish should be renowned for its sweetness, flavor, and texture.

At 5 A.M. on a sweltering Chicago morning, darkness wavers to light as the 50-foot fishing tug, *Seeker*, plies its way down the Chicago River, while newspaper delivery trucks and taxis cross bridges above. The air is already warm and muggy, though an early coolness skips over the bow.

We're on our way to fish for yellow perch in Lake Michigan. The season has been sparse so far, with daily catches of 50 to 100 pounds. That's not much encouragement for a crew who works for shares, and who splits sixty-forty with the boat's owner, Larry Schweig.

The *Seeker* is the only boat in the locks between the river and the lake. It may be the only commerical boat in the Illinois waters of the lake today. "Even when nobody else is catching fish, we catch it on this boat," crew member Dick Hansen said. He points out the expensive technical equipment that makes that possible. The *Seeker* is considered the best-equipped tug on the lake.

There's a fish finder that registers 16 shades of color to identify different species of fish. A loran shows where nets were set the night before, and there is sonar and radar equipment too. A ship-to-shore telephone allows constant communication with the shore.

Yellow perch is a major commercial species in Lake Michigan along with chubs, which can be fished only deeper than 40 fathoms (240 feet) to avoid incidental catch of salmon and trout, which belong to sportsfishermen. Whitefish are fished primarily in the northern part of the lake, as well as some smelt.

As morning light creeps up the horizon illuminating a skyline of spires and suddenly bustling traffic, the *Seeker* heads north. It's a relaxing trip. Captain Allan Grow and Hansen sit in the pilot house smoking and watching the fish finder, while two crew members nap on top of the boat. Then suddenly a big yellow blob shows up on the screen. "There's perch there," Dick says. "We'll maybe get some good fishing in today."

Dick jumps down from the captain's seat and shovels ice into boxes so they're ready to receive fish. Sleek and efficient, the *Seeker* is completely enclosed, and very spare. There are no amenities, just a bucket one takes up top, for privacy.

A hydraulic roller attached to the outside of the boat pulls the nylon gillnet out of the water. Inside is a long, stainless-steel table, stacks of empty boxes, hooks to hang up buoys, and a huge box filled with ice for the fish, but which now holds a carton of chocolate milk.

Before hauling any nets, the crew tape their fingers and hands, to protect them from tiny, clear spines on the perch that easily cause infection, and they don bright yellow aprons and gloves.

The first bright orange buoy that signals a net is spotted at 7 A.M. The crew get into position on either side of the table, their picks—blunted screw drivers—in hand. Allan steers the boat toward the wildly bobbing buoy. Dick hauls it in and attaches the net to the roller. He pushes a lever and with a loud clanking, the net is hauled aboard.

No one speaks, they just look. The net is silver with fish. The crew becomes a blur of moving hands and picks, flying fish, and pale blue netting that piles up quickly, before it's gathered up and stuffed into a box at the end of the table. The floor is slick with fish scales and water. The air remains surprisingly sweet, filled with the smell of fresh water and wet nets. As each box is filled, it gets a layer of ice on top, then is quickly shoved to the side of the boat and covered with a tarp to keep it cool.

Several hundred pounds of fish later the crew sets tomorrow's nets, then takes a break as they head for the next set. They smoke, wolf sandwiches, eye the fish finder like most people watch television. Their luck holds all day and the tug fills with perch.

By 2 P.M. a storm is brewing; the sky is suddenly black and the boat pitches from side to side. In the midst of a heavy

While waiting to pull in a net full of perch, I snapped this photo of the magnificent Chicago skyline as it looks from Lake Michigan.

run Grow decides it's too dangerous to hang around, and he speeds up the roller. Fish and net tumble onto the table faster than the crew can pick, until it's piled high. They pull in the roller, close up the sides of the boat and head for the locks and Chicago. It's hot outside, stifling in the boat, but the rain pouring down prohibits opening windows. The crew furiously picks fish from a two-foot-high pile of net on the table.

It's been 11 hours since the *Seeker* quietly entered Lake Michigan. Sixteen hundred pounds of fat, gleaming perch later, it docks. The crew continues picking fish for another hour, then they're weighed, iced, and packed into a cooler. Within 24 hours, they will be at the market as tiny, golden fillets.

Allan can't keep the satisfaction of a good day's fishing out of his voice. "We'd be doing great just to get 1,000 pounds a day," he said. "The luck has turned."

King Mackerel with Black Beans and Plantains

I had this dish at La Teresita, a Cuban café in West Tampa, Florida, that I learned about from mullet fisherman Mike Rabada, who is of Spanish extraction and who eats there once a week. He claims it is the best Cuban restaurant in the city, and he accompanied my husband Michael and me there one evening. I loved the herbed black beans and rice and the meaty, fried plantains, which set off the moist king mackerel perfectly. If you can't get king mackerel, use *ono*, which has similar meat, or swordfish, which will take less time to cook. Try this with a lightly chilled, Spanish white Rioja.

4 king mackerel or ono steaks (4 to 6 ounces each),
   cut about 1 inch thick
1 cup dried black beans
1 bay leaf
2 small dried hot red chiles
1 large yellow onion, diced
1 large green bell pepper, cored, seeded, and diced
Salt and freshly ground black pepper
3 medium-size ripe plantains
¼ cup clarified butter (see Index)
2 cups cooked white rice (see Index)
¼ cup Fish Stock (see Index)
¼ cup mild vegetable oil, such as safflower
¼ cup all-purpose flour
¼ cup diced red onion

1. Rinse the fish steaks and pat dry. Refrigerate until ready to cook them.

2. Wash and pick over the beans to remove any pebbles or soil. Combine the beans with 4 cups water in a medium-size, heavy-bottomed ovenproof saucepan over high heat. Bring to a boil; remove from the heat. Cover and let sit for 1 hour.

3. Drain the beans. Return them to the pan and add 4½ cups water, the bay leaf, chiles, yellow onion, and bell pepper. Cover partially and bring to a boil over medium heat. Reduce the heat to medium-low. Simmer the beans until tender, 55 to 60 minutes. If there is still liquid left in the pan, drain it off. Remove and discard the chiles. Season the beans with plenty of salt and pepper. Keep warm, covered, in a low oven.

4. Peel the plantains. Cut diagonally into ½-inch-thick slices. Heat the clarified butter in a large skillet over medium-high heat. Add the plantain slices and cook, just until golden, 4 to 6 minutes per side. Season with salt and pepper. Remove from the heat; keep warm in a low oven.

5. Combine the rice and fish stock in a medium-size non-aluminum saucepan over low heat. Cook until warmed through. Season with salt and pepper to taste.

6. Heat the oil in a large skillet over medium heat. In a shallow plate, combine the flour with ¼ teaspoon each of salt and pepper. Pat the fish steaks dry. Dredge in the seasoned flour. When the oil is hot, add the steaks and cook, turning them often so they are evenly golden on all sides, just until they are opaque through, 5 to 6 minutes.

7. To serve, place the rice on a serving plate; top with the black beans. Arrange the plantains around the edge of another serving platter, and place the king mackerel steaks in the middle. Top each steak with some of the red onion. Serve everything at once.

Makes 4 servings

Mackerel Braised in White Wine with Potatoes and Apples

A friend of mine says this dish makes her want to cozy up near a big fire on a cold winter evening. Its big, warming flavors make me agree with her.

Be sure to follow the directions closely here, and remove as many bones from the fish as possible. Also, don't think that the effort of cooking just one beet is for naught—it helps make this a very stunning, as well as delicious, dish. Try this with a chilled Vouvray or, for a special treat, a sparkling Vouvray.

4 mackerel fillets (7 to 8 ounces each)

2 large onions, peeled

2 large russet potatoes, peeled

2 firm tart cooking apples, peeled and cored

Salt and freshly ground black pepper

1 bottle semi-sweet white wine, such as Vouvray

3 tablespoons white wine vinegar

2 bay leaves

½ cup sour cream

1 medium beet, cooked, peeled, and diced, at room temperature

1 large bunch fresh chives, minced

1. Trim the mackerel fillets by cutting off the collar (near the head end) and the fin, if they are still there, and trimming ⅛ inch from the belly flap of the fillet. Skin side down, locate a dark strip that runs right down the middle of the fillet. There will be a strip of bones there, and you can remove them easily by cutting down to the skin on each side of the strip. Remove the bones with some meat attached. Be careful not to cut through the skin. Rinse the mackerel and pat dry.

2. Very thinly slice the onions and potatoes. Slice the apples slightly thicker than the onions and potatoes.

3. Place the potatoes and onions, in that order, in a large, heavy-bottomed non-aluminum skillet that has a cover. Season lightly with salt and pepper.

4. Add the wine, vinegar, bay leaves, and enough water to cover the vegetables. Cover and bring to a boil over high heat. Reduce the heat to medium, and simmer for 10 minutes. Add the apples and additional water to cover. Cover and continue cooking until the potatoes are cooked through, 30 to 45 minutes.

5. Season the mackerel fillets on the meat side with salt and pepper. Place them, skin side up, on top of the apples. Cover and cook until the mackerel fillets are opaque through, about 5 minutes.

6. To serve, use a spatula to lift a mackerel fillet and the vegetables and apples it is resting on from the skillet to the center of a warm dinner plate. Divide the sour cream among the plates, placing a dollop near the head end of the mackerel fillet. Arrange the beets completely around the sour cream, extending them on the plate above the mackerel fillet. Pour the fish and vegetable cooking liquid over the beets. Sprinkle generously with chives. Serve immediately.

Makes 4 servings

Sweet and Sour Tilapia with Lychee

This dish has the flavor and allure of the Hawaiian Islands, where a wonderful mix of Asian cultures produces an incredible variety of exotic foods. The recipe comes from the Hawaiian Aquaculture Development Program, which works closely with tilapia farmers, to help them develop their aquafarms and to promote their products.

Lychees lend a touch of surprise to the mild, tender tilapia in its egg batter. If you can't find tilapia, use ocean perch or rock cod. Try this with a chilled Riesling or a pale ale.

4 tilapia, ocean perch, or rock cod fillets (3½ ounces each)
2 large eggs
¾ teaspoon salt
2 tablespoons all-purpose flour
2 cups mild vegetable oil, such as safflower, for frying
1 cup drained, canned or fresh lychees
1 cup syrup from canned lychees or 1 cup sugar syrup (see Note)
⅓ cup white wine vinegar
1½ tablespoons sugar
¼ teaspoon salt
2 tablespoons cornstarch
1 small bunch fresh chives, finely minced (optional), for garnish
1 orange calendula (pot marigold) flower, petals separated, for garnish (optional)

1. Rinse the tilapia fillets and pat dry. Cut into 2 x 1 x ¼-inch pieces.
2. In a bowl, whisk together the eggs and salt with 2 tablespoons water. Gradually whisk in the flour, whisking until no lumps remain. Set the batter aside.
3. Heat the oil in a wok, electric deep-fat fryer, or a heavy-bottomed deep saucepan over medium-high heat until just before it smokes, about 375°F.
4. While the oil heats, cut the lychees into thin strips. Reserve, covered, so they don't dry out.
5. To fry the fish, dip several pieces into the batter. Slide them into the hot oil, frying the fish in batches until golden and cooked through, about 4 minutes. Drain on paper towels. Keep the fish warm in a low oven while you continue frying.
6. In a medium-size, heavy-bottomed non-aluminum saucepan, whisk together the lychee syrup, vinegar, sugar and the salt. Whisk in the cornstarch until smooth. Just before all of the fish is fried, place the saucepan over medium heat. Bring to a boil, stirring constantly. The sauce will thicken almost immediately. Remove from the heat and keep warm.
7. To serve, thin the sauce if necessary with water or liquid from the lychees—it should be thick and somewhat viscous, but not gluey. Pour half the sauce on a serving platter. Mound the fish on top of it. Pour the remaining sauce over the fish; sprinkle the lychees over all. Garnish with the chives and calendula petals. Serve immediately.

Makes 4 servings

Note: To make sugar syrup, boil 1 cup water with ¼ cup sugar until the sugar dissolves and the mixture is slightly thick, about 10 minutes.

Napi's Ocean Pout Taratour

This recipe is from Napi's restaurant in Provincetown, Massachusetts. Napi's is owned and operated by Helen and Napi Van Dereck, who refer to their establishment as "Provincetown's most unusual restaurant."

One of the more unusual things about Napi's is the ocean pout on the menu. Ocean pout is an abundant fish of extremely high quality, yet it rarely shows up in a fish market, and even less frequently on a restaurant menu. It's unprepossessing—rivaling monkfish in its lack of natural allure—and it has sinewy, muscular meat, with a pleasant and mild flavor, truly reminiscent of veal.

Overcoming its looks is up to the people out at sea; overcoming its texture is a simple matter of pounding it gently. Familiar East Coast species like cod, haddock, and flounder are not abundant enough to supply the rapidly increasing seafood market. There is the chance they will rebound, if some pressure on them is diverted to other species such as ocean pout.

When I called Napi's to get the details for this recipe, they not only gave them to me, but when I mentioned I couldn't find ocean pout anywhere, Helen immediately said, "I've got 200 pounds in the freezer, I'll just send you some." And she did, all the way from Provincetown to Seattle.

I'm grateful to the Van Dereck's for this recipe, which is Turkish in origin, delectable, and simple to prepare, and for the chance to champion the homely, but tasty ocean pout. If you can't find ocean pout, try this with tuna. Try a light, dry California Zinfandel with this!

1 ocean pout or tuna loin (1 pound), cut into 4 equal pieces
2 large cloves garlic, minced
½ cup lightly toasted tahini (sesame seed paste)
¼ to ½ cup fresh lemon juice
2 large eggs, beaten
2 tablespoons milk
⅓ cup all-purpose flour
¼ teaspoon salt
⅓ cup sesame seeds
2 tablespoons coarsely ground black pepper
¼ cup mild vegetable oil, such as safflower
½ cup loosely packed flat-leaf parsley leaves, for garnish

1. Rinse the ocean pout and pat dry. Place each piece between 2 sheets of waxed paper and gently pound to between $1/16$ and $1/8$ inch thick. (If you are using tuna, there is no need to pound it.) Refrigerate until ready to use.

2. In a medium-size bowl, whisk together the garlic, tahini, and ¼ cup lemon juice until it is the consistency of very heavy cream and somewhat tart, but not so tart it makes your mouth pucker. Add more lemon juice or up to 3 tablespoons water to thin it, and if it is still too thick and you don't want to add more lemon juice, add more water. Reserve the taratour sauce.

3. In a bowl whisk the eggs with the milk. Pour the mixture into a shallow bowl. In a shallow dish, mix together the flour, salt, sesame seeds, and black pepper.

4. Heat the oil in a large, heavy-bottomed skillet over medium-high heat.

5. While the oil is heating, dip the fish first in the egg wash and then in the flour mixture, making sure to coat well on both sides. You may need to press the flour mixture onto the fish.

6. When the oil is hot but not smoking,

add the fish. It will shrink somewhat, but don't worry, that is normal. Cook until golden on each side and opaque through, 4 to 5 minutes per side. (If using tuna, cooking time is the same.) Drain on paper towels.

7. While the fish is cooking, gently heat the taratour sauce in a non-aluminum saucepan over medium heat. Stir occasionally.

8. To serve, pour some of the taratour sauce in the center of 4 warm dinner plates. Place a piece of ocean pout on top. Garnish the plates with the parsley leaves, placing them around the fish and on the sauce. Serve immediately.

Makes 4 servings

Mako Shark with Sake and Lemon Juice

Dick Yoshimura, owner of Mutual Fish Company in Seattle, Washington, has dealt in fish all his life. He used to sell fish at the waterfront, when it was an active fishing port. When the port closed some years ago he moved to south Seattle, and his clientele followed him, for he has some of the best, most varied seafood in the city.

Mr. Yoshimura is quick with a smile but he doesn't say much—he's usually too busy cleaning, filleting, or steaking fish, or making sure the shop runs smoothly. Every once in a while though, he'll let a pearl slip—and this recipe is one of them. A necessary trick, however, is to season the fish at the table. I pass a small pitcher of sake around the table, and follow it with a small dish of lemon juice, so everyone can season their fish to taste. (I suggest about 2 teaspoons of sake and ¼ to ½ teaspoon of lemon juice per serving.) A generous sprinkling of salt on top of the sake and lemon juice really completes the dish, but I leave that to the discretion of each person.

I serve this with rice and Spinach Salad (see Index). Try warmed sake with this, or a lightly chilled, delicate German Kabinett.

4 mako shark or swordfish steaks (4 to 6 ounces each)
Scant ½ teaspoon mild vegetable oil, such as safflower
Garlic chives and flowers, for garnish
8 teaspoons sake, for seasoning at table
2 teaspoons fresh lemon juice, for seasoning at table
Salt

1. Rinse the shark steaks and pat dry. Rub lightly all over with the oil.

2. Bring 2 cups of water to a boil in the bottom of a steamer or fish poacher. Place the shark steaks in the steamer and cook until they are just opaque through, 4 to 5 minutes. Remove from the heat.

3. Place each steak in the center of a warm dinner plate. Garnish the plate with 3 garlic chives and a chive flower. Serve, letting each diner season with 2 teaspoons sake, ¼ to ½ teaspoon lemon juice, and salt.

Makes 4 servings

Albacore or Bluefin Tuna Misoyaki

*I*t seems like every restaurant in Waikiki Beach offers fish *misoyaki*, usually made with black cod (sablefish) or tuna. *Misoyaki* is a Japanese term that refers to the fish being marinated overnight in a sweet white miso sauce, then quickly cooked. The result is deeply flavored and absolutely heavenly.

Because tuna is quite rich, I find four-ounce portions ideal. However, use a six-ounce portion if you have large appetites to satisfy. You may scrape off the excess miso sauce before cooking the tuna if you like, though it is delicious. I prefer to leave it on.

I like to serve this with Spinach Salad (see Index), placing half the salad on either end of a warmed, oblong serving platter, and arranging the tuna steaks in the middle. Try a lightly chilled, clean, young Chadonnay, or a white Burgundy, such as Rully.

4 tuna steaks (4 to 6 ounces each)
⅔ cup white miso paste, preferably shiro white miso paste from Hawaii, such as Maru-Hi brand
3 tablespoons sugar
2 tablespoons minced fresh ginger
1 tablespoon sake
¼ cup mild vegetable oil, such as safflower

1. Rinse the tuna steaks and pat dry.
2. In a medium-size bowl, combine the miso, sugar, ginger, and sake and mix well. Slather the tuna steaks with the sauce. Place the steaks in a single layer in a non-aluminum dish or pan. Cover and refrigerate for 24 hours.
3. To cook the tuna, heat the oil in a large heavy-bottomed skillet over medium heat. When the oil is hot but not yet smoking, add the tuna steaks; cook until golden, about 3 minutes on each side. Serve immediately.

Makes 4 servings

Tuna with 40 Garlic Cloves

*T*his is an unabashed variation on a classic French dish that is usually made with chicken. It is hearty, homey, and delightfully different. There are two ways to make this dish—the "proper" way, which results in moist, flavorful, tuna-flavored tuna and tender garlic, and calls for less cooking time, as the recipe is written; or the other way, which turns the tuna steaks crisp and garlic flavored—slightly on the dry side, but pleasantly. (This is done by increasing the cooking time, adding the tuna to the pan with the garlic, keeping it covered for the first 10 minutes, and then cooking it as per the recipe.) Either way, try this with a chilled white Burgundy, such as Montagny.

2 tablespoons unsalted butter
¼ cup olive oil
41 large cloves garlic, unpeeled
1 cup dry white wine, such as a French Riesling
4 tuna steaks, preferably albacore (4 to 6 ounces each), cut 1 inch thick, rinsed and patted dry
Salt and freshly ground black pepper
8 slices French bread
½ cup minced fresh parsley

1. In a large, deep-sided skillet, melt the butter with the oil over medium-high heat. When the fats are hot but not smoking, add 40 cloves of the garlic and stir to coat on all

sides. If you want the tuna to be crisp and garlic-flavored, season it liberally with salt and pepper on both sides and add it at the same time you add the garlic. Cover the pan and cook for 10 minutes. Otherwise, reduce the heat to medium, and cook, stirring occasionally, until the garlic begins to turn golden, about 10 minutes.

2. Slowly add the wine. Stir, gently scraping up any brown bits from the bottom of the pan. Season the tuna steaks liberally with salt and pepper. Add to the pan with the garlic. Partially cover, and cook, turning once, until the tuna is opaque through, the garlic cloves are golden and soft, and the wine and cooking juices are deep golden and have reduced by about half, about 15 minutes.

3. While the tuna is cooking, toast the bread on both sides. Peel the remaining 1 clove garlic and cut in half. Rub the toast on both sides with garlic.

4. To serve, arrange the tuna and garlic on a heated platter. Pour the sauce over all. Garnish the platter with the slices of toast. Sprinkle with the parsley. Serve immediately.

Makes 4 servings

Curried Tuna with Currants

*T*his exotic treatment for tuna caused a guest at our house to ask, "Why don't people use curry with fish more often? It's so delicious." I took that as a vote of confidence! I serve this dish frequently, using fresh or flash-frozen albacore tuna. The curry is so subtle and aromatic it gently infuses the fish, without overpowering its gentle flavor. The currants add a wonderful texture and play of sweetness. Jon Rowley, a Seattle seafood consultant with an abiding affection for tuna, gave me the idea for this recipe. Serve with plenty of basmati rice, a garnish of tart apple slices, and a chilled American Gewürztraminer.

4 albacore tuna steaks (6 to 8 ounces each), skin removed, rinsed and patted dry
2 shallots, thinly sliced
2 bay leaves
2 large sprigs fresh thyme or ½ teaspoon dried
2 cups dry white wine
2 tablespoons unsalted butter
¼ cup finely chopped carrot
⅓ cup finely chopped onion
½ cup loosely packed flat-leaf parsley leaves, finely minced
1 tablespoon curry powder, preferably Madras or Sharwood brand
1 teaspoon coriander seed, crushed
½ cup currants
1 cup crème fraîche or sour cream

1. Place the tuna steaks in a large, deep, non-aluminum dish. Add the shallots, bay leaves, and thyme; pour the wine over all. Marinate the tuna in the refrigerator for 1 hour, turning the steaks once after 30 minutes if the wine doesn't completely cover them.

2. Melt the butter in a medium-size, heavy-bottomed, non-aluminum skillet over medium-high heat. Add the carrot, onion, parsley, and curry powder. Cook, stirring often, until the onions begin to turn translucent, about 5 minutes.

3. Pour in the tuna marinade and bring to

a boil. Reduce the heat to medium, so the mixture is boiling gently. Sprinkle on the coriander seed. Add the tuna and cook until opaque through, about 10 minutes, turning once after 5 minutes if the cooking liquid doesn't completely cover the tuna.

4. While the tuna is cooking, place the currants in a small bowl and cover them with boiling water or very hot tap water.

5. Transfer the tuna to a plate. Cover with foil and keep warm in a low oven. Bring the tuna cooking liquid to a boil over medium-high heat. Boil until reduced by about one-third. Drain the currants. Add to the cooking liquid. Add ½ cup of the *crème fraîche*. Boil, stirring, until reduced by about half. The sauce should be the consistency of thin cream.

6. To serve, arrange the tuna steaks on a heated serving platter. Remove the thyme and the bay leaves from the sauce. Pour the sauce over the tuna steaks. Serve the remaining ½ cup *crème fraîche* alongside. Alternatively, place each tuna steak in the center of a warm dinner plate. Pour sauce over each steak; top with a large dollop of *crème fraîche*. Serve immediately.

Makes 4 servings

Tuna with Pine Nut and Anchovy Sauce

Willie Fisch, a delightful man who is a naval architect in Seattle, is a seafood cook by passion. He described this sauce, then served it one night at his home which overlooks Elliott Bay, and I was transfixed. I knew it would be good—Mr. Fisch describes food with such precision and flair that you can almost taste it—but I hardly expected the flavors I found. The sauce is fabulous over tuna, but don't stop there. It complements any full-bodied fish. And if there is any leftover sauce, which is doubtful, it makes a scrumptious dip for fresh-toasted bread. Serve a salad made with escarole and dressed with vinaigrette. A dish this delectable deserves a Quarts de Chaume, a Clos de Sainte Catherine if you can find one, or a late-harvest Riesling.

4 tuna steaks (3½ to 4 ounces each), cut 1 inch thick
6 anchovy fillets packed in oil, drained
¼ cup dry white wine
1 cup pine nuts
⅛ teaspoon ground cinnamon
Small pinch of ground cloves
1 tablespoon balsamic vinegar
3 tablespoons drained capers
¾ cup plus 2 tablespoons extra-virgin olive oil
Salt and freshly ground black pepper
2 tablespoons minced fresh parsley leaves, for garnish

1. Rinse the tuna steaks and pat dry. Refrigerate until ready to use.

2. Soak the anchovies in the wine for 15 minutes, to rid them of excess salt. Drain, discarding the wine.

3. In a food processor, combine the anchovies, pine nuts, cinnamon, cloves, vinegar, and capers. Purée, pulsing on and off. With the machine running, slowly add the ¾ cup of oil in a thin stream, and process until the mixture is quite thick, but pourable. Season with salt and pepper to taste; reserve.

4. Liberally season the tuna steaks on both sides with salt and pepper. Heat the remaining olive oil in a heavy-bottomed skillet over medium-high heat. When the oil is hot but not smoking, add the tuna steaks and

cook until the tuna is cooked as you like it, about 4 minutes per side if you like it cooked until opaque. If you prefer the tuna slightly undercooked, reduce the cooking time accordingly.

5. To serve, pour the sauce onto a warm serving platter. Place the tuna steaks on top; sprinkle with the parsley. Serve immediately.

Makes 4 servings

Pompano with Achiote and Jalapeño Sauce

This is another creation from Robert Del Grande, chef/owner of Cafe Annie in Houston, Texas. I love the exotic play of flavors in the Gulf of Mexico pompano with musky *achiote* and searing jalapeño chile. The heat of the chile is tempered by hard-cooked egg, cream, and chicken stock. If you can't find pompano, substitute mahimahi or swordfish. The cooking times are the same. Serve this with a light Mercurey or a dry Sauternes such as Château R.

Achiote Sauce:

¼ cup achiote (annatto seeds)
6 tablespoons fresh orange juice
1½ cups chicken stock
3 small cloves garlic
1½ teaspoons paprika
½ teaspoon salt

Fish:

4 pompano or mahimahi fillets, or swordfish steaks (6 to 7 ounces each), rinsed and patted dry

Jalapeño Sauce:

2 tablespoons unsalted butter
1 small jalapeño chile, cored, seeded, and diced
2 tablespoons diced onion
¼ cup chicken stock
¼ cup heavy or whipping cream
1⅓ cups cilantro leaves, minced
1 large hard-cooked egg, diced
1 teaspoon fresh lime juice
Salt

1. Make the *Achiote* Sauce: Combine the *achiote*, orange juice, and 1 cup of the chicken stock in a medium-size non-aluminum saucepan over medium-high heat. Bring to a boil. Boil until the pan is almost dry, 15 to 20 minutes. The remaining mixture will be sticky and chunky with the *achiote*.

2. Transfer the mixture to blender or food processor. Add the garlic, paprika, and salt; purée until quite smooth and flecked with bits of *achiote*. Stir in the remaining ½ cup chicken stock.

3. Preheat the broiler.

4. Liberally brush the *achiote* sauce onto the meat side of the pompano fillets. Broil, skin side down, until opaque to the center, 6 to 8 minutes total. If using swordfish or mahimahi, spread the *achiote* liberally on both sides, and broil, turning once after about 4 minutes. Continue broiling until the fish is opaque throughout, about 4 minutes. Cover loosely with aluminum foil and keep warm in a low oven.

5. Make the jalapeño sauce: In a medium-size saucepan, melt the butter over medium-high heat. Add the jalapeño and onion and sauté until the onion is translucent, about 4 minutes. Add the chicken stock; bring the mixture to a boil. Boil until reduced by half, about 4 minutes. Whisk in the heavy cream;

bring to a boil again. Reduce the heat to low. Mince the cilantro leaves, and stir them with the egg and lime juice into the jalapeño sauce. Season with salt to taste.

6. When the fish fillets are cooked, transfer each to a warm dinner plate. Spoon sauce over each fillet. Serve immediately.

Makes 4 servings

Brandade de Morue

*B*randade, a silken salt cod and garlic purée, is comfort food for me. I learned to love it in France, where I ate it every chance I had. This recipe results in a *brandade* that is almost fluffy—so light it seems like a cod pudding. You will be tempted to heap it on your plate—it smells of cod and garlic and looks heavenly—but begin slowly, for it will fill you up more quickly than you think. I like to serve *brandade* as a first course, though it is wonderful at lunch, along with a green salad. Try it for brunch too—it goes surprisingly well with champagne, toast, and fruit. At lunch or dinner try *brandade* with a simple white table wine.

1 pound skinless and boneless salt cod
1 cup milk
1 cup olive oil
4 large cloves garlic
½ teaspoon freshly grated nutmeg
2 teaspoons fresh lemon juice
Freshly ground black pepper
4 slices bread, toasted and rubbed with 1 clove garlic
¼ cup oil-cured black olives

1. Soak the cod in plenty of cold water, changing the water several times, for 1 to 2 days.

2. Drain well. Place the cod in a saucepan, add cold water to cover, and bring to a boil over high heat. Reduce the heat to medium; simmer the cod until softened slightly, about 10 minutes. Drain the cod. When cool enough to handle, break into flakes, discarding any skin or bones.

3. Scald the milk in a medium saucepan over medium-high heat. At the same time, heat the olive oil in a small saucepan over medium heat, until hot but not smoking.

4. Place the salt cod and the garlic in the bowl of a food processor. With the machine running, add the hot oil in a thin stream. Pulse on and off, so the cod isn't over-beaten. When the oil is incorporated and the mixture is quite smooth, slowly add the milk in a thin stream, pulsing on and off to avoid overmixing the *brandade*. It should be light, white, and fluffy—like pudding.

5. Add the nutmeg and the lemon juice to the *brandade*; pulse 1 to 2 times. Season with pepper. Scrape the *brandade* into a shallow serving bowl, mounding it in the center.

6. Cut the toast into triangles. To serve, arrange the toast triangles with a point up, around the base of the *brandade*. Garnish with the olives. Serve immediately.

Makes 6 to 8 servings

Sole Fillets with Plums and Apricots

*O*n my way home from the fish market I stopped by our corner grocery, and when I walked in I was surrounded by the summery aroma of plums and apricots. I'd had another plan for the petrale sole I'd just purchased, but it fell by the wayside when visions of a luscious fruit sauce entered my mind. I love the colors and play of textures in this dish, and the surprising versatility of the sauce, which does as much to enhance the delicacy of sole fillets as it does to soften the meatiness of a tuna or swordfish steak. Try this with a rich, luscious Chardonnay.

4 sole fillets (6 to 7 ounces each), preferably petrale sole
3 tablespoons unsalted butter
1 large shallot, minced
4 ounces ripe apricots, pitted and quartered
4 ounces ripe plums, pitted and quartered
1 tablespoon port wine
1 teaspoon sugar
Salt and freshly ground white pepper
Borage blossoms, calendula petals, or flat-leaf parsley leaves, for garnish

1. Rinse the sole fillets and pat dry.
2. Melt 1 tablespoon of the butter in a medium-size saucepan over medium heat. Add the shallot and sauté until it begins to soften, 2 to 3 minutes. Stir in the apricots, plums, and port. Cover and cook, stirring occasionally, until the fruit is soft, about 15 minutes.
3. Scrape the mixture into the bowl of a food processor. Purée until very smooth. Return the purée to the saucepan. Stir in the sugar and 1 tablespoon butter. Season with salt and white pepper to taste. Keep warm over low heat.
4. Melt the remaining 1 tablespoon butter in a large skillet over medium heat. Add the sole fillets, season with salt and pepper, and cook until opaque on one side, 4 to 5 minutes. Gently turn, season with salt and pepper, and cook until they are opaque through, 2 to 3 minutes.

5. Divide the sauce among 4 warm dinner plates, spreading it out on the center of the plate. Top with the sole fillets. Garnish with the borage blossoms.
Makes 4 servings

Peixo Conservado em Vinagre - Portuguese Spiced, Pickled Fish

Portuguese may not be the first culture one thinks of in connection with Hawaii, but it has had an important influence on the island cuisines, particularly that of the island of Hawaii. Though this dish is Mediterranean in style, the Hawaiian sun shines on it, and it takes practically no time to prepare. Try this with boiled potatoes and an American Gewürztraminer.

2 pounds fresh true or lingcod, Alaska or red snapper, or grouper, boned
6 whole cloves, crushed
1 teaspoon dried hot pepper flakes
1 bay leaf
4 fresh sage leaves, coarsely chopped, or 1/8 teaspoon dried
2 teaspoons salt
4 large sprigs fresh thyme or 1/4 teaspoon dried
2 cloves garlic, coarsely chopped
1 1/2 cups white wine vinegar
1/4 cup olive oil
1 small bunch fresh parsley (optional), leaves finely minced, for garnish

1. Rinse the fish and pat dry. Remove any bones; cut the fish into serving-size pieces. Place the fish in a single layer in an oven-proof porcelain or enameled baking dish.

2. In a mortar or spice grinder, lightly crush the cloves, pepper flakes, bay leaf, and dried sage, if you are using it. Sprinkle over the fish. Sprinkle on the fresh sage, salt, thyme sprigs, and the garlic; pour the vinegar over all. Cover and refrigerate for 12 hours.

3. If the fish has marinated in a dish that can be used on top of the stove, place over medium-high heat and bring the fish and the marinade to a boil. Otherwise, transfer the fish and the marinade to a large non-aluminum skillet and bring to a boil. Remove from the heat. Drain the fish, discarding the marinade.

4. Heat the olive oil in a large skillet until hot but not smoking. Add the fish and cook until opaque through, turning once, about 3 minutes on each side.

5. Transfer the fish to a warmed platter. Garnish with the parsley. Serve immediately, accompanied with boiled potatoes.

Makes 4 to 6 servings

Steamed Salmon with Mustard Cream and Peas Triad

I tried the salmon dish I created aboard the *Triad* (see box) at home, steaming instead of baking it, and with a more relaxed fish, it proved a very tasty treat indeed. Try this with a chilled American Chardonnay or a white Burgundy.

The Story of the Too-Fresh Fish

T his recipe was created aboard the fishing vessel *Triad*, in the Pacific Ocean outside of Sitka Sound, Alaska. I was on a three-day visit aboard the *Triad*, watching skipper Bruce Gore and deckhand Tom Reinholdt catch salmon, hand-bleed them, and freeze them on the boat. Since they were both working and because my cooking arm was getting itchy, I volunteered to prepare dinner.

The refrigerator yielded frozen peas, cream, mustard, and onions, and, of course, there was plenty of fresh fish. I came up against an unexpected problem, however. Tom had pulled aboard a pink salmon, or "humpie," about an hour before dinner. Marveling over such fresh fish, I seasoned it and put it in a moderately warm oven to bake, then proceeded with the sauce. When I pulled the fish from the oven some 8 minutes later it appeared to be cooked through, and the fillets were slightly uplifted at the edges. I cut into it and was astonished to see it crumble into bits. It was cooked to dryness in spots, almost raw in others. What a strange beast this is, I thought. Bruce remarked they'd had another one just like it, and it turns out that the problem was—if you can believe it—fish that was too fresh. It hadn't gone through rigor mortis on deck and did so very rapidly in the oven. The tension of that accelerated process quite literally caused the meat to explode within itself.

It was a memorable meal on all accounts, and the sauce got rave reviews.

4 pieces salmon fillet (5 ounces each)

Scant ½ teaspoon mild vegetable oil, such as
 safflower

1 tablespoon unsalted butter

2 scallions, trimmed, the white bulbs and light green
 stems cut into thin rounds

1 cup fresh or frozen green peas

1 teaspoon Dijon mustard

½ cup heavy or whipping cream

Salt and freshly ground black pepper

1. Rinse the salmon fillets and pat dry. Rub them all over with the oil. Refrigerate until ready to use.

2. Melt the butter in a medium-size skillet over medium heat. Add the scallions and cook, stirring constantly, until they begin to soften and turn a darker shade of green, about 3 minutes. Add the peas and cook, stirring occasionally, until they begin to turn bright green, about 5 minutes.

3. Blend the mustard with the cream in a small bowl. Add to the scallions and peas. Mix well and bring to a boil. Cook until the cream is reduced by about one-third and has thickened enough to coat the back of a spoon, about 5 minutes. Season with salt and pepper to taste. Keep warm over low heat.

4. Meanwhile, pour water into the bottom of a steamer or fish poacher and bring to a boil. Season the fillets with salt and pepper; place in the steamer. Cook until opaque through, about 5 minutes.

5. To serve, transfer the fillets to 4 warm dinner plates, placing them in the center of the plates. Divide the sauce among the plates, pouring it over and to the side of the fillets. Serve immediately.

Makes 4 servings

Mahimahi with Preserved Turnip

Since she married Brooks Takenaka, the general manager of the United Fishing Agency's fish auction in Honolulu, Cynthia Takenaka has learned more about cooking seafood than most of us will learn in a lifetime. She took me on a rollicking tour of Honolulu's markets (fish and otherwise) and urged me to buy all kinds of unfamiliar ingredients, insisting I try them, insisting they were wonderful. Her ideas have all proven true. This one, where the subtle saltiness of the turnip enhances the delicate sweetness of mahimahi, is no exception. Try this with warmed sake.

4 ounces fresh spinach, well rinsed but not dried,
 stemmed

4 ounces young beet greens, well rinsed but not dried

1 tablespoon soy sauce

1 tablespoon rice wine vinegar

1 mahimahi fillet (1 pound), cut into 4 equal pieces

Scant ½ teaspoon mild vegetable oil, such as
 safflower

1 preserved turnip, (available in most Asian grocery
 stores), cut into thin slivers

1. Place the spinach and the beet greens in a large non-aluminum saucepan over medium-high heat. Cover and cook in the water that clings to their leaves just until wilted, about 5 minutes. Remove from the heat and pour off any excess liquid. Add the soy sauce and vinegar and toss. Reserve, keeping the greens warm over very low heat, if necessary.

2. At the same time you are cooking the greens, bring 2 cups of water to a boil in a

steamer or fish poacher. Rub the mahimahi all over with the oil. Place on the steamer rack and sprinkle with all but a large pinch of the slivered turnip. Place in the steamer, cover, and steam until opaque through, about 4 minutes.

3. To serve, transfer the greens to a serving platter. Top them with the mahimahi fillets and the steamed, preserved turnip. Garnish with the remaining slivered turnip. Serve immediately.

Makes 4 servings

Halibut with Cucumber Cream

I love cucumbers any time, any fashion, though I am particularly fond of them cooked. They are subtle but assertive, and there is nothing to beat their elegant color, which is similar to the color of fresh, fresh halibut. There are a couple of secrets to success here. Don't overcook the cucumber pieces—they should be cooked through, but not mushy; season the sauce liberally with salt and white pepper; don't omit the final grating of cucumber into the sauce—it adds a delicate touch and texture to the dish. Try this with a lightly chilled Sancerre.

4 halibut steaks (6 ounces each), cut 1 inch thick

4 large cucumbers, peeled, halved lengthwise, and seeded

1 cup Fish Stock (see Index)

2 cups heavy or whipping cream

Salt and freshly ground white pepper

Salad burnet or flat-leaf parsley leaves, for garnish

1. Rinse the halibut steaks and pat dry.

2. Cut 6 of the cucumber halves into ¼-inch-thick slices.

3. Bring the fish stock to a boil in a large, heavy-bottomed non-aluminum skillet over medium-high heat. Boil until reduced by one-third. Add the cream and cook, stirring, until the mixture has reduced by one-third and thickened somewhat. Reduce the heat to medium so the sauce is just above a simmer. Add the sliced cucumbers and poach until crisp-tender, about 8 minutes.

4. Add the halibut steaks to the cream sauce and turn to coat with the sauce. Cover and cook until opaque through, 5 to 8 minutes.

5. Using a slotted spatula, gently transfer the halibut steaks to a large, warm serving platter or 4 warm dinner plates. Keep warm in a low oven.

6. Grate the reserved cucumber into the cream sauce. Stir and cook for 2 to 3 minutes. Season with salt and pepper to taste. Pour the sauce over the halibut steaks, arranging the cucumber pieces on and around the halibut. Garnish with salad burnet leaves. Serve immediately.

Makes 4 servings

Shad with Sorrel Mousse

*T*he tried and true way to cook shad, a delightfully sweet-meated fish, is to bake it for hours in the oven, dissolving the hundreds of tiny, floating bones in the meat. Well, this also dissolves most of the meat's texture, and I don't recommend it. My solution to shad bones, since boneless fillets are impossible to get in Seattle, is to pick out what I can, and consider the meat just reward. Some fish are just a little difficult to eat, that's all.

Sorrel is often cooked or served along with fish, because it's thought the oxalic acid in it dissolves the bones. Well, teaming them here is symbolic—I did it because of the wonderfully complementary flavors. Try an Alsatian Riesling or an Italian Pinot Grigio along with this dish, and enjoy it, bones and all!

2 shad fillets (1 to 1½ pounds each)
5 tablespoons unsalted butter
12 ounces sorrel leaves, stemmed, washed and patted dry
2 tablespoons dry white wine
2 large egg whites
Salt and freshly ground black pepper

1. Remove as many bones as possible from the shad fillets, cutting them out with a knife and using a strawberry huller, fish bone puller, or needle-nose pliers. Rinse and pat dry.

2. Melt 2 tablespoons of the butter in a large, non-aluminum saucepan over medium heat. Add the sorrel and cook, stirring occasionally, until darkened and reduced to a purée, about 10 minutes. Remove from the heat; reserve in the saucepan.

3. Melt 2 tablespoons of the butter in a large skillet over medium-high heat. When the butter foams, add the shad and the wine. Cook until the fish is opaque, 8 minutes.

4. Just before the shad is cooked, whisk the egg whites with a pinch of salt until the whites are stiff. Bring the sorrel to a boil over medium-high heat. Remove from the heat; add the egg whites, whisking vigorously. Return the mixture to medium-high heat and bring to a boil, whisking constantly. Season with salt and pepper to taste. Transfer the sorrel mousse to a warm serving platter.

5. In a small saucepan, melt the remaining 1 tablespoon butter over medium heat. To serve, lay the shad fillets on top of the sorrel mousse. Drizzle with the melted butter. Serve immediately.

Makes 4 servings

Shad with Shad Roe, Bacon, and Capers

Shad roe have a wonderful, hearty, slightly earthy flavor that suggested the sauce in this dish. The roe and bacon anchor the dish, and the capers, lemon juice, and sweet, tender-meated shad make it sprightly and delicious. When buying shad roe, make sure they were removed from the fish as soon as it was caught, or they can have an unpleasant bitterness. They should have a deep, rosy hue. Grapple with the bones in the shad if you must, before the fillets are cooked, though I suggest cooking them, and picking your way through as you eat the shad—it's much more rewarding that way! Try this with a dry Sauternes, such as Château R.

2 shad fillets (about 1 pound each)
Roe of 1 shad
½ teaspoon salt
4 ounces slab bacon, rind removed, cut into 1½ x ¼ x ¼-inch pieces
2 tablespoons fresh lemon juice
2 tablespoons dry white wine
1 tablespoon drained capers
Salt and freshly ground black pepper

1. If you don't have boneless shad fillets, remove as many bones as possible, cutting them out with a knife and using needle-nose pliers, a strawberry huller, or fish bone puller made for removing fish bones. Rinse the fillets and pat dry. Refrigerate until ready to use.

2. Place the roe, 2 cups water, and the salt in a medium saucepan. Cover and bring the roe to a boil over medium-high heat. Reduce the heat and simmer until the roe turns dark brown on the outside, about 8 minutes. To check for doneness, make a shallow cut into the center of the roe to check for color. It should be deep red inside. Drain. Cut the roe into bite-size pieces; reserve.

3. In a medium-size skillet over medium-high heat, cook the bacon until crisp and golden. Using a slotted spoon, remove the bacon from the pan; drain on paper towels. Reduce the heat to medium. Add the lemon juice, wine, capers, and the shad fillets to the pan. Cover and cook until the fillets are nearly opaque, about 8 minutes. Add the bacon and shad roe. Cover and cook until the fillets are opaque and the bacon and roe are heated through, about 1 minute.

4. Transfer the shad fillets to a warm serving platter. Stir the cooking juices with the capers, bacon, and shad roe, scraping up any brown bits from the bottom of the pan. Season with salt and pepper to taste. Pour over the shad fillets. Serve immediately.

Makes 4 servings

Steamed Rock Cod

*T*his recipe was inspired by Judy Lew, the director of Uwajimaya Cooking School in Seattle, and a friend who is always willing to share an idea or advice about recipes. She suggests using the following technique—a simple way to make a very impressive dish—on fillets and steaks as well, and with any cod, snapper, or rockfish. If you are using a whole fish and it exceeds the length of the plate it will steam on, curl it around slightly—it doesn't matter if the tail fin sticks out a bit from the top of the steamer. Try a simple, very dry white wine with this dish.

Rock Cod:

2½- to 3-pound rock cod or rockfish, cleaned, with head on

Scant 1 teaspoon mild vegetable oil, such as safflower

1 scallion, trimmed and coarsely chopped

2 slices fresh ginger (1 inch x ¼ inch each), peeled, and cut into julienne

1 clove garlic, thinly sliced

¼ teaspoon freshly ground white pepper

Sauce:

2 tablespoons Japanese sesame oil

2 tablespoons mild vegetable oil, such as safflower

1 bunch scallions, trimmed, the white bulbs and light green stems cut into fine julienne

1 slice fresh ginger (1 inch x 1 inch), peeled and cut into julienne

2 large cloves garlic, cut into julienne

⅓ cup soy sauce

1. Prepare the Rock Cod: Bring 4 cups water to a boil in a wok or steamer fitted with a steamer rack over medium-high heat.

2. Rinse the rock cod and pat dry. Rub lightly all over with the oil. Place the chopped scallion, ginger, and sliced garlic in the stomach cavity; place the fish on a heatproof plate. Place the plate on the steamer rack. Cover and steam until the fish is

opaque all the way through, 20 to 25 minutes. (Make sure the steam is circulating around the fish, and check the water after about 15 minutes to be sure there is plenty left in the steamer. Add additional boiling water if necessary.)

3. Remove the cod from the steamer. Sprinkle with the white pepper. Cover loosely with foil to keep it warm.

4. Make the Sauce: Heat the oils in a small saucepan over medium-high heat until very hot but not smoking. While the oils are heating, pour off any water that has collected around the fish, and pat the plate dry. Sprinkle the fish with the scallions, ginger, and garlic; pour the soy sauce over all. Pour the hot oils over the ingredients on top of the fish; they will sizzle. Serve immediately.

Makes 4 servings

Snapper à La Lille Finne Pete

I stepped off the plane in Petersburg, Alaska, a complete stranger. I walked across the runway to the airline terminal, marveling at the clear air and snow-capped mountains in the distance, and was surprised to see a cheery woman there holding a sign with my name on it. She'd heard over the local radio that I was coming and had come to offer me a room in her home during my stay.

That was just the beginning of Ruth Sandvik's hospitality. That day she took me for a long walk on the "loop" road around Petersburg. It cuts through the scruffy brush—called muskeg—and wends its way past a tent city, where the workers who flood Petersburg each summer to work in the fish processing plants live, near a marsh where huckleberries were just turning ripe, and near a sandy beach where rocks bearing petroglyphs could be seen at low tide.

We spied a baby brown bear ambling off into the woods and a bald eagle hunkered on a dock just outside the city, and Ruth talked about her 50 years in Petersburg. When she wasn't at her full-time job as the school librarian, she helped her fisherman husband, Oscar, as he came and went on fishing trips, and raised their three children. She made this dish with halibut on my first evening in Petersburg, though she said it is as good with snapper or rockfish. "Lille Finne Pete, the cook on my husband's fishing boat, was famous for this recipe—he made it all the time," she said.

Serve this with Cucumber Salad (see Index) and a simple, chilled dry white wine.

2 snapper, halibut, or rockfish steaks (about 9 ounces each), boned and halved
3 tablespoons fresh lemon juice
3 tablespoons Worcestershire sauce
½ cup all-purpose flour
¼ teaspoon salt
Freshly ground black pepper
4 tablespoons clarified butter (see Index)
Borage blossoms, for garnish

1. Rinse the fish steaks and pat dry.

2. Combine the lemon juice and the Worcestershire sauce in a shallow dish. Combine the flour, salt, and pepper in another shallow dish.

3. Heat 3 tablespoons of the butter in a medium-size skillet over medium-high heat. While the butter is heating, dip the pieces of fish first in the lemon and Worcestershire sauce mixture, and then in the flour, shaking off any excess flour.

4. Cook fish until golden on both sides and opaque through, about 3 minutes per side.

5. Remove from the pan to a platter. Grind pepper over the fish; drizzle with the remaining 1 tablespoon butter. Garnish with the borage blossoms. Serve immediately.

Makes 4 servings

China Moon Tea- and Spice-Smoked Fish

*B*arbara Tropp is a Chinese scholar, fabulous cook, and owner of the café, China Moon, in San Francisco. She serves this tea-smoked fish as an appetizer there, accompanied by a delicate green salad and herb mayonnaise. I like to serve it as a light luncheon main course.

This recipe is very simple to prepare—it does take some planning, however, for it must be served at room temperature or, better yet, the day after it is smoked, slightly chilled from the refrigerator. And it takes a heavy-duty pot or wok that can withstand the high heat required to get the smoking ingredients going. The flavor is so subtle, and so elegantly perfumed that I prefer to serve it without any sauce at all. Try it with a lightly chilled Pinot Grigio, or for a change, a pitcher of warmed sake.

1½ pounds black cod steaks, cut at least 1 inch thick
1½ tablespoons Chinese rice wine or high-quality dry sherry
¼ cup soy sauce
1 tablespoon sugar
1 tablespoon kosher (coarse) salt
2 medium scallions, trimmed and cut into 2-inch lengths
4 quarter-size slices fresh ginger

Smoking Mixture:

⅓ cup dried black tea leaves
⅓ cup raw white or brown rice
⅓ cup packed light or dark brown sugar
1 teaspoon Szechuan peppercorns (available at Asian grocery stores), crushed
1 cinnamon stick (2 inches long), broken into small bits
2 lengths (3 x 4 inches) fresh or dried orange or tangerine zest (see Note), broken into small pieces
1½ teaspoons Japanese sesame oil

1. Rinse the fish and pat it dry. Refrigerate until ready to use.

2. Combine the rice wine, soy sauce, sugar, and salt in a flat glass or enamel baking dish large enough to hold the fish in a single layer. Stir to dissolve the sugar. Hit the scallions and ginger with the blunt handle end or broad side of a cleaver or heavy knife to spread the fibers and bring the juices to the surface; add to the soy sauce mixture. Place the fish steaks in the dish and turn once to coat with the marinade. Arrange the fish with half the scallions and ginger under them and the other half on top. Cover and marinate at room temperature for at least 1 hour, spooning the marinade over the fish every 15 minutes. The fish can be marinated for up to 2 hours in this mixture in the refrigerator. You only need to turn it once.

3. Drain the marinade from the fish and discard it. Oil a steamer or a steaming rack that fits into a wok with a scant amount of mild vegetable oil. Place the black cod steaks on the rack. (If you don't have a steaming rack, make one from a metal cooling rack covered with aluminum foil that has many holes poked in it so the fish can drain. The fish must not sit in its own juices as it steams.) Bring 1½ cups of water to a boil in the bottom of the wok. Place the rack over the water, cover, and steam until the black cod is almost opaque through (still under-cooked), about 10 minutes. Remove the fish from the wok; discard the water.

4. Prepare the wok (or a cast-iron Dutch oven or other heavy-duty pot) for smoking the fish. Dry the wok and the lid and line them with 2 layers of regular aluminum foil, leaving an overhang of about 5 inches over the edge of the wok or pot. Line the lid with 1 layer of regular aluminum foil, leaving the same overhang around the entire edge of the lid.

5. Combine all of the smoking ingredients and spread them evenly in the bottom of the wok. Put the rack with the fish on it into the wok about 1 inch above the smoking mix-ture, propping the rack above the smoking mixture if necessary with balls of aluminum foil set under four sides of the rack.

6. Set the uncovered wok over high heat and cook until the sugar begins to bubble and send up smoke in several places, any-where from 4 to 10 minutes. Cover the wok securely, and crimp the foil loosely shut, leaving an inch-wide "escape hatch" for the smoke to come out. Smoke the fish for 10 minutes, turn off the heat under the wok and let sit for 5 minutes, to continue cooking.

7. Uncrimp the foil. (You may want to do this outdoors or near an open window, an-gling it away from you, though there is really minimal smoke that emerges.) The fish should be a deep golden brown. If it is light, or if tasted it doesn't taste smoky, add 3 to 4 tablespoons of white or brown sugar to the smoking mixture, return the heat to high until smoke appears, re-cover and crimp the foil. Continue smoking for about 5 minutes.

8. To serve, remove the skin from the black cod. Divide the meat into 6 portions. Serve accompanied with a green salad (see Index).

Makes 4 servings

Note: To dry zest strips, place them on a wire rack in a warm spot, such as the top of the refrigerator, for 6 to 8 hours. They should be dry but not brittle.

9

ACCOMPANIMENTS

Maybe you feel that nothing goes better with fried fish than coleslaw, french fries, and some tartar sauce. Or that a pile of white rice has to accompany a fish fillet. Well, you're about to have your mind changed because when it comes to seafood, there are no limits to accompaniments.

Seafood is endlessly fascinating to work with, because it allows so much room for a play of flavors, textures, and colors. I like to balance rich with light, spicy with refresh-ing, warm with cool. Because the flavors of seafood are distinct, yet often very subtle, accompaniments must complement and enhance, rather than interfere. In other words, they must be simple and prepared with the best ingredients.

You'll find plenty of sauces and vegetables, salads and starches, and desserts in this chapter. While I've given specific suggestions as to when they should be served, they are ex-tremely versatile, and open to your own ideas and experiments.

Lemon Bread

This tender, delectable bread is almost like cake. It goes with a Wisconsin Fish Boil and is a surprisingly good addition to the meal because of its lemon tang. This recipe makes two small loaves, which is usually about half the required amount whether there are two or four people, so I always double the recipe!

⅔ cup (about 1¼ sticks) unsalted butter, at room temperature
1⅔ cups sugar
Grated zest of 2 lemons
1 tablespoon fresh lemon juice
3 large eggs
2½ cups all-purpose flour
¾ teaspoon salt
1½ teaspoons baking powder
¾ cup milk

1. Preheat the oven to 350°F. Lightly oil two 8½ x 4½-inch loaf pans.
2. In a large bowl, cream the butter until light. Add the sugar and beat until thoroughly mixed and light. Mix in the lemon zest and juice. One at a time, add the eggs, mixing thoroughly after each addition.
3. Combine the dry ingredients and add them to the creamed mixture alternately with the milk, beginning and ending with the dry ingredients. Do not over-mix or the bread will be tough.
4. Divide the batter between the loaf pans. Bake until golden and a skewer inserted in the center comes out clean, about 45 minutes.
Makes 2 loaves

Hush Puppies for Fried Fish and Clam Chowder

In the South and Southeast, fish is always served with hush puppies and a cup of steaming coffee. The quality of good hush puppies is a much disputed issue that centers around the subject of onions and sugar. Most Southerners say that only Yankees would put sugar in their hush puppies. Maybe they're right, but in researching hush puppies I found many Southern recipes calling for a touch of sweetening, and to my taste it makes all the difference. Onions don't raise quite the same furor—they are a matter of taste rather than demographics. In any case, these hush puppies are feather light and delicious. They'll disappear, so you may want to make a double batch.

3 cups mild vegetable oil such as safflower, for frying
1½ cups medium-grind yellow cornmeal
½ cup all-purpose flour
1 teaspoon sugar
½ teaspoon salt
2 teaspoons baking powder
1 teaspoon baking soda
1 large egg, beaten
2 tablespoons unsalted butter, melted
½ medium onion, grated
½ to ¾ cup milk

1. Pour the oil into a deep-fat fryer or deep saucepan. Bring the oil to 350°F.
2. In a large bowl, sift together the dry ingredients. Add the egg, melted butter, grated onion, and ½ cup of the milk. Mix together quickly, until the dough is stiff

enough to hold its shape, though sticky to touch. Add additional milk 1 tablespoon at a time, if necessary.

3. Working in batches and using 2 soup-spoons or tablespoons, shape the dough into balls about the size of an egg. Drop in the hot fat and fry, turning until golden brown and cooked through, 3 to 4 minutes. Let the oil heat up between batches.

Makes about 1 dozen

Friselli

These peppery biscuits are an essential ingredient to Calamari Stuffed with Mozzarella (see Index). They are also a delicious substitute for crackers. Try them with sturgeon mousse or along with a seafood salad—I like them with cold Brandade or with Pickled Salmon too (see Index for both these recipes).

1 cup lukewarm water
1 package active dry yeast
1 teaspoon salt
2 to 2½ cups unbleached all-purpose flour
3½ teaspoons coarsely ground black pepper

1. Combine the water and yeast in a large mixing bowl or the bowl of a heavy-duty mixer. Add the salt. Add 1 cup of the flour and the pepper; mix well. Add the second cup of flour, mix well, then add any additional flour until the dough becomes too stiff to stir.

2. Place the dough on a lightly floured surface and knead, adding additional flour if the dough is too sticky, until smooth and satiny, about 10 minutes. (The dough can be prepared and kneaded in a heavy-duty mixer

fitted with a dough hook.)

3. Place the dough in a bowl, cover, and let rise at room temperature for 1 hour, or until doubled in bulk.

4. Punch down the dough. Let rise again, covered, for 1½ hours, or until it doubles in bulk.

5. Preheat the oven to 375°F.

6. To make the friselli, divide the dough into 4 equal pieces. Shape them into long, narrow loaves about 8 x 1½ inches. Let rise until slightly less than doubled in bulk, 15 to 20 minutes.

7. Slash the top of the loaves several times. Bake until golden and hollow sounding when you tap them, 30 to 35 minutes. Remove from the oven and let cool slightly. Reduce the oven temperature to 350°F.

8. Cut each loaf into ½-inch slices. Arrange on 2 clean baking sheets. Bake the friselli, turning once, until crisp, about 10 minutes on each side. Remove from the oven and let cool. Friselli will keep for several days in an airtight container.

Makes about 64

Brendan Walsh's Red Pepper Brioche

This brioche is essential to Brendan Walsh's Lobster Salad (see Index). However, it makes more than enough for the salad, and I like to serve it along with the meal following the salad, or save it for breakfast the next morning. It's delicious toasted, with butter and honey.

1 package active dry yeast

2 tablespoons lukewarm water

1 tablespoon sugar

4 cups all-purpose flour

2 teaspoons salt

6 large eggs

1 cup (2 sticks) butter

2 red bell peppers, roasted, seeded, and peeled (see Index)

1. In the large bowl of an electric mixer, combine the yeast, lukewarm water, and sugar. Stir to combine and set aside to proof for 5 minutes.

2. Stir in 1 cup of the flour. Then stir in the salt. With the mixer on low speed, add the remaining 3 cups flour alternately with the 6 eggs. Continue beating, increasing the speed once the flour is incorporated, until the dough is blended, but somewhat sticky. Remove the butter from the refrigerator and set it aside to soften slightly.

3. If your mixer has a dough hook, knead the dough at medium-high speed for 10 minutes, until it pulls off the dough hook and slaps against the side of the bowl in a solid mass. Otherwise, knead the dough by hand for at least 15 minutes, or until it no longer adheres to the work surface.

4. Cut the butter into thin slices. With the mixer at medium speed, begin adding the butter, slice by slice, beating until the dough is quite soft and the butter is no longer visible, 5 to 10 minutes.

5. Place the dough in a large bowl, cover with a damp towel, and set aside in a warm, draft-free place to rise until doubled, about 2 hours.

6. Mince the roasted red peppers.

7. Punch down the dough. Mix in the red peppers, using your hand as though it were a mixing spoon. Cover the dough and let it rise

until almost doubled, about 1½ hours.

8. Generously butter two 8½ x 4½-inch loaf pans. Place half the dough in each pan. Let the loaves rise until nearly double, about 45 minutes.

9. Preheat the oven to 350°F about 15 minutes before the dough is finished with its third rising.

10. Bake until the loaves sound hollow when tapped, about 40 minutes. Remove from the pans and let cool on a wire rack.

Makes 2 loaves

Tarragon Crêpes

*T*hese crêpes will dress up any seafood recipe. Tarragon is a traditional seafood herb, but try these crêpes with thyme, savory, or chervil.

There are some tricks to crêpe-making. If the pan is too hot the batter will cook as soon as it hits the pan, not allowing you to swirl it around. The resulting crêpe will be too thick, have holes in it, and may burn. If the pan is not hot enough the batter will sit there and get tough. So, carefully regulate the heat under the pan—the batter should sizzle when it hits the pan and you should have enough time to quickly swirl the batter around in the pan before it sets. If you're not quite fast enough and your crêpe has small holes in it, go ahead and smooth some uncooked batter over the holes, if possible. If not, worry not. The crêpes will be fine, and your technique will rapidly improve. I usually discount the first crêpe; my wrist action improves further into the batch.

¾ cup plus 2 tablespoons all-purpose flour

¼ teaspoon salt

2 large eggs, lightly beaten

¾ to 1 cup milk

2 tablespoons unsalted butter, melted

¼ cup fresh tarragon leaves

¼ cup clarified butter (see Index), for frying

¾ cup ricotta cheese, seasoned with salt and freshly
   ground black pepper to taste

1. Combine the flour and the salt in a large mixing bowl and make a well in the center. Add the eggs and ½ cup of the milk. Stir, gradually incorporating the flour into the mixture. Mix the melted butter with ¼ cup milk and quickly incorporate it into the flour mixture. Set the batter aside for 1 hour.

2. Thin the batter with additional milk, if necessary, to make it the consistency of thin pancake batter. Don't use more than 1 cup milk total. Finely mince the tarragon. Fold into the batter.

3. Place a crêpe pan over medium-high heat. Add 1 tablespoon clarified butter and heat until it is hot but not smoking. Pour off any excess butter. Pour in 2 tablespoons batter and immediately swirl the pan so the batter evenly covers the bottom. Cook until the crêpe bubbles on the top side and is golden underneath, about 2 minutes. Flip the crêpe and cook until golden on the second side, about 10 seconds. Turn the crêpe out onto a plate and keep warm in a low oven. Repeat until all of the batter is used, adding clarified butter to the pan as necessary.

4. To serve the crêpes, spread 2 heaping teaspoons of the ricotta cheese mixture on each crêpe. Fold in half and then in half again, to form a small triangle. Serve warm.

Makes about 12 crêpes (4 to 6 servings)

Oven-Fried Potatoes and Garlic

*F*ried potatoes are wonderful any time, but they are especially good, and appropriate, alongside just-grilled fish. They are not only satisfying, but the generous addition of garlic slices gives them an extra punch.

2 pounds new potatoes, scrubbed

1 tablespoon kosher (coarse) salt

½ cup olive oil

8 large cloves garlic, thinly sliced crosswise

Salt and freshly ground black pepper

½ cup loosely packed flat-leaf parsley leaves, minced

1. Place the potatoes in a large saucepan. Add water to cover and the kosher salt. Bring to a boil over high heat; cook until the potatoes are nearly, but not quite, tender, about 15 minutes. Test them with a skewer, which should meet some resistance in the middle. Drain the potatoes and let them cool.

2. Preheat the oven to 500°F.

3. When the potatoes are cool enough to handle, cut into thin slices.

4. Pour ¼ cup of the oil into a 12½ x 8½-inch glass baking dish. Place the potatoes in the dish, coating them with the oil. Sprinkle the garlic over the top; season generously with salt and pepper. Add the remaining ¼ cup oil, pouring it all over the potatoes. If any potatoes aren't coated with oil, turn once so they are completely covered.

5. Bake the potatoes until golden on both sides, 15 to 20 minutes, checking them occasionally to be sure they don't get too brown.

6. To serve, sprinkle with the parsley.

Makes 4 servings

Potato Pancakes

While potato pancakes are great for just about any fish meal, they particularly shine when teamed with fried fish, applesauce, and a cool, crisp coleslaw.

2 pounds russet potatoes, peeled and coarsely grated
1 medium onion, coarsely grated
3 cloves garlic, finely minced
3 tablespoons all-purpose flour
1 teaspoon salt, or to taste
Freshly ground black pepper
4 large eggs
½ cup clarified butter (see Index)
½ cup mild vegetable oil, such as safflower, for frying
½ cup crème fraîche (see Index) or sour cream, for garnish
Applesauce (see Index)

1. Place the potatoes in a cotton tea towel, bring the edges up around the potatoes to form a bag, and squeeze the bag to force out as much liquid as you can. The potatoes should be quite dry when you are finished.

2. Combine the potatoes, onion, garlic, flour, salt, and pepper to taste in a large bowl, tossing to mix well. Whisk together the eggs in a small bowl. Add to the mixture and mix thoroughly.

3. Heat 1 tablespoon each of the butter and oil in a large skillet over medium-high heat until hot but not smoking. Using a slotted spoon, drop level spoonfuls of the potato mixture into the pan. Pat the mixture out to form 3-inch patties about ¼ inch thick. They will be slightly ragged, but this gives the pancakes delicious crisp edges. Stir the pancake mixture before you spoon it out each time, as the eggs separate from the rest of the ingredients.

4. Working in batches, cook until deep golden and cooked through, 4 to 5 minutes per side. Add more butter and oil as needed. Regulate the heat carefully so the pancakes don't get too brown on the outside without cooking on the inside. Drain the pancakes on paper towels; keep warm in a single layer on a baking sheet in a low oven. When all of the pancakes are made, serve immediately, with crème fraîche or sour cream and applesauce alongside.

Makes about 12

Rosemary Potato Salad

This salad is wonderful all by itself for a simple lunch. But it's better alongside grilled fish, and it's so easy, it makes itself. The secret is not to overcook the potatoes—cook them until they are just this side of soft all the way through—a slight crispness in the interior is fine. Let them marinate in the dressing for at least two hours—or make the salad in the morning to serve in the evening.

1½ pounds new potatoes, scrubbed
1 tablespoon kosher (coarse) salt
3 tablespoons extra-virgin olive oil
1½ teaspoons balsamic vinegar
1 large clove garlic, minced
1 tablespoon fresh rosemary leaves, coarsely chopped, or ½ teaspoon dried
Salt and freshly ground black pepper
¼ cup oil-cured black olives, pitted and quartered lengthwise

1. Combine the potatoes, 8 cups of water, and the salt in a large saucepan over high heat. Bring to a boil and cook the potatoes until nearly cooked through but still firm in the center, about 15 minutes. Drain and let cool slightly.

2. Whisk together the oil, vinegar, garlic, rosemary, and salt and pepper to taste in a medium-size bowl. Stir in the olives.

3. When the potatoes are cool enough to handle, cut them into ¼-inch-thick slices with a very sharp knife. Add the potatoes to the dressing and toss gently but thoroughly. Season with salt and pepper to taste. Cover and marinate for at least 2 hours, stirring occasionally. Just before serving, quickly toss the potatoes.

Makes 4 servings

White Rice

White rice goes with just about everything, and there are so many times where it is more appropriate than any other kind of starch. I nearly always make basmati rice, for I love its nuttiness, and find that it can be assertive or subtle, depending on the needs of the rest of the meal.

2 cups basmati rice, rinsed
¼ teaspoon salt

1. Place the rice, 3½ cups water, and the salt in a large, heavy-bottomed saucepan over high heat. Bring to a boil and boil until the rice has absorbed most of the water and there are bubble holes on top of the rice, about 10 minutes.

2. Cover the rice and reduce the heat to medium. Cook for 10 minutes.

3. Turn off the heat under the rice, but leave it covered. Let sit for 10 minutes. Serve immediately.

Makes 6 servings

Coleslaw

Coleslaw is a wonderful accompaniment to fried and grilled seafoods. I love it year round—sometimes served at room temperature, sometimes chilled. The secret to a good coleslaw is to let it ripen for at least two hours before eating. Sometimes I make it the morning of the day I plan to serve it. To transform this coleslaw into a uniquely Northwest salad, add 2 small cans of drained, pink shrimp, and toss well.

1 cup best-quality mayonnaise (or use homemade
    mayonnaise, see Note)
2 to 4 teaspoons fresh lemon juice
3 tablespoons heavy or whipping cream
2 tablespoons minced fresh chives
1 teaspoon celery seed
½ teaspoon dry mustard
Salt and freshly ground black pepper
1 small green cabbage, cored and trimmed
1 small white boiling onion, peeled

1. In a small bowl, whisk together the mayonnaise, 2 teaspoons of the lemon juice, the cream, chives, celery seed, and dry mustard until very smooth. Season with salt and pepper to taste. You may want to add additional lemon juice.

2. Slice the green cabbage as thin as you possibly can—paper-thin slices are best. Do the same with the onion; separate the rings. Combine the cabbage and onion in a large

bowl. Add the dressing and toss until the cabbage is thoroughly coated. Cover and refrigerate for at least 2 hours, stirring once or twice.

3. Serve either chilled or at room temperature.

Makes 4 to 6 servings

Note: To make mayonnaise, follow steps 1 and 2 of the Tartar Sauce recipe (see Index). Use the ingredients through the olive oil, plus an additional ½ cup corn oil.

Crunchy Jicama Salad

*J*icama is a juicy-crisp tuber that reminds me of an unsweetened apple. It is incredibly refreshing, particularly alongside grilled fish.

1 small jicama, peeled
¼ cup fresh lime juice
About ¼ teaspoon cayenne pepper

1. Cut the jicama into ¼-inch slices. Stack the slices and cut into ½-inch-thick sticks.

2. Arrange the jicama in overlapping concentric circles on a large plate. Drizzle the lime juice evenly over the sticks; sprinkle with the cayenne. Serve chilled or at room temperature.

Makes 4 to 6 servings

Fresh Tomato Salad

*T*his salad is best in late summer, with vine-ripened tomatoes bursting with warm, sun-kissed juice and flavor. Serve it alongside any grilled or baked fish.

2 vine-ripened beefsteak tomatoes, cored
¼ cup Herb Oil (see Index)
Salt and fresh coarsely ground black pepper
Leaves of 1 small bunch flat-leaf parsley, for garnish

1. Cut the tomatoes into ¼-inch-thick slices. Arrange in concentric circles on a serving plate.

2. Drizzle with the herb oil; season generously with salt and pepper. Garnish the plate with the parsley leaves. Serve at room temperature.

Makes 4 servings

Green Salad with a Vinaigrette

*T*his is a basic salad recipe that can be varied in a hundred ways. As is, this salad is a wonderful accompaniment to fried seafood or seafood soups. It is also ideal served after a main course.

6 cups mixed salad greens, such as spinach, arugula, green and red leaf lettuce, mâche, baby kale, purslane, or romaine
¼ cup extra-virgin olive oil
2 tablespoons best-quality red wine vinegar
1 clove garlic, finely chopped
Salt and freshly ground black pepper

1. Rinse and dry the greens. Tear into bite-size pieces; place in a large bowl.

2. In a small bowl, whisk together the oil, vinegar, garlic, and salt and pepper to taste. Pour over the greens and toss to coat with the dressing. Serve immediately.

Makes 4 to 6 servings

Arugula Salad

A rugula, or roquette, rocket, or garden rocket, is a wonderful tasting salad green, maybe the best. I like it fresh out of the garden any time, even in midsummer when the leaves are so hot they almost burn your tongue. It is best in late spring and early fall, of course, when the leaves have a little sugar coursing through them. With it's smoky, spicy flavor, arugula has an uncanny affinity for seafood. It is particularly suited to bluefish, but serve it with any grilled fish. Because it has an intense flavor, the serving portions are quite small.

3 tablespoons extra-virgin olive oil
2 teaspoons balsamic vinegar
1 small clove garlic, minced
Salt and freshly ground black pepper
4 cups loosely packed arugula leaves, rinsed and torn
*   into manageable pieces*

Whisk together the oil and the vinegar in a small salad bowl. Add the garlic and stir. Season with salt and pepper to taste. Add the arugula and toss well. Serve immediately.

Makes 4 servings

Fresh Beets with Their Greens

T his raw beet salad is as stunning to the eye as it is to the palate. Be sure to choose young beets that are sweet and firm, and use the youngest, greenest leaves as a bed for the salad. This goes well with simply broiled seafood.

12 ounces young beets with their green tops
2 tablespoons best-quality red wine vinegar
3 tablespoons extra-virgin olive oil
1 small shallot, finely minced
Salt and freshly ground black pepper
2 to 3 sprigs fresh dill (optional), for garnish

1. Trim the greens from the beets and reserve. Peel the beets, rinse, and pat dry with paper towels. Finely grate the beets.

2. Whisk together the vinegar, oil, and shallot in a medium-size bowl. Season with salt and pepper to taste. Add the beets and toss until thoroughly coated.

3. Wash and dry about 2 cups of the reserved beet greens. Trim the stems from the leaves and stack the leaves on top of one another. Cut them in fine slices.

4. Arrange the greens in the center of a dinner plate or serving platter. Arrange the beet salad on top, leaving a narrow edge of beet greens showing. Garnish with fresh dill sprigs if desired. Serve immediately.

Makes 4 to 6 servings

Cucumber Salad

This is an old-fashioned cucumber salad that is excellent with just about any seafood dish. The crunch of cucumber with its clean, green taste is light and refreshing, and the sauce is mildly sweet and tangy. This salad is equally good chilled or at room temperature.

2 large unwaxed cucumbers, rinsed and patted dry
½ cup distilled white vinegar
2 tablespoons sugar
¼ teaspoon salt
¼ teaspoon freshly ground white pepper
1 tablespoon finely chopped flat-leaf parsley

1. Score the length of the cucumbers with the tines of a fork. Cut the cucumbers into very thin slices. Place them in a medium-size bowl.
2. In a small bowl, combine the vinegar, sugar, salt, pepper, and 2 tablespoons water. Pour over the cucumbers. Sprinkle with the parsley and toss. Refrigerate for 2 to 3 hours.
   Makes 4 servings

Soy- and Sake-Dressed Spinach Salad

This is a wonderfully fresh and refreshing salad, with an exotic hint of sesame oil. It goes well alongside a variety of seafood dishes or as an appetizer to a seafood meal.

1 tablespoon soy sauce
2 tablespoons sake
½ teaspoon Japanese sesame oil
½ teaspoon sugar
1 pound spinach, stemmed and washed
1 tablespoon toasted white sesame seeds

1. Combine the soy sauce, sake, sesame oil, and sugar in a bowl; mix well.
2. Steam the spinach in the water that clings to its leaves until the leaves are bright green and still retain some of their shape, about 5 minutes. Drain, then squeeze gently to extract some of the liquid. Transfer the spinach to a cutting board. Coarsely chop.
3. Whisk the soy sauce mixture and add the spinach. Toss until the spinach is thoroughly coated with the sauce.
4. To serve, either divide the spinach into 4 small bowls or serve as a side dish. Sprinkle with the toasted sesame seeds and serve.
   Makes 4 servings

Tzaziki

Tzaziki is a refreshing accompaniment to grilled fish and to spicy foods. It's cool, light, and pungent with garlic and dill. Try it with Grilled Greek Grouper, Grilled Bluefish, Rosemary Baked Mullet or Turkish Fish in Parchment (see Index).

1 large cucumber, peeled and diced
2 cups plain yogurt
3 large cloves garlic, minced
¼ to ½ teaspoon dill seed, to taste

Combine all of the ingredients in a large bowl. Serve at room temperature.
Makes 3 cups

Applesauce for a Wisconsin Fish Fry

I love warm, fresh applesauce that's full of chunks and made from old-fashioned, tart-sweet Gravenstein apples. This sauce goes perfectly with fried fish, as it is served in Wisconsin. If you can't get tart apples, add a dash of lemon juice at the very end, to taste. I don't care for cinnamon in applesauce when it's to go with fried fish and potato pancakes, but that choice is yours.

You may increase this recipe indefinitely, if you want applesauce to spare.

2 pounds tart apples, such as Gravensteins,
  Braeburns, Jonagolds, or Granny Smiths
2 tablespoons unsalted butter
4 tablespoons sugar, or to taste
Ground cinnamon, to taste (optional)

1. Peel, core, and thinly slice the apples.
2. Melt the butter in a medium-size, heavy-bottomed saucepan over medium heat. Stir in the apple slices, cover, and cook, stirring occasionally, until soft but still chunky, about 15 minutes.
3. Add the sugar, sweetening the applesauce to taste. Remove from the heat. Serve hot, warm, or cold.

Makes about 3 cups

Roasted Peppers

B ell peppers are crisp, fresh, and succulent right off the plant. Roasting gives them a silken, sweet quality. I like roasted peppers simply tossed in top-quality extra-virgin olive oil and served as an accompaniment to grilled seafood, though they are good any number of ways. What follows are directions for roasting any bell pepper.

1 firm bell pepper

1. Preheat the broiler.
2. Place the pepper on a piece of aluminum foil at least 3 inches under the broiler element. Turn often, until the skin is charred on all sides and bubbles loose from the meat of the pepper. Be careful not to let the skin get too black, or it may be difficult to remove.
3. Remove the foil from the broiler with the pepper on it. Wrap the foil loosely around the pepper to steam and loosen the skin, 10 to 15 minutes.
4. When the pepper is cool enough to handle, remove the stem end (most of the seeds will come with it) and discard. Peel the skin off the meat of the pepper, using your fingers. If it sticks, use the blade of a sharp knife to scrape off the skin.
5. Scrape all the seeds and the ribs from the inside of the pepper with the blade of a sharp knife, so you are left with the meat of the pepper, which will be very limp. Proceed with any recipe calling for roasted peppers.

Skorthalia

T his zesty potato sauce comes from Greece and according to Minas Sarris, a first-generation Greco-American, former fisherman, and party boat operator in Tarpon Springs, Florida, it is traditionally served over grilled fish. Mr. Sarris, who makes *skor-*

thalia by the vat in summertime, insists it be blended with a fork just until the lemon juice, olive oil, and vinegar are incorporated, so the sauce remains chunky. I like *skorthalia* at room temperature over fish that's hot from the grill and sprinkled with fresh, coarsely chopped walnuts. Try serving it with freshly grilled lingcod, grouper, or snapper.

Salt
2 large potatoes, peeled and quartered
½ cup fresh lemon juice
½ cup Fish Stock (see Index)
½ cup olive oil
1 tablespoon white wine vinegar
8 cloves garlic, minced
½ cup walnuts, coarsely chopped (optional)

1. Bring 2 cups of water and ½ teaspoon salt to a boil in a medium-size saucepan over medium-high heat. Add the potatoes and cook, covered, until tender, 20 minutes.
2. While the potatoes are cooking, whisk together the lemon juice, ¼ cup of the fish stock, olive oil, and vinegar in a medium-size bowl.
3. When the potatoes are cooked, drain well. Place in a second medium-size bowl and use a fork or potato masher to crush the potatoes into small chunks. Sprinkle the garlic over them. Add the lemon juice mixture and use a fork or potato masher to incorporate it into the potatoes. The *skorthalia* should be thick and somewhat chunky, but smooth enough to resemble a sauce. Thin with additional fish stock if desired. Sprinkle with walnuts, if using.
   Makes 2½ cups

Pesto

This version of the classic recipe for pesto embodies the glory of summer, and it goes well with fish prepared in just about any fashion. Make plenty in summer when basil is fresh and full of flavor, and freeze it for winter use. Omit the pine nuts, which should be added fresh just before you use the pesto. When you measure the basil, gently push on the leaves without crushing them.

2 cups loosely packed fresh basil leaves
½ cup olive oil
2 tablespoons pine nuts
3 cloves garlic, peeled
¼ to ½ teaspoon salt
½ cup freshly grated Parmesan cheese
Freshly ground black pepper

1. Place the basil, olive oil, pine nuts, garlic, and ¼ teaspoon of the salt in the bowl of a food processor. Process to a fine purée.
2. Scrape the mixture into a medium-size bowl. Stir in the cheese. Season with salt and pepper to taste.
   Makes ¾ cup

Adolfo Calles' Aïoli

Adolfo Calles is the chef and owner of La Gaviota, a charming little Spanish restaurant in Seattle. He is passionate about gooseneck barnacles, and he serves them with this wonderful, garlicky *aïoli*. Try this with grilled fish or use it as a dip for steamed shellfish.

1 whole large egg, at room temperature

1 large egg yolk, at room temperature

1½ tablespoons fresh lemon juice

10 cloves garlic

½ teaspoon salt

1 teaspoon Dijon mustard

1 cup extra-virgin olive oil

Combine the egg, egg yolk, lemon juice, garlic, salt, and mustard in the bowl of a food processor. Purée. With the processor running, slowly add the olive oil in a thin stream until the aïoli is thick and creamy, but not quite as thick as regular mayonnaise.

Makes 1⅓ cups

Tartar Sauce

This tartar sauce is an essential ingredient to the Wisconsin Fish Fry. But don't stop there—serve it as a dip, with fresh vegetables, as a spread for a sandwich, or add it to leftover fish for a salad or a sandwich. I suggest making your own mayonnaise, but you can also use 1¼ cups top-quality prepared mayonnaise here, instead of making your own.

2 large egg yolks, at room temperature

2 tablespoons fresh lemon juice

Salt and freshly ground black pepper

1 cup extra-virgin olive oil

½ teaspoon minced fresh parsley

2 tablespoons minced dill pickle

1 tablespoon drained capers, minced

1 tablespoon finely chopped red onion

1 clove garlic, minced

1. To make the mayonnaise, place the egg yolks in the bowl of a food processor. Add 1 tablespoon of the lemon juice and a sprinkling of salt and pepper. Process until thoroughly combined.

2. With the machine running, slowly add the olive oil in a very thin stream. The mixture will emulsify and become quite thick. When the olive oil is all incorporated, add the remaining 1 tablespoon lemon juice.

3. Scrape the mayonnaise into a medium-size bowl. Add the remaining ingredients and mix well. Season with salt and pepper to taste. This will keep for a week in the refrigerator, covered.

Makes about 1⅓ cups

Mustard Sauce

I suggest using one small bunch of fresh dill in this wonderfully piquant sauce, but you may want to adjust the amount to your own taste. Serve it with Gravlax and Pickled Smelt.

¼ cup coarse whole-grain mustard

1 tablespoon plus 2 teaspoons sugar

2 tablespoons plus 1 teaspoon white wine vinegar

1 cup mild vegetable oil, such as safflower

1 small bunch fresh dill, stems removed

Salt and freshly ground white pepper

Whisk together the mustard, sugar, and vinegar in a small bowl. Add the oil in a thin stream, whisking constantly, so the sauce emulsifies. Whisk in the dill and season with salt and white pepper to taste.

Makes 1⅓ cups

Miso Sauce for Misoyaki

This sauce, which is based on a golden, fermented mixture of rice and soybeans, has a wonderful sweetness reminiscent of apples. It is a Japanese-influenced sauce widely used in Hawaii, primarily to marinate black cod (sable fish) and tuna. Salmon also makes excellent *misoyaki*. This recipe makes enough for 1 to 1½ pounds of fish. Don't think there is too much—it should generously cover the fish with some to spare.

⅔ cup white miso paste from Hawaii, preferably
  Maru-Hi brand
3 tablespoons sugar
2 tablespoons minced fresh ginger
1 tablespoon sake

Place all of the ingredients in a small mixing bowl and mix well. Cover and store in the refrigerator for up to 2 days.
Makes about 1 cup

Herb Oil

Brendan Walsh uses this herb oil on at least one of the dishes he serves at Arizona 206, a Manhattan restaurant. It highlights his warm lobster salad, giving it an aromatic burst of flavor. I like to have it around to use on grilled fish or meat, in a salad dressing, or as a dip for just-baked sourdough bread.

2 long sprigs fresh rosemary
2 long sprigs fresh oregano
8 sprigs fresh thyme
2 cups extra-virgin olive oil

Place the herbs in a jar or bottle that will hold slightly more than 1 pint. Cover with the olive oil, seal and let sit for at least 1 week, unrefrigerated, before using. Once infused, refrigerate. It will last indefinitely.
Makes 1 pint

Salsa

This subtle salsa is another from Brendan Walsh, chef at Arizona 206, in Manhattan. I like it on grilled, poached, or broiled fish, for a summery sprightliness.

1 large tomato, peeled, seeded, and coarsely chopped
¼ teaspoon minced serrano chile
2 teaspoons fresh lime juice
1 cup loosely packed fresh cilantro leaves, coarsely
  chopped
Salt and freshly ground black pepper, to taste

Mix together all of the ingredients in a small bowl. Use the day it is made.
Makes about 1¼ cups

Teriyaki Marinade

Use this marinade, which is deep, flavorful, and exotic, with just about any fish. Marinate darker fish, such as bluefish or mackerel, for 2 to 3 hours. White fish, such as snapper, hake, haddock, or lingcod, should marinate for just 2 hours.

⅔ cup soy sauce

2 teaspoons sugar

¼ cup sake

2 tablespoons grated fresh ginger

4 large cloves garlic, finely minced

Mix all of the ingredients together in a medium bowl. Stir in ⅔ cup water.

Makes 1 ⅓ cups or enough to marinate 4 fish fillets

Pia's Ginger Purée

Pia Carroll, chef at the Sooke Harbour House on Vancouver Island, British Columbia, always has a jar of this sauce in her refrigerator. She adds it to cream or butter sauces, then uses them with all kinds of subtly flavored shellfish and fish. It adds zip and allure, and you'll be glad you have it on hand. Stir the sauce before using it, and as a general rule, add about ½ teaspoon per serving to whatever sauce you are making, or to taste.

8 ounces fresh ginger, peeled and thinly sliced

¼ cup sugar

1 cup rice wine vinegar

1 cup dry white wine

1. Combine the ginger, sugar, vinegar, wine, and 1 cup water in a medium-size saucepan over medium heat. Cover and bring to a boil. Cook until the ginger softens but retains its shape, about 30 minutes. Remove from the heat and let cool.

2. Purée the ginger with ¼ cup of the cooking liquid in the bowl of a food processor. Scrape the purée into a jar and stir in the remaining cooking liquid. Cover and refrigerate until ready to use. The purée should be the consistency of thin cream. It will last several weeks in the refrigerator.

Makes 1 ⅓ cups

Red Pepper and Toasted Sesame Sauce

This is a sauce with Hawaiian flair—use it on any grilled fish, from mackerel to salmon.

2 teaspoons white sesame seeds

3 medium scallions, trimmed, the white bulbs and light green stems finely minced

2 teaspoons sesame oil

¼ teaspoon cayenne pepper

1 teaspoon sugar

1 clove garlic, minced

2 teaspoons minced fresh ginger

2 tablespoons soy sauce

1. Place the sesame seeds in a small skillet over medium-high heat. Toast, stirring constantly, until golden. Remove from the heat.

2. Very finely crush 1 teaspoon of the toasted sesame seeds in a mortar and pestle.

3. Reserving 1 tablespoon of the scallions and the remaining 1 teaspoon toasted sesame seeds, combine all of the remaining ingredients in a small saucepan. Stir in 2 tablespoons water. Place over low heat until hot.

4. When hot, pour over grilled or broiled fish. Garnish with the reserved scallions and sesame seeds.

Makes ½ cup, enough for 4 servings of grilled fish

Pastry for a Two-Crust Pie

This makes a beautiful, and very forgiving, pastry crust. Use it for any sweet or savory pie.

2 cups all-purpose flour
¼ teaspoon salt
⅓ cup unsalted butter, chilled and cut in small pieces
⅓ cup lard, chilled and cut in small pieces
⅓ to ½ cup ice water

1. Combine the flour and salt in the bowl of a food processor. Pulse on and off just to mix them together.
2. Add the butter and lard, and pulse until the mixture resembles coarse meal. (You don't want to over blend this pastry.)
3. Slowly pour in ⅓ cup of the water and pulse to incorporate it into the flour mixture. Process just until the mixture looks crumbly, but adheres when you press it together between your fingers, without feeling damp. Add more water 1 tablespoon at a time, if necessary.
4. Gather the pastry into a ball. Wrap in waxed paper and chill it for at least 1 hour.
Makes enough pastry for a 2-crust, 10-inch pie

Crème Fraîche

To my way of thinking tangy, rich *crème fraîche* is an essential ingredient to have on hand. It softens sauces and enriches soups, it is wonderful on top of fresh-grilled

fish, garnished with a teaspoon of caviar, or whisked into a salad dressing at the last minute. And when it comes to dessert, the possibilities are endless.

2 cups heavy or whipping cream (ultrapasteurized cream is not satisfactory)
3 tablespoons cultured buttermilk

1. Whisk together the heavy cream and the buttermilk in a medium-size bowl. Cover with a cotton kitchen towel and let stand at room temperature in a warm spot—on top of the refrigerator or on top of a gas stove with a pilot light—until it thickens, 8 to 12 hours, depending on the temperature.
2. Cover the *crème fraîche* and refrigerate for several hours, until thickened. It will keep, tightly covered, in the refrigerator for 1 week.
Makes 2 cups

Lime Soufflé

This recipe is based on a lemon soufflé I used to make while an apprentice at La Varenne Ecole de Cuisine in Paris. Though I love lemon, I prefer the deep tang of lime in this pillowy, not-too-sweet hot soufflé. It makes a dramatically delicious finish to any meal, but particularly one starring seafood. One of the most wonderful things about this recipe is its adaptability—I usually complete the soufflé up to three hours before I plan to bake it, refrigerate it, enjoy my meal, then pop it in a preheated oven. You'll amaze your guests by making it all look so easy! A properly cooked soufflé is somewhat runny in the center, and the cooking time indicated here will give that result. If you prefer the soufflé cooked through, increase the cooking time by about 4 minutes.

½ cup sugar
4 tablespoons (½ stick) unsalted butter
⅓ cup fresh lime juice
Grated zest of 2 limes (about 2 teaspoons zest)
4 large egg yolks
6 large egg whites
Pinch of salt

1. Preheat the oven to 425°F.

2. Heavily butter a 6-cup soufflé dish. Sprinkle with 1 tablespoon of the sugar, and discard any excess.

3. Melt the butter, 3 tablespoons of the sugar, and the lime juice in a small non-aluminum pan over medium heat. Remove the pan from the heat. Add the lime zest and whisk in the egg yolks. Return the mixture to low heat and cook, stirring constantly, until thickened to the consistency of very thick cream. This will happen quite quickly; do not cook the mixture too long or it will curdle. Immediately pour the mixture into a bowl, so it won't continue cooking in the heat from the pan.

4. To finish the soufflé, whip the egg whites and salt with a whisk or an electric mixer using the whisk attachment until nearly stiff. Sprinkle on the remaining 4 tablespoons sugar and continue beating until the egg whites are glossy, about 30 seconds.

5. Fold one-third of the egg whites into the lime mixture to lighten it. Pour the mixture into the remaining egg whites and fold gently, to mix thoroughly. Gently spoon the mixture into the soufflé dish, smoothing out the top. With the back of your thumb-nail, make a small trench around the edge of the soufflé; mound the batter you remove in the center of the soufflé. This will ensure that the soufflé rises evenly. Bake until the soufflé is puffed and golden, 12 minutes.

6. To serve, bring the soufflé immediately to the table. Using two serving spoons of similar size, break open the top of the soufflé and scoop up some of the more cooked top and some of the interior.

Makes 4 servings

Hazelnut Tart

This tart is soul-satisfying yet light, its sweet, toasty, hazelnut-studded layer topped with fresh, clean strawberry purée and crowned with more fresh berries.

1¼ cups hazelnuts
Unbaked 10½-inch pastry shell (see Index)
⅔ cup sugar
½ pound (2 sticks) unsalted butter, at room temperature
1 large whole egg
1 large egg yolk
2 tablespoons dry sherry
1 tablespoon all-purpose flour
1 pound (about 1½ pints) fresh strawberries, rinsed and hulled
Confectioners' sugar, to taste (optional)

1. Preheat the oven to 350°F.

2. Place the hazelnuts in an ovenproof pan and toast them until they are golden, and the skins split, 12 to 15 minutes. Remove them from the oven and wrap them in a tea towel to steam, about 5 minutes. Then rub them in the towel to remove as much of the skin as possible. Discard the skin. Raise the oven temperature to 425°F.

3. Line the pastry shell with aluminum

foil, pressing it lightly against the sides, right up to the rim. Fill the shell with dried beans or pastry weights and bake until light golden, about 20 minutes. Remove from the oven and remove the foil and weights. Set aside to cool on a wire rack. Reduce the oven temperature to 375°F.

4. In a food processor, coarsely grind the hazelnuts with 1 tablespoon of the sugar so that some of the nuts are finely ground and some are in coarse chunks. Set aside.

5. In a large bowl, cream the butter with the remaining sugar until light and fluffy. Beat in the whole egg and then the egg yolk. Then add the sherry and beat again. Sift in the flour and mix well. Add the hazelnut and sugar mixture and mix well.

6. Spread the hazelnut filling in the cooled pastry shell. Bake on the center rack until the filling is deep golden in color and firm at the edges, 20 to 25 minutes. The filling will be slightly soft in the center, which is fine. Remove from the oven and set aside to cool on a rack.

7. In a food processor, purée half of the strawberries, adding confectioner's sugar to taste, if necessary. Thinly slice the remaining berries, cutting them from top to bottom.

8. Just before serving, spread the berry purée over the cooled tart. Arrange the sliced berries in concentric overlapping circles on top of the purée, and serve.

Makes 6 to 8 servings

Orange Cake with Marmalade Fool

This is an easy dessert to prepare and its fresh citrus flavor makes it an ideal ending to a seafood dinner.

¾ cup plus 1 tablespoon granulated sugar
1½ cups unbleached all-purpose flour
1½ teaspoons baking powder
Pinch of salt
7 ounces (1¾ sticks) unsalted butter, at room temperature
3 large eggs
½ teaspoon vanilla extract
Zest of 1 orange, minced
¾ cup heavy cream, preferably not ultrapasteurized
3 tablespoons best-quality orange marmalade
2 tablespoons confectioners' sugar (optional)

1. Preheat the oven to 350°F. Generously butter a 9-inch round cake pan. Sprinkle with 1 tablespoon of the granulated sugar.

2. On a sheet of waxed paper, sift together the flour, baking powder, and salt.

3. In a large bowl, cream the butter with the remaining ¾ cup granulated sugar until light. One at a time, add the eggs, mixing well after each addition. Beat in the vanilla and orange zest. Fold in the flour mixture.

4. Pour the batter into the prepared cake pan, smoothing the top. Bake until the cake is deep golden and springs back when you touch it lightly, or until a cake tester inserted in the middle comes out clean, 30 to 35 minutes. Remove from the oven and run a knife around the edge of the cake to loosen it from the pan. Cool on a wire rack.

5. Make the marmalade fool: Whip the cream until it is thick and holds soft peaks. Fold in the marmalade.

6. Turn the cake out onto a serving plate. Dust with the confectioners' sugar if desired. Serve the marmalade fool alongside.

Makes 6 to 8 servings

Gâteau Ste. Marie

I rarely find a chocolate cake at a restaurant that satisfies my admittedly demanding palate. But the first time I had this, after a wonderful meal at Campagne, a restaurant in Seattle's Pike Place Market, my palate was won over. I have adapted pastry chef Lisa Siegel's recipe just slightly and suggest you make this cake early on the day it is to be served.

¾ cup golden raisins

1 tablespoon Triple Sec

1 cup hazelnuts

⅔ cup sugar

6 ounces semisweet chocolate (preferably Lindt or Tobler)

8 tablespoons (1 stick) unsalted butter, at room temperature

3 large eggs

Grated zest of 1 orange

¼ cup fresh bread crumbs

Chocolate Glaze:

6 ounces semisweet chocolate (preferably Lindt or Tobler)

8 tablespoons (1 stick) unsalted butter, at room temperature

1. Soak the raisins in the Triple Sec for 30 minutes.
2. Preheat the oven to 350°F.
3. Lightly butter a 9-inch cake pan. Line the bottom of the pan with a piece of parchment paper. Lightly butter the paper.
4. In a food processor, combine the hazelnuts with 1 tablespoon of the sugar. Process until finely ground.
5. Melt the chocolate in a heavy-bottomed small saucepan over low heat. Re-move from the heat as soon as it is melted; let cool to room temperature.
6. In a large bowl, cream the butter with the remaining sugar until pale yellow and fluffy. One at a time, add the eggs, beating well after each addition. One at a time, add the ground hazelnuts, the melted chocolate, the orange zest, the bread crumbs, and the raisins, mixing well after each addition.
7. Turn the mixture into the prepared cake pan and bake on the center rack of the oven until the cake has puffed slightly and has a slight crust on top, about 30 minutes. Test for doneness by inserting a metal skewer into the center of the cake. The skewer will not come out completely dry—it will be moist in some spots. Remove the cake from the oven and cool on a wire rack.
8. While the cake is cooling, make the glaze. Melt the chocolate with the butter, stirring occasionally, in a small, heavy-bottomed saucepan over low heat. Remove from the heat when melted, and stir to blend well. Set aside to cool. Spread evenly over the top and sides of the cooled cake.

Makes 8 servings

Fall Plum Tart

T his tart is a year-round specialty at our house—I make it with first-of-the-season plums, which always coincide with crisp, fragrant, summer days in Seattle. I often make this in winter too, with frozen plums, as an antidote to the gray drizzle, for the splendor of summer emanates from the aroma of sweet plums.

Pastry:

1 ¾ *cups unbleached all-purpose flour*

¼ *teaspoon salt*

½ *cup sugar*

¼ *teaspoon ground allspice*

8 *tablespoons (1 stick) unsalted butter, chilled and cut into bits*

4 *large egg yolks*

Filling:

1 *large egg*

½ *cup plus 2 tablespoons heavy or whipping cream*

1 *tablespoon sugar*

3 ½ *cups pitted, halved Italian prune plums*

1. Make the Pastry: Combine the flour, salt, sugar, and allspice in a food processor. Add the butter and process, pulsing on and off, until the mixture resembles coarse cornmeal. Add the egg yolks and pulse on and off until thoroughly incorporated and the mixture resembles couscous.

2. Transfer the dough to a 10½-inch tart tin with a removable bottom. Gently and quickly press the dough into the tin, being sure to press it up the sides of the tin. Refrigerate the pastry for 1 hour.

3. Preheat the oven to 350°F.

4. Pierce the pastry with the tines of a fork and line it with aluminum foil. Fill the shell with dried beans or pastry weights and bake until golden around the edges, about 20 minutes. Remove the crust from the oven and let cool on a wire rack.

5. Make the Filling: Whisk together the egg, cream, and sugar in a small bowl. Arrange the halved plums in concentric circles over the pastry crust, beginning at the outside edge. Carefully pour the egg and cream mixture over the plums. Bake in the center of the oven until the cream mixture is golden,

about 30 minutes. Cool to room temperature before serving.

Makes 6 to 8 servings

Plum Ice Cream

The plum tree in our garden always yields a surfeit of dusty purplish plums, but they never go to waste. We eat them sweet and bursting with juice right from the tree, I make tarts, breads, and jams, and what plums aren't used in season are frozen for future use. Plum ice cream is a favorite at our house. It is absolutely wonderful on its own, with a few slices of fresh plum over the top, and it is ethereal in combination with the luscious Plum Tart.

5 *cups whole Italian prune plums, pitted and halved*

3 *cups milk*

½ *cup heavy or whipping cream*

1 *vanilla bean, halved*

4 *large egg yolks*

⅔ *cup sugar*

1. In a food processor, chop the plums until they are a thick, chunky purée. You should have 1½ cups of plum purée.

2. To make the ice cream, scald the milk and the heavy cream with the vanilla bean in a heavy-bottomed saucepan over medium-high heat. Remove from the heat, cover and set aside to infuse for 10 minutes.

3. Whisk together the egg yolks and the sugar in a large bowl until thickened and pale yellow.

4. Remove the vanilla bean from the milk and add the milk to the egg yolk and sugar mixture, whisking constantly. Return this mixture to the saucepan and cook, stirring

constantly, over low heat until the custard has thickened enough to coat the back of a spoon, at least 5 minutes. Be careful not to overcook or the custard will curdle.

5. Immediately pour the custard into a large bowl. Let cool to room temperature. Refrigerate until cold. The recipe can be made up to this point several hours or the night before churning it.

6. Before freezing the ice cream, stir the plum purée into the custard sauce, then freeze according to the manufacturer's instructions.

Makes about 1 quart of ice cream—4 servings

Lemon Ice Cream with Chocolate Sauce

*T*his elegant, refreshing dessert combines two of my favorite flavors, the two I crave the most after a satisfying seafood meal. The rich, warm chocolate sauce here is a perfect foil for the gentle tang of fresh lemon ice cream, and it's surprisingly quick and easy to prepare.

Ice Cream:

2⅔ *cups whole milk*
½ *cup Crème Fraîche (see Index) or heavy or*
   whipping cream
Strips of zest from 2 lemons
4 *large egg yolks*
½ *cup sugar*
¼ *cup fresh lemon juice*

Chocolate Sauce:

5 *ounces semisweet chocolate*
1 *tablespoon unsalted butter*
½ *cup Crème Fraîche (see Index)*
1 *teaspoon vanilla extract*

1. Make the ice cream: Combine the milk, *crème fraîche,* and half the zest in a heavy-bottomed saucepan. Place over medium-high heat and scald the milk. Remove from the heat, cover, and set aside to infuse for 10 minutes.

2. Meanwhile, in a large bowl, whisk together the egg yolks and the sugar until thick and pale yellow. Strain the hot milk mixture, discarding the zest. Whisk the mixture into the egg yolks and sugar. Return to the saucepan and cook, stirring constantly, over medium-low heat until the custard thickens enough to coat the back of a spoon. Be careful not to curdle the custard.

3. Immediately transfer the mixture to a bowl so it won't continue to cook from the heat of the pan, and let cool to room temperature. Refrigerate until the custard is well chilled, 3 to 4 hours.

4. Finely mince the remaining lemon zest and stir it into the chilled custard, along with the lemon juice. Mix well and freeze in an ice cream maker, following the manufacturer's directions.

5. While the ice cream is freezing, make the chocolate sauce. Combine the chocolate, butter, and ¼ cup water in a heavy-bottomed saucepan over low heat. Cook, stirring occasionally, until melted together, taking care that it doesn't burn. Stir in the crème fraîche and the vanilla and heat through. Remove from the heat and reserve. Serve either warm or at room temperature.

Makes 3½ cups of ice cream; 1 cup chocolate sauce

Northwest Crayfish

*I*f anyone asked you where crawfish comes from you'd probably say "Louisiana" without missing a beat. You'd be right. But the crawfish's cousin, the crayfish, comes from the Northwest, and many aficionados insist its tail meat is sweeter than that of Louisiana's bayou brand.

Crayfisherman Guy Taylor begins each day early. He quietly edges his aluminum boat out of the dock at Westport, Oregon, and glides it into Westport Slough on his way to the mighty Columbia River, and he pulls line after line of traps on the way.

The boat he designed and built is equipped with an electric winch that pulls traps out of the water for him. This is a dramatic innovation in a fishery where most fishermen still pull their traps by hand. Even with a winch it's difficult work—those traps weigh 10 pounds and up, and that's not including the drag of the water. If it's a good line in waters heavily populated with crayfish, they'll weigh much more.

Like most crayfishermen, Guy makes the small traps, which are about 3 feet long, out of 1-inch wire mesh. Little plastic funnels at either end reach into the trap, allowing the crayfish in and barring their retreat. He uses larger mesh than most—the standard is 7/8 inch—because it allows smaller, illegal crayfish to escape so Taylor doesn't have to sort his catch.

Guy Taylor baits one of his crayfish traps before lowering it back into the Columbia River.

By day's end he'll have about 250 pounds of the golden brown, clawed creatures in his boat. By 5 P.M. those crayfish are in a cooler in Westport. By evening or early morning they're in Portland, 71 miles away, at Jake's Famous Crawfish and Seafood (Jake's is a holdout for the Louisiana spelling). Jake's considers Guy a highliner—one of the best—of their crayfish suppliers, and they sell most of his prime catch to Norway. One batch was out of the Columbia and on a plane to the royal palace within hours, for a state event. Said Guy, "I never did get a thank you note from the king, but I know they were eatin' my crayfish."

Lexicon

What makes a cookbook useful, besides wonderful recipes, is knowing what ingredients to use when those called for aren't available. This is particularly true with a seafood cookbook, since seafood is available regionally and seasonally. This lexicon will go a long way toward making the recipes in this book as useful in Maine as they are in Texas, or Kansas City, or Seattle. Consult it when you want to find out where a certain fish, shellfish, or crustacean comes from, when it's available fresh or flash-frozen, how to prepare it, or what to use as a substitute for it. Use it for the recipes in this book, and for those in other books, too. It will take some of the mystery out of cooking with seafood, and it will open up a new world of seafood species and recipes.

ABALONE *(Haliotis rufescens)*

ALIAS: red abalone
FAMILY: univalve.
RANGE: West Coast.
PHYSICAL CHARACTERISTICS: one shell covering meat; inner shell mother-of-pearl; 6 to 8 ounces.
MEAT COLOR AND FAT CONTENT: pale ivory, firm; moderately lean.
PREFERRED COOKING METHODS: steaming, sautéing.
SUBSTITUTES: geoduck.
AVAILABILITY: sporadically year-round.
COMMENTS: tiny abalone farm-raised in California, available year-round; must be cooked quickly (about 30 seconds) or will toughen; pounding unnecessary; freezes well.

ALASKA POLLOCK *(Theragra chalcogramma)*

ALIAS: Walleye pollock
FAMILY: cod.
RANGE: northern California to northwestern Alaska.
PHYSICAL CHARACTERISTICS: generally less than 2 pounds.
MEAT COLOR AND FAT CONTENT: white; lean.
PREFERRED COOKING METHODS: poaching, sautéing.
SUBSTITUTES: sole, flounder, other cod.
AVAILABILITY: fresh-frozen, year-round.
COMMENTS: almost exclusively frozen at sea, in huge blocks that are cut and processed into fish portions and sticks; small, thin frozen fillets sometimes available—they cook more quickly than other cod; more distinctive flavor than other cod; mostly harvested by Japanese, who grind it into fish paste later transformed into surimi and used as shellfish substitute.

ALBACORE *(Thunnus alalunga)*

ALIAS: white-meat tuna; see Common Hawaiian Fish box (see Index)
FAMILY: mackerel.
RANGE: temperate waters off Atlantic and Pacific coasts, Hawaii.
PHYSICAL CHARACTERISTICS: dark blue on upper body with greenish hue toward tail, cream colored belly, tiny yellow finlets along edges of tail; 40 to 50 pounds.
MEAT COLOR AND FAT CONTENT: ivory meat turns white when cooked, small-flaked, firm; moderately fatty.

PREFERRED COOKING METHODS: uncooked as sashimi, baking, braising, sautéing, broiling, marinated, and grilled.
SUBSTITUTES: other tuna, shark, marlin, swordfish (dryer than albacore).
AVAILABILITY: fresh, June to October.
COMMENTS: much albacore canned as "white-meat tuna;" cooks quickly; dryer than most tuna.

AMERICAN PLAICE *(Hippoglossoides platessoides)*

ALIAS: dab
FAMILY: flounder.
RANGE: Atlantic from Grand Banks off Newfoundland to Cape Cod.
PHYSICAL CHARACTERISTICS: reddish to gray-brown; 2 to 3 pounds.
MEAT COLOR AND FAT CONTENT: white, fine-flaked; lean.
PREFERRED COOKING METHODS: frying, sautéing, baking.
SUBSTITUTES: other flounder.
AVAILABILITY: year-round.

ANCHOVY *(Engraulis mordax)*

ALIAS: northern anchovy
FAMILY: anchovy.
RANGE: Queen Charlotte Islands to Baja California.
PHYSICAL CHARACTERISTICS: slim, silvery; 4 to 6 inches long.
MEAT COLOR AND FAT CONTENT: dark; high-fat.
PREFERRED COOKING METHODS: if available fresh, deep-fried; rinsed and used as seasoning.
SUBSTITUTES: fresh: whitebait; canned, none.
AVAILABILITY: seldom available fresh.
COMMENTS: Most anchovies are salted, then canned in oil, to be used as seasoning; benefit from soaking in milk or white wine for 15 minutes to remove salt.

ANGEL SHARK *(Squatina californica)*

FAMILY: shark.
RANGE: off the coast of California.
PHYSICAL CHARACTERISTICS: resembles skate; large wings, long, shark-like tail; 3½ feet; 25 pounds.
MEAT COLOR AND FAT CONTENT: white, firm; lean.
PREFERRED COOKING METHODS: steaming, baking, broiling, sautéing.
SUBSTITUTES: other shark, swordfish, tuna.

AVAILABILITY: year-round.

COMMENTS: new addition, within last 10 years, to California shark fishery; now biggest shark landing in California.

ARROWTOOTH FLOUNDER (Atheresthes stomias)

ALIAS: turbot, French sole
FAMILY: flounder.
RANGE: central California north to Alaska.
PHYSICAL CHARACTERISTICS: averages 2 to 4 pounds.
MEAT COLOR AND FAT CONTENT: white, soft; lean.
PREFERRED COOKING METHODS: frying, broiling, baking.
SUBSTITUTES: flounder.
AVAILABILITY: year-round.

ATLANTIC COD (Gadus morhua)

ALIAS: small cod, scrod, market cod, large cod (see Comments)
FAMILY: cod.
RANGE: in North Atlantic from Hudson straits to New England, sometimes to North Carolina. Imported from Denmark, Iceland, Norway.
PHYSICAL CHARACTERISTICS: up to 40 inches in length; 3 to 20 pounds.
MEAT COLOR AND FAT CONTENT: white, firm; lean.
PREFERRED COOKING METHODS: poaching, baking, sautéing, braising; in soups and chowders.
SUBSTITUTES: other cod, lingcod, petrale sole, snapper, grouper.
AVAILABILITY: year-round, peak season—March to November in mid-Atlantic, April to December in New England.
COMMENTS: Sold under different names according to size: small cod, less than 1½ pounds; scrod, 1½ to 2½ pounds; market cod, 2½ to 10 pounds; large cod, 10 to 25 pounds. Fillets sold as jumbo (1 pound and more) and regular.

ATLANTIC HALIBUT (Hippoglossus hippoglossus)

FAMILY: flounder.
RANGE: Labrador to the New Jersey Coast and to Greenland.
PHYSICAL CHARACTERISTICS: averages 5 to 9 feet long; 200 pounds.
MEAT COLOR AND FAT CONTENT: white, big-flaked, tender; lean.

PREFERRED COOKING METHODS: steaming, baking, poaching, frying.
SUBSTITUTES: large-flaked cods, grouper, snapper (will all take longer to cook than halibut).
AVAILABILITY: frozen, year-round; fresh, from April to December.
COMMENTS: cooks very quickly.

ATLANTIC HERRING (Clupea harengus harengus)

FAMILY: herring.
RANGE: northern Labrador to North Carolina.
PHYSICAL CHARACTERISTICS: dark green to steel blue on back; 6 to 12 inches long.
MEAT COLOR AND FAT CONTENT: dark meat turns ivory when cooked; fatty.
PREFERRED COOKING METHODS: smoking, grilling, pickling, baking.
SUBSTITUTES: smelts, sardines in some cases.
AVAILABILITY: fresh, December to April, July to November; frozen, sporadically year-round.
COMMENTS: more perishable than most fish; small herring sometimes packed as sardines.

ATLANTIC MACKEREL (Scomber scombrus)

FAMILY: mackerel.
RANGE: north Atlantic from St. Lawrence River to Cape Hatteras; abundant in New England.
PHYSICAL CHARACTERISTICS: greenish-blue along back, dark toward tail; series of wavy, zebra-like lines on sides; averages 1½ to 3½ pounds.
MEAT COLOR AND FAT CONTENT: reddish meat turns ivory when cooked; short-grained; fatty.
PREFERRED COOKING METHODS: grilling, braising, broiling, baking, sautéing.
SUBSTITUTES: mullet, sardines, bluefish, tuna in some instances (see Peppers Stuffed with Tuna).
AVAILABILITY: fresh, June to November in New England, April to August and October to December in mid-Atlantic; frozen, year-round.
COMMENTS: usually sold whole; freezes extremely well.

ATLANTIC POLLOCK (Pollachius virens)

ALIAS: Boston blue, blue cod
FAMILY: cod.
RANGE: usually shallow waters from Nova Scotia to Chesapeake Bay; most common between Cape Cod and Cape Sable, Nova Scotia.
PHYSICAL CHARACTERISTICS: 1 to 3 feet long; 4 to 12 pounds.

Farmed Atlantic Salmon

An increasing amount of farmed Atlantic salmon, most of it from Norway though the Scots farm it too, is being sold at fish markets and restaurants. The Norwegians are the world's experts at raising and transporting salmon to its destination while it's still so fresh, it looks like it just jumped from the water.

Usually, it hasn't been more than a few hours since it did. And the salmon arrive with every scale in place, the eyes bright and the meat firm, almost quiveringly fresh, the dream of chefs and fish processors who aren't within easy reach of wild salmon.

Farmed salmon swim about in saltwater pens. They are confined and their food is controlled. What is firm, flavorful, and vibrant in nature is by comparison, subdued and lackluster in farmed salmon. Some liken the difference between wild and farm-raised salmon to wine: farmed salmon is non-vintage wine—perfectly edible, even quite good. A good wild salmon is a great vintage with all the implied subtleties of flavor, texture, and aroma.

Farmed salmon is a very real threat to commercial fishermen, who can't guarantee their catch and its availability, and who can't always keep their prices low. One hopes the demand for farmed and wild salmon will keep everyone in business, fish farmers and fishermen alike.

MEAT COLOR AND FAT CONTENT: grayish, turns white when cooked; lean.
PREFERRED COOKING METHODS: poaching, braising, steaming, baking, sautéing.
SUBSTITUTES: other cod, lingcod, petrale sole, snapper, and grouper.
AVAILABILITY: May to December.
COMMENTS: resembles haddock and is often illegally substituted for Atlantic cod and haddock.

ATLANTIC SALMON (*Salmo salar*)

FAMILY: salmon.
RANGE: Greenland to Maine, farmed throughout the world.
PHYSICAL CHARACTERISTICS: dark blue on top with silvery sides and belly; average 1 to 12 pounds up to 60 pounds.
MEAT COLOR AND FAT CONTENT: pale pink meat, large flakes, mild flavor; fatty.
PREFERRED COOKING METHODS: baking, poaching, braising, grilling, broiling, sautéing, frying.
SUBSTITUTES: other salmon, whitefish, trout, barracuda, weakfish, spotted seatrout.
AVAILABILITY: year-round.
COMMENTS: only native Atlantic salmon; most farmed salmon (from Norway, Scotland, etc.); Atlantic salmon generally not as flavorful as Pacific salmon.

BARRACUDA (*Sphyraena argentea*)

ALIAS: Pacific barracuda, California barracuda, see Common Hawaiian Fish box (see Index)
FAMILY: barracuda.
RANGE: southern California, Mexico, Hawaiian waters.
PHYSICAL CHARACTERISTICS: long, slim, upper back bluish green, or silvery gray; protruding lower jaw; 2 to 6 feet, up to 12 feet; 4 to about 8 pounds.
MEAT COLOR AND FAT CONTENT: white; fatty.
PREFERRED COOKING METHODS: grilling, steaming, baking, broiling, sautéing.
SUBSTITUTES: salmon.
AVAILABILITY: summer.

BAY SCALLOP (*Argopecten irradians*)

FAMILY: mollusk.
RANGE: In protected bays and shallow waters, from New England to North Carolina, though they are most abundant from Cape Cod to Long Island.

PHYSICAL CHARACTERISTICS: shell grows to about 4 inches across; muscle (what we call the scallop) quite small, about ¼ inch across.
MEAT COLOR AND FAT CONTENT: ivory with a golden tinge; lean.
PREFERRED COOKING METHODS: steaming, sautéing, baking.
SUBSTITUTES: other scallops.
AVAIILABILITY: fresh, fall through early spring, though specific seasons vary by state; frozen, year round.
COMMENTS: bay scallops only spawn once during their 1½ to 2 year lifespan, and after the spawn a line-like growth ring is left on the shell. Only scallops with these growth rings may be harvested, to protect the resource. Bay scallops are bagged in their shells, brought ashore each afternoon and manually shucked. They can reach the market within 24 hours of being harvested, and are nearly always fresher than sea scallops. The calico scallop (Aequipecten gibbus), harvested in the Gulf of Mexico, is often sold as the bay scallop, though it lacks the sweetness and firm texture, isn't considered as high quality, and is a slightly darker color. Calico scallops are available fresh December through May.

BELON OYSTER (Ostrea edulis)

ALIAS: European flat oyster
FAMILY: bivalve.
RANGE: native to Atlantic and Mediterranean; farmed on both U.S. coasts.
PHYSICAL CHARACTERISTICS: flat, round, dark brownish to greenish shell; 4 inches long.
MEAT COLOR AND FAT CONTENT: silvery gray to green; moderately lean.
PREFERRED COOKING METHODS: uncooked, on the half shell.
SUBSTITUTES: other oysters.
AVAILABILITY: fall and winter.
COMMENTS: slow growing; sharp, distinctive taste.

BIGEYE TUNA (Thunnus obesus)

ALIAS: see Common Hawaiian Fish box (see Index)
FAMILY: mackerel.
RANGE: tropical and semitropical waters; Gulf of Mexico; Hawaii.
PHYSICAL CHARACTERISTICS: muted bluish-silver, tiny yellow finlets along both sides of tail; 30 to 50 pounds, up to 400 pounds.
MEAT COLOR AND FAT CONTENT: dark red, short-grained, firm; moderately fatty.

PREFERRED COOKING METHODS: uncooked in sashimi; braising, baking, sautéing; marinated and grilled or broiled.
SUBSTITUTES: other tuna, swordfish, marlin, shark, king mackerel.
AVAILABILITY: year-round.
COMMENTS: one of largest tuna; cooks quickly.

BLACK COD (Anoplopoma fimbria)

ALIAS: sablefish (accepted), butterfish (in California, unaccepted)
FAMILY: skilfish.
RANGE: Baja California to Alaska.
PHYSICAL CHARACTERISTICS: Nearly black, velvety skin, slim; 3 to 7 pounds.

Hawaiian Deep Sea Fish

Hapu'upu'u, ulua, onaga, uku, and opakapaka all inhabit deep waters surrounding the Hawaiian Islands. Their meat is generally more moist than that of surface fish, and the meat of onaga and uku is so fine, fatty, and delicate, it is served as sashimi. The color of the meat ranges from white to pink when uncooked, and white when cooked, and it is generally much more delicately flavored than surface fish.

Other deep-sea fish from Hawaii to look for:

EHU: short tail red snapper
GINDAI: Hawaiian tai snapper
KAKU: barracuda
KAMANU: rainbow runner, also called Hawaiian salmon for its pale pink meat
LEHI: long tail pink or silvermouth
ONAGA: red snapper

MEAT COLOR AND FAT CONTENT: white meat; high-fat.
PREFERRED COOKING METHODS: smoking, steaming, grilling, sautéing.
SUBSTITUTES: salmon, bluefin tuna, sturgeon, black bass.
AVAILABILITY: fresh, from spring through fall; fresh-frozen year-round.
COMMENTS: *not* a member of the cod family. Most black cod shipped to Japan. Smoked black cod, called smoked sable, is popular in Midwest and along East Coast. An increasingly popular fish.

BLACK GROUPER *(Mycteroperca bonaci)*

FAMILY: sea bass.
RANGE: Florida to Brazil.
PHYSICAL CHARACTERISTICS: dark brown; up to more than 100 pounds, averages 20.
MEAT COLOR AND FAT CONTENT: white, big-flaked; lean.
PREFERRED COOKING METHODS: grilling, poaching, broiling, baking, sautéing.
SUBSTITUTES: large-flaked cods (such as haddock), snapper, redfish, halibut (will cook in less time than black grouper).
AVAILABILITY: year-round.
COMMENTS: not the highest quality grouper.

BLACK SEA BASS *(Centropristis stratus)*

ALIAS: black bass
FAMILY: bass.
RANGE: Maine to Florida and eastern Gulf of Mexico.
PHYSICAL CHARACTERISTICS: bluish to dark brown; stripes along sides.
MEAT COLOR AND FAT CONTENT: white; fatty.
PREFERRED COOKING METHODS: steaming, baking, sautéing, smoking, grilling, broiling.
SUBSTITUTES: black cod, grouper.
AVAILABILITY: year-round.

BLACKTIP SHARK *(Carcharhinus limbatus)*

FAMILY: shark.
RANGE: Gulf of Mexico, along Florida coast into Caribbean.
PHYSICAL CHARACTERISTICS: beige-gray with pale belly, thin skin, black tip on each fin; no dorsal ridge as most shark have; seldom over 6 feet; 80 pounds.
MEAT COLOR AND FAT CONTENT: pinkish with some bright red contrasting meat just under skin, turns ivory when cooked; lean.

PREFERRED COOKING METHODS: steaming, baking, sautéing, braising, marinated and broiled.
SUBSTITUTES: other shark, swordfish, marlin and tuna.
AVAILABILITY: fresh, December through April from the Atlantic coast of Florida.
COMMENTS: other inferior shark often substituted for blacktip, such as bull, which has darker, thicker skin, and hammerhead sharks with bright white, tough meat, not pinkish. Look for small concentric circles with clearish gristle between circles in substitutes; black tip has no gristle. Another substitute is silky shark—bright white, high quality, fragile meat that falls apart if grilled. Shark carry urea in skin and will smell of ammonia if not handled properly.

BLUEFIN TUNA *(Thunnus thynnus)*

FAMILY: mackerel.
RANGE: temperate and subtropical waters of the Atlantic, as far north as Nova Scotia in warm weather.
PHYSICAL CHARACTERISTICS: deep blue on top, silvery on sides and belly; 100 up to 1,500 pounds.
MEAT COLOR AND FAT CONTENT: dark red, firm; moderately fatty.
PREFERRED COOKING METHODS: uncooked as sashimi; braising, baking, marinated and grilled, broiling, sautéing.
SUBSTITUTES: other tuna, swordfish, marlin, shark.
AVAILABILITY: fresh, June to September.
COMMENTS: largest tuna; migrate across Atlantic; cooks quickly.

BLUEFISH *(Pomatomus saltatrix)*

FAMILY: bluefish.
RANGE: Open waters from Florida to Cape Cod, sometimes to Nova Scotia.
PHYSICAL CHARACTERISTICS: silvery blue, stout; up to 4 feet; up to 27 pounds, average 3 to 6.
MEAT COLOR AND FAT CONTENT: dark, bluish-reddish meat; fatty.
PREFERRED COOKING METHODS: grilling, broiling, smoking.
SUBSTITUTES: sturgeon, salmon, black cod (though texture is less firm).
AVAILABILITY: fresh, as fillets, year-round.
COMMENTS: meat lightens during cooking; pleasant, distinctive flavor.

BLUE CRAB *(Callinectes sapidus)*

FAMILY: crustacean.

RANGE: Cape Cod to Florida and Gulf of Mexico.
PHYSICAL CHARACTERISTICS: bright vivid blue to brownish with scattered blue and cream markings, turns bright red when cooked; 6 to 8 inches across back.
MEAT COLOR AND FAT CONTENT: white; moderately fatty.
PREFERRED COOKING METHODS: live whole: steaming, boiling, sautéing.
SUBSTITUTES: any crab.
AVAILABILITY: fresh during spring, summer, and fall.
COMMENTS: soft-shell crab is blue crab just after molt, when it has emerged from hard shell and has only a soft shell; completely edible except for face and gills; range from 3 to 6 inches; should be purchased live or fresh-frozen. Available mid-April through mid-September. (For more on soft-shell crab see Index.) Latin name *Callinectes* means "beautiful swimmer."

BLUE WAREHOU—see New Zealand fish box (see Index).

BUFFALOFISH *(Ictiobus cyprinellus, I. niger, or I. bubalus)*
FAMILY: sucker
RANGE: rivers of Mississippi Valley.
PHYSICAL CHARACTERISTICS: hefty, steely gray with large scales; up to 70 pounds, averages 2 to 8 pounds.
MEAT COLOR AND FAT CONTENT: white; moderately fatty.
PREFERRED COOKING METHODS: frying, steaming.
SUBSTITUTES: carp.
AVAILABILITY: fresh, year-round.
COMMENTS: sweet, soft meat; quite bony near head.

BUTTER CLAM *(Saxidomus giganteus)*
ALIAS: clam
FAMILY: bivalve.
RANGE: West Coast.
PHYSICAL CHARACTERISTICS: shell relatively smooth with fine-etched lines.
MEAT COLOR AND FAT CONTENT: pinkish ivory, tender, dark siphon; lean.
PREFERRED COOKING METHODS: uncooked on half shell when small; steaming, sautéing, frying.
SUBSTITUTES: other clams, geoduck.
AVAILABILITY: year-round.

COMMENTS: native to West Coast.

CALIFORNIA HALIBUT *(Paralichthys californicus)*
FAMILY: flounder.
RANGE: Washington to Baja California.
PHYSICAL CHARACTERISTICS: similar to Pacific halibut; 2 to 5 feet; 5 to 72 pounds.
MEAT COLOR AND FAT CONTENT: white, big-flaked, tender; lean.
PREFERRED COOKING METHODS: steaming, poaching, baking, frying.
SUBSTITUTES: large-flaked cods, grouper, snapper (all will take longer to cook than halibut).
AVAILABILITY: fresh, May to December; frozen, year-round.
COMMENTS: not as good as Pacific or Atlantic halibut. Usually sold in fillets.

CANARY ROCKFISH *(Sebastes pinniger)*
ALIAS: Pacific snapper, Alaska snapper
FAMILY: rockfish.
RANGE: West Coast.
PHYSICAL CHARACTERISTICS: round-bodied, heavy-finned, reddish skin, large scales.
MEAT COLOR AND FAT CONTENT: white, large-flaked; lean.
PREFERRED COOKING METHODS: steaming, frying, baking, sautéing.
SUBSTITUTES: cod, snapper.
AVAILABILITY: generally year-round.
COMMENTS: skin-on fillets are the most common substitute for red snapper.

CARP *(Cyprinus carpio)*
RANGE: fresh waters of Great Lakes, Mississippi River Valley.
PHYSICAL CHARACTERISTICS: olive green to brown coloring, paling to yellowish pink on belly; 2 to 8 pounds.
MEAT COLOR AND FAT CONTENT: white; lean.
PREFERRED COOKING METHODS: frying, baking, broiling, smoking.
SUBSTITUTES: buffalofish.
AVAILABILITY: year-round, best in winter.
COMMENTS: best carp from cold waters; imported to U.S. from Germany in nineteenth century, took over and threatened indigenous species, nationwide movement to eradicate resulted in its lack of popularity. Traditionally used in gefilte fish and as centerpiece for grand Asian meals.

Common Hawaiian Fish

AHI

ALIAS: refers primarily to yellowfin and bigeye tuna, though albacore sometimes called *ahi*

JAPANESE NAMES: *mebachi*—bigeye; *hon maguro*—bluefin; *kehada*—yellowfin; *tombo*—albacore.

FAMILY: mackerel.

COMMENTS: among the largest fish in Hawaiian waters; important fishery in Hawaii; commonly sold for sashimi—custom at the United Fishing Agency Ltd. fish auction in Honolulu to cut a small section out of the tail of each fish so buyers can grab a small piece of meat and rub it between their fingers to assess: 1. texture—the tackier the meat, the fresher; 2. fat content—the fattier the better; 3. color—the redder the better.

AKU

ALIAS: Skipjack tuna (see Index)

JAPANESE NAME: *otaro.*

FAMILY: tuna.

COMMENTS: meat prized in Hawaii for sashimi, often more than *ahi*, particularly in winter when fattiest; meat darker red than *ahi*.

A'U

ALIAS: refers to striped, Pacific, and blue marlin

FAMILY: marlin.

RANGE: tropical and temperate waters worldwide.

PHYSICAL CHARACTERISTICS: striped marlin diminutive—120 to 130 pounds—compared with Pacific blue or black marlin that range from 100 to 1,000 pounds.

MEAT COLOR AND FAT CONTENT: firm, white to orange (in winter, when fattiest); lean in warmer months, fatty in winter.

PREFERRED COOKING METHODS: marinated and grilled or broiled; baking, frying, sautéing, steaming.

SUBSTITUTES: swordfish, tuna, shark.

AVAILABILITY: fresh, year-round; best in winter.

COMMENTS: marlin over 150 pounds tend to be tough, with connective tissue, which looks white, between the "rings" of meat.

HAPU'UPU'U *(Epinephlaus guernus)*

ALIAS: Hawaii's sea bass, or grouper

FAMILY: sea bass.

RANGE: Hawaiian bottom fish.

MEAT COLOR AND FAT CONTENT: white, firm, moist; lean.

PREFERRED COOKING METHODS: thinly sliced at low heat or will become tough; braising, poaching, sautéing.

SUBSTITUTES: grouper, monkfish.

COMMENTS: similar to grouper; certain cuts, when cut into small pieces, resemble monkfish.

HAWAIIAN SUN FISH

ALIAS: tilapia

FAMILY: perch relative.

RANGE: aquacultured.

PHYSICAL CHARACTERISTICS: reddish skin; 1 to 4 pounds.

MEAT COLOR AND FAT CONTENT: white, sweet, fine-flaked; lean.

PREFERRED COOKING METHODS: steaming, baking, grilling, broiling.

SUBSTITUTES: rockfish, small snapper.

AVAILABILITY: sporadically, year-round.

COMMENTS: copyrighted name for red tilapia.

MAHIMAHI *(Coryphaena hippurus)*

FAMILY: dolphin.

RANGE: tropical and subtropical waters, close to surface off coasts of California and Hawaii, Gulf of Mexico, and south Atlantic.

PHYSICAL CHARACTERISTICS: bright, yellowish green coloring against silvery gray; female has large, sloping forehead; male big, square head; 5 to 40 pounds, larger than 15 pounds most desirable.

MEAT COLOR AND FAT CONTENT: white, tender, sweet; lean.

PREFERRED COOKING METHODS: baking, braising, sautéing, frying, marinated and grilled.

SUBSTITUTES: pompano, snapper, cod.

AVAILABILITY: fresh, year-round.

COMMENTS: no relation to Flipper, who was/is a

porpoise; female more desirable than male, higher yield; dry meat cooks quickly, benefits from sauce or marinade.

ONO *(Acanthocybrium solandri)*
ALIAS: wahoo
FAMILY: mackerel.
RANGE: worldwide, tropical and subtropical waters.
PHYSICAL CHARACTERISTICS: long, slender, silvery; up to 100 pounds though average much smaller.
MEAT COLOR AND FAT CONTENT: ivory turning white when cooked, firm; lean.
PREFERRED COOKING METHODS: marinated and grilled; broiling, braising, frying, sautéing, steaming, smoking.
SUBSTITUTES: mackerel, tuna, swordfish, shark, mahimahi.
AVAILABILITY: fresh, year-round.
COMMENTS: cooks quickly; benefits from marinade if grilled or broiled; *ono* means "good to eat" in Hawaiian.

OPAKAPAKA
ALIAS: pink snapper
FAMILY: snapper.
RANGE: bottom fish.
MEAT COLOR AND FAT CONTENT: white; lean in warmer weather, fatty in winter.
PREFERRED COOKING METHODS: steaming, baking, braising, sautéing, grilling (when fatty).
SUBSTITUTES: snapper, rockfish, ocean perch.

SPEARFISH
ALIAS: Short nose billfish
JAPANESE NAME: *hebi.*
COMMENTS: similar to marlin, can be prepared the same way.

TA'APE
ALIAS: snapper, Tahitian perch
FAMILY: snapper.
RANGE: Tahiti, Hawaiian waters.
PHYSICAL CHARACTERISTICS: small; up to 1 pound.
MEAT COLOR AND FAT CONTENT: white; lean in warmer months, fatty in winter.
PREFERRED COOKING METHODS: sautéing, stir-frying, steaming.

SUBSTITUTES: other small fish such as aweo-weo, small snapper.
AVAILABILITY: fresh, year-round.

UKU
ALIAS: gray snapper
FAMILY: snapper.
RANGE: Hawaiian waters.
MEAT COLOR AND FAT CONTENT: white; fatty.
PREFERRED COOKING METHODS: steaming, sautéing, grilling, broiling, baking.
SUBSTITUTES: other snapper, rockfish, ocean perch, black bass.
AVAILABILITY: summer.
COMMENTS: fattier than other snapper.

ULUA
ALIAS: jack crevally
JAPANESE NAME: *Hoshi* or *Omilu.*
FAMILY: jack or *Carangidae.*
RANGE: bottom fish in tropical and subtropical waters.
PHYSICAL CHARACTERISTICS: up to 40 pounds, though usually smaller.
MEAT COLOR AND FAT CONTENT: white; fatty.
PREFERRED COOKING METHODS: uncooked as sashimi; braising, steaming, baking, sautéing, grilling, broiling.
SUBSTITUTES: tuna, swordfish, snapper, black bass.
AVAILABILITY: fresh, year-round.
COMMENTS: PAPIO is young ulua; another ulua to look for is DOBIE ULUA; highly prized in Hawaii; pompano relative.

CATFISH (Ictalurus punctatus)

ALIAS: channel catfish

RANGE: wild, in Great Lakes south to Virginia and west to Mexico. Farmed in more than 40 states.

PHYSICAL CHARACTERISTICS: long, dull bluish-gray on top with lighter belly; young have dark, trout-like spots; tough skin; "whiskers" are sabre-sharp; wild catfish, 8 ounces to 40 pounds, farmed catfish, 2 to 3 pounds.

MEAT COLOR AND FAT CONTENT: white; lean.

PREFERRED COOKING METHODS: frying, baking, grilling, broiling.

SUBSTITUTES: trout.

AVAILABILITY: year-round.

COMMENTS: farmed catfish fine when prepared traditionally—filleted, rolled in cornmeal, and fried until crisp. Otherwise, meat soft, flabby and uninteresting. Small (8 ounces to 1 pound), wild catfish resemble wild trout. Their meat is delicate with slight, pleasant earth flavor balanced by vibrant texture.

CAVIAR: see STURGEON ROE

CHUM SALMON (Oncorhynchus keta)

ALIAS: dog salmon, keta

FAMILY: salmon.

RANGE: West Coast.

PHYSICAL CHARACTERISTICS: silver, thick bodied; 10 to 15 pounds.

MEAT COLOR AND FAT CONTENT: pale pink, coarse; moderately fatty.

PREFERRED COOKING METHODS: smoking, grilling, broiling.

SUBSTITUTES: any salmon, trout, whitefish, weakfish, spotted seatrout.

AVAILABILITY: fresh, summer and fall.

COMMENTS: not the best salmon; not recommended for eating fresh unless right out of the water.

CLAM: see BUTTER CLAM, GEODUCK, LITTLENECK CLAM, MANILA CLAM, QUAHAUG CLAMS, RAZOR CLAM

COD: a family of fish which includes many common American white-meated fish including Atlantic cod, cusk, haddock, hake, Pacific cod, pollock, scrod, schrod.

CODFISH ROE: see ROE.

CONCH: see WHELK

CRAB: see BLUE CRAB, DUNGENESS CRAB, KING CRAB, STONE CRAB CLAWS, TANNER CRAB

CRAWFISH (Procambrus clarkii, Louisiana; Pacifisticus leniusculus, Northwest)

ALIAS: crayfish, mudbug, crawdad

FAMILY: crustacean.

RANGE: southern states, primarily Louisiana; Washington, Oregon, northern California.

PHYSICAL CHARACTERISTICS: reddish-brown turns bright red when cooked; 3 to 6 inches in Louisiana, 3½ to 10 inches in Northwest.

MEAT COLOR AND FAT CONTENT: white; moderately fatty.

PREFERRED COOKING METHODS: boiling, sautéing.

SUBSTITUTES: shrimp, lobsterette tails in some cases.

AVAILABILITY: February through May for wild southern crawfish; January to June for farmed southern crawfish; May through October for Northwest crawfish (crayfish).

COMMENTS: wild crawfish generally considered tastier than the farmed version; southern crawfish farmed in rice paddies on alternate years—they hibernate in mud and come back the following year; Northwest crawfish larger and broader through shoulders than southern cousins; tail provides most meat, though meat in claws and body juices, which are sucked out, are flavorful.

CUSK (Brosme brosme)

FAMILY: cod.

RANGE: North Atlantic from Greenland to Cape Cod, sometimes to New Jersey.

PHYSICAL CHARACTERISTICS: shaped like fat eel without thinning at tail of most fish; greenish-brown to pale yellow fading to cream color on sides; averages 1½ to 5 pounds, up to 30 pounds.

MEAT COLOR AND FAT CONTENT: soft, white, delicate, lean meat; fattier than most cod.

PREFERRED COOKING METHODS: poaching, sautéing, baking, braising, broiling.

SUBSTITUTES: other cod, lingcod, petrale sole.

AVAILABILITY: fresh, April to December in New England, March to November in mid-Atlantic.

COMMENTS: available frozen in fillets and fish sticks. Much cusk imported.

DOGFISH (Squalus acanthias)

ALIAS: spiny dogfish

What's in a Name?

Blue point was originally a patented name for the oysters produced at the Blue Point Oyster Company at Blue Point, Great South Bay, Long Island, which went out of business in 1942. Legally, no oyster can be called blue point, though Eastern oysters are commonly given that name.

FAMILY: shark.
RANGE: Gulf of Mexico, Atlantic Coast, and Pacific Coast.
PHYSICAL CHARACTERISTICS: gray to brown on top, white below with white spots along the sides; smaller, flatter than most sharks; 2 to 3 feet; 7 to 10 pounds.
MEAT COLOR AND FAT CONTENT: white; moderately lean.
PREFERRED COOKING METHODS: frying, smoking.
SUBSTITUTES: other shark, king mackerel.
AVAILABILITY: fresh, year-round in Gulf of Mexico; November to April in mid-Atlantic; April to December in New England; June to August on West Coast.
COMMENTS: popular in England as the fish in fish and chips; underutilized in this country, but available.

DOVER SOLE *(Microstomus pacificus)*
ALIAS: Pacific flounder
FAMILY: flounder.
RANGE: Alaska to California.
PHYSICAL CHARACTERISTICS: light to dark brown on eyed side; 2 to 10 pounds.
MEAT COLOR AND FAT CONTENT: white, fine-flaked; lean.
PREFERRED COOKING METHODS: steaming, sautéing, frying, baking.
SUBSTITUTES: other flounder, sole.
AVAILABILITY: year-round.
COMMENTS: meat inconsistent—it can cook up tender and delicate, at other times it turns to mush in pan. No way to tell beforehand if this will happen. Not recommended if other sole or flounder available.

DUNGENESS CRAB *(Cancer magister)*
FAMILY: crustacean.
RANGE: Alaska to California.
PHYSICAL CHARACTERISTICS: heavy shell, purplish fading to red-tinged ivory, turns bright red when cooked; 6¼ inches across back; averages 2 pounds.
MEAT COLOR AND FAT CONTENT: white; moderately fatty.
PREFERRED COOKING METHODS: whole—steaming, boiling; in pieces—sautéing.
SUBSTITUTES: any crab.
AVAILABILITY: fresh, summer and fall from Alaska, winter from Washington and Oregon; fresh-frozen, year-round.
COMMENTS: only males are harvested; 25 percent of weight yields edible meat; Alaska Dungeness slightly sweeter than others.

EASTERN OYSTER *(Crassostrea virginica)*
ALIAS: Atlantic oyster, blue point oyster
FAMILY: bivalve.
RANGE: Canadian East Coast south through Gulf of Mexico to Texas.
PHYSICAL CHARACTERISTICS: shells round and flat to deep and cupped.
MEAT COLOR AND FAT CONTENT: ranges from silvery to tan to deep green; moderately fatty.
PREFERRED COOKING METHODS: uncooked on half shell; steaming, grilling, poaching, frying.
SUBSTITUTES: other oysters.
AVAILABILITY: year-round; best from September through April.
COMMENTS: some oysters farmed; named for bays of origin or bays transferred to before harvest; some oysters harvested with huge tongs swung over side of boat by hand.

EASTERN SQUID *(Loligo pealei)*
ALIAS: squid, calamari, calamar
FAMILY: cephalopod.
RANGE: Atlantic Coast.
PHYSICAL CHARACTERISTICS: slim, rocket-shaped body with fin on either side of narrow end; transparent purple-spotted skin; two large eyes and ink sac in head, surrounded by wreath of 10 tentacles with suction cups; transparent "pen" inside body considered shell; 8 inches long.
MEAT COLOR AND FAT CONTENT: milky white turns bright white when cooked; moderately fatty.
PREFERRED COOKING METHODS: sautéing, frying, baking, grilling.

SUBSTITUTES: other squid.
AVAILABILITY: fresh-frozen, year-round.
COMMENTS: squid toughens if cooked too long, but will pass through toughness if cooked longer when baking, braising, sautéing; if frying, 1 minute usually is sufficient; if accidental overcooking results in toughness, continue cooking so total cooking time is at least 20 minutes; squid will become tender again, though its texture not as good.

ENGLISH SOLE (Parophrys vetulus)

ALIAS: lemon sole
FAMILY: flounder.
RANGE: Alaska to northern Mexico.
PHYSICAL CHARACTERISTICS: 15 inches; 12 ounces.
MEAT COLOR AND FAT CONTENT: white; lean.
PREFERRED COOKING METHODS: frying, sautéing, baking, steaming.
SUBSTITUTES: other flounder, sole.
AVAILABILITY: year-round.
COMMENTS: no relation to East Coast lemon sole.

FINNAN HADDIE

ALIAS: smoked haddock
FAMILY: cod.
MEAT COLOR AND FAT CONTENT: soaking in light salt brine gives it a golden color on the outside, whitish on the inside; lean.
PREFERRED COOKING METHODS: poaching in milk is traditional.
AVAILABILITY: year-round.
COMMENTS: named for the Scottish town of Findon, where haddock is landed, and the Scottish word for haddock, "haddie." Finnan haddie produced on East Coast most often made with cod.

FLOUNDER: see AMERICAN PLAICE, ARROWTOOTH FLOUNDER, CALIFORNIA HALIBUT, DOVER SOLE, ENGLISH SOLE, FLUKE, GRAY SOLE, PACIFIC HALIBUT, PACIFIC SANDDAB, PETRALE SOLE, SOUTHERN FLOUNDER, STARRY FLOUNDER, WINTER FLOUNDER, YELLOWTAIL FLOUNDER: no commercially harvested sole in U.S. waters; flatfish from U.S. waters marketed as sole is flounder; flounder generally wider and more round than sole, which are thicker through body; flounder meat more coarse than sole, though they are interchangeable in most cases; sole more delicate than flounder and requires gentler cooking; flounder begin life looking like roundfish, slowly their skeleton twists, one eye migrates to other side, and they swim on what was their side.

FLUKE (Paralichthys dentatus)

ALIAS: summer flounder
FAMILY: flounder.
RANGE: Maine to northern Florida, most common off New England; deep water in winter, shallow water in summer.
PHYSICAL CHARACTERISTICS: spots on body; 20 to 25 inches; 2 to 5 pounds.
MEAT COLOR AND FAT CONTENT: white; lean.
PREFERRED COOKING METHODS: baking, poaching, frying.
SUBSTITUTES: other flounder, sole.
AVAILABILITY: year-round

FLYING FISH ROE: see ROE

GASPERGOO (Aplodinotus grunniens)

ALIAS: freshwater sheepshead, freshwater drum, gou, goo
FAMILY: drum.
RANGE: large rivers and lakes from Hudson Bay to the Gulf of Mexico.
PHYSICAL CHARACTERISTICS: oblong body with slightly humped back, gray-bronze with blue and silver highlights; 8 ounces to 20 pounds.
MEAT COLOR AND FAT CONTENT: white, small-flaked; lean.
PREFERRED COOKING METHODS: steaming, frying, sautéing, grilling.
SUBSTITUTES: rockfish, tilapia.
AVAILABILITY: most available in spring and summer.
COMMENTS: only drum found in freshwater.

GEODUCK (Panope generosa)

ALIAS: king clam
FAMILY: clam.
RANGE: California to Alaska.
PHYSICAL CHARACTERISTICS: up to 3 feet long including protruding siphon, averages 6 to 10 inches; 1 to 3 pounds.
MEAT COLOR AND FAT CONTENT: pinkish golden to ivory; lean.
PREFERRED COOKING METHODS: uncooked as sashimi; steaming, sautéing.
SUBSTITUTES: other clams.
AVAILABILITY: year-round.

Oysters with No Sex Appeal

Oyster lovers who refrain from eating the bivalves during warm weather, when they are soft and milky, may be in for a surprise. Sandy Downing and Stan Allen, research associates at the University of Washington in Seattle, have developed an all-season oyster that reportedly stays firm and sweet year-round.

These oysters, unromantically but correctly called triploids, have an extra set of chromosomes. To produce them, fertilized eggs that begin with one set of chromosomes are briefly shocked with high water pressure, heat, or a chemical, which gives the eggs a second set of chromosomes. The result is a sterile oyster with three sets of chromosomes rather than two.

Despite excitement about the triploids, particularly in the Northwest oyster industry, some growers are skeptical. They say the triploids are neither firm nor soft, but something in-between. They are also concerned with the success rate in converting diploids to triploids, now about 50 percent. Sandy Downing is concerned too, and she is currently trying to develop a tetraploid oyster which, when mated with a regular, diploid oyster, would naturally produce a triploid.

The real verdict on triploids? They are sweet and mild and they do retain their firmness more than normal diploid oysters, but they aren't crisp and they have a curious golden color. As they become more available, however, they will provide a reasonable, year-round substitute for spawny diploids.

COMMENTS: siphon crisp and crunchy; body meat rich and buttery; some "geoduck steaks" available frozen, but not usually of good quality; most clams in canned clam chowder actually geoduck.

GRAY SNAPPER *(Lutjanus griseus)*
ALIAS: mangrove snapper
FAMILY: snapper.
RANGE: Florida and Caribbean.
PHYSICAL CHARACTERISTICS: medium to dark gray, red tinges close to belly; 8 to 10 pounds.
MEAT COLOR AND FAT CONTENT: white, large-flaked; lean.
PREFERRED COOKING METHODS: steaming, braising, baking, sautéing, broiling.
SUBSTITUTES: other snapper, cod, lingcod, petrale sole, or grouper (especially scamp).
AVAILABILITY: year-round.

GRAY SOLE *(Glyptocephalus cynoglossus)*
ALIAS: witch flounder
FAMILY: flounder.
RANGE: Atlantic waters.
PHYSICAL CHARACTERISTICS: white underside, top grayish brown.
MEAT COLOR AND FAT CONTENT: white; lean.
PREFERRED COOKING METHODS: frying, baking, poaching, steaming.
SUBSTITUTES: other flounder, sole.
AVAILABILITY: year-round.
COMMENTS: a major East Coast flounder.

GREEN LIPPED MUSSEL
ALIAS: New Zealand green mussel
FAMILY: bivalve.
RANGE: New Zealand waters.
PHYSICAL CHARACTERISTICS: bright, kelly green shell edges; large, up to 3 to 4 inches long.
MEAT COLOR AND FAT CONTENT: large, meaty, ivory; moderately lean.
PREFERRED COOKING METHODS: steaming, sautéing, frying, pickling, smoking.
SUBSTITUTES: other mussels, clams.
AVAILABILITY: year-round.
COMMENTS: recent import from New Zealand.

GROUPER, member of sea bass family; see BLACK GROUPER, JEWFISH, NASSAU GROUPER, RED GROUPER, SCAMP, WARSAW GROUPER, YELLOWMOUTH GROUPER. Other grouper include GAG, MARBLED GROUPER, OLIVE GROUPER,

Other New Zealand Fish to Look for

Blue Warehou: versatile, pinkish-white meat becomes white when cooked, lean; good when baked, sautéed, fried, steamed.

Ling or Kingclip: white, firm flesh; good when smoked, grilled, broiled.

New Zealand Hake: (the same fish is caught in Chile and marketed in the U.S. as Antarctic Queen) white, moist flesh with delicate texture; good when sautéed, fried, baked, steamed.

Oreo Dory: similar to John Dory with smooth, fine-flaked meat; good when poached, baked, steamed, sautéed, fried.

Red Cod: white, flaky, lean meat, moist flesh and delicate texture; good when sautéed, baked, steamed.

Silver Warehou: white, firm, fatty; good when broiled, baked, braised, grilled, sautéed, fried.

Tuna: yellowfin, southern bluefin, albacore; good when baked, broiled, braised, sautéed, grilled (if marinated).

SNOWY GROUPER, YELLOWEDGE GROUPER, and WHITE GROUPER. They are all lean with similar flavor and texture, and can be used interchangeably.

HADDOCK *(Melanogrammus aeglefinus)*
ALIAS: snapper, schrod (see below)
FAMILY: cod.
RANGE: North Atlantic waters from Newfoundland sometimes as far south as Cape Hatteras, North Carolina.
PHYSICAL CHARACTERISTICS: purplish-gray skin with narrow, black lateral line and large black patch called "devil's thumbprint" or "St. Peter's mark"; 4 to 10 pounds.

MEAT COLOR AND FAT CONTENT: white, large-flaked; lean.
PREFERRED COOKING METHODS: poaching, baking, steaming, broiling.
SUBSTITUTES: Atlantic pollock, Atlantic cod, lingcod, grouper, snapper.
AVAILABILITY: fresh, April to November in mid-Atlantic, April to December in New England; frozen, year-round.
COMMENTS: haddock always sold skin-on. Sold by different names according to size: snapper, less than 1½ pounds; schrod, 1½ to 2 pounds; large haddock, more than 2½ pounds.

HAKE *(Urophycis tenuis)*; RED HAKE *(Urophycis chuss)*
ALIAS: Whiting, white hake
FAMILY: cod.
RANGE: Newfoundland to North Carolina; throughout the world.
PHYSICAL CHARACTERISTICS: grayish to olive, pale line along sides; about 2 pounds.
MEAT COLOR AND FAT CONTENT: white, slightly soft; lean.
PREFERRED COOKING METHODS: poaching, braising, baking, sautéing, frying.
SUBSTITUTES: other cod, lingcod, petrale sole.
AVAILABILITY: fresh, June to November; frozen, year-round.
COMMENTS: much hake is fresh-frozen at sea in huge blocks, then processed into portions, fillets, sticks. Frozen hake imported from South America.

HALIBUT: see ATLANTIC HALIBUT, PACIFIC HALIBUT

HAWAIIAN BLUE PRAWNS *(Macrobrachium rosenbergii)*
FAMILY: crustacean.
RANGE: originally freshwater species from Malaysia; farmed in Hawaii.
PHYSICAL CHARACTERISTICS: bright blue tail; whole prawn about 6 inches long.
MEAT COLOR AND FAT CONTENT: translucent gray turns pink and white when cooked; moderately fatty.
PREFERRED COOKING METHODS: steaming, boiling, sautéing, frying, baking, grilling.
SUBSTITUTES: any shrimp, crawfish tails, lobsterette tails.

AVAILABILITY: year-round.
COMMENTS: most, not all, Hawaiian blue prawns grown by Am-Orient, on Oahu, and sold at local markets or from roadside stands; exported to mainland sporadically; some prawns labeled Hawaiian blue prawns are thought to be from Viet Nam, Cambodia, Thailand—these usually frozen with one claw trimmed.

HERRING: a family of light-meated, distinctively flavored fish; see ATLANTIC HERRING, PACIFIC HERRING, PACIFIC SARDINE, SHAD

HOKI (*Macruronus novaezealandiae*)
FAMILY: cod.
RANGE: New Zealand waters.
PHYSICAL CHARACTERISTICS: small, slender.
MEAT COLOR AND FAT CONTENT: white; lean.
PREFERRED COOKING METHODS: frying, sautéing.
SUBSTITUTES: any cod, flounder.
AVAILABILITY: frozen, year-round.
COMMENTS: currently the fish in many "fishwiches" at fast-food restaurants and in surimi; will be appearing more frequently in frozen fish sections as frozen "loin" or fillet; second major fisheries product from New Zealand, which will supply U.S. with increasing amounts of fish.

JACK MACKEREL (*Trachurus symmetricus*)
ALIAS: Monterey mackerel, Spanish mackerel, Pacific jack mackerel
FAMILY: jack or *Carangidae*.
RANGE: Southeast Alaska to Chile.
PHYSICAL CHARACTERISTICS: metallic blue to dark green and silvery on bottom, resembles other mackerel.
MEAT COLOR AND FAT CONTENT: reddish meat cooks to ivory; fatty.
PREFERRED COOKING METHODS: braising, grilling, broiling, smoking.
SUBSTITUTES: sardines, mullet, other mackerel.
AVAILABILITY: fresh-frozen and canned, year-round.
COMMENTS: a great deal of jack mackerel is canned; good but not the finest mackerel.

JEWFISH (*Epinephelus itajara*)
ALIAS: grouper, giant sea bass
FAMILY: sea bass.
RANGE: Florida and Gulf of Mexico to Brazil.

PHYSICAL CHARACTERISTICS: largest grouper, grayish with brownish mottling.
MEAT COLOR AND FAT CONTENT: white, large-flaked; lean.
PREFERRED COOKING METHODS: baking, frying, poaching, steaming, sautéing.
SUBSTITUTES: large-flaked cods (such as haddock), snapper, redfish, halibut (needs to cook longer than jewfish)
AVAILABILITY: year-round.
COMMENTS: most common in Florida and along the Gulf, not usually available elsewhere; one of the sweetest groupers.

KING CRAB (*Paralithodes camtschaticus*)
ALIAS: Alaska King crab
FAMILY: crustacean.
RANGE: cold waters of northern Pacific.
PHYSICAL CHARACTERISTICS: bright red, knobby shell; small body atop long, spider-like legs; up to 20 pounds, averages 10 pounds.
MEAT COLOR AND FAT CONTENT: white, sweet; moderately fatty.
PREFERRED COOKING METHODS: pre-cooked; no cooking necessary, just warming.
SUBSTITUTES: any crabmeat.
AVAILABILITY: fresh, from September to January; fresh-frozen, year-round.
COMMENTS: most King crab processed and frozen aboard ships; harvested for the legs, which, when fresh, yield sweet, succulent meat; if not carefully frozen, meat will be dry; populations were down but seem to be reviving.

KING MACKEREL (*Scomberomorus cavalla*)
ALIAS: kingfish (regional along Atlantic Coast and Gulf of Mexico)
FAMILY: mackerel.
RANGE: Gulf of Mexico, along Atlantic Coast to North Carolina, sometimes as far north as Gulf of Maine.
PHYSICAL CHARACTERISTICS: dark blue, slender, silver bellies; 10 to 80 pounds.
MEAT COLOR AND FAT CONTENT: reddish meat cooks to ivory; small-flaked; moderately fatty.
PREFERRED COOKING METHODS: braising, baking, grilling, sautéing, smoking.
SUBSTITUTES: tuna, swordfish, marlin, other mackerel.

AVAILABILITY: fresh, from December to March; frozen, year-round.

COMMENTS: king mackerel benefits from marinating if it is to be grilled or broiled; cooks quickly; has a mild, distinctive flavor.

KING SALMON (Oncorhynchus tshawytscha)

ALIAS: chinook, tyee, spring

FAMILY: salmon.

RANGE: West Coast, from Alaska to California.

PHYSICAL CHARACTERISTICS: deep green to blue-black with dark spots on back; silvery belly; solid, thick; tough, arrowhead-shaped scales on larger kings.

MEAT COLOR AND FAT CONTENT: vivid pink; fatty.

PREFERRED COOKING METHODS: grilling, broiling, poaching, steaming, sautéing, baking.

SUBSTITUTES: other salmon, trout, whitefish, barracuda, sturgeon, weakfish, spotted seatrout.

AVAILABILITY: fresh, from March through October; fresh-frozen, year-round.

COMMENTS: one of the best, richest salmon; occasionally white king salmon available; meat white, though indistinguishable from the meat of red king.

KINGCLIP: see New Zealand Fish box (see Index)

LAKE TROUT (Salvelinus namaycush)

FAMILY: char.

RANGE: northern U.S., from Maine to Idaho, into Alaska; introduced throughout the country.

PHYSICAL CHARACTERISTICS: grayish blue to green with light spots; 8 to 20 pounds.

MEAT COLOR AND FAT CONTENT: pale ivory to deep pink; fatty.

PREFERRED COOKING METHODS: grilling, baking, broiling, steaming, braising, sautéing, frying.

SUBSTITUTES: salmon, trout, small, wild catfish.

AVAILABILITY: year-round.

COMMENTS: not a member of the trout family; is primarily a sport fish.

LINGCOD (Ophidon elongatus)

FAMILY: greenling.

RANGE: Baja California to Alaska, most common in Washington and Alaska.

PHYSICAL CHARACTERISTICS: mottled brown to orange to bluish green with pale undersides; 5 to 40 pounds.

MEAT COLOR AND FAT CONTENT: pale green to white meat that cooks up bright white, large-flaked; lean.

PREFERRED COOKING METHODS: poaching, steaming, baking, frying, sautéing, broiling.

SUBSTITUTES: sole, cod, halibut, snapper, grouper.

AVAILABILITY: year-round.

COMMENTS: not a cod; extremely versatile; the pale green meat supposed to be sweeter than white, though difference seems negligible.

LITTLENECK CLAM (Protothaca staminea)

ALIAS: clam

FAMILY: bivalve.

RANGE: California to Alaska.

PHYSICAL CHARACTERISTICS: grayish brown rounded shell; small.

MEAT COLOR AND FAT CONTENT: ivory meat, brownish siphon; lean.

PREFERRED COOKING METHODS: steaming, sautéing.

SUBSTITUTES: other clams.

AVAILABILITY: year-round.

COMMENTS: not as tender as little neck quahaugs.

LOBSTER (Homarus americanus)

ALIAS: American lobster

FAMILY: crustacean.

RANGE: Atlantic coast from Newfoundland to North Carolina, most abundant off Maine coast.

PHYSICAL CHARACTERISTICS: greenish blue to reddish brown; turn bright red when cooked; 2 to 3 pounds, up to more than 25 pounds.

MEAT COLOR AND FAT CONTENT: white; moderately fatty.

PREFERRED COOKING METHODS: live whole: boiling or steaming; meat only: sautéing, steaming, baking, poaching, braising.

SUBSTITUTES: monkfish, crab in some cases.

AVAILABILITY: fresh, year-round.

COMMENTS: lobster imported from Canada; getting smaller each year; largest ever reported weighed 42 pounds; simple preparations best.

LOBSTERETTE (Nephrops aculeata)

ALIAS: Florida lobsterette, scampi.

FAMILY: crustacean.

RANGE: deep waters along continental shelf from New Jersey south to the Caribbean.

PHYSICAL CHARACTERISTICS: greenish blue to reddish brown; turn bright red when cooked; under 1 pound.

MEAT COLOR AND FAT CONTENT: white; moderately fatty.
PREFERRED COOKING METHODS: boiling or steaming, sautéing.
SUBSTITUTES: large shrimp, lobster, crawfish tails.
AVAILABILITY: frozen, year-round.
COMMENTS: fresh-frozen tails primarily available.

LUMPFISH ROE: see ROE

MACKEREL: see ATLANTIC MACKEREL, JACK MACKEREL, KING MACKEREL, PACIFIC MACKEREL, SPANISH MACKEREL

MAKO SHARK (Isurus glaucus)
FAMILY: shark.
RANGE: Gulf of Mexico, Atlantic Coast, and Pacific Coast.
PHYSICAL CHARACTERISTICS: up to 12 feet long; 150 to 200 pounds.
MEAT COLOR AND FAT CONTENT: pale pink to white, ivory when cooked, fine-flaked, tender; lean.
PREFERRED COOKING METHODS: sautéing, steaming, baking or marinated and grilled.
SUBSTITUTES: swordfish, king mackerel, marlin, tuna.
AVAILABILITY: fresh: year-round in the Gulf of Mexico; November to April in the mid-Atlantic; June to November in New England; June to August on the West Coast.
COMMENTS: meat dark pink with quarter-size blood-line (dark meat) in center of each side of steak; often sold illegally for swordfish, which it resembles; shark carry urea in skin and must be dressed immediately or will take on ammonia smell and flavor.

MANILA CLAM (Tapes phillippinarium)
ALIAS: clam
FAMILY: bivalve.
RANGE: British Columbia to California.
PHYSICAL CHARACTERISTICS: light gray; more oblong than other clams.
MEAT COLOR AND FAT CONTENT: ivory meat, brownish siphon, tender; lean.
PREFERRED COOKING METHODS: uncooked on the half shell; steaming, sautéing, frying.
SUBSTITUTES: other clams, geoduck.
AVAILABILITY: year-round.
COMMENTS: originally from Japan; came with oysters at turn of the century.

MONKFISH (Lophius americanus)
ALIAS: goosefish, sea devil, anglerfish, frogfish, "poor man's lobster"
FAMILY: goosefish.
RANGE: Newfoundland to North Carolina, most common in Maine and Massachusetts.
PHYSICAL CHARACTERISTICS: huge head, gaping mouth with sharp teeth, long eel-like tail.
MEAT COLOR AND FAT CONTENT: white, firm; moderately lean.
PREFERRED COOKING METHODS: braising, sautéing, baking, poaching.
SUBSTITUTES: scallops or lobster in certain recipes.
AVAILABILITY: fresh, year-round in the mid-Atlantic; April to December in New England; most common in summer.
COMMENTS: only tail meat used (head thrown overboard); sometimes a thin membrane must be removed, though usually done by fish merchant; sweet taste and texture from preferred diet of mollusks, vaguely reminiscent of certain shellfish and can be used in some recipes as a substitute, such as Curried Scallops and Warm Lobster Salad (see Index). Be warned—when used as a substitute, it does not taste the same, takes longer to cook than most fish, and must be cooked thoroughly or it will be tough. Extremely valuable, but no established American fishery for it, by-catch of East Coast flounder fishery; considered underutilized.

MULLET (Mugil cephalus)
ALIAS: striped mullet
FAMILY: mullet.
RANGE: Gulf of Mexico to North Carolina, and California.
PHYSICAL CHARACTERISTICS: light silvery-blue, faint stripes along sides; 1 foot; up to 3 pounds.
MEAT COLOR AND FAT CONTENT: reddish; fatty.
PREFERRED COOKING METHODS: grilling, smoking.
SUBSTITUTES: mackerel, sardines.
AVAILABILITY: year-round, best in fall and winter.
COMMENTS: regional delicacy; harvested primarily for its roe (see Index).

MULLET ROE
FISH: striped mullet (Mugil cephalus)
PHYSICAL CHARACTERISTICS: roe contained in two lobes, bright yellow; from 2 to 8 ounces total weight.

SUBSTITUTES: shad roe.

AVAILABILITY: fall.

TRADITIONAL AND RECOMMENDED PREPA-
RATIONS: dredged in cornmeal or flour and fried;
sautéed.

COMMENTS: most mullet roe is frozen and shipped
to Taiwan, where it is a delicacy. Mullet milt, prepared
in same manner as mullet roe, is an excellent Southeast
regional specialty that resembles sweetbreads.

MUSSEL *(Mytilus edulis)*

ALIAS: blue mussel

FAMILY: bivalve.

RANGE: Nova Scotia to North Carolina and West
Coast.

PHYSICAL CHARACTERISTICS: brittle, thin dark
blue to brownish shell; 1 to 3 inches long.

MEAT COLOR AND FAT CONTENT: ivory to
bright orange; moderately lean.

PREFERRED COOKING METHODS: steaming,
sautéing, frying, smoking.

SUBSTITUTES: clams.

AVAILABILITY: year-round; best from October
through April.

COMMENTS: most mussels on West Coast are
farmed and have milder flavor; most dredged on East
Coast are larger and have a stronger flavor.

MUTTON SNAPPER *(Lutjanus analis)*

ALIAS: muttonfish

FAMILY: snapper.

RANGE: south Florida throughout tropical Atlantic.

PHYSICAL CHARACTERISTICS: gray back, yellowish red near belly; up to 25 pounds, averages 5 to
10 pounds.

MEAT COLOR AND FAT CONTENT: white, large-
flaked; lean.

PREFERRED COOKING METHODS: steaming,
braising, baking, broiling, sautéing.

SUBSTITUTES: snapper, cod, lingcod, petrale sole,
or grouper (especially scamp).

AVAILABILITY: year-round.

COMMENTS: fine meat, very similar to red snapper.

NASSAU GROUPER *(Epinephelus striatus)*

ALIAS: grouper

FAMILY: sea bass.

RANGE: common in Florida waters and the Bahamas.

PHYSICAL CHARACTERISTICS: brown with
blackish markings; up to 50 pounds, averages 5 to 10.

Name That Shrimp

Look out for the Chilean nylon and the
Australian Banana!

Those aren't clothing or fruit, they're
shrimp, and as our appetite for the
feathery-legged crustaceans increases,
we're more likely to see a panoply of exot-
ics on menus and at fish markets.

Fleshy prawn *(Penaeus chinensis)*: from Taiwan's northern coast, grows to about 7
inches in length.

Kuruma prawn *(Penaeus japonicus)*: found
in the Pacific waters around Japan, reaches
almost 9 inches in length.

White or banana prawn *(Penaeus mer-
guiensis)*: found closer to Australia and is the
most important species in the region, can
grow to be 9 inches long.

Giant tiger prawn *(Penaeus monodon)*: primarily from the southwestern Pacific,
reaches over 13 inches in length.

Indian white shrimp *(Penaeus indicus)*:
found in the Indian Ocean, reaches about
9 inches in length.

Deepwater rose shrimp *(Parapenaeus
longirostris)*: found off the northern coast of
Africa, reaches over 7 inches in length.

Southern pink shrimp *(Penaeus notialis)*:
found in the southern portion of the Atlantic, reaches over 7 inches in length.

Chilean nylon shrimp *(Heterocerpus reedi)*
and **Argentine red shrimp** *(Pleoticus muelleri)*:
both found toward the southern portion of
South America, and grow larger than 7
inches.

Blue shrimp *(Penaeus stylirostris)* and
whiteleg shrimp *(Penaeus vannamei)* are the
two most commercially important shrimp
in the area; both reach about 9 inches.

MEAT COLOR AND FAT CONTENT: white, large-flaked, sweet; lean.
PREFERRED COOKING METHODS: grilling, broiling, baking, sautéing, frying, steaming.
SUBSTITUTES: any large-flaked cod (such as haddock), snapper, redfish, halibut (cooks in less time than Nassau grouper).
AVAILABILITY: year-round.
COMMENTS: one of the finest groupers.

NEW ZEALAND HAKE: see New Zealand Fish box (see Index)

OCEAN PERCH (*Sebastes marinus*)

ALIAS: redfish, golden redfish, red perch, rosefish
FAMILY: rockfish.
RANGE: deep water from Labrador to Gulf of Maine, and east.
PHYSICAL CHARACTERISTICS: orange-red, round bodied, red skinned, heavy, sharp fins, large scales; up to 14 pounds, averages 1 to 4 pounds.
MEAT COLOR AND FAT CONTENT: white, moderately firm; lean.
PREFERRED COOKING METHODS: steaming, baking, poaching, frying.
SUBSTITUTES: snapper, cod.
AVAILABILITY: year-round.
COMMENTS: not a member of the perch family; versatile; subtle, nutty flavor; commonly used in Chinese cuisine; deep water redfish (*Sebastes mentella*) and Acadian redfish (*Sebastes fasciatus*) also marketed as ocean perch.

OCEAN POUT (*Macrozoarces americanus*)

ALIAS: ling (New England)
FAMILY: eelpout.
RANGE: Atlantic from North Carolina to the Arctic.
PHYSICAL CHARACTERISTICS: resembles a huge eel with a head.
MEAT COLOR AND FAT CONTENT: golden, short-flaked; lean.
PREFERRED COOKING METHODS: sautéing, baking.
SUBSTITUTES: no substitute; can be substituted for fish used in highly spiced recipes such as The Moor's *Peixe Com Molho*, or with compound butters such as the Green Lake Grill's Sturgeon with Caper Butter Sauce (see Index).
AVAILABILITY: fresh, sporadically; fresh-frozen, year-round.

COMMENTS: regionally available, underutilized, will likely become more popular as common fish become more scarce; must be pounded gently before cooking; takes longer to cook than most fish; texture similar to chicken.

OCTOPUS (*Octopus dofleini*, West Coast; *Octopus vulgaris*, East Coast)

FAMILY: cephalopod.
RANGE: West Coast: Baja California to Alaska; East Coast: New England to Gulf of Mexico.
PHYSICAL CHARACTERISTICS: 8 tentacles on large globular body; milky white meat turns bright white when cooked; purplish skin.
MEAT COLOR AND FAT CONTENT: white, sweet, crisp; moderately lean.
PREFERRED COOKING METHODS: boiling, braising. Japanese method calls for rubbing vigorously with salt then boiling just until it turns white.
SUBSTITUTES: none.
AVAILABILITY: fresh, sporadically year-round; fresh-frozen, year-round.
COMMENTS: usually available pre-cooked—can be sliced and eaten as is; meat tender, not tough; ink sac inside head—ejects octopus-shaped cloud of ink when frightened—same ink can be used in cooking.

OLYMPIA OYSTER (*Ostrea lurida*)

FAMILY: bivalve.
RANGE: Northwest.
PHYSICAL CHARACTERISTICS: tiny, size of quarter; dark brownish to greenish shell; round; flat.
MEAT COLOR AND FAT CONTENT: dark silver gray to green; moderately lean.
PREFERRED COOKING METHODS: uncooked on the half shell.
SUBSTITUTES: Belon oyster.
AVAILABILITY: fall and winter.
COMMENTS: relative of Belon oyster; once flourished on West Coast, over-harvested during the Gold Rush era when schooners from San Francisco filled their holds and took the oysters with them; so small, usually 13 to 15 served as a dozen; sharp, distinctive flavor reminiscent of Belon.

ORANGE ROUGHY (*Hoplostethus atlanticus*)

ALIAS: slimehead (New Zealand)
FAMILY: slimehead.
RANGE: New Zealand waters.
PHYSICAL CHARACTERISTICS: rough, bright orange skin.

MEAT COLOR AND FAT CONTENT: white, tender; lean.
PREFERRED COOKING METHODS: sautéing, poaching, baking, frying.
SUBSTITUTES: cod, snapper, sole, flounder, lingcod.
AVAILABILITY: frozen, year-round.
COMMENTS: available in U.S. as fresh-frozen fillets; almost no flavor.

OREO DORY: see New Zealand Fish box (see Index)

OYSTER: see BELON, EASTERN, OLYMPIA, PACIFIC, SEXLESS

PACIFIC COD (*Gadus macrocephalus*)
ALIAS: true cod
FAMILY: cod.
RANGE: California to the north Pacific.
PHYSICAL CHARACTERISTICS: brown to light gray; 5 to 10 pounds.

Trash Fish

Ocean pout are considered a "trash fish," or fish that fishermen throw away because there is little or no consumer demand and therefore no market value.

Long ago, lobster were considered trash and good for nothing but chicken feed. More recently, monkfish was a trash fish in the U.S., and now we can't get enough. Obscure species are often trash fish until someone somewhere tastes them and realizes that they offer some incredible flavors and textures.

Searobins, dogfish, skate, and whiting are still considered trash fish in America, though they are gradually becoming more popular and will someday be readily available at fish markets.

MEAT COLOR AND FAT CONTENT: white; lean.
PREFERRED COOKING METHODS: steaming, poaching, sautéing, frying, broiling.
SUBSTITUTES: other cod, lingcod, petrale sole, snapper, grouper.
AVAILABILITY: fresh, year-round.
COMMENTS: very similar to Atlantic cod; primarily salted at turn-of-the-century, now mostly frozen at sea or fresh, as fillets.

PACIFIC HALIBUT (*Hippoglossus stenolepis*)
FAMILY: flounder.
RANGE: Bering Sea to California.
PHYSICAL CHARACTERISTICS: similar to Atlantic halibut; 5 to 80 pounds.
MEAT COLOR AND FAT CONTENT: white to pale green, cooks up white, tender, large-flaked; lean.
PREFERRED COOKING METHODS: poaching, steaming, baking, frying, sautéing.
SUBSTITUTES: snapper, large-flaked cod, grouper, (all will take longer to cook than halibut).
AVAILABILITY: fresh, from May to December; frozen, year-round.
COMMENTS: one of the best halibut.

PACIFIC HERRING (*Clupea harengus pallasi*)
FAMILY: herring.
RANGE: Kotzebue Bay, Alaska, to northern California.
PHYSICAL CHARACTERISTICS: dark green to silvery blue on back with silver sides and belly; 6 to 12 inches long.
MEAT COLOR AND FAT CONTENT: dark meat cooks up ivory; fatty.
PREFERRED COOKING METHODS: grilling, smoking, pickling.
SUBSTITUTES: smelt, sardines in some cases (for grilling).
AVAILABILITY: fresh, sporadically during December, January, April.
COMMENTS: more perishable than other fish. Most herring caught in Alaska for their roe, which is sent to Japan.

PACIFIC MACKEREL (*Scomber japonicus*)
ALIAS: Monterey mackerel, American mackerel
FAMILY: mackerel.
RANGE: California.
PHYSICAL CHARACTERISTICS: long, missile-shaped, resembling small tuna; dark blue back, bottom silvery; vertical, zebra-like black lines on sides.

MEAT COLOR AND FAT CONTENT: reddish cooks up to ivory; fatty.
PREFERRED COOKING METHODS: braising, grilling, smoking, broiling.
SUBSTITUTES: sardines, mullet, bluefish.
AVAILABILITY: fresh-frozen, year-round.
COMMENTS: fine-eating, distinctive flavor; freezes extremely well.

PACIFIC OCEAN PERCH (*Sebastes alutus*)

FAMILY: rockfish.
RANGE: Bering Sea to southern California.
PHYSICAL CHARACTERISTICS: red-skinned; 14 to 20 inches; 2 to 3 pounds.
MEAT COLOR AND FAT CONTENT: white, large-flaked; lean.
PREFERRED COOKING METHODS: steaming, frying, baking, sautéing.
SUBSTITUTES: cod, snapper.
AVAILABILITY: year-round.
COMMENTS: *Not* a member of the perch family; skin-on fillets often substituted for red snapper or called redfish; often dressed catfish-style—whole, skinned, head off; sweet meat.

PACIFIC OYSTER (*Crassostrea gigas*)

ALIAS: Japanese oyster, West Coast oyster
FAMILY: bivalve.
RANGE: West Coast.
PHYSICAL CHARACTERISTICS: shell generally deeply cupped, grayish white to dark gray, ruffled edges; 2 inches to 10 inches long.
MEAT COLOR AND FAT CONTENT: silver gray to tan to silver green; moderately fatty.
PREFERRED COOKING METHODS: uncooked on half shell; steaming, grilling, baking, poaching, smoking, frying.
SUBSTITUTES: other oysters.
AVAILABILITY: fresh, year-round, best in fall and winter.
COMMENTS: imported from Japan to save West Coast oyster industry; named for bays of origin.

PACIFIC SANDDAB (*Citharichthys sordidus*)

ALIAS: sanddab
FAMILY: flounder.
RANGE: Alaska to southern California.
PHYSICAL CHARACTERISTICS: orange and black spots on the dark side; up to 2 pounds, average under 12 ounces.

Helpful Bivalves

The Waddell Mariculture Center raises oysters in shrimp ponds. The oysters gorge on the plankton-rich water and when they're not eating, they pump water and regurgitate small, compressed packets of food for the shrimp, in an apparently symbiotic relationship. The oysters grow rapidly in the shrimp ponds and are market-ready within about 10 months.

MEAT COLOR AND FAT CONTENT: white, fine, sweet; lean.
PREFERRED COOKING METHODS: frying, sautéing whole.
SUBSTITUTES: small sole, flounder.
AVAILABILITY: fresh, year-round.

PACIFIC SARDINE (*Sardinops sagax*)

FAMILY: herring.
RANGE: Alaska to southern California.
PHYSICAL CHARACTERISTICS: round, stubby, greenish blue back and spotted silver sides and belly.
MEAT COLOR AND FAT CONTENT: darkish, cooks up ivory; fatty.
PREFERRED COOKING METHODS: grilling, braising, broiling.
SUBSTITUTES: small mackerel.
AVAILABILITY: winter.
COMMENTS: more perishable than other fish.

PETRALE SOLE (pronounced "petrawlie") (*Eopsetta jordani*)

FAMILY: flounder.
RANGE: Baja California to Alaska.
PHYSICAL CHARACTERISTICS: 2 to 8 pounds.
MEAT COLOR AND FAT CONTENT: white with pale pink stripe running length of fillet, larger flaked than most sole, tender; lean.
PREFERRED COOKING METHODS: poaching, sautéing, baking, broiling, steaming.
SUBSTITUTES: sole, flounder, snapper.

AVAILABILITY: year-round.
COMMENTS: one of the best flounders.

PINK SALMON *(Oncorhynchus gorbuscha)*

ALIAS: humpback, humpies
FAMILY: salmon.
RANGE: Northwest Coast to Alaska.
PHYSICAL CHARACTERISTICS: silvery, develops hump on back during spawning season; small; 3 to 7 pounds.
MEAT COLOR AND FAT CONTENT: pale pink, fine-textured; moderately fatty.
PREFERRED COOKING METHODS: steaming, baking, poaching, grilling, broiling, sautéing.
SUBSTITUTES: other salmon, trout, whitefish, barracuda, weakfish, spotted sea trout.
AVAILABILITY: fresh, summer and fall; fresh-frozen, year-round.
COMMENTS: fine eating if extremely fresh; odd metallic odor; perishable.

POMPANO *(Trachinotus carolinus)*

ALIAS: Florida pompano, common pompano
FAMILY: jack or *Carangidae.*
RANGE: Virginia to Texas, most common in Florida.
PHYSICAL CHARACTERISTICS: round, flat, light metallic silvery skin; 12 inches long; 2 to 3 pounds.
MEAT COLOR AND FAT CONTENT: white, firm; moderately fatty.
PREFERRED COOKING METHODS: steaming, baking, grilling, broiling.
SUBSTITUTES: snapper, cod.
AVAILABILITY: year-round.
COMMENTS: simple preparations are best.

QUAHAUG CLAMS *(Mercenaria mercenaria)*

ALIAS: little neck, cherrystone, chowder clam, according to size with little neck the smallest
FAMILY: bivalve.
RANGE: East Coast.
PHYSICAL CHARACTERISTICS: brownish, ringed, round shells; little neck, 1-inch across; cherrystone, 2½ inches across; chowder clam, over 3 inches across.
MEAT COLOR AND FAT CONTENT: pinkish ivory, tender in little neck and some cherrystone; tough in some cherrystone and chowder; lean.
PREFERRED COOKING METHODS: half shell for little neck and tender cherrystone; steaming or sautéing for same; chopping and quick poaching or braising (soups, sauces) for chowder clam; frying.

Northwest Oysters

Pacific oysters destined to be packed in jars, where shell shape is unimportant, are grown in clumps, nestled in the gravelly mud and silt of tidewater flats. They develop slowly, taking up to three years to mature, and still account for the bulk of the nearly one billion oysters sent to market each year from Washington state, the largest producer in the Northwest. But oyster lovers's tastes have created a strong demand for oysters on the half shell.

Randy Shuman, president of Shoalwater Bay Oysters, in Bay Center, Washington, was the first in Washington state to grow his Pacifics the "French Table" way, singly, in heavy mesh bags that sit on metal racks above tidal flats. Unencumbered by silt, the oysters grow rapidly and can be harvested after 10 months.

Bill Webb, owner of Westcott Bay Sea Farms, grows his oysters—a hybrid Pacific oyster that is a cross between a meaty Kumomoto and a fast-growing myagi—in Japanese lantern nets. They grow singly, hanging in the water, and can devote their entire energy to rapid growth of firm, fatty meat.

Olympia oysters are another story. Duane Fagergren, whose Calm Cove Oyster Company is near Olympia, Washington, is one grower in the state coaxing the variety back to its native waters.

Cultivated in traditional fashion, Olympias are grown behind dikes in the shallow pools of tideland areas. They require coddling, constant temperatures, and protection from predators. Even with such attention, they take four years to reach maximum size—rarely larger than a quarter.

SUBSTITUTES: other clams, geoduck.
AVAILABILITY: year-round.
COMMENTS: chowder clams must be ground or chopped before using.

RAZOR CLAM *(Siliqua patula, West Coast; Ensis directus, East Coast)*
FAMILY: bivalve.
RANGE: East and West coasts.
PHYSICAL CHARACTERISTICS: East Coast razor has long, rounded, thin white shell, 2 to 10 inches long; on West Coast long, narrow, square-edged shells, similar length.
MEAT COLOR AND FAT CONTENT: ivory, tender; lean.
PREFERRED COOKING METHODS: steaming, sautéing, frying.
SUBSTITUTES: other clams, geoduck, abalone.
AVAILABILITY: fresh, from April through October.
COMMENTS: sweet and juicy; cooks quickly; too tough for half shell; typically steamed on East Coast, dredged in flour and fried on West Coast.

When Is a Sardine not a Sardine? When it's a Herring.

The name "sardine" refers to small members of the herring family that range between 4 and 6 inches in length. The term was reputedly coined when the sardine fishing industry began on the island of Sardinia around the 14th century. Herring packed in Maine are rarely small enough to be called sardines, so they are canned and marketed as sardine "steaks." These tiny little steaks—usually packed in mustard or chili sauce—are cut from large herring.

RED COD: see New Zealand Fish box (see Index)

RED GROUPER *(Epinephelus morio)*
ALIAS: grouper
FAMILY: sea bass.
RANGE: Florida and the Caribbean.
PHYSICAL CHARACTERISTICS: reddish brown with pale mottled markings; up to 50 pounds.
MEAT COLOR AND FAT CONTENT: white, large-flaked, sweet; lean.
PREFERRED COOKING METHODS: grilling, baking, poaching, frying, broiling, sautéing.
SUBSTITUTES: large-flaked cod (such as haddock), snapper, redfish, halibut (cooks in less time than red grouper).
AVAILABILITY: year-round.
COMMENTS: one of the best groupers.

RED SNAPPER *(Lutianus campechanus)*
FAMILY: snapper.
RANGE: Gulf of Mexico to North Carolina.
PHYSICAL CHARACTERISTICS: red upper body and head, fins tinged with yellow, red eyes, pale pink to white belly; up to 30 pounds.
MEAT COLOR AND FAT CONTENT: white, large-flaked; lean.
PREFERRED COOKING METHODS: baking, steaming, braising, broiling, sautéing.
SUBSTITUTES: snapper, cod, lingcod, petrale sole, or grouper (especially scamp).
AVAILABILITY: year-round.
COMMENTS: most desirable, expensive snapper; fillets from other red-skinned fish often called "red snapper," true red snapper always sold whole or as skin-on fillets, and the skin is never scored or marred; beware skinless red snapper fillet—it's something else.

ROCKFISH: see CANARY ROCKFISH, YELLOW-EYE ROCKFISH
OTHER ROCKFISH
   Widow rockfish: alias "brownie," abundant from Alaska to Baja California.
   Yellowtail rockfish: alias "greenie," abundant from southern California to Vancouver Island.

ROE: see MULLET ROE, SALMON ROE, SHAD ROE, STURGEON ROE
OTHER FISH ROE
   Codfish roe: smoky paste-like roe, sometimes sold as tarama, and a principal ingredient in taramasalata, a

creamy Greek purée. (In Greece, tarama is made with gray mullet roe, unavailable in the U.S.).

Lumpfish roe: tiny granules, usually dyed black, red, or gold, can be used in any recipe calling for caviar; gentle draining recommended.

Flying Fish roe: hot-orange crunchy granules that can be used in any recipe calling for caviar, though best as colorful garnish; slightly strong flavor.

SALMON: see ATLANTIC SALMON, CHUM SALMON, KING SALMON, PINK SALMON, SILVER SALMON, SOCKEYE SALMON

SALMON ROE

ALIAS: Salmon caviar
FISH: salmon.
PHYSICAL CHARACTERISTICS: bright, glossy orange globes about the size of a small pea.
SUBSTITUTES: any fish roe.
AVAILABILITY: year-round.
TRADITIONAL AND RECOMMENDED PREPARATIONS: no preparation needed; used as garnish, in sauces, atop hot white rice, in omelettes.
COMMENTS: salmon eggs are soaked in brine and packed in tubs; keeps one month in home refrigerator; freezes well; chum salmon roe most popular; silver salmon roe used also.

SCAMP *(Mycteroperca phenax)*

ALIAS: grouper
FAMILY: sea bass.
RANGE: Carolinas to the Gulf of Mexico.
PHYSICAL CHARACTERISTICS: grayish; small; 1 to 10 pounds.
MEAT COLOR AND FAT CONTENT: white, slightly soft; lean.
PREFERRED COOKING METHODS: baking, frying, broiling.
SUBSTITUTES: cod, snapper, halibut (cooks longer than halibut).
AVAILABILITY: year-round.
COMMENTS: relatively rare, popular in Florida.

SEA SCALLOP *(Pecten magellanicus)*

ALIAS: giant or smooth scallop
FAMILY: mollusk.
RANGE: from Georges Bank off the East Coast and along the New Jersey and Virginia Coast.
PHYSICAL CHARACTERISTICS: shell can reach 8 inches across; the adductor muscle, or "eye," (what we refer to as the scallop) can reach 2 inches across.

MEAT COLOR AND FAT CONTENT: ivory; moderately lean.
PREFERRED COOKING METHODS: steaming, sautéing, baking, broiling, grilling
SUBSTITUTES: other scallops, monkfish in certain recipes.
AVAILABILITY: fresh, March or April through the summer; frozen, year-round.
COMMENTS: sea scallops are harvested and shucked on board ship, by hand, though research is being done on automatic shucking machines. Peruvian scallops are also sold as sea scallops, which they resemble. The Pacific sea scallop or weathervane scallop *(Pecten caurinus),* which is about the same size as the Atlantic sea scallop and of very similar flavor and sweetness, is found from Alaska to Oregon, though in short supply. It is rare, and available primarily in the Northwest.

Fishing for Herring Roe

Fishing for herring roe in Alaska is a free-for-all. The season lasts just a couple of hours each year, and during that time fortunes are won or lost. Hundreds of boats crowd the water while dozens of spotter planes fly dangerously close to each other overhead, looking for schools of roe-laden herring and transmitting their location to the boat that hired them.

Once the season opens, the boats throw nets overboard—it is so frantic that boats have been known to capsize or push each other out of the way in the rush. Once the opening is over, the herring are taken ashore and processed. The roe is frozen and most of it is shipped to Japan, where it is sold for very high prices. The Alaska herring itself is discarded—it has little economic value, and it isn't worth the time needed to process it.

Eggs on Eggs?

The American custom of garnishing caviar with hard-cooked eggs, minced onions, and lemon slices originated when there was an abundance of poor-quality caviar on the market some time in the 1920s. The garnishes covered any of the caviar's failings. Now, if you have top-quality caviar, its subtle, sublime flavor needs no garnish at all.

SEA URCHIN

ALIAS: purple urchin (*Strongylocentrotus purpuratus*); green urchin (*Strongylocentrotus drobachiensis*)
FAMILY: echinoderm (marine mammal).
RANGE: East and West coasts.
PHYSICAL CHARACTERISTICS: purplish to greenish to brown; round, spiny; 2 inches to 8 inches.
MEAT COLOR AND FAT CONTENT: roe: golden to bright orange; fatty.
PREFERRED COOKING METHODS: uncooked on bread, toast, as sushi or on hot white rice.
SUBSTITUTES: none.
AVAILABILITY: generally, from August through April.
COMMENTS: to reach roe, cut circle out of bottom of shell—viscera will come with it; tongues of roe cling to top of shell, can be scooped out; fresh sea urchin will have spines intact, which will move when touched.

SHAD (*Alosa sapidissima*)

ALIAS: "porcupines of the sea," American shad
FAMILY: herring.
RANGE: shallow waters of Atlantic coast from St. Lawrence River to Florida; also ascends many rivers and streams; Mexican border to Cook Inlet, Alaska.
PHYSICAL CHARACTERISTICS: round, metallic bluish-green luster on back, silvery sides and belly, large scales; 18 to 22 inches long; 3 to 6 pounds.
MEAT COLOR AND FAT CONTENT: white, sweet, tender; fatty.
PREFERRED COOKING METHODS: baking, braising, grilling, smoking, sautéing.
SUBSTITUTES: salmon, trout.
AVAILABILITY: fresh, from February to June in the mid-Atlantic; April in New England; May and June on West Coast.
COMMENTS: shad are very bony—bones "float" in meat making each unboned mouthful a spiny surprise; boned fillets available in East, in West whole fish sold; most shad harvested in the West are shipped East.

SHAD ROE

FISH: American shad (*Alosa sapidissima*)
PHYSICAL CHARACTERISTICS: two deep red egg sacs; 2 to 10 ounces per pair.
SUBSTITUTES: mullet roe.
AVAILABILITY: from February to June in the mid-Atlantic; April in New England, May and June on West Coast.
PREFERRED COOKING METHODS: dredged in flour and fried; poached and added to scrambled eggs or sauce; grilled.
COMMENTS: thoroughly wash before cooking.

SHARK: see ANGEL SHARK, BLACKTIP SHARK, DOGFISH, MAKO SHARK, THRESHER SHARK

SHRIMP (BROWN SHRIMP *Penaeus aztecus*; PINK SHRIMP *Penaeus duorarum*; SPOT SHRIMP *Pandalus platyceros*)

ALIAS: prawns, scampi
FAMILY: crustacean.
RANGE: worldwide; from North Carolina south to Gulf of Mexico (most important fishery); Washington and Alaska.
PHYSICAL CHARACTERISTICS: generally light pinkish red to reddish brown in color, or grayish blue, with tinges of blue or green on tail and legs; East Coast and Gulf shrimp average 6 to 10 inches long, West Coast shrimp average 3 to 6 inches long.
MEAT COLOR AND FAT CONTENT: translucent pink to gray when uncooked, pink and white when cooked; moderately fatty.
PREFERRED COOKING METHODS: steaming, boiling, frying, sautéing, baking, grilling.
SUBSTITUTES: crawfish tails, lobsterette tails.
AVAILABILITY: fresh sporadically throughout year, generally in spring and summer; frozen, year-round.
COMMENTS: shrimp are a worldwide commodity, from as far away as Thailand and Cambodia to Georgia and Alaska; most frozen and thawed at the market; many farm-raised throughout the world.

Oyster Primer

Going into an oyster bar can be as confusing as walking into a wine shop, and just as intimidating if you don't know your oysters.

Most oysters consumed in the U.S. are commercially grown. Although there are just four species, there are dozens of different types, and to distinguish them in the marketplace, they are named for their bays of origin or for the bays where they are fattened. Since each oyster picks up the flavor of the water it was grown in, it is helpful to recognize their names.

Generalities can be made about oysters. Those from the Pacific Northwest tend to be mild, meaty, crisp, and sweet; those from California are similar, with slightly stronger flavors; oysters from the Gulf and the Southeast are generally softer, with an earthier flavor; those from the Mid-Atlantic and Northeast are quite crisp and distinctively salty. These generalities should serve only as reference, for there are as many variances in flavor as there are oysters.

The four species of oysters commonly available in the U.S. are the Olympia oyster, the only oyster native to the Northwest; the Japanese, now called Pacific oyster from the West Coast; the Atlantic oyster, now generically called blue point oyster; and the European flat oyster, usually called a Belon.

Atlantic Oysters

Alabama Gulf: A mild, almost bland, meaty oyster from Bayou La Batre and Mobile Bay.

Apalachicola: An Atlantic oyster with a teardrop-shaped, deep-cupped shell. It has a sweet, coppery taste.

Black bay: A mild, deep-flavored oyster with a tinge of sweetness, from Black Bay, Louisiana.

Blue point: The generic name for the Atlantic oyster.

Box: From North Carolina and Long Island, this oyster has a slightly mild, muddy flavor, and is somewhat tough.

Bras d'Or: A sweet, mild oyster from Cape Breton, Nova Scotia.

Bristol: A plump, crisp, fairly salty oyster with a pleasant, strong flavor, from South Bristol, Maine.

Chatham: From Chatham, Massachusetts, these are briny with a delicate, sweet aftertaste.

Chesapeake Bay (Kent Island): An oyster with a mild, clean, and sweet flavor, from Maryland and Virginia.

Chilmark: A very briny, crisp oyster from Martha's Vineyard, Massachusetts.

Chincoteague: There are two similar varieties of Chincoteagues. Those from Chincoteague Bay are less consistent than those from the ocean side (which are also called Salts). Both varieties are sweet, crisp and clean.

Cotuit: A native Atlantic Coast oyster from Cotuit Harbor in Massachusetts, the cotuit is a good size and fairly salty with a fresh clean taste.

Emerald Point: A small, delicate oyster from Emerald Point Bay, Mississippi.

Florida Gulf: A medium-size oyster with a long, narrow shell from Horseshoe Beach, Wakulla Bay, Florida. It is firm, with a mild briny flavor.

Hog Island Sweetwater: A small, plump oyster with a sweet, crisp flavor and slightly smoky aftertaste.

Indian River: A briny, medium-size oyster from Cape Canaveral, Florida.

James River: A fairly salty but sweet, slightly soft oyster from Virginia.

Lake Borgnes: An Atlantic oyster from Louisiana, it has a round, curved shell and a mild, almost bland flavor.

Long Island: A mildly salty oyster from the Connecticut side of the Long Island Sound.

Louisiana Gulf: A big, plump, and flabby oyster with a musky, brackish aftertaste, from the Mississippi bayous.

Malpeque: A small oyster with a clean, coppery taste, from Prince Edward Island, Canada.

Nelson Bay: A good-sized, meaty oyster from Nelson Bay, Alabama, that is mild, but has a slightly strong aftertaste.

Port Norris: A plump, mild oyster from New Jersey with the pleasant flavor of seaweed.

Rhode Island Select: A plump oyster with a clean, slightly salty flavor, from southeast Rhode Island.

Texas Gulf: A very meaty, somewhat flabby and salty oyster, with an indistinct flavor, from Galveston Bay and Corpus Christi, Texas.

Wellfleet: A slightly salty, crisp oyster from Cape Cod, Massachusetts.

European Flat Oysters

Belon: A European flat oyster. The name Belon comes from the Belon River in Brittany, northern France. In France the name is protected by law—only oysters grown in the Belon River estuary have a right to the name, and they are a very distinctive, prized oyster. Though European flat oysters cultivated in the U.S. are often called Belon, it is misnomer. They are the same species as the Belon, but the resemblance stops there. European flat oysters raised in Maine and New Hampshire have a very lemony, metallic taste, more distinct than those raised on the West Coast, which are mild.

Westcott European Flat: A variety that is similar to the oyster grown in the Belon River, in northern France. It has a flat shell and the meat is firm and crisp, the flavor deliciously metallic.

Olympia Oyster

Olympia: Related to the European flat oysters, the Olympia is the only oyster indigenous to the West Coast, and is considered a rare delicacy. It has a distinct, though mild, metallic flavor, and it rarely grows to be larger than a quarter.

Pacific Oysters

Golden Mantle: A small, delicate oyster from Vancouver, B.C., whose shell is slightly golden, hence the name. It has a crisp, gamy flavor that can be somewhat fishy.

Hamma-hamma: A mild Pacific oyster from Washington State, with a firm, crisp texture and a touch of saltiness.

Kumamoto: A tiny, deep-cupped Pacific hybrid grown in California and Washington. Its plump, ivory-colored meat is milder than most Pacifics and has a slightly sweet aftertaste.

Lasqueti oyster: This oyster is raised in a suspended culture in Penn Cove in Washington state. Its flavor is more distinct, cleaner and brighter than the Penn Cove Select, and it has slightly more sweetness, because it is raised off the beach.

Magaki: An oyster generally imported from New Zealand when northern hemisphere oysters aren't in peak condition. It is similar to a Pacific oyster in flavor and looks.

Pacific: The Pacific was brought to the West Coast from Japan in the 1920s, to bolster the ailing oyster industry. It is now the most common oyster on the West Coast and the bulk of these mild oysters are shucked, jarred, and sold in markets throughout the country.

Penn Cove Select: A beach-grown Pacific oyster from Washington State's Penn Cove, with a full, slightly sweet flavor, and pleasant saltiness.

Portuguese: Crisp, meaty and plump, this oyster from Vancouver, B.C., has a distinct, briny taste.

Preston Point: A clean, sweet oyster from Tomales Bay, California.

Quilcene: A crisp, refreshing oyster from Quilcene Bay, Washington, that tastes mildly salty and coppery.

Rock Point: Another mildly salty, clean, crisp oyster, with a slight coppery taste, from Dabob Bay, Puget Sound, Washington.

Shoalwater Bay: An oyster from Willapa Bay, Washington, this is one of the Northwest's meatiest oysters. It has a mild saltiness with a sweet, fruity aftertaste.

Westcott Bay: A very meaty, sweet and mild oyster with a tiny hint of a metallic aftertaste, from San Juan Island, Washington.

Westcott Bay Petite: A smaller version of the Westcott Bay oyster.

Westcott Bay Reserves: A year-round, triploid (sexless) oyster, generally softer than other oysters, from San Juan Island, Washington.

Willapa Bay: A mild, clean and sweet oyster, from Willapa Bay, Washington.

Yaquina Bay: A firm, bland, moderately salty oyster, from Yaquina Bay, Oregon.

Note: This list was compiled with the help of Stephen Cohen, seafood buyer for the Oyster Bar in Grand Central Station, New York City.

Wild Shrimp

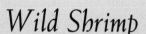

Shrimpers and the National Marine Fisheries Service are currently waging a battle that may result in a decline in the number of wild U.S. shrimp available. NMFS is requiring that all shrimpers equip their nets with a box-like contraption called a Turtle Excluder Device (TED). This is in response to declining populations of loggerheads, hawksbills, green sea turtles, leatherbacks, and Kemp's Ridley turtles, that environmentalists say are being decimated by shrimpers.

Shrimpers disagree. They say the turtle populations are hurt by several things, mainly the bulkheads and seawalls built along the shores of Florida that have blocked turtles off from their traditional egg-laying beaches. Bright city lights near shore confuse baby turtles, shrimpers say, causing them to go toward the lights, often getting run over by cars in the process.

Shrimpers cite a 20 percent decrease in shrimp catch because of the TEDs. Environmentalists claim the TEDs keep turtles and other fish out of the shrimp nets, so, while the entire catch may be less, it is heavier in shrimp.

The battle is ongoing. Louisiana shrimpers have offered to fund a turtle hatchery in exchange for dropping the TED requirements. The coming years will show the future of the Gulf and South Atlantic shrimp fishery. The future of shrimp farming, in Ecuador and Taiwan, is already assured.

SILVER SALMON (*Oncorynchus kisutch*)

ALIAS: coho
FAMILY: salmon.
RANGE: Alaska to central California.
PHYSICAL CHARACTERISTICS: long, wider than most salmon, sleek; 8 to 12 pounds.
MEAT COLOR AND FAT CONTENT: light pink; fatty.
PREFERRED COOKING METHODS: baking, braising, poaching, steaming, grilling, broiling, sautéing.
SUBSTITUTES: other salmon, sturgeon, barracuda, whitefish, weakfish, spotted sea trout.
AVAILABILITY: fresh, in summer; fresh-frozen, year-round.

SILVER WAREHOU: see New Zealand Fish box (see Index)

SKATE (BIG SKATE *Raja binoculata;* CLEARNOSE SKATE *Raja eglanteria;* BARNDOOR SKATE *Raja laevis;* WINTER SKATE *Raja ocellata*)

ALIAS: ray or raie
FAMILY: ray.
RANGE: North Carolina to Maine and West Coast (big skate).
PHYSICAL CHARACTERISTICS: flat, diamond shaped; blue-purple with black dots to mottled brown or gray; 8 inches to 5 feet long.
MEAT COLOR AND FAT CONTENT: striated, pinkish meat turns white when cooked, sweet; lean.
PREFERRED COOKING METHODS: steaming, baking, braising.
SUBSTITUTES: flounder, sole, can be used in some scallop and salmon recipes.
AVAILABILITY: year-round; best in winter.
COMMENTS: only wing portions edible; meat better and firmer 2 to 3 days after it is caught; carries urea in tissue and wings must be cut off immediately or meat will become contaminated; suspected that skate meat substituted for scallops, though skate grain horizontal, scallop vertical; has no bone, just flat piece of cartilage running horizontally through wings; simple preparations and baking in parchment paper suggested.

SKIPJACK TUNA (*Euthynnus pelamis*)

ALIAS: see Common Hawaiian Fish box (see Index)
FAMILY: mackerel.

RANGE: tropical and subtropical waters; Hawaii, southern California, Gulf of Mexico.

PHYSICAL CHARACTERISTICS: dramatic blue back with subtle red slashes; smaller and rounder than other tuna; up to 40 pounds, averages 6 to 8.

MEAT COLOR AND FAT CONTENT: red, firm; moderately fatty, high-fat in winter.

PREFERRED COOKING METHODS: uncooked as sashimi; braising, baking, sautéing, broiling, or marinated and grilled.

SUBSTITUTES: other tuna, shark, swordfish, marlin, king mackerel.

AVAILABILITY: year-round.

COMMENTS: cooks quickly; often canned.

SMELT

FAMILY: smelt.

RANGE: saltwater and freshwater; East and West Coasts, Great Lakes, bays from Mexico to Canada.

PHYSICAL CHARACTERISTICS: tiny, salmon lookalikes; flashing silver sides with olive green undertone; 4 to 6 inches long; 2 to 6 ounces.

MEAT COLOR AND FAT CONTENT: ivory, mild, tender; fatty.

PREFERRED COOKING METHODS: frying, sautéing, baking, pickling, grilling.

SUBSTITUTES: small herring.

AVAILABILITY: fresh, in fall in Maine and New York; in summer on West Coast; February to April in Great Lakes region; fresh-frozen, year-round.

COMMENTS: other smelt include whitebait (*Allosmerus elongatus*) tiny, 2 inches long, usually deep-fried; silver smelt (*Hypomesus pretiosus*) considered the best; capelin (*Mallotus villosus*); rainbow smelt (*Osmerus mordax*); eulachon, hooligan, ooligan (*Thaleichthys pacificus*), very fatty, eaten in Alaska, also called candlefish because Northwest Indians dried them, inserted a wick, and used as a light source (still smoked, fermented, pressed for oil, called ooligan oil).

SNAPPER: see GRAY SNAPPER, MUTTON SNAPPER, RED SNAPPER, VERMILION SNAPPER, YELLOWTAIL SNAPPER

SOCKEYE SALMON (*Oncorhynchus nerka*)

ALIAS: red salmon

FAMILY: salmon.

RANGE: Alaska to California.

PHYSICAL CHARACTERISTICS: long, slim, bluish black to silvery; 5 to 12 pounds.

Sardine Saying

"The sardine's whiskers" was a turn-of-the-century saying used in the same way as "the cat's meow."

MEAT COLOR AND FAT CONTENT: vivid red meat, fine-flaked; moderately fatty.

PREFERRED COOKING METHODS: steaming, broiling, grilling, baking, poaching, sautéing, braising.

SUBSTITUTES: other salmon, barracuda, trout, whitefish, sturgeon, weakfish, spotted sea trout.

AVAILABILITY: fresh, from June to November; fresh-frozen, year-round.

COMMENTS: up until the last 10 years, most sockeye was canned, because color doesn't fade during cooking; still canned, but also common fresh; cooks quickly.

SOLE: see FLOUNDER

SOUTHERN FLOUNDER (*Paralichthys lethostigma*)

FAMILY: flounder.

RANGE: North Carolina to Texas.

PHYSICAL CHARACTERISTICS: plain, olive green on dark side; up to 3 pounds, averages 1½ pounds.

MEAT COLOR AND FAT CONTENT: white; lean.

PREFERRED COOKING METHODS: baking, frying, sautéing, poaching.

SUBSTITUTES: flounder.

AVAILABILITY: year-round.

COMMENTS: similar to summer flounder or fluke.

SPANISH MACKEREL (*Scomberomorus maculatus*)

FAMILY: mackerel.

RANGE: Gulf of Mexico, southern Florida, north to Cape Cod though rarely north of the Chesapeake Bay; along Pacific Coast from San Diego to Galápagos.

PHYSICAL CHARACTERISTICS: rounder than other mackerel, blue to silver with yellowish or olive spots; up to 11 pounds, averages 3.

MEAT COLOR AND FAT CONTENT: reddish, cooks up ivory; fatty.

PREFERRED COOKING METHODS: grilling, braising, baking, broiling, smoking.
SUBSTITUTES: fresh sardines, mullet, bluefish.
AVAILABILITY: fresh-frozen, year-round.
COMMENTS: available, but not major mackerel on West Coast.

SPINY LOBSTER *(Panulirus argus)*

ALIAS: rock lobster
FAMILY: crustacean.
RANGE: tropic and subtropical waters from North Carolina south to Brazil, through southern Gulf of Mexico.
PHYSICAL CHARACTERISTICS: brownish shell with multi-colored markings; long antennae; under 5 pounds.
MEAT COLOR AND FAT CONTENT: white; moderately fatty.
PREFERRED COOKING METHODS: boiling, steaming, sautéing.
SUBSTITUTES: any lobster, crawfish tails, large shrimp.
AVAILABILITY: fresh-frozen, year-round.
COMMENTS: only tail meat is consumed; spiny lobster tails imported from Australia; good value, good quality.

SPOTTED SEA TROUT *(Cynoscion regalis)*

FAMILY: drum.
RANGE: south of Virginia to Gulf of Mexico.
PHYSICAL CHARACTERISTICS: long, slim, black spots on back; 1 to 6 pounds.
MEAT COLOR AND FAT CONTENT: white, fine-flaked, tender; moderately fatty.
PREFERRED COOKING METHODS: steaming, baking, grilling, broiling, sautéing, frying, braising.
SUBSTITUTES: snapper, trout, salmon.
AVAILABILITY: fresh, from June to December; fresh-frozen, year-round.
COMMENTS: similar to weakfish.

SQUID *(Loligo opalescens;* see also Eastern squid)

ALIAS: California squid, calamari, calamar
FAMILY: cephalopod.
RANGE: West Coast.
PHYSICAL CHARACTERISTICS: slim, rocket-shaped body with fin on either side of narrow end; transparent purple spotted skin, milky white when fresh; two large eyes, ink sac in head; wreath of 10 tentacles with tiny suction cups surrounding head;

From Sturgeon Roe to Caviar

Caviar production, transforming sturgeon roe into crisp, salty globes, is an art, and there are no written recipes. Those who produce it work with masters for years to learn the job.

To make it, fresh sturgeon eggs are placed on a screen with the mesh just larger than the individual eggs. The eggs are washed to separate them from the surrounding membrane. After draining, the eggs are salted using about 5 ounces of fine-grain salt for every 10 pounds of eggs. The Russians, traditionally the masters of caviar, claim that only salt from northern Russian salt seas produces real caviar, and they don't share their salt.

The eggs are placed in an airtight container and refrigerated at about 26°F for about a week, when they reach their gastronomic peak. If handled "like a baby," caviar will keep for one month in a home refrigerator.

Iran has also traditionally been a producer of caviar, but because of its political situation, the quality and supply is inconsistent.

Some caviar is produced in the U.S., made either from sturgeon or paddlefish (a Midwest sturgeon relative) roe.

At the turn of the century, tons of sturgeon eggs were produced in the Pacific Northwest from the huge sturgeon catches there. They were processed into poor-quality, highly salted "caviar" and served at saloons, much like popcorn and peanuts, to encourage beer drinking.

transparent "pen" inside body of squid considered its shell; 6 to 8 inches long.

MEAT COLOR AND FAT CONTENT: milky white, cooks up bright white, tender; moderately fatty.

PREFERRED COOKING METHODS: sautéing, frying, baking.

AVAILABILITY: fresh, from February to June in Monterey Bay, November through February in southern California; fresh-frozen, year-round.

COMMENTS: squid toughens if cooked too long, but will pass through toughness if cooked longer when baking, or sautéing; if frying, 1 minute usually sufficient; if accidental overcooking results in toughness, continue cooking so total cooking time is at least 20 minutes; squid will become tender again, though its texture not as good.

STARRY FLOUNDER *(Platichthys stellatus)*

FAMILY: flounder.

RANGE: southern California to Alaska.

PHYSICAL CHARACTERISTICS: rough dark skin marked with star-shaped blotches; 1 to 2 pounds.

MEAT COLOR AND FAT CONTENT: white, soft; lean.

PREFERRED COOKING METHODS: baking, broiling, steaming, frying, sautéing.

SUBSTITUTES: other flounder.

AVAILABILITY: year-round.

COMMENTS: not considered the best quality flounder; can have dull taste.

STONE CRAB CLAWS *(Menippe mercenaria)*

FAMILY: crustacean.

RANGE: Florida waters and off Carolina coasts.

PHYSICAL CHARACTERISTICS: only claws harvested; white with orange and black tips.

MEAT COLOR AND FAT CONTENT: white, sweet, mild; moderately fatty.

PREFERRED COOKING METHODS: pre-cooked aboard boat.

SUBSTITUTES: any crabmeat.

AVAILABILITY: frozen, year-round.

COMMENTS: one claw twisted off crab, crab returned to water under common assumption it will regenerate another claw; generally served as appetizer.

STURGEON (ATLANTIC STURGEON, *Acipenser oxyrhynchus;* GREEN STURGEON, *Acipenser mediostris;* WHITE STURGEON *Acipenser transmontanus)*

FAMILY: sturgeon.

RANGE: Atlantic—large rivers and coastal waters from St. Lawrence River to South Carolina, into Gulf of Mexico; white and green—bays, rivers, and lakes from Alaska to Central California.

PHYSICAL CHARACTERISTICS: prehistoric looking, covered with big, hard scales so rough they're sold as "natural nail files"; long snout, long, slim bodies; Atlantic—olive green with reddish tinges and white belly, 4 to 8 feet long, 150 pounds; white—grayish brown with white belly, 3 to 6 feet long, up to 200 pounds; green—olive green with scattered red and white markings, 3 to 5 feet long, 50 to 100 pounds.

MEAT COLOR AND FAT CONTENT: Atlantic: whitish pink cooks to white, firm; fatty; white—pink cooks to white, firm; fatty; green: reddish meat cooks to ivory, firm; fatty.

PREFERRED COOKING METHODS: baking, braising, broiling, sautéing, smoking.

SUBSTITUTES: shark, marlin, swordfish (all more lean than sturgeon).

AVAILABILITY: Atlantic—year-round, most abundant in spring; white and green—late summer, fall, winter

COMMENTS: Atlantic sturgeon is in short supply; its meat earthier tasting than white sturgeon; white sturgeon generally very mild; green sturgeon very earthy, usually smoked; sturgeon toughens if grilled over high heat—lower heat better; sturgeon meat keeps well, better after 2 to 3 days.

STURGEON ROE

FISH: white, beluga, sevruga, osetra sturgeon.

PHYSICAL CHARACTERISTICS: small black to grayish brown translucent, glossy globes about the size of buckshot.

SUBSTITUTES: any fish roe except shad, carp, or mullet.

AVAILABILITY: year-round.

TRADITIONAL AND RECOMMENDED PREPARATIONS: used as a garnish atop fish pâtés, in soups, omelettes, atop blini, served alone, usually with vodka.

COMMENTS: most caviar comes from beluga, sevruga, and osetra, common in the Mediterranean and Caspian Seas; U.S.D.A. states that only processed, imported sturgeon roe may be called caviar, though the term is loosely used for most fish roe; caviar should be whole, crisp, and firm so they pop when eaten.

SWORDFISH *(Xiphias gladius)*

FAMILY: swordfish.

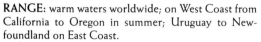

RANGE: warm waters worldwide; on West Coast from California to Oregon in summer; Uruguay to Newfoundland on East Coast.
PHYSICAL CHARACTERISTICS: up to 15 feet; 200 to 400 pounds.
MEAT COLOR AND FAT CONTENT: ivory to light pink, dark meat under skin; firm, short-grained; fatty.
PREFERRED COOKING METHODS: sautéing, baking, broiling, marinated and grilled.
SUBSTITUTES: shark, tuna.
AVAILABILITY: year-round.
COMMENTS: cooks quickly; "sword" accounts for one-third of the length of the fish.

TANNER CRAB (Chionoecetes tanneri)
ALIAS: snow crab
FAMILY: crustacean.
RANGE: southwest Alaska to the Bering Sea.
PHYSICAL CHARACTERISTICS: small body, long, thin legs and claws; golden shell; up to 2 feet across; up to 3 pounds.
MEAT COLOR AND FAT CONTENT: white, sweet; moderately fatty.
PREFERRED COOKING METHODS: live whole: boiling, steaming; generally legs are pre-cooked.
SUBSTITUTES: any crab.
AVAILABILITY: fresh, seldom available; frozen, year-round.
COMMENTS: already picked meat, sometimes fresh; frozen in clusters (2 to 3 legs and part of the body), cocktail claws (just the claw), legs, split legs (cut in half lengthwise).

THRESHER SHARK (Alopius vulpinus)
ALIAS: common thresher
FAMILY: shark.
RANGE: Pacific waters.
PHYSICAL CHARACTERISTICS: up to 1,000 pounds.
MEAT COLOR AND FAT CONTENT: pinkish-white with red layer under the skin, white when cooked; fine-flaked, tender; lean.
PREFERRED COOKING METHODS: steaming, baking, sautéing, frying, braising, grilling if marinated first.
SUBSTITUTES: marlin, swordfish, tuna.
AVAILABILITY: generally, in summer.
COMMENTS: common thresher most common and most tasty; another species, bigeye thresher, is caught on East Coast. Sharks carry urea in their skin and must be dressed immediately or will taste of ammonia.

TILAPIA (Oreochromus niloticus, O. aureus, O. mossabica most common)
ALIAS: cherry snapper, sunshine snapper (fillets)
FAMILY: perch relative.
RANGE: naturally, from Egypt to the Cape of Good Hope; farmed, worldwide.
PHYSICAL CHARACTERISTICS: most commonly charcoal gray with large scales; 1 to 2 pounds.
MEAT COLOR AND FAT CONTENT: white, sweet, short-flaked; lean.
PREFERRED COOKING METHODS: steaming, sautéing, baking, broiling.
SUBSTITUTES: snapper, cod, ocean perch, rock fish, trout.
AVAILABILITY: year-round.
COMMENTS: in the wild, tilapia live in any kind of fresh water, from clean to brackish, and can have an off taste; increasing amount of farmed tilapia available; white, clean, sweet meat of good quality; better than most farmed fish; tilapia reputedly the fish of the biblical loaves and fishes story.

TROUT (Salmo gairdneri)
ALIAS: rainbow trout
FAMILY: trout.
RANGE: primarily Idaho, though throughout the U.S.
PHYSICAL CHARACTERISTICS: dark olive-silver back with dark spots, luminescent band along each side; 1 to 5 pounds.
MEAT COLOR AND FAT CONTENT: white to pale orange, short-grained; moderately fatty.
PREFERRED COOKING METHODS: steaming, baking, braising, grilling, broiling, frying, sautéing.
SUBSTITUTES: catfish, tilapia, shad, salmon.
AVAILABILITY: year-round.
COMMENTS: all rainbow trout in marketplace are farm-raised; 90 percent of trout from Idaho; landlocked steelhead; native to Northwest U.S.

TUNA: see BIGEYE, ALBACORE, BLUEFIN, SKIPJACK, YELLOWFIN, New Zealand and Common Hawaiian Fish boxes (see Index)

VERMILION SNAPPER (Rhomboplites aurorubens)
ALIAS: b-liners
FAMILY: snapper.
RANGE: North Carolina to Brazil.
PHYSICAL CHARACTERISTICS: pale red throughout, silvery belly; up to 30 pounds.
MEAT COLOR AND FAT CONTENT: white, medium-flaked; lean.

Tuna on Terminal Island

Pan Pacific stands alone, the only working processing plant on what used to be "tuna cannery row," at Terminal Island, California. Most tuna is now canned in American Samoa and Puerto Rico, where labor is cheap.

Pan Pacific buys local fresh tuna in season, and frozen tuna at other times. Every part of the fish is put to use. The tender loin meat is canned and the viscera and oil are processed and sold as a cattle feed supplement. The dark blood line meat goes into pet food.

When whole tuna arrive at Pan Pacific, they are cleaned and laid on tall racks that fit inside huge steam ovens.

Once out of the oven, they're wheeled into a cavernous processing room where 80 women stand on either side of three conveyor belts. The tuna are loaded onto the belts, and the women remove the skin while the fish are still warm or it won't come off. They remove any waste and separate light meat from dark, then the loins continue down the line.

A sharp blade cuts them into chunks. The chunks are put in cans, and flakes of meat are sprinkled on top, to fill the can. The meat is tested for its natural salt content, before additional salt is added to reach a total of one percent salt.

The filled, sealed cans are put in a retort, processed, cooled, and labeled. Once cooled, each can is inspected for a good seal before being packed.

PREFERRED COOKING METHODS: steaming, braising, baking, sautéing, broiling.
SUBSTITUTES: snapper, cod, lingcod, petrale sole, or grouper (especially scamp).
AVAILABILITY: year-round.
COMMENTS: one of the most frequent substitutes for red snapper.

WARSAW GROUPER (Epinephelus nigritus)
ALIAS: grouper
FAMILY: sea bass.
RANGE: from Florida southward to Brazil.
PHYSICAL CHARACTERISTICS: large, up to 200 to 300 pounds; dark gray to brown with white spots.
MEAT COLOR AND FAT CONTENT: white, large-flaked, sweet; lean.
PREFERRED COOKING METHODS: poaching, baking, frying, steaming, grilling, broiling.
SUBSTITUTES: large-flaked cod (such as haddock), snapper, other grouper, halibut (cooks in less time than warsaw grouper).
AVAILABILITY: fresh, year-round.
COMMENTS: illegally substituted for jewfish; the meats are similar in flavor.

WEAKFISH (Cynoscion regalis)
ALIAS: seatrout, gray trout
FAMILY: drum.
RANGE: northern Atlantic.
PHYSICAL CHARACTERISTICS: long, slim, silvery with dark spots on back; 1 to 6 pounds.
MEAT COLOR AND FAT CONTENT: white, fine-flaked; fatty.
PREFERRED COOKING METHODS: steaming, baking, frying, sautéing, grilling, broiling.
SUBSTITUTES: snapper, salmon, trout.
AVAILABILITY: generally, fresh from May to December; fresh-frozen, year-round.
COMMENTS: name comes from weak mouth, which rips easily to release hook; fine, delicate flavor similar to brook trout; stands up well to spicy sauces.

WHELK (Buccinum undatum)
FAMILY: mollusk.
RANGE: from Maine to Gulf of Mexico; prefers cold water.
PHYSICAL CHARACTERISTICS: reddish to pink vaguely conical shell with brown coloring.
MEAT COLOR AND FAT CONTENT: blotchy white streaked with black; generally under 8 ounces.

PREFERRED COOKING METHODS: steaming, sautéing, baking, braising.
SUBSTITUTES: conch, abalone.
AVAILABILITY: fresh, from spring through fall; frozen, year-round.
COMMENTS: conch (*Strombus gigas*), relative to whelk; habitat Florida Keys and Caribbean; meat larger than whelk and white; most imported from Caribbean, Honduras, Haiti; milder flavor, interchangeable; recommended to freeze conch and whelk before cooking to tenderize them.

WHITEFISH (*Coregonus clupeaformis*)

FAMILY: Salmonidae family.
RANGE: deep lakes throughout New England and across the northern United States.
PHYSICAL CHARACTERISTICS: up to 20 pounds, averages 1½ to 5; thick, flexible silver body.
MEAT COLOR AND FAT CONTENT: white, delicate, sweet; fatty.
PREFERRED COOKING METHODS: steaming, poaching, grilling, sautéing, baking, broiling.
SUBSTITUTES: salmon, trout.
AVAILABILITY: fresh, year-round, best in spring and fall.
COMMENTS: has golden roe called "whitefish caviar" or "golden caviar."

WHITEFISH ROE

FISH: whitefish (*Coregonus clupeaformis*)
ALIAS: "golden caviar" or "whitefish caviar."
PHYSICAL CHARACTERISTICS: tiny golden globes; sometimes dyed black; mild flavor; crunchy.
SUBSTITUTES: any fish roe.
AVAILABILITY: year-round.
TRADITIONAL AND RECOMMENDED PREPARATIONS: used as garnish.

WIDOW ROCKFISH: see ROCKFISH

WINTER FLOUNDER (*Pseudopleuronectes americanus*)

ALIAS: blackback, lemon sole (see below)
FAMILY: flounder.
RANGE: Atlantic coast, commonly from Newfoundland to Chesapeake Bay, as far south as Georgia.
PHYSICAL CHARACTERISTICS: 12 to 15 inches; up to 5 pounds, averages 1 to 3.
MEAT COLOR AND FAT CONTENT: white, fine; lean.

PREFERRED COOKING METHODS: frying, baking, sautéing, broiling.
SUBSTITUTES: flounder, sole.
AVAILABILITY: year-round.
COMMENTS: one of the best flounders; called lemon sole when weighs more than 3 pounds.

YELLOWEYE ROCKFISH (*Sebastes riberrimus*)

ALIAS: Pacific snapper, Alaska snapper
FAMILY: rockfish.
RANGE: Alaska to California.
PHYSICAL CHARACTERISTICS: round-bodied, heavy-finned, reddish skin; 1 to 4 pounds.
MEAT COLOR AND FAT CONTENT: white; lean.
PREFERRED COOKING METHODS: steaming, frying, sautéing, baking.
SUBSTITUTES: cod, snapper.
AVAILABILITY: year-round.
COMMENTS: one of the most common substitute for red snapper; highest quality rockfish.

YELLOWFIN TUNA (*Thunnus albacares*)

ALIAS: see Common Hawaiian Fish box (see Index)
FAMILY: mackerel.
RANGE: temperate and subtropical waters worldwide; as far north as New Jersey in warm weather; Gulf of California.
PHYSICAL CHARACTERISTICS: bluish silver with bright yellow stripe along sides, and curved yellow anal and dorsal fins; 30 pounds up to 400 pounds.
MEAT COLOR AND FAT CONTENT: reddish—darker than albacore, lighter than bluefin; moderately fatty.
PREFERRED COOKING METHODS: braising, baking, sautéing, broiling, marinated and grilled.
SUBSTITUTES: other tuna, swordfish, marlin, shark, king mackerel.
AVAILABILITY: fresh, in summer on West Coast; year-round in Hawaii and on East Coast.
COMMENTS: cooks quickly.

YELLOWMOUTH GROUPER (*Mycteroperca interstitialis*)

ALIAS: grouper
FAMILY: sea bass.
RANGE: Florida, Gulf of Mexico and south.
PHYSICAL CHARACTERISTICS: grayish, very small; 4 to 10 pounds.
MEAT COLOR AND FAT CONTENT: white, sweet, large-flaked; lean.

PREFERRED COOKING METHODS: grilling, baking, frying, steaming, sautéing, broiling.
SUBSTITUTES: other grouper, large-flaked cod (such as haddock), snapper, halibut (cooks in less time than yellowmouth grouper).
AVAILABILITY: year-round.
COMMENTS: one of the most common and best groupers.

YELLOWTAIL FLOUNDER

FAMILY: flounder.
RANGE: Labrador to Virginia.
PHYSICAL CHARACTERISTICS: oval, grayish olive to green; about 1 pound.
MEAT COLOR AND FAT CONTENT: white; lean.
PREFERRED COOKING METHODS: frying, baking, broiling, sautéing, poaching.
SUBSTITUTES: other flounder.

AVAILABILITY: year-round.

YELLOWTAIL ROCKFISH: see ROCKFISH

YELLOWTAIL SNAPPER *(Ocyurus chrysurus)*

FAMILY: snapper.
RANGE: Florida and Caribbean.
PHYSICAL CHARACTERISTICS: yellow tinged with gray; up to 6 pounds.
MEAT COLOR AND FAT CONTENT: white, delicate; lean.
PREFERRED COOKING METHODS: steaming, braising, baking, broiling.
SUBSTITUTES: snapper, cod, lingcod, petrale sole, or rockfish.
AVAILABILITY: year-round.
COMMENTS: more perishable than other fish.

INDEX

D

E

F

A Long Island Bonnacker

Nearly every day before dawn on Long Island, in New York, Mickey Miller sets out fishing in his snub-nose "garvey" with his dog Brutus. They go to Northwest Bay near the Hamptons, which in early fall is as lonesome and picturesque as a Wyeth painting.

Miller is one of the Bonnackers, the fabled fishermen of Long Island. He traps fish in his trap nets which are set in the bay 1,000 feet apart. Miller checks his traps in the early morning, before cormorants, fishing birds that are locally known as "shags," have had their chance.

Trapping is a fishing method that is disappearing on Long Island. "There aren't more than 20 trap fishermen on the whole island now," Mr. Miller said. "It's a good way to fish—we can release undesirables or fish that are too small, and we get more for our fish because they're alive when we catch 'em. Besides, it's a passive fishing method, and it gives me more time with my family."

As Miller talks he poles his boat quietly around a trap, using a stake with a spike on the end of it to pull up the net until he gathers it all around the boat. This first net is full of fat striped bass, the traditional fish of the Bonnacker. He used to make his living from this fish, but he can't keep any of the "stripers" now because of a state moratorium preventing their commercial catch. He reached out to touch one of the bass as though petting it, distracted for a moment, but then checked to see what else was in the net. He pulled out a sea robin, a lovely, bird-like fish with fins that stretch out like fans from the side of its head. "This will be a fish of the future," he said as he set it in the boat.

"I stick with fishing because I'm hoping people will start eating fish that they haven't previously eaten. If they do, it could save the industry. Besides, there's my fringe benefit—nature."

The rest of the morning he pulls small dogfish—a smooth member of the shark family that he once considered trash and threw right back—out of the net, along with more sea robins and several pounds of blowfish, that puff up like water balloons when they're landed.

At day's end he will sell a selection of his fish to Stewart's Market in nearby Amagansett. He will dress the dogfish and put them on a truck headed that night to the Fulton Fish Market in Manhattan. The next morning they'll be sold to Koreans and Chinese, both of whom have traditionally eaten the firm, white meat. The Germans eat plenty of dogfish too, smoked, and the British batter and fry it for fish and chips. Both countries have begun to buy it from the United States, and it's also emerging here as a more popular fish. That's good news for Miller.

M